Guide to the
Court of Sessions Records
of
Sonoma County, California

1850–1863

Steven M. Lovejoy

HERITAGE BOOKS
2020

HERITAGE BOOKS
AN IMPRINT OF HERITAGE BOOKS, INC.

Books, CDs, and more—Worldwide

For our listing of thousands of titles see our website
at
www.HeritageBooks.com

Published 2020 by
HERITAGE BOOKS, INC.
Publishing Division
5810 Ruatan Street
Berwyn Heights, Md. 20740

Copyright © 2020 Steven M. Lovejoy

Cover image: Hiram White indictment, November term 1860,
Sonoma County Court of Sessions

Heritage Books by the author:
Guide to the Court of Sessions Records of Sonoma County, California, 1850–1863
Index to the Probate Court Records of Sonoma County, California, 1847–1879
Index to the Public Official Bonds of Sonoma County, California, 1850–1892

International Standard Book Number
Paperbound: 978-0-7884-0144-2

Table of Contents

Introduction

Court records are incredibly rich in information useful for genealogical research. They can, however, be hard to locate and, once found, difficult to navigate, especially since most are not indexed. For these reasons they are probably the most under-utilized of all genealogical records. The Sonoma County Genealogical Society has made some of the early Sonoma County court records more easily accessible to the researcher by indexing the records of several 19th century Sonoma County courts.[1] This publication adds to the series by presenting a guide to the Sonoma County Court of Sessions records.

The Court of Sessions was one of the first courts established in California by the 1849 California Constitution. As organized by the California Legislature in 1850, the Court of Sessions in each county was presided over by the county judge. He was assisted by two associate justices elected from among the county's justices of the peace. After receiving an indictment or presentment from the county's Grand Jury, the Court heard criminal cases of assault, assault and battery, breach of the peace, riot, affray, petit larceny, and all misdemeanors punishable by a fine not exceeding $500 or imprisonment not exceeding three months or both such fine and imprisonment. The Court of Sessions was abolished in 1863 when the California Legislature reorganized the California courts.

This publication comprises three sections. The first section is a table which gives for each Sonoma County Court of Sessions case its California State Archives case file number, the name(s) of the defendant(s), the charge, the date of the indictment or presentment, and the volume(s) and page number(s) in the existing Sonoma County Court of Sessions bound volumes (minute books, judgment book, and register) in which each case is recorded. The second section is a narrative arranged chronologically describing the proceedings of each Court of Sessions term. The third section provides a name index for the entire publication.

---

[1] See three publications by the Sonoma County Genealogical Society, *Index to the District Court Records of Sonoma County, California, 1850–1879* (Berwyn Heights, Maryland: Heritage Books, 2016), *Index to the Superior Court Records of Sonoma County, California, Volume 1: 1880–1889* (Berwyn Heights, Maryland: Heritage Books, 2017), and *Index to the Superior Court Records of Sonoma County, California, Volume 2: 1890–1899* (Berwyn Heights, Maryland: Heritage Books, 2017).

How to Use this Guide

When searching for a specific individual in the records of the Sonoma County Court of Sessions consult the name index at the back of this publication first. As spelling in the 19th century was not standardized, researchers should look for all possible variations of a name. Names could be spelled a variety of ways even within the same document. The spelling of the names in this guide is generally that which was most commonly used in the records. Where no one spelling predominates, the variation or variations are given, for example, Antonio Valasques (var. Valasquez, Velasquez).

If stated in the records, the names of Court and county officials, defendants, Grand Jurors, and Grand Jury witnesses involved in every Court of Sessions case have been captured. No attempt, however, was made to record the names of the many others associated with the cases such as defense lawyers, trial jurors, bond sureties, and trial witnesses. After identifying a name of interest in the name index, the researcher should turn to the page or pages specified in the first and second sections of this publication.

The first section, "Table of Court of Sessions Cases," is a seven-column tabular listing of the Sonoma County Court of Sessions cases. The first column of the table gives each case's California State Archives case file number. The Court of Sessions did not number its cases. These case file numbers are strictly an artifact of the processing of the case files by the State Archives staff. The case file number, however, is the key to finding the original case documents. A case file may contain more than one case. Indictments and other court papers for cases that were transferred to the Sonoma County District Court for trial, such as murder cases, or to the Sonoma County County Court on 1 January 1864 after the Court of Sessions was abolished, generally will be found among the District Court and County Court case files at the State Archives. The second and third columns of the table give the names of the defendants and the charges brought against them. The plaintiff in all these criminal cases is officially "The People of the State of California," but this is usually shortened to "The People" or just "People." The fourth column gives the date the indictment was filed. The fifth, sixth, and seventh columns give the volume and page numbers in the four existing bound volumes of Sonoma County Court of Sessions records (a register, two minute books, and a judgment book) on which each case is recorded. See "Records Utilized" for full descriptions of these bound volumes.

A number of cases files contain only miscellaneous documents, not necessarily from the Sonoma County Court of Sessions, and no Sonoma County Grand Jury indictments. All of the usually small number of documents in each of these case files are described briefly within the table.

Several cases which are listed at the end of the table do not have case file numbers. These are cases in which no documents associated with the cases were received by the State Archives and therefore did not receive case file numbers. Most of these cases, even though they were recorded in one or more of the Court of Sessions bound volumes, were either dismissed by the

Court or transferred to the Sonoma County District Court before generating any Court of Sessions documents.

The second section, "Court of Sessions Terms," summarizes in narrative form the proceedings of each term of the Sonoma County Court of Sessions for which there are existing records. The information given for each term varies. For some terms, especially those of the early 1850s, little information is available as there are no Court minute books, very few Court documents to consult, and newspaper coverage was scant. Once the Court minute books begin in October term 1857, the information for each Court term is fairly complete.

The information given for each Court term includes:

1.) the total number of and specific days the Court was in session
2.) a listing of the Court and County officials involved in the term's proceedings
3.) a listing of the Grand Jurors called, but not empaneled
4.) a listing of the Grand Jurors empaneled
5.) the Grand Jury report
5.) a summary of each case whose indictment was received by the Court that term

The summary of each case is composed of information from a variety of sources including the Court records themselves, newspaper accounts, prison records, and pardon applications and may include some, if not all, of the following:

1.) the title of the case
2.) the charge against the defendant as given in the indictment
3.) the California State Archives case file number for the case
4.) the specific charges in the indictment
5.) the date the indictment was filed, usually the same day it was presented to the Court
6.) a listing of the witnesses examined before the Grand Jury
7.) newspaper accounts of the crime, arrest, and trial
8.) court proceedings
9.) the outcome of the trial
10.) the defendant's sentence, if convicted
11.) the dates of incarceration, if sentenced to a prison term
12.) the pardon application outcome, if applicable

Researchers are advised to use this Guide only as a starting point when researching Sonoma County Court of Sessions records, to examine each and every original record or document associated with a case for themselves, and to make their own conclusions. The case files especially may contain hidden gems such as eyewitness testimonies which are not summarized in this publication.

Records Utilized

1. Sonoma County Court of Sessions records

When the Sonoma County courthouse records were examined in December of 1917 for inclusion in the *Guide to the County Archives of California*, five bound volumes of Sonoma County Court of Sessions records were identified.[2] Four of these volumes survive and are housed at the Sonoma County Archives. The fifth, a fee book for the years 1857–1859, which was in the basement of the Sonoma County courthouse in 1917, has since been lost, misplaced, or misidentified. Strangely, the Sonoma County Court of Sessions case files were not inventoried for the *Guide* in 1917, but they do exist and are housed at the California State Archives in Sacramento.

a. Sonoma County Court of Sessions minute books

i. Volume D, entries dated 5 October 1857 through 9 August 1859, 242 hand-written numbered pages, no index, Sonoma County Archives accession # 1508.

ii. Volume E, entries dated 3 October 1859 through 8 December 1863, 710 stamped pages, no index, Sonoma County Archives accession # 1507. This volume appears to be repurposed. Turning the volume over there is another set of stamped numbers running in the opposite direction. On the spine, the words "Book A" have been rubbed out.

b. Sonoma County Court of Sessions register

No volume number or letter, entries dated 9 July 1857 through 3 February 1862, 358 stamped pages, pages 1–51 are an index, pages 52–54 and 206–358 are blank, Sonoma County Archives accession # 1496. This volume, arranged by case, gives the dates actions were taken and court papers were filed in a number of Court of Sessions cases.

c. Sonoma County Court of Sessions judgment book

No volume number or letter, entries dated 27 August 1858 through 11 January 1859, entries only on the first eight pages, the remainder of the volume is blank, separate index by defendant tied in to volume, Sonoma County Archives accession # 1509. This volume gives the Sonoma County Court of Sessions judgments in the following eight cases, along with the date of the judgment and the charge against the defendant for each:

People vs. James Knowles, 27 Aug 1858, [assault and battery]
People vs. James B. Boggs, 28 Aug 1858, assault and battery
People vs. R. E. Harrison, 28 Aug 1858, assault with intent to commit great bodily injury
People vs. Griffith P. Sanders, 13 Oct 1858, assault with intent to commit great bodily injury

---

[2] Owen C. Coy, *Guide to the County Archives of California* (Sacramento: California Historical Survey Commission, 1919), 525.

People vs. William Harris, 15 Oct 1858, grand larceny
People vs. William Harris, 15 Oct 1858, grand larceny
People vs. L. W. Freeman, 15 Oct 1858, grand larceny
People vs. Edward McLaughlin, 11 Jan 1859, assault with intent to commit great bodily injury

d. Sonoma County Court of Sessions case files

The original documents filed in each Court of Sessions case are housed at the California State Archives in two banker's boxes containing 291 case files distributed among 22 file folders. These case files may include such items as complaints, Justice's Court documents, indictments, presentments, warrants, subpoenas, bail bonds, recognizances, jury instructions, demurrers, depositions, requests for continuances, writs of attachment, and transcripts of testimony. Some case files consist of only one sheet of paper, while others contain a hundred sheets or more.

According to the Sonoma County Courts Finding Aid in the County Records binder at the California State Archives, when the State Archives received the Sonoma County Court of Sessions case files, most likely in the late 1960s or early 1970s, the documents were folded, and, for the most part, all of the documents in each case were bundled and tied together.[3] The documents of each case were unfolded and flattened, and the cases were arranged roughly in order of date filed. Each case's documents were separated by a sheet of paper, assigned a case file number, and put into an archival folder. The Court of Sessions did not number its cases, and so the case file number is strictly an artifact of the processing of the case files by the State Archives staff. A case file may contain more than one case. Documents misfiled or not belonging in a case file are noted in the Table of Court of Sessions Cases.

2. Sonoma County Grand Jury reports

The original Grand Jury reports are scattered among various files in several boxes of unprocessed Sonoma County Court records housed at the California State Archives. Transcriptions of some of the reports can be found in the Court of Sessions minute books and in the local newspapers. Microfilmed copies can be examined at the Sonoma County Clerk-Recorder's Office in Santa Rosa.

3. Sonoma County District Court and County Court records

Some Court of Sessions cases, murder cases for example, were transferred to the Sonoma County District Court for trial, and cases pending in the Court of Sessions when it was abolished at the end of 1863 were transferred to the County Court. The surviving Sonoma County District Court and County Court minute books and other bound volumes are housed at the Sonoma County Archives. The original case files for these two courts are housed at the California State Archives.

---

[3] The Sonoma County District Court, County Court, Justice's Court, and some Superior Court cases files were received by the State Archives at the same time and were processed similarly. The processing of these records by the State Archives staff apparently was not completed, as there remain several boxes of unprocessed Sonoma County Court records at the State Archives.

4. California Supreme Court records

A number of Sonoma County Court of Sessions or District Court cases were appealed to the California Supreme Court. The records of this Court, including its minute books and case files, are housed at the California State Archives. Many of the case files contain a transcript on appeal, which was sent to the Supreme Court by the lower Court and includes a transcription of all the relevant documents and court minutes from the case in the lower Court. This document can be especially important when the original documents from the lower Court are now lost or missing.

5. Governor's pardon application files

Among the California Governor's Office records housed at the California State Archives in Sacramento is a series entitled "Applications for Pardon, Historical Case Files (1850–ca. 1935)." This series consists of case files of persons who have petitioned the Governor for a pardon or commutation. Each case file generally contains the petition for pardon to the Governor by the convict or his representative and letters from family, friends, and others recommending the granting of the pardon or commutation. Sometimes transcripts of the court proceedings, letters from prison officials, and even the official pardon itself can be found in the case files. A name index to these Governor's pardon application files is on microfilm at the State Archives.

6. Newspaper articles

Newspaper reports of court proceedings can be very useful for filling in the details of cases when those details are lacking in the available court records. Newspaper articles can also provide colorful, and sometimes unreliable, accounts of the events that were the cause of the court proceedings. The first newspaper published in Sonoma County was the *Sonoma Bulletin* by A. J. Cox in Sonoma from 1852 to 1855.[4] Unfortunately, few issues survive. Articles and snippets from this newspaper can be found, however, quoted in other newspapers of the time such as the *Daily Alta California* and *Sacramento Daily Union*. Within a year or two of the demise of the *Sonoma Bulletin*, other newspapers began publication in Sonoma County, most notably *The Petaluma Weekly Journal and Sonoma County Advertiser* (published weekly in Petaluma beginning on 18 August 1855, later called *The Sonoma County Journal*) and *The Sonoma Democrat* (published weekly in Santa Rosa beginning on 22 October 1857, later called *Sonoma County Democrat* and *The Sonoma County Democrat*).

The following is a list of the newspapers utilized as digital images in the preparation of this publication, along with the website names and home page URLs where these images can be found. Referenced websites were accessed on 15 February 2020.

---

[4] Edward C. Kemble, *A History of California Newspapers, 1846–1858* (Los Gatos, California: The Talisman Press, 1962), 222. This book is a reprint of the supplement to the *Sacramento Daily Union* newspaper of 25 December 1858, edited and with a forward by Helen Harding Bretnor.

At *California Digital Newspaper Collection* (http://cdnc.ucr.edu): *The Sonoma Democrat, Sonoma County Democrat, The Sonoma County Democrat, The Marin County Journal, Daily Alta California, The Wide West, The Daily Union, Sacramento Daily Union, Marysville Daily Appeal,* and *The Weekly Colusa Sun*

At *Newspapers.com* (http://www.newspapers.com): *The Petaluma Weekly Journal and Sonoma County Advertiser, The Sonoma County Journal,* and *The Petaluma Argus*

At *GenealogyBank* (http://www.genealogybank.com): *Daily Evening Bulletin*

7. California State Prison registers

Over thirty persons were sent to the California State Prison at San Quentin from Sonoma County after being convicted of serious crimes in Sonoma County courts from 1850 through 1863. The original executive department copies of the State Prison registers are housed at the California State Archives. Each convict received at the State Prison is listed in a register along with their nativity, their crime, when they were received, the term of their sentence, the county from which they were sent, and their age, occupation, height, complexion, color of eyes, and color of hair. The remarks column of the register usually gives the date prisoners were discharged, either after serving their full sentence, by pardon, or escape. These registers have been microfilmed, and the microfilm can be viewed at the State Archives. Digital images produced from this microfilm can be accessed at *Ancestry.com* (https://www.ancestry.com/search/collections/californiaprison/).

8. California statutes

The California statutes can be found in bound volumes in law libraries across California and the United States. Digital images of these bound volumes can be accessed at a number of websites such as *Google Books* (http://books.google.com), *Internet Archive* (http://archive.org), and most completely at *California State Assembly Office of the Chief Clerk* (http://clerk.assembly.ca.gov).

Legal Terms

Attachment: The act or process of taking, apprehending, or seizing persons or property, by virtue of a writ, summons, or other judicial order, and bringing the same into the custody of the law; used either for the purpose of bringing a person before the court, or acquiring jurisdiction over the property seized, to compel an appearance, to furnish security for debt or costs, or to arrest a fund in the hands of a third person who may become liable to pay it over. Also the writ or other process for the accomplishment of the purposes above enumerated, this being the more common use of the word.[5]

Bail bond: A bond executed by a defendant who has been arrested, together with other persons as sureties, naming the sheriff, constable, or marshal as obligee, in a penal sum proportioned to the damages claimed or penalty denounced, conditioned that the defendant shall duly appear to answer to the legal process in the officer's hands, or shall cause special bail to be put in, as the case may be.[6]

Bench warrant: A process issued by the court itself, or "from the bench," for the attachment or arrest of a person, either in case of contempt, or where an indictment has been found, or to bring in a witness who does not obey the subpoena. So called to distinguish it from a warrant issued by a justice of the peace, alderman, or commissioner.[7]

Capias: Latin for "that you take." The general name for several species of writs, the common characteristic of which is that they require the officer to take the body of the defendant into custody. They are writs of attachment or arrest.[8]

Demurrer: A response in a court proceeding in which the defendant does not dispute the truth of the allegation but claims it is not sufficient grounds to justify legal action.[9]

Felony: A crime, or public offence, which is punishable with death or imprisonment in the state prison. Every other crime is a misdemeanor.[10]

Indictment: An accusation in writing found and presented by a grand jury, legally convoked and sworn, to the court in which it is impaneled, charging that a person therein named has done some

---

[5] Henry Campbell Black, *A Dictionary of Law Containing Definitions of the Terms and Phrases of American and English Jurisprudence, Ancient and Modern* (St. Paul, Minnesota: West Publishing Co., 1891), 102–103, "attachment."

[6] Black, *A Dictionary of Law*, 113–114, "bail-bond."

[7] Black, *A Dictionary of Law*, 126–127, "bench warrant."

[8] Black, *A Dictionary of Law*, 168, "capias."

[9] *Merriam-Webster's Collegiate Dictionary*, 11th ed., "demurrer."

[10] James H. Deering, Walter S. Brann, and R. M. Sims, *The Penal Code of California. Enacted in 1872: As Amended up to and Including 1905, with Statutory History and Citation Digest up to and Including Volume 147, California Reports* (San Francisco: Bancroft-Whitney Company, 1906), p. 41, § 17, "Felony and misdemeanor defined."

act, or been guilty of some omission, which, by law, is a public offense, punishable on indictment.[11]

Nolle prosequi: Latin for "in practice." A formal entry upon the record, by the plaintiff in a civil suit or the prosecuting officer in a criminal action, by which he declares that he "will no longer prosecute" the case, either as to some of the counts, or some of the defendants, or altogether.[12]

Presentment: An informal statement in writing, by the grand jury, representing to the court that a public offense has been committed, which is triable in the county, and that there is reasonable ground for believing that a particular individual named or described therein has committed it. A presentment differs from an indictment in that it is an accusation made by a grand jury of their own motion, either upon their own observation and knowledge, or upon evidence before them.[13]

Recognizance: A species of bail bond or security given by the prisoner either on being bound over for trial or on his taking an appeal.[14]

Subpoena: A writ or order directed to a person and requiring his attendance at a particular time and place to testify as a witness.[15]

Venire: Latin for "to come, to appear in court." The name of a judicial writ for summoning a jury, more commonly called a "venire facias," directed to the sheriff of the county in which a cause is to be tried, commanding him that he cause to come before the court a certain number of good and lawful men of the county, qualified by law, to serve as jurors.[16]

Warrant: A writ or precept issued by a magistrate, justice, or other competent authority, addressed to a sheriff, constable, or other officer, requiring him to arrest the body of a person therein named, and bring him before the magistrate or court, to answer, or to be examined, touching some offense which he is charged with having committed.[17]

Writ: A precept in writing, couched in the form of a letter, running in the name of the king, president, or state, issuing from a court of justice, and sealed with its seal, addressed to a sheriff or other officer of the law, or directly to the person whose action the court desires to command, either as the commencement of a suit or other proceeding or as incidental to its progress, and requiring the performance of a specified act, or giving authority and commission to have it done.[18]

---

[11] Black, *A Dictionary of Law*, 616, "indictment."
[12] Black, *A Dictionary of Law*, 818, "nolle prosequi."
[13] Black, *A Dictionary of Law*, 931, "presentment."
[14] Black, *A Dictionary of Law*, 1002, "recognizance."
[15] Black, *A Dictionary of Law*, 1130–1131, "subpoena."
[16] Black, *A Dictionary of Law*, 1213, "venire" and "venire facias."
[17] Black, *A Dictionary of Law*, 1234, "warrant."
[18] Black, *A Dictionary of Law*, 1246, "writ."

Abbreviations and Marks

et al.   abbreviation for either of the Latin terms *et alius* meaning "and another" or *et alii* meaning "and others"[19]

dba   abbreviation for "does business as"

Hon.   abbreviation for Honorable, an honorific used by judges and other public officials

NS   New Series

OS   Old Series

v.   a common abbreviation of "versus" in the titles of causes and reported cases[20]

var.   abbreviation for variant, inserted in parentheses before variant or alternate spellings of a word, usually a surname, thus John Smith (var. Smyth) indicates both names, John Smith and John Smyth, are found in the records

[*sic*]   a Latin term meaning "so," "thus," or "in this manner," inserted in brackets following a misspelled or wrongly used word in the original[21]

[?]   a question mark within brackets indicates some information, such as the name of the person, usually the forename, is not given in the record, thus [?] Smith means only Smith's surname is found in the record

[ ]   letters or words between brackets indicates those letters or words are not part of the original document and have been inserted by the author to improve clarity or to add information

*   an asterisk after a case file number indicates that there are no documents in that case file

The names of the months of the year in this guide have been shortened to three-letter abbreviations as follows:

Jan	January	May	May	Sep	September
Feb	February	Jun	June	Oct	October
Mar	March	Jul	July	Nov	November
Apr	April	Aug	August	Dec	December

---

[19] Black, *A Dictionary of Law*, 438, "et al." and "et alius."
[20] Black, *A Dictionary of Law*, 1209, "v."
[21] *The Chicago Manual of Style*, 17th ed. (Chicago: The University of Chicago Press, 2017), 733.

History of the Court of Sessions

In 1849, a Court of Sessions was established in every California county by the state's first constitution, which directed that the County Judge of each California county along with two Justices of the Peace "shall hold Courts of Sessions with such criminal jurisdiction as the Legislature shall prescribe."[22] On 11 April 1850, the California Legislature dutifully fulfilled its constitutional obligation and passed "An Act to organize the Court of Sessions."[23] This act stipulated that each Court of Sessions was to be composed of the County Judge, acting as the presiding Judge, and two Justices of the Peace, as Associates Justices, elected by all the Justices of the Peace of the County. The County Clerk was to be the clerk of the Court of Sessions, and the County Sheriff, or his deputy, was required to attend each term of the Court and execute all writs and processes issued.

In addition to its judicial role, the Court, in lieu of a Board of Supervisors, was to have broad administrative duties in each county which included powers to:

1.) make such orders respecting the property of the County as they may deem expedient, in conformity with any law of the State, and to take care of, and preserve such property,

2.) examine, settle, and allow all accounts chargeable against such County, and to direct the raising of such sums, by taxation on property, real and personal, in such County, not to exceed, however, the one-half of the tax levied by the State on such property, as may be necessary to defray all expenses and charges against such County,

3.) examine and audit the accounts of all officers having the care, management, collection, and disbursement of any money belonging to the County, or appropriated by law, or otherwise, for its use and benefit,

4.) have the control and management of public roads, turnpikes, ferries, canals, roads, and bridges, within the County, where law does not prohibit such jurisdiction; and to make such orders as may be necessary and requisite to carry such control and management into effect,

5.) divide the County into townships, and to create new townships, and change the divisions of the same, as the convenience of the County may require,

6.) establish and change election precincts,

7.) control and manage the property, real and personal, belonging to the County, and to purchase and receive by donation, any property, real and personal, for the use and benefit

---

[22] Constitution of the State of California, 1849, Article VI (Judicial Department), section 8.

[23] *The Statutes of California, Passed at the First Session of the Legislature, Begun the 15th Day of Dec. 1849, and Ended the 22nd Day of April, 1850, at the City of Pueblo San José* (San José: J. Winchester, State Printer, 1850), pp. 210–211, Chap. 86, "An Act to Organize the Court of Sessions" (hereafter cited as *The Statutes of California, First Session*).

of the County: *Provided*, however, that the Court of Sessions shall not have power to purchase any real or personal property, except such as may be absolutely necessary for the use of the County,

8.) sell, and cause to be conveyed, any real estate, goods, or chattels belonging to their County, appropriating the proceeds of such sale to the use of the same,

9.) cause to be erected and furnished, a Court House, Jail, and such other public buildings as may be necessary, and the same to be kept in repair, and

10.) do and perform all such other acts and things as may be requisite and necessary to the full discharge of the powers and jurisdiction conferred on such Court, and which may be enjoined on it by law.

On 3 May 1852, the California Legislature transferred these County administrative duties in many California counties, including Sonoma County, to Boards of Supervisors in each county when it passed "An Act to create a Board of Supervisors for the Counties of this State, and to define their duties and powers."[24] The Boards were to be composed of five members elected at the next general election and at each subsequent general election. Supervisors were to hold office for the term of one year. No Justices of the Peace, Clerks, Sheriffs, or other County Officers were eligible for the office of Supervisor. Sonoma County elected its first Board of Supervisors on 14 June 1852.[25] The Board, composed of David O. Shattuck, William A. Hereford, Leonard P. Hanson, and James Singley, met for the first time on 5 July 1852 to take charge of the County's affairs, ending the role of the Sonoma County Court of Sessions in County administration.[26]

Several articles of the 1849 California Constitution were amended in 1862. Article six, concerning the reorganization of the judicial department, as amended, effectively abolished the Court of Sessions by omitting it from the list of California courts vested in judicial power in section one of that article. Section nineteen of that same article, however, allowed the various existing courts, including the Court of Sessions, to continue to function until the election and qualification of the officers of the new courts. When the courts of justice of the state of California were reorganized by the California Legislature in 1863, the Courts of Sessions were abolished effective 1 January

---

[24] *The Statutes of California, Passed at the Third Session of the Legislature, Begun on the Fifth of January, 1852, and Ended on the Fourth Day of May, 1852, at the Cities of Vallejo and Sacramento* (San Francisco: G. K. Fitch & Co., and V. E. Geiger & Co., State Printers, 1852), pp. 87–89, Chap. XXXVIII, "An Act to create a Board of Supervisors for the Counties of this State, and to define their duties and powers" (hereafter cited as *The Statutes of California, Third Session*).

[25] Sonoma County, California, certificates of election for David O. Shattuck, William A. Hereford, and James Singley dated 19 June 1852 and L. P. Hanson dated 24 June 1852; Sonoma County Archives, Santa Rosa.

[26] Robert A. Thompson, *Historical and Descriptive Sketch of Sonoma County, California* (Philadelphia: L. H. Everts and Co., 1877), 18.

1864.[27] All cases pending in the Courts of Sessions at the end of the year 1863 were transferred to the County Courts on 1 January 1864.[28]

---

[27] *The Statutes of California, Passed at the Fourteenth Session of the Legislature, 1863: Begun on Monday, the Fifth Day of January, and Ended on Monday, the Twenty-seventh Day of April* (Sacramento: Benj. P. Avery, State Printer, 1863), pp. 333–346, Chap. CCLX, "An Act Concerning the Courts of Justice of this State, and Judicial Officers" (hereafter cited as *The Statutes of California, Fourteenth Session*).

[28] *The Statutes of California, Passed at the Fifteenth Session of the Legislature, 1863–4: Began on Monday, the Seventh Day of December, Eighteen Hundred and Sixty-three, and Ended on Monday, the Fourth Day of April, Eighteen Hundred and Sixty-four* (Sacramento: O. M. Clayes, State Printer, 1864), pp. 1–4, Chap. 1, "An Act providing for the Transfer of Cases, on the first day of January next, to the Courts established by the present Constitution" (hereafter cited as *The Statutes of California, Fifteenth Session*).

Jurisdiction of the Court of Sessions

The 1850 act organizing the Court of Sessions conferred on the Court jurisdiction over all cases of assault, assault and battery, breach of the peace, riot, affray, petit larceny, and all misdemeanors punishable by a fine not exceeding $500 or imprisonment not exceeding three months or both such fine and imprisonment.[29]

On 1 July 1851, the California Legislature repealed the 1850 act and gave to the Court of Sessions jurisdiction to: 1.) inquire, by the intervention of a Grand Jury, of all public offences committed or triable in its County, 2.) try and determine indictments found therein, for all public offences, except murder, manslaughter, and arson, and to try and determine indictments in these excepted cases against a person holding the office of District Judge, and 3.) hear and determine appeals from the Justice's, Recorder's, and Mayor's Courts in cases of a criminal nature.[30] Indictments for murder, manslaughter, and arson were to be transmitted to the District Court for trial, except those against District Court judges.[31]

Two years later on 19 May 1853, the California Legislature repealed the 1851 act concerning the courts of justice and judicial officers and passed another act of the same name, which was to take effect on 6 June 1853.[32] The jurisdiction of the Court of Sessions remained the same except that in all counties except San Francisco County, indictments for "crimes as may by law be punishable by death" were added to those which the Court of Sessions could not try and determine.[33] Those indictments would be transmitted to the District Court for trial. In San Francisco County's Court of Sessions all indictments for public offences could be tried and determined. Indictments for murder, manslaughter, arson, or any crime that may be punishable by death found against a District Court judge were to be transmitted to another District Court for trial.

The California Legislature amended the 1853 act concerning the courts of justice and judicial officers less than a year later on 13 April 1854, essentially restoring the jurisdiction of the Court of Sessions back to that of the 1851 act with the exception that indictments for murder,

---

[29] *The Statutes of California, First Session*, pp. 210–211, Chap. 86, "An Act to Organize the Court of Sessions."

[30] *The Statutes of California, Passed at the Second Session of the Legislature: Begun on the Sixth Day of January, 1851, and Ended on the First Day of May, 1851, at the City of San Jose* (n.p.: Eugene Casserly, State Printer, 1851), pp. 31–34, Chap. 2, "An Act amending an Act entitled 'An Act concerning the Courts of Justice of this State and Judicial Officers'," specifically p. 34, § 11 (hereafter cited as *The Statutes of California, Second Session*). This act amended a previous act by adding the hearing and determining of appeals from Mayor's Courts in cases of a criminal nature to the jurisdiction of the Court of Sessions. See, *The Statutes of California, Second Session*, pp. 9–31, Chap. 1, "An Act concerning the Courts of Justice of this State, and Judicial Officers," specifically p. 19, § 66.

[31] *The Statutes of California, Second Session*, pp. 9–31, Chap. 1, "An Act concerning the Courts of Justice of this State, and Judicial Officers," specifically p. 19, § 67.

[32] *The Statutes of California, Passed at the Fourth Session of the Legislature, Begun on the Third Day of January, 1853, and Ended on the Nineteenth Day of May, 1853, at the Cities of Vallejo and Benicia* (San Francisco: George Kerr, State Printer, 1853), pp. 287–305, Chap. CLXXX, "An Act Concerning the Courts of Justice of this State, and Judicial Officers" (hereafter cited as *The Statutes of California, Fourth Session*).

[33] *The Statutes of California, Fourth Session*, pp. 287–305, Chap. CLXXX, "An Act Concerning the Courts of Justice of this State, and Judicial Officers," specifically p. 295, sections 52 and 53.

manslaughter, and arson found against District Court judges were to be transmitted to another District Court for trial rather than tried and determined in the Court of Sessions.[34]

The 1853 act concerning the courts of justice and judicial officers was again amended on 14 February 1860 to add "fighting a duel, and killing or wounding any person therein" to the list of indictments for public offences the Court of Sessions could not try or determine.[35] Indictments found for murder, manslaughter, fighting a duel, and killing or wounding any person therein, or arson were to be transmitted to the District Court for trial, except those found against a District Court judge, when they were to be transmitted to another District Court for trial.

When the Courts of Sessions were abolished at the end of 1863 the jurisdiction "to inquire, by the intervention of a Grand Jury, of all public offences committed or triable in their respective counties" and "to try and determine all indictments found therein, for all public offences, except treason, misprision of treason, murder, and manslaughter" was given to the County Courts.[36] The jurisdiction "to hear and determine all cases, civil and criminal, appealed thereto, in the manner provided by law, from Courts held by Justices of the Peace, Recorders, and other inferior Municipal Courts" was also conferred on the County Courts.

---

[34] *The Statutes of California Passed at the Fifth Session of the Legislature, Begun on the Fourth Day of January, 1854, and Ended on the Fifteenth Day of May, 1854, at the Cities of Benicia and Sacramento* (Sacramento: B. B. Redding, State Printer, 1854), pp. 28–29, Chap. XX, "An Act to amend an Act entitled 'An Act concerning the Courts of Justice of this State and Judicial officers,' passed May, nineteenth, eighteen hundred and fifty-three," specifically p. 29, sections 7 and 8 (hereafter cited as *The Statutes of California, Fifth Session*).

[35] *The Statutes of California, Passed at the Eleventh Session of the Legislature, 1860, Begun Monday, the Second Day of January, and Ended on Monday, the Thirtieth Day of April* (Sacramento: Charles T. Botts, State Printer, 1860), p. 31, Chap. LV, "An Act to amend an Act entitled 'An Act concerning the Courts of Justice of this State and Judicial officers,' approved May nineteenth, on thousand eight hundred and fifty-three, and an Act amendatory thereof, approved April thirteenth, one thousand eight hundred and fifty-four" (hereafter cited as *The Statutes of California, Eleventh Session*).

[36] *The Statutes of California, Fourteenth Session*, pp. 333–346, Chap. CCLX, "An Act Concerning the Courts of Justice of this State, and Judicial Officers," specifically p. 337, sections 32 and 35.

Terms of the Court of Sessions

Unlike the California courts of today which are open for business year-round, the Court of Sessions met every other month or quarterly for only a few days or a couple of weeks at a time depending on the number of cases heard. These court meetings were referred to as "terms." On 11 April 1850, the California Legislature determined the beginning dates of these terms for each California county for the first time and set the first terms of the Court of Sessions in every California county except San Francisco and Sacramento Counties for the trial of all criminal cases to be heard. Over the years of the existence of the Sonoma County Court of Sessions the California Legislature amended the beginnings of its terms four times, as shown in the table below.

Beginnings of Sonoma County Court of Sessions Terms	Date Act Approved
Second Mondays of February, April, June, August, October, and December[37]	11 April 1850
First Mondays of February, April, June, August, October, and December[38]	11 March 1851 (took effect on 1 July 1851)[39]
First Mondays of February, April, June, August, October, and December[40]	19 May 1853 (took effect on 6 June 1853)
First Mondays of January, April, July, and October[41]	9 April 1856
First Mondays of February, May, August, and November[42]	12 April 1859

---

[37] *The Statutes of California, First Session*, pp. 210–211, Chap. 86, "An Act to Organize the Court of Sessions."

[38] *The Statutes of California, Second Session*, pp. 9–31, Chap. 1, "An Act Concerning the Courts of Justice of this State, and Judicial Officers," specifically pp. 20–21, § 73.

[39] *The Statutes of California, Second Session*, pp. 31–34, Chap. 2, "An Act Amending an Act entitled, 'An Act Concerning the Courts of Justice of this State and Judicial Officers'," specifically p. 34, § 12.

[40] *The Statutes of California, Fourth Session*, pp. 287–305, Chap. CLXXX, "An Act Concerning the Courts of Justice of this State, and Judicial Officers," specifically pp. 296–297, section 59.

[41] *The Statutes of California, Passed at the Seventh Session of the Legislature, Begun on the Seventh Day of January, One Thousand Eight Hundred and Fifty-six, and Ended on the Twenty-first Day of April, One Thousand Eight Hundred and Fifty-six, at the City of Sacramento* (Sacramento: James Allen, State Printer, 1856), p. 117, Chap. XCIX, "An Act Fixing the Time of Holding the Several Courts Authorized to be Held by the County Judge in the County of Sonoma" (hereafter cited as *The Statutes of California, Seventh Session*).

[42] *The Statutes of California, Passed at the Tenth Session of the Legislature, 1859, Begun on Monday, the Third Day of January, and Ended on Tuesday, the Nineteenth Day of April* (Sacramento: John O'Meara, State Printer, 1859), pp. 225–226, Chap. CCXIX, "An Act fixing the Terms of the County Court, Probate Court, and Court of Sessions, in Counties therein named."

Crimes and Punishments

In genealogical research it is important to understand the laws of the time and place in which one is researching. The laws of today's California are quite different from those that were in effect during the existence of the Courts of Sessions, 1850 through 1863.[43] In "An Act concerning Crimes and Punishments" passed on 16 April 1850 the first California Legislature defined the crimes, or public offences, and set out their punishments, for the soon-to-be new state of California.[44] The following list gives the definitions of many of the common crimes prosecuted in the Sonoma County Court of Sessions and their punishments as given by statute in this 1850 act along with any amendments or changes before 1864.

Grand larceny: Every person who shall feloniously steal, take, and carry, lead, or drive away the personal goods or property of another, of the value of fifty dollars or more, shall be deemed guilty of grand larceny, and upon conviction thereof shall be punished by imprisonment in the State prison for any term not less than one year, nor more than ten years.[45] In 1851, the words "or by death, in the discretion of the jury" were added to the end of the statute.[46] In 1856, the words added to the statute in 1851 were deleted, and the maximum sentence was changed to no more than fourteen years.[47]

Petit larceny: Every person who shall feloniously steal, take, and carry, lead, or drive away the personal goods or property of another, under the value of fifty dollars, shall be deemed guilty of petit larceny, and upon conviction thereof shall be punished by imprisonment in the county jail not more than six months, or by fine not more than five hundred dollars, or by both such fine and imprisonment.[48] In 1851, the words "or by any number of lashes not exceeding fifty upon the bare back, or by such fine or imprisonment and lashes, in the discretion of the jury" were added after the words "five hundred dollars."[49] In 1856, the words added to the statute in 1851 were deleted.[50]

---

[43] For current California law concerning crimes and punishments see, Legislative Counsel Bureau, *California Legislative Information* (http://leginfo.legislature.ca.gov : accessed 23 January 2019), path: California Law > Code Search > Penal Code – PEN > Part 1. Of Crimes and Punishments [25-680].

[44] *The Statutes of California, First Session*, pp. 229–247, Chap. 99, "An Act concerning Crimes and Punishments."

[45] *The Statutes of California, First Session*, pp. 229–247, Chap. 99, "An Act concerning Crimes and Punishments," specifically p. 235, § 60.

[46] *The Statutes of California, Second Session*, pp. 406–407, Chap. 95, "An Act to Amend an Act 'An Act concerning Crimes and Punishments'," specifically § 2.

[47] *The Statutes of California, Seventh Session*, pp. 219–221, Chap. CXXXIX, "An Act to Amend an Act entitled 'An Act Concerning Crimes and Punishments,' Passed April 16th, 1850," specifically p. 220, sec. 7.

[48] *The Statutes of California, First Session*, pp. 229–247, Chap. 99, "An Act concerning Crimes and Punishments," specifically p. 235, § 61.

[49] *The Statutes of California, Second Session*, pp. 406–407, Chap. 95, "An Act to Amend an Act 'An Act concerning Crimes and Punishments'," specifically p. 407, § 3.

[50] *The Statutes of California, Seventh Session*, pp. 219–221, Chap. CXXXIX, "An Act to Amend an Act entitled 'An Act Concerning Crimes and Punishments,' Passed April 16th, 1850," specifically p. 220, sec. 8.

Robbery: Robbery is the felonious and violent taking of money, goods, or other valuable thing from the person of another, by force or intimidation. Every person guilty of robbery shall be punished by imprisonment in the State prison for a term not less than one year, nor more than ten years.[51] In 1851, the words "or by death, in the discretion of the jury" were added to the end of the statute.[52] In 1856, the words added to the statute in 1851 were deleted, and the maximum sentence was changed to life.[53]

Murder: Murder is the unlawful killing of a human being, with malice aforethought, either express or implied. The unlawful killing may be effected by any of the various means by which death may be occasioned.[54] The punishment for any person convicted of the crime of murder shall be death.[55] In 1856, the degrees of the crime of murder and punishments thereof were defined as "All murder which shall be perpetrated by means of poison, or lying in wait, torture, or by any other kind of wilful, deliberate and premeditated killing, or which shall be committed in the perpetration or attempt to perpetrate any arson, rape, robbery or burglary, shall be deemed murder of the first degree; and all other kinds of murder shall be deemed murder of the second degree" and "Every person convicted of murder of the first degree, shall suffer death, and every person convicted of murder of the second degree shall suffer imprisonment in the State Prison for a term not less than ten years and which may extend to life."[56]

Manslaughter: Manslaughter is the unlawful killing of a human being without malice expressed or implied, and without any mixture of deliberation. It must be voluntary, upon a sudden heat of passion, caused by a provocation apparently sufficient to make the passion irresistible; or involuntary in the commission of an unlawful act, or a lawful act without due caution or circumspection.[57] Every person convicted of the crime of manslaughter shall be punished by imprisonment in the State prison for a term not exceeding three years, and fined not exceeding five thousand dollars.[58] In 1856, the maximum sentence was changed to ten years, and the fine was eliminated.[59]

---

[51] *The Statutes of California, First Session*, pp. 229–247, Chap. 99, "An Act concerning Crimes and Punishments," specifically p. 235, § 59.

[52] *The Statutes of California, Second Session*, pp. 406–407, Chap. 95, "An Act to Amend an Act 'An Act concerning Crimes and Punishments'," specifically p. 406, § 1.

[53] *The Statutes of California, Seventh Session*, pp. 219–221, Chap. CXXXIX, "An Act to Amend an Act entitled 'An Act Concerning Crimes and Punishments,' Passed April 16th, 1850," specifically p. 220, sec. 6.

[54] *The Statutes of California, First Session*, pp. 229–247, Chap. 99, "An Act concerning Crimes and Punishments," specifically p. 231, § 19.

[55] *The Statutes of California, First Session*, pp. 229–247, Chap. 99, "An Act concerning Crimes and Punishments," specifically p. 231, § 21.

[56] *The Statutes of California, Seventh Session*, pp. 219–221, Chap. CXXXIX, "An Act to Amend an Act entitled 'An Act Concerning Crimes and Punishments,' Passed April 16th, 1850," specifically p. 219, sec. 2.

[57] *The Statutes of California, First Session*, pp. 229–247, Chap. 99, "An Act concerning Crimes and Punishments," specifically p. 231, § 22.

[58] *The Statutes of California, First Session*, pp. 229–247, Chap. 99, "An Act concerning Crimes and Punishments," specifically p. 231, § 26.

[59] *The Statutes of California, Seventh Session*, pp. 219–221, Chap. CXXXIX, "An Act to Amend an Act entitled 'An Act Concerning Crimes and Punishments,' Passed April 16th, 1850," specifically p. 219, sec. 3.

Mayhem: Mayhem consists of unlawfully depriving a human being of a member of his or her body, or disfiguring or rendering it useless. If any person shall unlawfully cut out or disable the tongue, put out an eye, slit the nose, ear, or lip, or disable any limb or member of another, or shall voluntarily and of purpose put out an eye or eyes, every such person shall be guilty of mayhem, and on conviction shall be punished by imprisonment in the State Prison for a term not less than one year, nor more than five years.[60] In 1856, the State Prison term was changed to "not to exceed fourteen years."[61]

Assault: An assault is an unlawful attempt, coupled with a present ability to commit a violent injury on the person of another.[62] In 1856, the words "and every person convicted thereof, shall be fined in a sum not exceeding five hundred dollars or imprisoned in the County Jail not exceeding three months" were added to the statute.[63]

Assault with intent: An assault, with an intent to commit murder, rape, mayhem, robbery, or to commit felony larceny, shall subject the offender to imprisonment in the State Prison for a term not less than one year, nor more than fourteen years.[64] In 1855, the words "the infamous crime against nature" were inserted between the words "rape" and "mayhem" in the list of felonies, and the word "grand" was inserted before the word "larceny."[65]

Assault with a deadly weapon: An assault with a deadly weapon, instrument, or other thing, with an intent to inflict upon the person of another a bodily injury, where no considerable provocation appears, or where the circumstances of the assault show an abandoned and malignant heart, shall subject the offender to imprisonment in the State Prison not exceeding two years, or to a fine not exceeding five thousand dollars, or to both such fine and imprisonment.[66]

---

[60] *The Statutes of California, First Session*, pp. 229–247, Chap. 99, "An Act concerning Crimes and Punishments," specifically pp. 233–234, § 46.

[61] *The Statutes of California, Seventh Session*, pp. 219–221, Chap. CXXXIX, "An Act to Amend an Act entitled 'An Act Concerning Crimes and Punishments,' Passed April 16th, 1850," specifically p. 219, sec. 4.

[62] *The Statutes of California, First Session*, pp. 229–247, Chap. 99, "An Act concerning Crimes and Punishments," specifically p. 234, § 49. No specific punishment was called out for assault in this Act.

[63] *The Statutes of California, Seventh Session*, pp. 219–221, Chap. CXXXIX, "An Act to Amend an Act entitled 'An Act Concerning Crimes and Punishments,' Passed April 16th, 1850," specifically p. 220, sec. 5.

[64] *The Statutes of California, First Session*, pp. 229–247, Chap. 99, "An Act concerning Crimes and Punishments," specifically p. 234, § 50.

[65] *The Statutes of California, Passed at the Sixth Session of the Legislature, Begun on the First Day of January, One Thousand Eight Hundred and Fifty-Five, and Ended on the Seventh Day of May, One Thousand Eight Hundred and Fifty-Five, at the City of Sacramento* (Sacramento: B. B. Redding, State Printer, 1855), pp. 105–106, Chap. LXXXII, "An Act to amend an Act concerning Crimes and Punishments, passed April 16th 1850," specifically p. 106, sec. 2 (hereafter cited as *The Statutes of California, Sixth Session*).

[66] *The Statutes of California, First Session*, pp. 229–247, Chap. 99, "An Act concerning Crimes and Punishments," specifically p. 234, § 50.

Assault and battery: Assault and battery is the unlawful beating of another, and a person duly convicted thereof shall be fined in any sum not exceeding one thousand dollars, or imprisoned in the County Jail not exceeding one year.[67]

False imprisonment: False imprisonment is an unlawful violation of the personal liberty of another, and consists in confinement or detention without sufficient legal authority. Any person convicted of false imprisonment shall pay all damages sustained by the person so imprisoned, and be fined in any sum not exceeding five thousand dollars, or imprisoned in the County Jail for a term not exceeding one year.[68]

Burglary: Every person who shall in the night time forcibly break and enter, or without force (the doors and windows being open) enter into any dwelling house, or any other house whatever, or tent, or vessel, or other water craft, with intent to commit murder, robbery, rape, mayhem, larceny, or other felony, shall be deemed guilty of burglary, and upon conviction thereof, shall be punished by imprisonment in the State prison for a term not less than one nor more than ten years.[69] In 1858, the words "room, apartment or tenement" were added to the list of places that could be entered, and the words "grand or petit larceny, or any felony" replaced the words "murder, robbery, rape, mayhem, larceny, or other felony."[70]

Altering marks and brands: Every person who shall mark or brand, alter or deface the mark or brand of any horse, mare, colt, jack, jennet, mule, or any one or more head of neat cattle or sheep, goat, hog, shoat, or pig, not his or her own property, but belonging to some other person, or cause the same to be done, with intent thereby to steal the same, or to prevent identification thereof by the true owner, shall, on conviction thereof, be punished by imprisonment in the State prison for a term not less than one year, nor more than five years.[71]

Perjury: Every person having taken a lawful oath, or made affirmation in any judicial proceeding, or in any other matter where by law an oath or affirmation is required, who shall swear or affirm willfully, corruptly, and falsely, in a matter material to the issue or point in question, or shall suborn any other person to swear or affirm as aforesaid, shall be deemed guilty of perjury or

---

[67] *The Statutes of California, First Session*, pp. 229–247, Chap. 99, "An Act concerning Crimes and Punishments," specifically p. 234, § 51.

[68] *The Statutes of California, First Session*, pp. 229–247, Chap. 99, "An Act concerning Crimes and Punishments," specifically p. 234, § 52.

[69] *The Statutes of California, First Session*, pp. 229–247, Chap. 99, "An Act concerning Crimes and Punishments," specifically p. 235, § 58.

[70] *The Statutes of California, Passed at the Ninth Session of the Legislature, 1858, Begun on Monday, the Fourth Day of January, and Ended on Monday, the Twenty-Sixth Day of April* (Sacramento: John O'Meara, State Printer, 1858), p. 206, Chap. CCXLV, "An Act to amend an Act entitled 'An Act concerning Crimes and Punishments,' passed April sixteenth, A. D. one thousand eight hundred and fifty" (hereafter cited as *The Statutes of California, Ninth Session*).

[71] *The Statutes of California, First Session*, pp. 229–247, Chap. 99, "An Act concerning Crimes and Punishments," specifically pp. 235–236, § 65.

suborrnation of perjury (as the case may be), and upon conviction thereof shall be punished by imprisonment in the State Prison for any term not less than one nor more than fourteen years.[72]

Other crimes, or public offences, such as gaming and raffling, were first defined, and their punishments set, in the years after the passage of the 1850 act concerning crimes and punishments.

Gaming: All banking games, and games having a per centage, are hereby prohibited within this State, except as hereinafter provided, and any person offending against this section shall, upon conviction, be deemed guilty of a misdemeanor, and shall, for each and every offence, be punished by a fine of not less than one hundred nor more than one thousand dollars, or with imprisonment in the County jail for not less than three nor more than six months.[73]

In 1855, this statute was repealed and replaced with: Every person who shall open or cause to be opened, any gaming bank or game of chance, the whole or part of which belongs to him, in any house or other place whatsoever, whether said house or place be owned or usually occupied by said person or not; and likewise every person who shall deal for, or otherwise conduct, or assist in conducting the affairs of such bank or game; and also every person who shall permit such bank or game to be opened in any house under his control, may be prosecuted by indictment by the Grand Jury of the county in which the offense shall have been committed; or before any Justice of the Peace, or Recorder's Court of said county; and on conviction, upon evidence of one or more credible witnesses, shall be fined in a sum not exceeding five hundred dollars, nor less than one hundred dollars for the first offense, and double such amount for each subsequent offense; and in all cases, the house or place, in which such illegal gaming is carried on or held, except it be done without the knowledge of the owner thereof, shall be held liable for the fines imposed on persons for such illegal gaming within the same.[74]

In 1857, some of the games prohibited were specifically named and gaming was made a felony by the addition of a State prison term as punishment: Every person who shall deal, play, carry on, open, or cause to be opened, or who shall conduct, either as owner or employee, whether for hire or not, any game of faro, monte, roulette, lansquenet, rouge et noir, or any banking game played with cards, dice, or any other device, whether the same be played for money, checks, credit, or any representative of value, shall be guilty of felony, and on conviction thereof shall be punished by imprisonment in the State Prison for a term not exceeding two years, and by fine not exceeding five thousand dollars.[75]

---

[72] *The Statutes of California, First Session*, pp. 229–247, Chap. 99, "An Act concerning Crimes and Punishments," specifically p. 239, § 82.

[73] *The Statutes of California, Second Session*, pp. 165–166, Chap. 8, "An Act to License Gaming," specifically p. 165, § 1.

[74] *The Statutes of California, Sixth Session*, pp. 124–125, Chap. CIII, "An Act to Suppress Gaming," specifically p. 124, sec. 1.

[75] *The Statutes of California, Passed at the Eighth Session of the Legislature, 1857, Begun on Monday, the Fifth Day of January, and Ended on Thursday, the Thirtieth Day of April* (Sacramento: James Allen, State Printer, 1857), pp. 267–268, Chap. CCXXX, "An Act to prohibit Gaming," specifically p. 267, sec. 1.

In 1860, the game of rondo was added to the listed of prohibited games and gaming was reduced to a misdemeanor: Each and every person who shall deal, play, or carry on, open or cause to be opened, or who shall conduct, either as owner or employé, whether for hire or not, any game of faro, monte, roulette, lansquenet, *rouge et noir*, rondo, or any banking game, played with cards, dice, or any other device, whether the same be played for money, checks, credit, or any other representative of value, shall be guilty of a mis-demeanor, and on conviction thereof shall be punished by a fine of not less than one hundred dollars, and not more than one thousand dollars, and shall be imprisoned in the county jail until such fine, together with the costs of prosecution, to be taxed against the defendant, shall be paid.[76] In 1863, a proviso was added such that the county jail imprisonment for non-payment of the fine shall not exceed one year.[77]

Raffling: In 1851, all lotteries were prohibited in the California. Any person who shall set up or promote any lottery, for money or property of real value, real or personal, and any person who shall aid, either by printing or writing, or shall in any way be concerned in the setting up, managing, or drawing of any such lottery, or who shall in any building, owned or occupied by him, or under his control, knowingly permit the setting up, managing, or drawing of any such lottery, shall be deemed guilty of a misdemeanor, and on conviction thereof, be punished by fine not less than five hundred dollars, nor more than five thousand dollars, or by imprisonment not to exceed six months, or by both such fine and imprisonment.[78]

In 1854, the term "lottery" was to be construed in this 1851 act "as to apply to and include within the provisions of that Act lotteries, raffles, and all devices whatever in the nature of a lottery or raffles."[79] In 1855, the original 1851 act prohibiting lotteries and the 1854 act explanatory to it were repealed and replaced with: It shall be unlawful for any person or persons, to dispose of any money, goods, personal property, real estate, or other valuables by lottery, raffle, or any game of chance, or by any drawn numbers represented by tickets or cards, or by throwing and counting of dice, or by any other scheme or means by which an uncertain disposition of said money, goods, personal property, real estate, or other valuables, is sought to be had. It shall also be unlawful for any person or persons to aid in any such scheme before-named, in any way whatever, either in printing, circulating, buying or selling, managing or drawing tickets or cards, or chances, in any lottery, raffle, gifts, enterprise or other unlawful means as above-named.[80] A violation of this statute shall be deemed a misdemeanor and "shall be punished by imprisonment in the County Jail not to exceed six months, and by fine in any sum not less than five hundred dollars, nor more than five thousand dollars." In 1861, the punishment was to be by

---

[76] *The Statutes of California, Eleventh Session*, p. 69–70, Chap. XCIX, "An Act to Prohibit Gaming," specifically p. 69, sec. 1.

[77] *The Statutes of California, Fourteenth Session*, p. 723, Chap. CCCCXLVI, "An Act to amend an Act entitled an Act to prohibit Gaming, approved March seventh, eighteen hundred and sixty."

[78] *The Statutes of California, Second Session*, p. 211, Chap. 28, "An Act to Prohibit Lotteries."

[79] *The Statutes of California, Fifth Session*, p. 58, Chap. LIII, "An Act explanatory of an Act entitled 'An Act to prohibit Lotteries,' passed March 11, 1851."

[80] *The Statutes of California, Sixth Session*, pp. 99–100, Chap. LXXV, "An Act to Prohibit Lotteries, Raffles, Gifts, Enterprises and other Schemes, of a like Character."

imprisonment or fine, and the fine was reduced to "any sum not exceeding five hundred dollars."[81]

---

[81] *The Statutes of California, Passed at the Twelfth Session of the Legislature, 1861: Begun Monday, the Seventh Day of January, and Ended on Monday, the Twentieth Day of May* (Sacramento: Charles T. Botts, State Printer, 1861), pp. 229–232, "An Act to prohibit Lotteries, Raffles, Gift Enterprises, and other schemes of like character," specifically p. 231, sec. 15 (hereafter cited as *The Statutes of California, Twelfth Session*).

County Judges of Sonoma County, 1850-1863

The 1849 California Constitution stipulated that the County Judge of each California county along with two Justices of the Peace "shall hold Courts of Sessions with such criminal jurisdiction as the Legislature shall prescribe," and on 11 April 1850, the California Legislature passed "An Act to organize the Court of Sessions" which directed that each Court of Sessions was to be composed of the County Judge, acting as the presiding Judge, and two Justices of the Peace, as Associates Justices, elected by all the Justices of the Peace of the County.[82]

Below is a list of the County Judges of Sonoma County who presided over the Sonoma County Court of Sessions from 1850 through 1863.

1. Henry A. Green was elected on 1 April 1850 and took his oath of office on 9 April 1850.[83] He died on 11 July 1851 at Sonoma of "liver complaint."[84] Martin E. Cooke was appointed on 6 August 1851 by Governor John McDougal to fill the vacancy caused by the death of H. A. Green, but Cooke declined to accept.[85]

2. William O. King was appointed on 13 August 1851 by Governor John McDougal to fill the vacancy caused by H. A. Green's death.[86] He took his oath of office on 16 August 1851.[87] King held only one term of the Court of Sessions (August term 1851).[88]

3. Charles P. Wilkins was elected on 3 September 1851.[89] He took his oath of office on 8 September 1851.[90] California Secretary of State records indicate that he resigned sometime before 13 September 1852 when Governor John Bigler appointed Phillip R. Thompson as the County Judge of Sonoma County.[91] Evidence suggests, however, that this appointment never took effect as no letter of resignation from Wilkins to Governor Bigler has been found among the

---

[82] Constitution of the State of California, 1849, Article VI (Judicial Department), section 8. *The Statutes of California, First Session*, pp. 210–211, Chap. 86, "An Act to Organize the Court of Sessions."

[83] Sonoma County, California, oath of office for H. A. Green as County Judge, 9 April 1850; Sonoma County Archives, Santa Rosa.

[84] "Died," *The Daily Alta California* (San Francisco, California), 18 July 1851, p. 2, col. 6. The death notice reads: "At Sonoma, on the 11th last, of liver complaint, the Hon. H. A. Green, Judge of Sonoma county."

[85] California, "Record" (Dec., 1849–Oct. 30, 1857), entry for Martin E. Cooke as a County Judge of Sonoma County, p. 44, 6 August 1851; Secretary of State Records, F3680-1; California State Archives, Sacramento.

[86] California, "Record" (Dec., 1849–Oct. 30, 1857), entry for William O. King as a County Judge of Sonoma County, p. 44, 13 August 1851; Secretary of State Records, F3680-1; California State Archives, Sacramento.

[87] Sonoma County, California, oath of office for William O. King as County Judge, 16 August 1851; Sonoma County Archives, Santa Rosa.

[88] J. P. Munro-Fraser, *History of Sonoma County* (San Francisco: Alley, Bowen & Co., 1880), 142.

[89] Sonoma County, California, certificate of election for Charles P. Wilkins as County Judge, 8 September 1851; Sonoma County Archives, Santa Rosa.

[90] Sonoma County, California, oath of office for Charles P. Wilkins as County Judge, 8 September 1851; Sonoma County Archives, Santa Rosa.

[91] California, "Executive Records" (Dec., 1849–July, 1876), entry for Phillip R. Thompson as a County Judge of Sonoma County, p. 208, 13 September 1852; Secretary of State Records, F3680-2; California State Archives, Sacramento.

Governor's correspondence and Wilkins continued to serve as County Judge until F. W. Shattuck was elected and commissioned.[92] Wilkins committed suicide on 1 August 1864 in Santa Rosa "by cutting his throat with a razor."[93]

4. Frank W. Shattuck was elected on 7 September 1853 and commissioned on 27 September 1853.[94] He resigned on 21 January 1855, effective 1 February 1855.[95] He died on 14 October 1893 in Petaluma "from a stroke of paralysis."[96]

5. John E. McNair was appointed by Governor John Bigler on 23 January 1855, vice Shattuck resigned, to take effect on 1 February 1855.[97] He took his oath of office on 30 January 1855.[98] He died on 6 May 1856 in San Francisco at the Tehama House of "pulmonary consumption."[99]

6. William Churchman was elected on 5 September 1855 to fill the Shattuck vacancy.[100] He was elected again on 5 October 1857 for a full term and took his oath of office on 30 March 1858.[101] He was once more elected on 7 September 1859 and took his oath of office on 3 October 1859.[102] He died on 4 November 1873 in Santa Rosa.[103]

---

[92] C. P. Wilkins's signature as County Judge can be found on documents included in Sonoma County probate case files from September 1851 through at least June 1853 and on oaths of office for various Sonoma County public officials from September 1851 through November 1853. Phillip R. Thompson's signature as County Judge appears on no known documents.

[93] "Death of Judge Wilkins," *The Sonoma County Democrat* (Santa Rosa, California), 6 August 1864, p. 2, col. 1. "Shocking Death of an Old Californian," *Daily Alta California* (San Francisco, California), 4 August 1864, p. 1, col. 1.

[94] California, "Record" (Dec., 1849–Oct. 30, 1857), entry for Frank W. Shattuck as a County Judge of Sonoma County, p. 45, 7 September 1853; Secretary of State Records, F3680-1; California State Archives, Sacramento.

[95] Frank W. Shattuck to Hon. John Bigler, Governor, letter of resignation, 21 January 1855; Governor's Office Records (1849–1974), Resignations (1849–1941), F3672:186; California State Archives, Sacramento.

[96] "Death of Judge F. W. Shattuck," *The Sonoma Democrat* (Santa Rosa, California), 21 October 1893, p. 1, col. 1. "Called Suddenly," *The Morning Call* (San Francisco, California), 15 October 1893, p. 9, col. 4.

[97] California, appointment of John E. McNair as County Judge of Sonoma County, 23 January 1855; Sonoma County Archives, Santa Rosa.

[98] Sonoma County, California, oath of office for John E. McNair as County Judge, 30 January 1855; Sonoma County Archives, Santa Rosa.

[99] "Died," *The Wide West* (San Francisco, California), 11 May 1856, p. 2, col. 7. The death notice reads: "In this city [San Francisco], May 6, of pulmonary consumption, Hon. John E. McNair, aged 26 years and 11 months." "Judge J. E. McNair," *The Petaluma (California) Weekly Journal and Sonoma County Advertiser*, 10 May 1856, p. 2, col. 2.

[100] "Official Vote of Sonoma County," *The Petaluma (California) Weekly Journal and Sonoma County Advertiser*, 29 September 1855, p. 2, col. 4.

[101] "Official Vote of Sonoma and Mendocino Counties," *The Sonoma County Journal* (Petaluma, California), 18 September 1857, p. 2, cols. 4–5. Sonoma County, California, oath of office for William Churchman as County Judge, 30 March 1858; Sonoma County Archives, Santa Rosa.

[102] "Election Returns: Sonoma County – Official," *The Sonoma Democrat* (Santa Rosa, California), 6 October 1859, p. 4, cols. 1–2. Sonoma County, California, oath of office for William Churchman as County Judge, 3 October 1859; Sonoma County Archives, Santa Rosa.

[103] "Died," *The Sonoma Democrat* (Santa Rosa, California), 8 November 1873, p. 5, col. 2. The death notice reads: "CHURCHMAN – In Santa Rosa, Nov. 4, aged 55 years, 3 months and 6 days. Deceased was a native of Indiana, and came to California in 1853 and has been since the time of his death a resident of Sonoma County."

Grand Jury

On 20 April 1850, the first California Legislature passed "An Act to regulate proceedings in Criminal Cases," which defined the terms used in and laid out the legal procedures to be followed in the prosecution of criminal cases.[104] A crime, or public offense, was defined as "an act or omission forbidden by law, and to which is annexed, upon conviction, either of the following punishments: 1. Death; 2. Imprisonment; 3. Fine; 4. Removal from office; or, 5. Disqualification to hold and enjoy any office of honor, trust, or profit, under this State." The Grand Jury of each county was given the power and duty "to inquire into all public offenses committed or triable within the county, and to present them to the Court, either by indictment or presentment." They were also required to "inquire into the case of every person imprisoned in the jail of the county on a criminal charge, and not indicted; into the condition and management of the public prisons within the county; and into the wilful and corrupt misconduct in office of public officers of every description within the county." Thus, the documents the researcher will find among the Grand Jury records comprise indictments, presentments, and reports documenting the Grand Jury inquiries.

The number of Grand Jurors making up the Grand Jury and the qualifications required to be a Grand Juror were changed several times by the California Legislature over the years the Court of Sessions was in existence. Initially in 1850, the Grand Jury was to be composed of between sixteen and twenty-three men, each of whom were required only to be a qualified elector of their county.[105] In 1851, the number of Grand Jurors was to be between twelve to eighteen, and each Grand Juror was required to be: 1.) a citizen of the United States, 2.) an elector of the County in which they were returned, 3.) over twenty-one and under sixty years of age, 4.) in the possession of their natural faculties, and 5.) never convicted of a felony or a misdemeanor involving moral turpitude.[106] In 1852, the number of Grand Jurors was to be between seventeen and twenty-three, and the Grand Juror qualifications remained the same as in 1851.[107] Finally in 1863, the number of Grand Jurors was to be between thirteen and fifteen, and each Grand Juror was required to be: 1.) a citizen of the United States, 2.) a qualified elector of the county, 3.) a resident of the township at least three months before being selected and returned, 4.) in possession of their natural faculties, 5.) sufficiently knowledgeable of the language in which the Court was held, and 6.) assessed on the last assessment roll of their township or county on real or personal property, or both, belonging to them, if a resident at the time of the assessment.[108]

---

[104] *The Statutes of California, First Session*, pp. 275–331, Chap. 119, "An Act to regulate proceedings in Criminal Cases."

[105] *The Statutes of California, First Session*, pp. 275–331, Chap. 119, "An Act to regulate proceedings in Criminal Cases," specifically p. 288, § 178 and § 181.

[106] *The Statutes of California, Second Session*, pp. 290–296, Chap. 30, "An Act concerning Jurors," specifically p. 290, § 1 and p. 293, § 21.

[107] *The Statutes of California, Third Session*, pp. 107–111, Chap. XLVII, "An Act Concerning Jurors," specifically p. 107, section 1 and p. 108, section 9.

[108] *The Statutes of California, Fourteenth Session*, pp. 630–640, Chap. CCCCV, "An Act concerning Grand and Trial Jurors," specifically p. 630, section 1 and p. 634, section 11.

By the 1851 "Act concerning Jurors," persons could be exempted from liability to act as Grand Jurors if they fell into one of the following categories: 1.) a judicial officer, 2.) any other officer of this State or of the United States, whose duties are at the time inconsistent with their attendance as a Juror, 3.) an attorney or counsellor, 4.) a minister of the Gospel or a priest of any denomination, 5.) a teacher in a college, academy, or school, 6.) a practicing physician, 7.) an officer, keeper, or attendant of an alms house, poor house, hospital, asylum, or other charitable institution, created by or under the laws of this State, and 8.) a captain, mate, or other officer, or any person employed on board of a steamer, vessel, or boat, navigating the waters of this State.[109] In 1852, officers, keepers, or attendants of any County Jail or of the State Prison and keepers of public ferries were added to the list.[110] Finally in 1863, express agents, mail carriers, telegraph operators, and toll gate keepers were added to the list.[111] A person could also be excused from acting as a Grand Juror "when for any reason, his interests or those of the public, will be materially injured by his attendance, or when his own health or the death or sickness of a member of his family, requires his absence."[112]

The 1850 act to regulate criminal case proceedings specified several other Grand Jury procedures.[113] Once the requisite number of Grand Jurors were empaneled, the Court was to appoint a foreman of the Grand Jury and administer this oath:

> You, as Foreman of the Grand Jury, shall diligently inquire into and true presentment make of all public offenses against the people of this State, committed or triable within this county, of which you shall have or can obtain legal evidence; you shall present no person through malice, hatred, or ill will, nor leave any unpresented through fear, favor, or affection, or for any reward or the promise or hope thereof; but in all your presentments you shall present the truth, the whole truth, and nothing but the truth, according to the best of your skill and understanding, so help you God.

The following oath was to then be administered to the other Grand Jurors present: "The same oath which your Foreman has now taken before you, on his part, you, and each of you, shall well and truly observe on your part, so help you God." After being empaneled and sworn, the Grand Jurors were to be charged by the Court by reading to them the statutes concerning the Grand Jury's powers and duties. They were to withdraw to a private room to conduct their inquiries, receiving "no other evidence than such as is given by witnesses produced and sworn before them, or furnished by legal documentary evidence." The Grand Jury could ask the advice of the Court or District Attorney, but neither of those officers were permitted to be present during the Grand

---

[109] *The Statutes of California, Second Session*, pp. 290–296, Chap. 30, "An Act concerning Jurors," specifically pp. 290–291, § 2.

[110] *The Statutes of California, Third Session*, pp. 107–111, Chap. XLVII, "An Act Concerning Jurors," specifically p. 107, section 2.

[111] *The Statutes of California, Fourteenth Session*, pp. 630–640, Chap. CCCCV, "An Act concerning Grand and Trial Jurors," specifically p. 630, section 3.

[112] *The Statutes of California, Second Session*, pp. 290–296, Chap. 30, "An Act concerning Jurors," specifically p. 291, § 3.

[113] *The Statutes of California, First Session*, pp. 275–331, Chap. 119, "An Act to regulate proceedings in Criminal Cases."

Jury sessions unless such advice was asked for. They were "to find an indictment when all evidence before them, taken together, was such as in their judgment would warrant a conviction by the trial jury." Upon the completion of the business before them, the Grand Jury was to be discharged by the Court. If an offense was committed during the sitting of the Court after the discharge of the Grand Jury, the Court could summon another Grand Jury.

Indictments and Presentments

By the 1850 "Act to regulate proceedings in Criminal Cases," an indictment (or presentment) required the concurrence of at least twelve Grand Jurors.[114] When so found, the indictment, usually written and signed by the District Attorney, was to be endorsed "a true bill" and signed by the Grand Jury Foreman. The names of the witnesses examined before the Grand Jury were to be inserted at the foot of the indictment before it was presented to the Court and was to "contain the title of the action, specifying the name of the Court to which the indictment is presented, and the names of the parties; a statement of the acts constituting the offense in ordinary and concise language, without repetition, and in such manner as to enable a person of common understanding to know what is intended." An example of an indictment presented to the Sonoma County Court of Sessions is shown below.

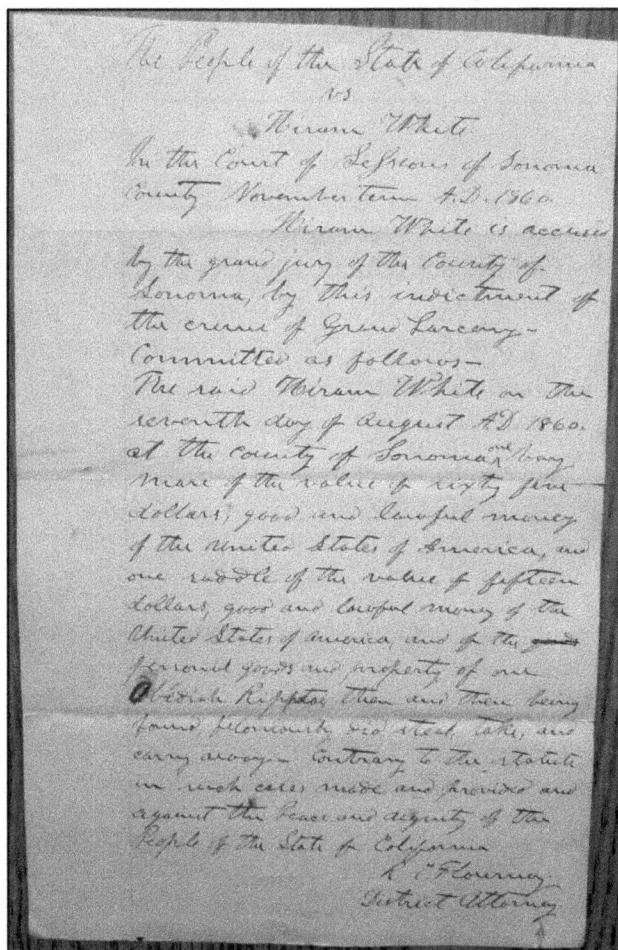

Hiram White indictment, November term 1860, Sonoma County Court of Sessions

---

[114] *The Statutes of California, First Session*, pp. 275–331, Chap. 119, "An Act to regulate proceedings in Criminal Cases."

Further Reading

Davis, W. N., Jr. "Research Uses of County Court Records, 1850–1879, and Incidental Intimate Glimpses of California Life and Society, parts I and II." *California Historical Quarterly* 52 (No. 3, Fall, 1973): 241–266 and (No. 4, Winter, 1973): 338–365.

Blume, William Wirt. "California Courts in Historical Perspective." *Hastings Law Journal* 22 (No. 1, November, 1970): 121–195.

Rose, Christine. *Courthouse Research for Family Historians: Your Guide to Genealogical Treasures.* San Jose, California: CR Publications, 2004.

Black, Henry Campbell. *A Dictionary of Law Containing Definitions of the Terms and Phrases of American and English Jurisprudence, Ancient and Modern.* 1st edition. St. Paul, Minnesota: West Publishing Co., 1891.

About the Author

Steven M. Lovejoy is a retired chemist living in Sebastopol, Sonoma County, California. He is currently (2020) the president of the Sonoma County Genealogical Society and a Sonoma County Historical Records Commissioner. He holds a PhD in synthetic organic chemistry from the University of Washington and a Certificate in Genealogical Research from Boston University. He can be contacted at stevelov@comcast.net.

Table of Court of Sessions Cases

State Archives Case File #	Defendants	Charges	Date Indictment or Presentment Filed	Register Page(s)	Minute Book Volume: Page(s)	Judgment Book Page
0A	James N. Cook	Assault with intent to commit murder	10 Jun 1852			
0B	George B. Farrar	Assault with intent to kill	24 Feb 1852			
0C	John S. Hittle (var. Hittell)	Petit larceny	February term 1852			
0D	Thomas H. Pyatt	Assault with intent to commit murder	9 Jun 1852			
0D	H. L. Lidstrom, C. H. Bartlett, Joseph Leprince, Oliver Bolio, [?] Blachier, M. Rickman (var. Ryckman)	Violation of the license law	2 Aug 1852			
1	John Hollingsworth	Rendering aid and assistance to a prisoner enabling his escape	5 Apr 1853			
2	Benjamin L. Moore	Murder	14 Jun 1853			
3	Francisco Caseres (alias Pancho, indicted as Francisco Carceras)	Petit larceny	12 Feb 1853			
4	William H. Conklin	Rendering aid and assistance to a prisoner enabling his escape	5 Apr 1853			
5	Adolph Blachen (var. Blashen, indicted as John Doe)	Selling liquor to an Indian	8 Feb 1853			
6	Robert Graham	Obstructing the navigation of the Sonoma river	7 Jun 1853			
7	S. R. McDonald	Grand larceny	9 Apr 1853			
7	S. R. McDonald, Nancy Jane Gwinnette, John Smith, James I. Smith, and William H. Conklin	Grand larceny and rendering aid and assistance to a prisoner enabling his escape	7 Apr 1853			
7A	J. B. Scott	Furnishing intoxicating liquor to an Indian	14 Apr 1853			
7A	J. B. Scott	Selling spiritous liquors at retail without a license	7 Apr 1853			
7B	DeWitt C. Thompson	Grand larceny	6 Apr 1853			
7C	G. T. Pauli and F. Schultz (dba Pauli and Schultz)	Retailing dry goods and spiritous liquors without a license	8 Feb 1853			
7D	Alexander C. McDonald	As County Treasurer using State funds for himself	3 Aug 1852			
7E	[?] Metcham	Retailing dry goods and spiritous liquors without a license	8 Feb 1853			
7F	Donald McDonald	Selling goods, wares, and merchandise without a license	7 Apr 1853			
7G	John McCurdy	Perjury	5 Apr 1853			
7H	[?] McCallister	Selling spiritous liquors without a license	7 Apr 1853			
7I	Christian Mertin	Furnishing intoxicating liquor to an Indian	14 Apr 1853			
7I	Christian Mertin	Furnishing intoxicating liquor to an Indian	14 Apr 1853			
7J	Nicholas J. T. Long and Norman Galusha	Petit larceny	6 Apr 1853			

State Archives Case File #	Defendants	Charges	Date Indictment or Presentment Filed	Register Page(s)	Minute Book Volume: Page(s)	Judgment Book Page
7K	[?] Lillie and [?] Godwin	Selling liquor by retail and vending goods, wares, and merchandise without a license	7 Apr 1853			
7L	John Leary (alias Jack Leary)	Petit larceny	12 Aug 1853			
7M	James Jackson, John Jackson, John Doe, Richard Roe, and Hiram Smith	Grand larceny	9 Apr 1853			
7N	Harmon Heald	Selling liquor, merchandise, and wares without a license	8 Apr 1853			
7O	Richard Fowler and [?] Harris	Retailing spiritous liquors without a license	8 Feb 1853			
7P	Thomas Hogan	Grand larceny	7 Apr 1853			
7Q	Nancy Jane Gwinnett, John Smith, James I. Smith, and William H. Conklin	Accessories after the fact in the commission of the crime of grand larceny	9 Apr 1853			
7Q	Nancy Jane Gwinnett	Perjury	7 Apr 1853			
7R	Lewis Adler	Retailing dry goods and spiritous liquors without a license	8 Feb 1853			
7S	Juan Beronda	Grand larceny	7 Apr 1853			
7T	Basil Barratt	Grand larceny	13 Jun 1853			
7U	Thomas Baylis and [?] Flogdell (dba Baylis and Flogdell)	Retailing dry goods and spiritous liquors without a license	8 Feb 1853			
7V	[?] Bugner	Selling, giving, or furnishing spiritous liquors to an Indian	7 Apr 1853			
7W	[?] Blachen and [?] Ducollet (dba Blachen and Ducollet)	Selling goods, wares, and merchandise without a license	7 Apr 1853			
7W	[?] Blachen and [?] Ducollet	Retailing dry goods and spiritous liquors without a license	8 Feb 1853			
7X	William Fraseir (var. Frazer)	Assault with intent to commit murder	14 Apr 1853			
7Y	[?] Cousins	Selling goods, wares, and merchandise contrary to the laws of the State	7 Apr 1853			
7Z	Walter Comstock (indicted as William G. Comstock)	Petit larceny	14 Apr 1853			
7AA	Walter Comstock (indicted as William G. Comstock)	Grand larceny	14 Apr 1853			
7BB	Raphael Celia	Petit larceny	8 Apr 1853			
7CC	Raphael Celia	Grand larceny	14 Apr 1853			
7DD	Robert G. Bynum, Hiram Smith, and James Jackson	Receiving stolen property	Apr term 1853			
7EE	William Bihler	Assault and battery	10 Aug 1853			
7FF	William Bihler	Assault and battery	10 Aug 1853			
7GG	[?] Breckenbridge	Selling spiritous liquors without a license	7 Apr 1853			
7HH	[?] Nathanson	Selling spiritous liquors at retail by the glass without a license	7 Apr 1853			

State Archives Case File #	Defendants	Charges	Date Indictment or Presentment Filed	Register Page(s)	Minute Book Volume: Page(s)	Judgment Book Page
7II	There is only one document in this case file, a writ of execution dated 12 Jun 1854 ordering the Sheriff of Sonoma County to collect a $50 fine from John Allen out of his personal and/or real property for contempt of Court by disregarding a summons as a Grand Juror for the June term 1854.					
8	John Williams	Grand larceny	9 Feb 1854			
8	John Williams	Petit larceny	9 Feb 1854			
8	Erroneously included in this case file is a subpoena dated 12 Feb 1852 commanding John M. Cantrell, Joseph Livreau, James A. Campbell, Pernell Campbell, George Miller, J. Beasley, William Potter, Moses Briggs, [?] Bolier, and Whan Mendocio to appear before the Hon. Peter Campbell, a Justice of the Peace in and for the County of Sonoma, at the Court house in the City of Sonoma on 13 Feb 1852 to give evidence in the cause the People v. Gustav Sarrebourse de Hautville (var. D'Audeville) and Joseph LeBrett concerning the murder of Lewis Legendre on or about the last of January [1852].					
9	Peter Campbell	Offering a bribe to an officer	9 Aug 1854			
9	Erroneously included in this case file is a summons dated 9 Sep 1850 issued by the Sonoma County District Court summoning Peter Campbell to appear before the District Court forthwith to show cause why he should not be removed from exercising the office of Justice of the Peace which the Grand Jury alleged he was illegally holding and exercising.					
10	The documents in this case file consist of papers filed in and proceedings had in the Court of Sessions of Marin County in the case of the People v. John Smith and Michael Jordon. In an indictment filed on 8 Aug 1854, the Marin County Grand Jury accused the defendants of obstructing public justice by entering the Marin County Court of Sessions court room at San Raphael while the Court was in session with a large number of people with force and arms in an unlawful and riotous manner, obstructing the progress of public justice and compelling the Court to adjourn. The case was transferred to the Sonoma County Court of Sessions on 4 Oct 1854.					
11	The documents in this case file consist of a transcript of the docket of the Hon. J. B. Boggs, a Justice of the Peace of Sonoma Township, dated 30 May 1854, concerning the case of the People v. H. Hirsh and two notices of appeal. The defendant was found guilty in the Justice's Court of selling goods without a license and fined $100 and the costs of the suit on 23 May 1854.					
11A	T. M. Leavenworth, William Leavenworth, and M. M. Cummings	Petit larceny	11 Aug 1854			
11A	T. M. Leavenworth, William Leavenworth, and M. M. Cummings	Malicious mischief	11 Aug 1854			
11B	[?] Hunter	Disquieting and disturbing a congregation by talking, cursing, and swearing with a loud voice	3 Oct 1854			
11C	Elisha Ely	Intentionally defacing, obliterating, tearing down, and destroying an advertisement for the sale of certain property to pay taxes	9 Aug 1854			
11D	Alejandro (an Indian)	Murder	8 Jun 1854			
11E	William Norman	Obtaining money or a draft or an order for money by false pretenses	9 Feb 1854			
11F	Isaac N. Randolph	Keeping a billiard table for pay at $1 a game without a license	9 Apr 1853			
11G	[?] Pierce and [?] Randolph	Selling spiritous liquors without a license	7 Apr 1853			
11H	Antonio Piña (var. Peña)	Grand larceny	8 Apr 1853			
11I	There is only one document in this case file, a writ of execution dated 9 Aug 1854 ordering the Sheriff of Sonoma County to collect a $50 fine from Lafayatt Barner (var. Barnard, Burnard) for disregarding a summons as a Grand Juror on 5 Jun 1854.					
11J	There is only one document in this case file, a writ of execution dated 9 Aug 1854 ordering the Sheriff of Sonoma County to collect a $50 fine from C. Irwin for disregarding a summons as a Grand Juror on 5 Jun 1854.					

State Archives Case File #	Defendants	Charges	Date Indictment or Presentment Filed	Register Page(s)	Minute Book Volume: Page(s)	Judgment Book Page
12	B. B. Bonham (a minister of the Gospel)	Joining in marriage a female under the age of 18 without the consent of her parents with whom she resided	5 Dec 1855			
13	James Hendry, Charles Jefferson, R. C. Smith, and Milroy Powell	False imprisonment	4 Jun 1855			
13	James Hendry, Charles Jefferson, R. C. Smith, and Milroy Powell	False imprisonment	4 Jun 1855			
13	James Hendry, Charles Jefferson, R. C. Smith, and Milroy Powell	False imprisonment	4 Jun 1855			
14*						
15	Alfred Davenport (var. Deavenport)	Grand larceny	4 Dec 1855			
16	This case file consists of six documents from the Justice's Court of Petaluma Township: 1.) an undated fee statement of J. G. Fair, a Constable of Vallejo Township, for three arrests, subpoenaing ten witnesses before examination, ten subpoena copies, and mileage on serving subpoenas, 2.) an undated order by the Hon. William Churchman, a Justice of the Peace of Petaluma Township, discharging Elijah H. Smith, who had been charged with grand larceny, after examination of John Merritt, there being no sufficient cause to believe Smith guilty, 3.) a bench warrant dated 12 May 1855 by the Hon. William Churchman, a Justice of the Peace of Petaluma Township, commanding the Sheriff or any Constable, Marshall, or Policeman to arrest Elijah H. Smith to answer to the complaint of James Hendry that Smith had committed grand larceny by stealing three of Hendry's horses, 4.) a subpoena for [?] Lampier or the Flying Duchman, H. Williams, Charles Jefferson and wife, J. Merritt, L. C. Lewis, [?] Walker, [?] Hill, [?] Nubill (var. Newbill), Dr. Galland, [?] Hagens (var. Hagans), John Babb, S. Beckwith, H. Ramer, and John M. Roberts to appear as witnesses dated 11 May 1855, 5.) a subpoena for Zadok Jackson, [?] Bartlette, Robert Leonak, [?] McMurry, Henry Holmes, William Arr, Jefferson Harden, William Hogeland, and William Faught to appear as witnesses dated 14 May 1855, and 6.) the complaint of James Hendry dated 12 May 1855 accusing Elijah H. Smith of stealing three of James Hendry's horses (value $175) on or about 17 Apr 1855. See case file # 13 for a related case.					
17	This case file consists of one document, a certified copy of the judgment in the case of the People v. Patrick P. Burk issued by the Hon. Frank W. Shattuck's Justice's Court of Petaluma Township filed on 15 Jun 1857. Patrick P. Burk was sentenced to 60 days confinement in the County Jail of Sonoma County for whipping his wife, Margaret Burk, on 1 Jun 1857. Burk died while in Jail seven days later on 8 Jun 1857.					
18	Francisco Esparsa (alias Chihuahua)	Grand larceny	4 Jun 1855			
19	This case file consists of the examinations of W. H. Hatch, J. C. Stuny, J. L. Rhoads, and S. W. Coolbroth by the Hon. George Robinson, a Justice of the Peace for Bodega Township, filed on 19 Dec 1855 concerning the alleged stealing of some sacks of potatoes by C. J. Zienwaldt. Justice Robinson ordered that Zienwaldt be held to answer to the charges.					
20	Jose Antonio and Surdo (Indians)	Murder	26 Apr 1855			
21	C. P. Vores (var. Vorse, Vorce)	Grand larceny	26 Apr 1855			
22	This case file consists of documents from the Justice's Court of the Hon. William Churchman, a Justice of the Peace [of Petaluma Township], concerning the alleged assault of Casper Louis by Joseph Scapacasa on 24 Jun 1855: 1.) a complaint and deposition by John Albany dated 26 Jun 1855 accusing Joseph Scapacasa of assaulting Casper Louis with a butcher knife on the evening of 24 Jun 1855 at Antonio Scapacasa's grocery store in Petaluma, 2.) examinations of the witnesses John Albany, Sebastiano Liquore, Caper Louis (signed name as Gaspar Lusis), John Murray, Charles R. Arthur, H. F. Cook, and Antonio Scapacasa (the accused's father, signed name as Antonio Schiapacasse) dated 27 Jun 1855, 3.) examinations of witnesses Angele Scapacasa (the accused's mother), Sebastiano Spignesi, and Alexander VanderNoot dated 28 Jun 1855, and 4.) a statement by Joseph Scapacasa (signed name as Joseph Schiapacase) dated 27 Jun 1855. Justice Churchman found no sufficient cause to find Scapacasa guilty of the charge and ordered him to be discharged.					
23	This case file consists of documents from the Justice's Court of the Hon. William Churchman, a Justice of the Peace of Petaluma Township, concerning the alleged stealing of three oxen by Alfred Edwards on or about 27 Mar 1855: 1.) a complaint and deposition by Thomas Frost dated 10 Apr 1855 accusing Alfred Edwards of stealing three oxen (value $185), property of Robert McCracken and Elisha Frost, from Thomas Frost's premises in Petaluma Township on or about 27 Mar 1855, 2.) a deposition by Cornelius Mason dated 10 Apr 1855, 3.) a warrant for the arrest of Alfred Edwards dated 10 Apr 1855, 4.) depositions by Robert McCracken, Elisha Frost, William Dampier, Thomas Frost, and Cornelius Mason dated 11 Apr 1855, and 5.) recognizance bonds of Thomas Frost, Elisha Frost, Robert McCracken, William Dampier, and Cornelius Mason dated 11 Apr 1855.					
23A	Scotch Smith	Rescue of a prisoner from the custody of an officer	5 Dec 1855			

State Archives Case File #	Defendants	Charges	Date Indictment or Presentment Filed	Register Page(s)	Minute Book Volume: Page(s)	Judgment Book Page
23B	Samuel Smith	Assaulting a Peace Officer	5 Dec 1855			
23C	Alexander Shaw and John Campbell	Murder	4 Apr 1855			
23C	Alexander Shaw	Murder	4 Apr 1855			
23D	John Campbell	Accessory to Murder	4 Apr 1855			
23E	Joseph H. P. Morris	Gaming house	5 Dec 1855			
23F	Charles M. Hudspeth	Assault and battery	4 Jun 1855			
23G*						
23H	King Emerson and Charles Smith	Gaming house	5 Dec 1855			
23I	William M. Ormsby	Grand larceny	8 Jun 1854			
23I	William M. Ormsby	Grand larceny	8 Jun 1854			
24	Samuel Finley	Furnishing intoxicating liquors to Indians	6 Feb 1856			
24	Joseph Finley and William Finley	Assault with a deadly weapon	9 Jul 1856			
24	Joseph Finley and William Finley	False imprisonment	9 Jul 1856			
24	Joseph Finley and William Finley	Exhibiting deadly weapons	9 Jul 1856			
25	William A. Buster (Treasurer of Sonoma County)	Using and loaning of money belonging to the State of California and the County of Sonoma for his own use and benefit	17 Oct 1856			
25	William A. Buster (Treasurer of Sonoma County)	Embezzlement	8 Apr 1857			
25	William A. Buster (Treasurer of Sonoma County)	Using and loaning of money belonging to the County of Sonoma	7 Apr 1857			
25	William A. Buster (Treasurer of Sonoma County)	Using and loaning of money belonging to the State of California	7 Apr 1857			
25	William A. Buster (Treasurer of Sonoma County)	Keeping a gaming house	8 Apr 1857			
26	George W. Baylor, Amos B. Ingram, Benjamin F. McCardie, [?] Buyes, and [?] Prather	Assault with intent to commit murder	15 Oct 1856			
26	George W. Baylor, A. B. Ingram, Benjamin F. McCardie, William Prather, and [?] Buyes	Assault with intent to commit murder	16 Oct 1856			
27	Robert Patton (var. Patten)	Grand larceny	4 Dec 1855			
28	Moses C. Briggs	Assault with intent to commit murder	6 Jan 1858	66	D: 31, 39-40, 41, 46, 60, 86-87	
28	Moses C. Briggs	Assault with a deadly weapon	6 Feb 1856			
28	Moses C. Briggs	Assault with a deadly weapon	14 Jan 1858			
28A	Joshua Lewis	Petit larceny	11 Oct 1856			
29	This case file consists of four documents which should be filed with case file # 49 (People v. Charles Spurgen and Robert Fowler): 1.) a subpoena dated 11 Oct 1856 summoning J. W. Beldon to appear and testify at the Court of Sessions in the case of People v. Robert Fowler on 13 Oct 1856, 2.) a bond for appearance dated 8 Oct 1856 in which John Hendley and Julio Carrillo undertake that Robert Fowler will appear in Court and failing that they will pay the People of the State of California $1,000, 3.) an undated defendant's request for instructions to the jury, and 4.) undated Court instructions to the jury in the case of People v. Robert Fowler.					

State Archives Case File #	Defendants	Charges	Date Indictment or Presentment Filed	Register Page(s)	Minute Book Volume: Page(s)	Judgment Book Page
29A	Joshua Perkins	Assault with a deadly weapon	9 Oct 1856			
30	Oliver Bolieu	Branding cattle not of his own property	10 Oct 1856			
31	This case file consists of three documents: 1.) a bench warrant dated 24 Mar 1856 issued by the Hon. Peter A. Forsee's Justice's Court of Mendocino Township for the arrest of Burk Miles, Andrew Miles, John Miles, and William H. Miles accused of assaulting Israel M. Millay with a rifle on 1 Feb 1856 and 24 Mar 1856, 2.) a bond for appearance filed 3 May 1856 in which Israel M. Millay undertakes to appear at the next Court of Sessions as a prosecuting witness in the case of the People v. John Miles and Harrison Miles and failing that he will pay the People of the State of California $200, and 3.) a bond for appearance filed 3 May 1856 in which Burk Miles and William Miles undertake that John Miles and Harrison Miles will appear in Court and answer to the charge of assaulting Israel M. Millay with a deadly weapon and failing that they will pay the People of the State of California $1,000.				
32	Baronet Barns, Reason Barns, and Jackson Estis	Assault with intent to commit murder	8 July 1856			
32	Baronet Barns, Reason Barns, and Jackson Estis	Assault with intent to commit murder	8 July 1856			
32A	Raphael Selalla	Grand larceny	7 Oct 1856			
32B	Samuel Finley	Keeping a gaming house	6 Feb 1856			
32C	Samuel Finley	Assault and battery	6 Feb 1856			
33	Amos Merrifield (var. Merryfield, alias Cheap John)	Selling spiritous liquors less than 1 mile from a camp meeting		64	D: 7, 16	
34	A. C. Freeland and William Freeland	Branding cattle not their own property	8 Apr 1857			
35	George Johnson (indicted as George A. Johnson)	Assault with intent to commit rape	7 Oct 1857	63	D: 7, 15, 17-19, 20	
36	James (var. John R.) Shaw	Keeping a gaming house	8 Apr 1857			
37	Davenport Cousins (var. Cousens)	Keeping a gaming house	8 Apr 1857			
38	Byrd Brumfield	Assault with a deadly weapon	9 Jul 1857	57	D: 6, 8, 13-14	
39	Jose Remeris and Fernando Remeris	Grand larceny	7 Jul 1857			
40	Jack (var. A. J.) Forrester (var. Forrister)	Keeping a gaming house	9 Jul 1857	55	D: 4, 5, 11	
41	Charles Spurgen and James Stephens	Assault with intent to commit murder	9 Jul 1857	56	D: 5, 11, 12, 21-23	
41	Charles Spurgen and James Stephens	Setting a spring gun	9 Jul 1857			
42	J. S. Ormsby	Assault and battery	8 Jul 1857	58	D: 6, 9	
43	Condy Coneghan	Grand larceny	8 Jul 1857			
44	James (var. John R.) Shaw	Keeping a gaming house	8 Apr 1857			
45	Lorenzo Failis	Grand larceny	8 Oct 1857			
46	George Powell	Petit larceny	7 Oct 1857			
47	Israel M. Malay	Petit larceny	9 Oct 1857	64	D: 28, 31, 33, 34-35	
47	Israel M. Malay	Malicious mischief	9 Oct 1857	65	D: 28, 31, 33, 35	
47	Erroneously included in this case file is a single undated sheet which reads: "Now comes Frank W. Shattuck and moves the Court that a committee be appointed to examine John W. Kendall as to his qualifications to practice as an atty. at law in the County of Sonoma as prescribed by law."					
48	William Townsend	Burglary	6 Jan 1857			
49	Charles Spurgen and Robert Fowler	Assault with a deadly weapon with intent to commit bodily injury	8 Oct 1856			

State Archives Case File #	Defendants	Charges	Date Indictment or Presentment Filed	Register Page(s)	Minute Book Volume: Page(s)	Judgment Book Page
49	Charles Spurgen and Robert Fowler	False imprisonment	8 Oct 1856			
50	Charles L. Lambert	Assault with intent to commit murder	8 Oct 1856			
50A	Vincent Lambert	Manslaughter				
51	William Leary (var. Larry)	Assault with a deadly weapon	8 Apr 1857	59	D: 6, 8-9, 10-11	
52	Angus McDonald	Assault and battery	11 Oct 1856			
52A	This case file consists of several documents filed in the Sonoma County Clerk's Office on 29 Nov 1851 concerning an 1851 Napa County Court of Sessions case (People v. William H. Richardson) which was transferred to the Sonoma County Court of Sessions for trial: 1.) a certified copy of the records of the Court of Sessions of Napa County of the case People v. William H. Richardson dated 27 Nov 1851, 2.) an affidavit by W. H. Richardson dated 7 Oct 1851 in which he petitions the Court for a change of venue to Sonoma County because he believes he cannot get a fair and impartial trial in Napa County, 3.) a Court order by the Hon. Johnson Horrell, County Judge, dated 17 Sep 1851, holding W. H. Richardson to answer to the charges brought against him and admitting him to bail, 4.) a recognizance bond of Fordyce J. Benjamin and Meier Goldsmith dated 17 Sep 1851 for their appearance to give evidence in the case of the People v. William H. Richardson, 5.) a bond of Henry H. Laurence and John E. Brown dated 17 Sep 1851 who undertake that William H. Richardson will appear and answer charges in the case of the People v. William H. Richardson, 6.) a complaint dated 17 Sep 1851 by M. Goldsmith accusing W. H. Richardson of assault and battery with the intent to kill on the person of one [Mr.] Gray at Napa City on 17 Sep 1851, 7.) an arrest warrant by the Hon. Johnson Horrell, County Judge, dated 17 Sep 1851, for the arrest of W. H. Richardson, with a notation on the back by N. McKimmey, Sheriff, that he had arrested W. H. Richardson on 17 Sep 1851, and 8.) depositions of Meier Goldsmidt, Henry Fowler, Fordyce J. Benjamin, Dr. David B. Hodges, E. W. McKinstry, M. H. N. Kendig, and Joseph Arnold dated 17 Sep 1851 concerning the assault on Mr. Gray by W. H. Richardson at the Union House in Napa City on the morning of 17 Sep 1851.				
53	Thomas Burns	Grand larceny	8 Jan 1858	110	D: 37, 50, 53, 57, 67	
53	Thomas Burns	Altering marks and brands	14 Jan 1858	111	D: 37, 50, 53-54	
53	Thomas Burns	Grand larceny	14 Jan 1858			
54	James Morris	Resisting an officer in the discharge of his official duties	12 Apr 1858	120	D: 51, 70, 71, 73, 74, 87, 89, 91, 105, 111, 120, 121, 125	
54	John Morris	Resisting an officer in the discharge of his official duties	12 Apr 1858	117	D: 51, 65, 70, 72, 73, 74, 87, 89, 91, 105, 111, 120, 121, 124-125	
55	John Dayton	Perjury	8 Jul 1858	90	D: 92	
55	Included this case file is a capias issued by the Court of Sessions dated 5 Oct 1858 commanding the Sheriff of Sonoma County to bring John Delahanty before the Court forthwith so that he may show cause why he did not obey the orders of the Court.[115] The Sheriff, E. L. Green, returned the capias the same day stating that he did not find John Delahenty. This capias belongs in case file # 56, People v. Edward McLaughlin.				
56	Edward McLaughlin	Assault with intent to commit great bodily injury	8 Jul 1858	94	D: 92, 93, 95, 96, 107, 108, 111-112	

---

[115] Sonoma County, California, Court of Sessions, Minute Book D: 108, The People v. Edward McLaughlin, court order to issue an attachment for John Delahanty, M. Barnes, and Dan Brown, 5 October 1858; Sonoma County Archives, Santa Rosa.

State Archives Case File #	Defendants	Charges	Date Indictment or Presentment Filed	Register Page(s)	Minute Book Volume: Page(s)	Judgment Book Page
56	Edward McLaughlin	Assault with intent to commit great bodily injury	7 Oct 1858	94, 136	D: 115, 116, 120, 123, 128-129, 130, 135, 141, 142, 143, 144, 146-147, 148, 150A	8
57*						
58	Walter S. Jarboe	Assault with intent to commit bodily injury	9 Jan 1858	77	D: 38, 46, 74, 75, 87	
59	O. P. Cash	Malicious mischief	14 Jan 1858	114	D: 50, 54, 60-61	
60	George W. M. Cowles	Raffling	13 Jan 1858	108	D: 48, 55	
61	James Davis	Raffling	9 Jan 1858	84	D: 38, 83, 85	
62	M. Doyle, James Knowles, John H. Richardson, C. I. Robinson, and Samuel Kern	Assault and battery	14 Jan 1858	115	D: 51, 57-59, 63	1
62	M. Doyle, James Knowles, John H. Richardson, C. I. Robinson, and Samuel Kern	Rescue	14 Jan 1858	118	D: 50, 57	
63	[?] King and [?] Harrington	Raffling	13 Jan 1858	73	D: 47, 55	
64	T. M. Leavenworth	Grand larceny	14 Jan 1858	69	D: 49, 56, 61, 67, 70, 72, 75, 76, 77, 82, 85, 87, 89, 90, 105, 107, 112, 113	
64	T. M. Leavenworth	Altering marks and brands	14 Jan 1858	70	D: 49, 62	
64	T. M. Leavenworth	Petit larceny	14 Jan 1858	71	D: 49, 62	
65	Robert E. Harrison	Assault with intent to commit murder	8 Jul 1858	86	D: 92, 94, 97-98, 99	3
66	Lewis W. Freeman	Grand larceny	13 Oct 1858	98	D: 110, 130, 132	7
67	Henry S. Gird	False representation	8 Jul 1858	89	D: 104, 107-108	
68	Smith D. Towne	Raffling	13 Jan 1858	107	D: 47, 56	
69	Robert Mills and Simon Taylor	False imprisonment	12 Apr 1858	81, 83	D: 70, 82, 83, 84, 91, 105, 106, 107, 111, 135, 138, 139, 140, 141, 151-152	
70	George Canning Smith	False representation	8 Jul 1858	91	D: 104, 108	
71	James Veeder	Selling liquor to an Indian	12 Apr 1858	80	D: 83, 84, 88	
72	Griffin P. Sanders (indicted as Griffith P. Sanders)	Assault with intent to commit great bodily harm	8 Oct 1858	123	D: 117, 118-119, 120, 127	4
73	Samuel Means	Petit larceny	12 Apr 1858	82	D: 83, 84, 88	
74	George W. McFarland	Passing counterfeit gold coin	8 Oct 1858	124	D: 110, 115, 116, 121, 126	
75	C. M. C. McVicar	Raffling	13 Jan 1858	72	D: 47, 55	
76	B. Newman	Raffling	13 Jan 1858	76	D: 48, 56	
77	H. L. Weston	Raffling	13 Jan 1858	75	D: 48, 56	

State Archives Case File #	Defendants	Charges	Date Indictment or Presentment Filed	Register Page(s)	Minute Book Volume: Page(s)	Judgment Book Page
78	Fred Johnson	Raffling	13 Jan 1858	74	D: 47, 56	
79	[?] Badger	Petit larceny	14 Jan 1858			
80	Jacob B. Palmer	Raffling	14 Jan 1858	109	D: 49, 56	
80	Jacob B. Palmer	Keeping, renting, and letting horses and carriages and saddle horses, etc. for hire without a license/violation of section 79 of the Revenue Act of 1861	7 Nov 1861		E: 301, 310, 319	
81	Thomas D. Williamson	Raffling	13 Jan 1858	78	D: 48, 56	
81A	William (var. Bill) Rains	Assault with intent to kill		93, 121	D: 109, 114, 122	
81B	James Arlington Delahanty (alias James Arlington)	Perjury	12 Jan 1859	95, 100	D: 137, 140, 141, 145-146, 149, 150, 153-154, 155, 156, 157-161, 168-170, 171, 182	
81C	James B. Boggs	Assault and battery	10 Apr 1858	122	D: 67, 68, 69	2
81D	Charles Broback	Assault with a deadly weapon with intent to commit bodily injury	8 Jul 1858	85	D: 92, 93, 95, 96	
81E	This case file consists of several documents concerning John S. Eagan (var. Egan): 1.) a petition by John S. Eagan to the Hon. William Churchman for a writ of habeas corpus with the judge's order to issue the writ dated 31 Jul 1858, 2.) a peace bond of John W. Titcomb and John Delahenty dated 15 Jul 1858 in which they indebt themselves to the People of the State of California for $1,000 on the condition that John S. Eagan will keep the peace, especially towards Sarah Eagan, for six months as ordered by William Haydon, Recorder of the City of Petaluma, on 14 Jul 1858, 3.) a certified copy of this peace bond, 4.) an undated acknowledgement of service by William G. Gordon, District Attorney, of a notice of an application for hearing of a motion to discharge John S. Eagan upon a writ of habeas corpus, 5.) a writ of habeas corpus by the Hon. William Churchman, County Judge, dated 31 Jul 1858 notifying E. L. Green, Sheriff of Sonoma County, to bring John Eagan before him on 2 Aug 1858, with notations on the back by the Hon. William Churchman ordering the Sheriff to discharge John S. Eagan from custody on 3 Aug 1858 and by E. L. Green, Sheriff, that he had done so, and 6.) another certified copy of the peace bond with the notation by E. L. Green, Sheriff of Sonoma County, dated 2 Aug 1858, that he had returned the writ of habeas corpus, a certified copy of the peace bond, and the body of John S. Eagan to his Hon. William Churchman.					
81F	This case file consists of only one document, an execution dated 1 Mar 1858 by the Hon. William Churchman, County Court Judge, commanding the Sheriff of Sonoma County to collect a fine of $25 and accruing costs imposed on Simon Taylor on 7 Oct 1857 for non-attendance as a trial juror during the October term 1857 of the Court of Sessions.[116] The Sheriff, E. L. Green, by his Under Sheriff, A. B. Nally, certified that he had received the execution on 1 Mar 1858 and returned it satisfied in full on 8 Mar 1858.					
82	Fenwick Fisher	Assault and battery	3 Aug 1859		D: 231, 232, 234, 238-239	
83	Gilbert Gillett	Assault with a deadly weapon with intent to commit murder	11 Nov 1859		E: 17	
84	Finis Ewing	Assault with a deadly weapon with intent to inflict bodily injury	9 Nov 1859	140	E: 6, 9, 12, 13-14, 15-16, 17	
85	John W. Ball, George H. Morrison (alias Tim Ryan), Frank Ward, and William S. Brown (a colored man)	Robbery	7 Apr 1859	105	D: 165, 166, 177; E: 37, 38	

---

[116] Sonoma County, California, Court of Sessions, Minute Book D: 13, The People v. Byrd Brumfield, court order imposing a $25 fine on Simon Taylor for not appearing or answering when called as a trial juror, 7 October 1857; Sonoma County Archives, Santa Rosa.

State Archives Case File #	Defendants	Charges	Date Indictment or Presentment Filed	Register Page(s)	Minute Book Volume: Page(s)	Judgment Book Page
85	John W. Ball, George H. Morrison (alias Tim Ryan), Frank Ward, and William S. Brown (a colored man)	Grand larceny	7 Apr 1859	126A	D: 165, 166, 173, 174-175, 179-180, 184, 185, 186, 187, 188, 189, 191-192, 193, 194-195, 196-197, 198-200, 201-206, 207-208, 210, 211, 213-216, 217-218, 220, 223, 224; E: 20, 38	
85	John W. Ball	Grand larceny	7 Apr 1859	128, 138	D: 165, 173, 174, 175, 179, 184, 186, 191-192, 193, 194-197, 204, 210, 215, 223, 224; E: 20	
85	George H. Morrison (alias Tim Ryan)	Grand larceny	7 Apr 1859	129	D: 165, 173, 174, 175, 179, 184, 185, 186, 198-200, 201, 202, 211, 223, 224; E: 38	
85	Frank Ward	Grand larceny (no. 1)	7 Apr 1859	130	D: 166, 173, 174, 175, 179, 184, 185, 186, 201, 202-203, 213-214, 215, 216, 220	
85	William S. Brown (a colored man)	Grand larceny	7 Apr 1859	135	D: 166, 173, 175, 180, 185, 188, 205-208, 214, 217-218	
85	John W. Ball, George H. Morrison (alias Tim Ryan), Frank Ward, and William S. Brown (a colored man)	Burglary	7 Apr 1859	127	D: 165, 166, 173-174, 175-177, 180-181, 183, 184, 186, 188, 189; E: 5-6, 10-11, 37, 38	
85	John W. Ball	Burglary	7 Apr 1859	132	D: 165, 173-174, 175-177, 180, 183, 184, 186, 189; E: 5-6, 10-11	
85	George H. Morrison (alias Tim Ryan)	Burglary	7 Apr 1859	133	D: 165, 173-174, 175-177, 181, 183, 184, 186, 189; E: 37	
85	Frank Ward	Burglary	7 Apr 1859	134	D: 166, 173-174, 175-177, 181, 184, 186, 189	
85	William S. Brown (a colored man)	Burglary	7 Apr 1859	131	D: 166, 173-174, 175-177, 181, 184, 188, 189	

State Archives Case File #	Defendants	Charges	Date Indictment or Presentment Filed	Register Page(s)	Minute Book Volume: Page(s)	Judgment Book Page
86	Henry Austin	Assault with a deadly weapon with intent to inflict bodily injury	8 Feb 1860		E: 27, 32, 34, 36, 44-45, 68-69, 77	
87	James McGowan (alias James Connelly) and Joseph H. Ball	Grand larceny	11 Apr 1859		D: 187	
87	Joseph H. Ball	Grand larceny	11 Apr 1859	112, 139	D: 200, 206, 216-217, 218, 221-222, 223	
87	James McGowan (alias James Connelly)	Grand larceny	11 Apr 1859	113	D: 224	
88	William J. Morris	Grand larceny	4 Aug 1859		D: 227, 232, 234, 240, 241	
89	R. B. Markle	Assault with an intent to kill			E: 6, 13, 38	
90	Antonio Valasques (var. Valasquez, Velasquez)	Petit larceny	6 Apr 1859	125	D: 172, 174, 183	
90A	William Harris	Grand larceny (no. 1)	8 Oct 1858	96	D: 109, 117, 118, 123, 131	5
90A	William Harris	Grand larceny (no. 2)	8 Oct 1858	97	D: 109, 117, 118, 123, 131	6
90A	William Harris	Grand larceny	2 Aug 1859		D: 227, 229, 230, 231, 236-238, 242	
90B	This case file consists of only one document, an eight-page transcript of records from the Court of Sessions of Santa Clara County in the case of the People v. Lewis Mahoney dated 28 Mar 1859 and filed in Sonoma County on 1 Apr 1859. In an indictment filed on 11 Nov 1856 the Grand Jury of Santa Clara County accused Lewis Mahoney (alias John Johnston) of stealing one of William Gillis's cows (value $100) on 20 Aug 1856. The trial jury found the defendant guilty on 15 Nov 1856, and the Court sentenced the defendant to five years' imprisonment in the State Prison on 18 Nov 1856. He was received by San Quentin on 2 Dec 1856 and escaped and was recaptured three times between 6 Jan 1856 and 24 Mar 1859.[117] He was pardoned by Governor John B. Weller on 26 Mar 1859 in return for his testimony against John W. Ball, George H. Morrison (alias Tim Ryan), Frank Ward, and William S. Brown who had been accused of stealing $3,000 of Berthold Hoen's in Santa Rosa on the night of 7 Nov 1858.[118] See case file #s 85 and 90D.					
90C	Bill (var. William) Williams (a colored man)	Rape	10 Feb 1860		E: 30, 31, 40	
90D	William S. Brown (a colored man)	Grand larceny	7 Apr 1859	135	D: 166, 173, 175, 180, 184, 188, 205-208, 214, 217-218	
90E	Louis Duthel (indicted as Louis Duchel)	Assault with intent to commit murder	2 Aug 1859		D: 227, 229-230, 231, 235-236, 237, 241-242	

[117] California, State Prison Register (1851–1867), Executive Department, entry no. 1044, Lewis Mahony, p. 72, received 2 December 1856; California State Archives, Sacramento.

[118] California, Supreme Court, case # 2489 (WPA # 7353), The People v. John W. Ball, copy of the record of the proceedings in the Court of Sessions of Sonoma County in the case of the People v. John W. Ball, 12 July 1859, pp. 5–6, copy of the Governor's pardon of Louis Mahoney dated 26 March 1859; California State Archives, Sacramento.

State Archives Case File #	Defendants	Charges	Date Indictment or Presentment Filed	Register Page(s)	Minute Book Volume: Page(s)	Judgment Book Page
90F	This case file consists of six documents concerning the case of the People v. Charles Patton which had been appealed from the Recorder's Court of Petaluma to the County Court of Sonoma County: 1.) a ten-page transcript of the proceedings of the case of the People v. Charles Patton in the Recorder's Court of Petaluma entitled "Statement of the Case on Appeal from Recorder's Court of Petaluma" filed 9 Mar 1859, 2.) a subpoena dated 18 Jul 1859 issued by the Sonoma County Court of Sessions commanding William S. Bryant and William Hill to appear and testify on the part of the defendant at the Court of Sessions in the case of the People v. Charles Patton on 1 Aug 1859, 3.) a subpoena dated 25 Jul 1859 issued by the Sonoma County Court of Sessions commanding Ely Smith to appear and testify on the part of the defendant at the Court of Sessions in the case of the People v. Charles Patton on 1 Aug 1869, 4.) a subpoena dated 5 Apr 1859 issued by the County Court of Sonoma County commanding William S. Bryant, Frank Demling, Jesse Jackson, and F. W. Deshills [var. T. W. Dashields] to appear and testify on the part of the plaintiff at the County Court of Sonoma County in the case of the People v. Charles Patton forthwith, 5.) a subpoena dated 1 Apr 1859 issued by the County Court of Sonoma County commanding Eli Smith, William Hill, and William S. Bryant to appear and testify on the part of the defendant and appellant at the County Court of Sonoma County in the case of the People v. Charles Patton on 4 Apr 1859, and 6.) an undated motion to dismiss in the case of the People v. Charles Patton filed 4 Aug 1859 by William Ross, District Attorney, who moved the Court to dismiss the case because the evidence was insufficient to convict the defendant.				
90G	Louis Piña	Gaming	9 Oct 1858	99	D: 122	
90G	Louis Piña	Gaming	4 Jan 1859	99	D: 136, 139-140	
90H	James Watson	Assault with a deadly weapon with intent to commit bodily injury	12 Apr 1859	137	D: 194, 197, 211, 212, 219, 220, 229, 234; E: 5, 8, 9	
90I	Phillips Williams	Gaming	9 Oct 1858		D: 122	
90I	Phil Williams	Gaming	4 Jan 1859		D: 139	
90J	Frank Ward	Grand larceny (no. 2)	9 Apr 1859	106	D: 185, 187, 201, 203	
91*						
92	James M. Stevens (indicted as James Stephens)	Assault and battery	10 Feb 1860		E: 25-26, 40, 42-43, 57, 58-59, 61, 73	
93	James Schivo	Assault with intent to commit murder	9 Nov 1860	161	E: 139, 147, 148, 152, 154, 156, 157-158, 165	
94	Andrew J. Markwell	Vending by retail spiritous, malt, and vinous liquors without a license	9 Aug 1860	158	E: 131, 141, 151	
95	John Morris	Assault with intent to commit murder	11 May 1860	155	E: 85, 93, 95, 97, 98, 103-104, 111, 114, 122-124, 125, 127, 129, 130, 134	
96	William P. Barnes	Assault with intent to commit murder			E: 27, 43	
97	John Morand	Gaming house	15 Nov 1860		E: 162	
98	Franklin W. Green	Assault with a deadly weapon with intent to commit bodily injury	9 Feb 1860		E: 29, 38, 39, 41, 56-57, 58, 60, 63, 64, 65	
99	Thomas J. Blackwell	Assault with a deadly weapon with intent to inflict bodily injury	11 May 1860	157	E: 97, 107-108, 110-111, 118	
100	Robert Fawcett and William Harris	Burglary	9 Feb 1860		E: 28, 29, 36-37, 39, 41, 46-47, 48, 49, 50-51	

State Archives Case File #	Defendants	Charges	Date Indictment or Presentment Filed	Register Page(s)	Minute Book Volume: Page(s)	Judgment Book Page
100	William Harris	Burglary	14 Feb 1860		E: 57, 64, 67, 68, 70-71, 77-78	
101	Milton Hall	Gaming	15 Nov 1860		E: 162	
102	Hiram Hill	Petit larceny	11 Feb 1860		E: 26, 44, 45, 46, 48, 53-54, 72	
103	John Hunter	Grand larceny	7 Aug 1860		E: 120, 124	
104	George W. Hagenmeyer	Assault with intent to commit a rape	14 Nov 1860		E: 160	
105	Juan Seron (indicted as John Serena)	Grand larceny	8 Feb 1860		E: 27, 33, 34, 36, 41-42, 65, 71, 73-74	
106	George Tomblins (var. Tomlins, indicted as George Tomblin)	Assault with intent to commit murder	8 May 1860	151	E: 85-86, 88, 89-90, 93, 98, 112-113, 115	
107	This case file consists of four documents: 1.) a letter dated 5 Mar 1860, Marysville, E. V. Sutter to Genl. Hinton, Santa Rosa, 2.) a copy of a Sutter County, California deed dated 1 Jul 1850, John A. Sutter and Anna Sutter, his wife, of Hock Farm, Sutter County, California to Henry E. Robinson, John S. Fowler, Eugene F. Gillespie, and John McDougal, 3.) a letter dated 5 Mar 1860, Marysville, Emil V. Sutter to Messrs. Hinton and Wilks, Attorneys at law, Santa Rosa, and 4.) an affidavit of notice by Thomas L. Thompson, publisher and proprietor of the *Sonoma County Democrat* newspaper, dated 22 Jun 1860, stating that a notice had run in the newspaper for three successive weeks immediately prior to 18 Jun 1860 concerning the application of William Benitz to the Sonoma County District Court to establish the genuineness of the land patent of Rancho de Munis, more commonly known as the Fort Ross Ranch.					
107A	Spencer P. Emerson	Assault with intent to commit rape	10 Nov 1860	163	E: 139, 150, 155, 163-164, 170, 237, 245, 269-270, 274	
107B	Perez Douglass	Assault with a deadly weapon with intent to inflict a bodily injury			E: 120, 126	
107C	John Linus	Assault with intent to commit murder	8 Nov 1860	160	E: 139, 146, 147, 149, 156-157, 158, 159	
107D	Ramon Arenas	Counterfeiting/passing counterfeit money	13 Feb 1860		E: 29-30, 50, 54, 55, 61, 66, 76, 82-83, 119	
107E	This case file consists of only one document, an execution dated 21 Mar 1860 by the Hon. William Churchman, Judge of the Court of Sessions, commanding the Sheriff of Sonoma County to collect a fine of $10 and accruing costs imposed on Agostin Harasthy on 6 Feb 1860 for non-attendance as a trial juror during the February term 1860 of the Court of Sessions.[119] The Sheriff, J. J. Ellis, by his Deputy Sheriff, J. W. Morris, certified that he had received the execution on 21 Mar 1860 and returned it fully satisfied on 16 Apr 1860.					
107F	Charles O'Neal	Grand larceny	8 Nov 1860	166	E: 146	
107G	James O'Sullivan	Assault with intent to commit murder	8 Feb 1860 and 14 Feb 1860		E: 26, 33, 35, 51-52, 57, 58, 64, 66, 74-75, 76, 79-80, 82	
107H	George O. Perkins	Gaming	11 May 1860	152	E: 86, 89, 90, 94, 97, 98-100, 102, 108-109, 110, 111, 118	

---

[119] Sonoma County, California, Court of Sessions, Minute Book E: 30, court order imposing a $10 fine on Agostin Harasthy for failing to answer when called as a trial juror for the February term 1860 of the Court of Sessions, 6 February 1860; Sonoma County Archives, Santa Rosa.

State Archives Case File #	Defendants	Charges	Date Indictment or Presentment Filed	Register Page(s)	Minute Book Volume: Page(s)	Judgment Book Page
107I	James W. Porter	Assault and battery	9 Aug 1860	159	E: 120, 128, 129, 133, 143-145, 146	
107J	Joseph Wood	Grand larceny	9 Aug 1860		E: 120, 128, 129	
107K	This case file consists of only one document, a capias dated 7 Nov 1860 issued by the Court of Sessions to the Sheriff of Sonoma County ordering him to bring C. I. Robinson, I. G. Wickersham, and R. H. King into Court forthwith to show cause why they should not be punished for not obeying a subpoena issued by the District Attorney to appear before the Grand Jury at the November term 1860 of the Court of Sessions. The Sheriff, John J. Ellis, certified that he had arrested them on 7 Nov 1860 and brought them before Court the same day.					
107L	This case file consists of only one document, a capias dated 6 Feb 1860 issued by the Court of Sessions to the Sheriff of Sonoma County ordering him to bring Mary E. Ross and Elizabeth Ross into Court forthwith to show cause why they did not attend as witnesses in the case of the People v. Bill Williams (case file # 90C). The Sheriff, John J. Ellis, by his Deputy, E. Latapie, certified that he had arrested them on 6 Feb 1860 and brought them before Court on 7 Feb 1860. Mary E. Ross, and her child, Elizabeth Ross, made a good and sufficient excuse, and the Court discharged them on 7 Feb 1860.[120]					
107M	This case file contains only one document, a capias dated 7 May 1860 issued by the Court of Sessions to the Sheriff of Sonoma County ordering him to bring J. G. Walker into Court forthwith to show cause why he did not obey the process of the Court (failing to answer when called as a Grand Juror for the May term 1860). The Sheriff, J. J. Ellis, by his Under Sheriff, M. Barnes, certified that he had arrested Walker on 7 May 1860 and had him in Court. After hearing Walker's excuse on 7 May 1860 the Court discharged him from the attachment.[121]					
107N	Hiram White	Grand larceny	14 Nov 1860		E: 160	
107O	Joseph Thompson	Burglary	9 May 1860	153	E: 86, 89, 91, 94, 96-97, 105	
107O	Joseph Thompson	Grand larceny	9 May 1860	154	E: 89, 90, 94-95, 104, 106-107	
107P	Charles Tabor (var. Taber)	Grand larceny	11 May 1860	156	E: 85, 97, 99, 119	
107Q	E. B. Thompson	Forgery			E: 139, 142, 153	
107R	This case file consists of only one document, an execution dated 21 Mar 1860 by the Hon. William Churchman, Judge of the Court of Sessions, requiring the Sheriff of Sonoma County to collect a fine of $10 and accruing costs of $2.75 imposed on John Allman on 6 Feb 1860 for contempt of Court (non-attendance as a trial juror during the February term 1860 of the Court of Sessions).[122] The Sheriff, J. J. Ellis, certified that he had received the execution on 22 Mar 1860 and returned it fully satisfied on 26 Mar 1860.					
108	William H. Meiering	Assault with a deadly weapon with intent to inflict bodily injury	7 Feb 1861	170	E: 172, 178, 179, 182, 189, 211-212, 213, 224-225, 226-227	
109	Herbert Mitchell	Attempting to aid and assist a prisoner to escape	7 May 1861	142	E: 240, 241, 247, 251, 252-253, 256-257	

---

[120] Sonoma County, California, Court of Sessions, Minute Book E: 30–31, court order discharging Mrs. Mary E. Ross and child for failing to attend before the Grand Jury, 7 February 1860; Sonoma County Archives, Santa Rosa.
[121] Sonoma County, California, Court of Sessions, Minute Book E: 84, court order discharging J. G. Walker from attachment, 7 May 1860; Sonoma County Archives, Santa Rosa.
[122] Sonoma County, California, Court of Sessions, Minute Book E: 31, court order imposing a $20 fine on John Allman and others for failing to answer when called as trial jurors for the February term 1860 of the Court of Sessions, 7 February 1860; Sonoma County Archives, Santa Rosa. The date of imposition and the amount of the fine in the execution do not match those in the Court of Sessions minute book.

State Archives Case File #	Defendants	Charges	Date Indictment or Presentment Filed	Register Page(s)	Minute Book Volume: Page(s)	Judgment Book Page
110	James R. Graham	Vending by retail spiritous, malt, and vinous liquors in quantities less than a quart without a license	13 Feb 1861		E: 193	
110	James R. Graham	Receiving stolen property knowing it to be stolen	7 Feb 1861	171	E: 178, 179, 184, 185, 186, 195, 214-215	
111	Patrick Sweeny and Jeremiah Sweeny (indicted as John Sweeny)	Vending by retail spiritous, malt, and vinous liquors in quantities less than a quart without a license	13 Feb 1861	184	E: 193, 205, 208	
112	John Sweeny (alias Long John) and James R. Graham	Grand larceny	7 Feb 1861	172	E: 173, 175, 178, 179-180, 183, 185-186, 200	
112	James R. Graham	Grand larceny	7 Feb 1861	174	E: 184, 199	
112	John Sweeny (alias Long John)	Grand larceny	7 Feb 1861	173	E: 195-197, 198, 199, 200, 203, 209, 230, 231, 232, 234	
113	Thomas Finchley	Selling liquor within one mile of a camp meeting	14 Nov 1860	168	E: 160, 170-171, 176, 181	
114	Henry Thornley	Assault with a deadly weapon with intent to commit murder	8 May 1861	149	E: 242, 262, 264, 283-284, 286-288, 290, 294, 308	
115	Andrew J. Markwell	Vending spiritous liquors without license	13 Feb 1861	185	E: 193, 205, 219-220, 221, 227	
116	William M. Main	Vending certain goods, wares, and merchandise without a license	8 Nov 1861		E: 303, 315-316	
116A	This case file consists of two subpoenas: 1.) a subpoena dated 4 Feb 1861 by District Attorney R. C. Flournoy commanding a number of people (Dr. Piper, Robert Robinson, Frank Robinson, J. A. Kleiser, [?] Brush, L. Boggs, Mike Barnes, Capt. John Markle, Tom Drew, J. Gould, [?] Searight, Dr. James Ramy, S. McClenlock, William Garson, James Taylor, A. J. Cox, James McDaniels, [?] Brookbanks, [?] Pixley, John Houck (var. Houx), [?] Holester, [?] Riley, J. Clark, Elisha Kay, E. H. Eubanks, Samuel McCullough, and [?] McFarland) to appear forthwith as witnesses before the Grand Jury in the case of the People v. John Doe, and 2.) a subpoena dated 6 Feb 1861 by District Attorney R. C. Flournoy commanding William Winn to appear forthwith as a witness before the Grand Jury, which the Sheriff, John J. Ellis, by his Deputy, A. L. Boggs, returned on 8 Feb 1861, stating that after a diligent search he had not found William Winn in Sonoma County.					
117	Frederick G. Blume	Assault with intent to commit murder	9 Nov 1860	162	E: 140, 143, 148, 149, 152, 160, 161, 162, 171, 176, 177, 190, 191-192, 193, 195	
118	Nancy A. Culbertson (formerly Nancy A. Moore and Nancy A. Bray)	Bigamy	10 Aug 1861	201	E: 277, 295	
119	Charles Jefferson	Altering marks and brands	10 Nov 1860	164, 169	E: 150, 171, 174, 175, 176, 182, 183, 187, 215-216, 217-218, 220, 228-229, 230-231	

State Archives Case File #	Defendants	Charges	Date Indictment or Presentment Filed	Register Page(s)	Minute Book Volume: Page(s)	Judgment Book Page
120	James D. Barnes	Assault with a deadly weapon with intent to commit murder	10 May 1861	150	E: 248	
121	Darias Clark	Selling spiritous, malt, and vinous liquors without a license	10 May 1861	146	E: 248	
122	Paul Heisel	Selling certain goods, wares, and merchandise by retail without a license	6 Nov 1861		E: 299, 300, 302-303, 311	
123	Mary Frances Hopper (formerly Mary Frances Johnson and Mary Frances Groves)	Bigamy	10 Aug 1861	203	E: 277	
124	James Culligan (indicted as James Calligan)	Vending spiritous liquors without a license	13 Feb 1861	188	E: 193, 201, 212, 213-214	
125	William F. Culbertson	Bigamy	10 Aug 1861	200	E: 277, 295	
126	William C. Jordan	Vending spiritous liquors by retail without a license	13 Feb 1861	183	E: 193, 204, 208, 222-223, 225, 238, 246, 250	
127	Jerry Linehan	Keeping, renting, and letting horses and carriages and saddle horses for hire without a license/violation of section 79 of the Revenue Act of 1861	7 Nov 1861		E: 301, 310, 320	
128	William R. Dodge (indicted as Henry Dodge)	Vending spiritous liquor without a license	13 Feb 1861	182	E: 193, 204, 207-208	
129	James M. Hannah	Assault with a deadly weapon with intent to inflict bodily injury	9 Aug 1861	199	E: 275, 279-280, 283, 289, 306-307	
130	John Hargrave	Grand larceny	7 May 1861	189	E: 236, 239, 242, 254, 268, 271, 276	
131	John B. Hopper	Bigamy	10 Aug 1861	202	E: 277	
132	Manville Doyle	Keeping, renting, and letting horses and carriages and saddle horses for hire without a license/violation of section 79 of the Revenue Act of 1861	7 Nov 1861		E: 301, 308-309, 318-319	
133	J. B. Hinkle	Renting and letting horses and carriages and saddle horses without a license	7 Nov 1861		E: 300, 301, 311-312	
134	William Allen, John McCombs, R. Combs, Walter Currier, Ed H. Grover, William Rodgers, and John Grennan	Resisting, opposing, and obstructing a duly authorized Deputy Sheriff in the execution of his duty	9 Nov 1861		E: 304	
134	William Allen, John McCombs, R. Combs, Walter Currier, Ed H. Grover, William Rodgers, and John Grennan	Unlawfully assembling to do an unlawful act and not dispersing on being commanded to do so by a duly authorized Deputy Sheriff	9 Nov 1861		E: 304	
135	Jesse Blanchard	Selling spiritous, malt and vinous liquors by retail without a license	13 Feb 1861	187	E: 193, 254, 262	

State Archives Case File #	Defendants	Charges	Date Indictment or Presentment Filed	Register Page(s)	Minute Book Volume: Page(s)	Judgment Book Page
136	Samuel Eberhart (var. Eberheardt) and Peter Gleason	Vending spiritous liquors without a license	13 Feb 1861	176, 179	E: 193, 200	
137	James Kelso	Assault and battery	7 Aug 1860		E: 120, 124, 126-127, 128	
137A	B. F. Tilton	Selling spiritous liquors without a license	10 May 1861	148	E: 248, 263, 273-274	
137B	Isaac Talbot (indicted as Isaac Tolbert)	Mayhem	8 Aug 1861	196	E: 261, 267, 268, 272-273, 275, 279	
137C	Fenwick Fisher	Gaming	15 Nov 1860	167	E: 162, 177-178, 182, 199, 238, 245, 271, 279, 281-283, 285, 287, 314	
137D	Francis Post (indicted as Frank Post)	Vending spiritous liquors by retail without a license	13 Feb 1861	186	E: 193, 206, 221-222	
137E	William J. Reynolds	Vending spiritous liquors by retail without a license	13 Feb 1861	178, 181	E: 193, 201, 203-204, 219, 223	
137F	Parker E. Weeks (indicted as P. Weeks)	Keeping, renting, and letting for hire horses and carriages and saddle horses, etc. without a license/violation of section 79 of the Revenue Act of 1861	7 Nov 1861		E: 301, 309, 319	
137G	David Wharf and Francis Green (indicted as William Green)	Grand larceny	9 Aug 1861	197	E: 273, 294	
137G	David Wharf	Grand larceny	9 Aug 1861	197	E: 312	
137G	Francis Green (indicted as William Green)	Grand larceny	9 Aug 1861	197	E: 315	
137H	John Wilson	Vending spiritous liquors without a license	13 Feb 1861	177, 180	E: 193, 201, 203, 218	
137I	Henry Yeagley	Keeping horses and carriages not used in the transportation of goods for rent and hire without a license	9 Nov 1861		E: 304, 316	
137J	This case file contains only one document, a capias dated 9 Nov 1861 issued by the Court of Sessions to the Sheriff of Sonoma County ordering him to bring [?] Buckland and [?] Bell into Court forthwith to show cause why they should not be punished for contempt in not obeying the process of the Court. The Sheriff, J. M. Bowles, by his Deputy Sheriff, S. F. Hood, certified that he had arrested Buckland and Bell on 9 Nov 1861 and had them in Court. They were both witnesses in the case of the People v. James M. Hannah (case file # 129).[123]					
137K	This case file contains only one document, a capias dated 8 Aug 1861 issued by the Court of Sessions to the Sheriff of Sonoma County ordering him to bring S. D. (var. H. D.) Lambert into Court forthwith to show cause why he should not be punished for contempt. The Sheriff, John J. Ellis, by his Deputy Sheriff, E. Latapie, certified that he had arrested Lambert on 8 Aug 1861 and had him in Court. Lambert had been called as a trial juror for the case of the People v. Spencer P. Emerson (case file # 107A) on 8 Aug 1861.[124]					

---

[123] Sonoma County, California, Court of Sessions, Minute Book E: 306, The People v. James M. Hannah, case proceedings, 9 November 1861; Sonoma County Archives, Santa Rosa, California.
[124] Sonoma County, California, Court of Sessions, Minute Book E: 270, The People v. Spencer P. Emerson, case proceedings, 8 August 1861; Sonoma County Archives, Santa Rosa.

State Archives Case File #	Defendants	Charges	Date Indictment or Presentment Filed	Register Page(s)	Minute Book Volume: Page(s)	Judgment Book Page
137L	This case file contains only one document, a capias dated 13 Aug 1861 issued by the Court of Sessions to the Sheriff of Sonoma County ordering him to bring James Lucas into Court forthwith to show cause why he should not be punished for contempt in not obeying the process and orders of the Court. The Sheriff, John J. Ellis, by his Deputy Sheriff, Daniel Rice, certified that he had arrested Lucas on 13 Aug 1861 and had him in Court. Lucas had been called as a trial juror for the case of the People v. Fenwick Fisher on 13 Aug 1861 and failed to appear.[125]					
138	Almer Clark (indicted as Adam Clark)	Selling spiritous liquors without a license	10 May 1861	147	E: 248, 263, 273	
139	B. F. Bonnell (var. Bonnel)	Violation of section 79 of the Revenue Act of 1861	8 Nov 1861	204	E: 303, 324, 326, 335	
140	Charles Brennan (var. Brannan)	Assault with a deadly weapon with intent to inflict a bodily injury	9 Aug 1861	198	E: 275, 288, 297, 313-314, 328, 329-330, 331-332	
141	Alexander Skaggs, I. N. Stapp, George Lawrence, Sylvester Prouse, and James Miller	Destroying the County Jail locks, hasps, bolts, and fastenings to cells			E: 393B, 405	
141	Alexander Skaggs, A. M. Green, I. N. Stapp, Elisha Givens, S. B. Martin, Warham Easley, James S. Buchanan, James Miller, Robert Neeley, Gip Young, C. C. Clark, George Lawrence, Daniel Prouse (var. Prowse), Sylvester Prouse (var. Prowse), John Hatfield, Peter T. Archambeau, [?] Phipps, William T. Garrison, Thomas Prince, K. Maxwell, Jesse Houghton (var. Hooton), George Clark, Isaac Miller, William Freshour, C. C. Freshour, B. W. Scott, Walker Wilson, Franklin Burk, Joseph Baugh, William Walters, Josiah McKinley, and Marion Anderson	Resisting an officer	9 Aug 1862		E: 374, 396, 397, 399	
141	Alexander Skaggs, A. M. Green, I. N. Stapp, Elisha Givens, S. B. Martin, Warham Easley, James S. Buchanan, James Miller, Robert Neeley, Gip Young, C. C. Clark, George Lawrence, Daniel Prouse (var. Prowse), Sylvester Prouse (var. Prowse), John Hatfield, Peter T. Archambeau, [?] Phipps, William T. Garrison, Thomas Prince, K. Maxwell, Jesse Houghton (var. Hooton), George Clark, Isaac Miller, William Freshour, C. C. Freshour, B. W. Scott, Walker Wilson, Franklin Burk, Joseph Baugh, William Walters, Josiah McKinley, and Marion Anderson	Unlawful assembly	9 Aug 1862		E: 374, 396, 397, 399	

---

[125] Sonoma County, California, Court of Sessions, Minute Book E: 282, The People v. Fenwick Fisher, court order to issue an attachment for James Lucas for failing to appear when summoned as a trial juror, 13 August 1861; Sonoma County Archives, Santa Rosa.

State Archives Case File #	Defendants	Charges	Date Indictment or Presentment Filed	Register Page(s)	Minute Book Volume: Page(s)	Judgment Book Page
142	John S. Taylor	Assault with a deadly weapon with intent to commit a bodily injury	9 Aug 1862		E: 374, 394, 399, 404, 446-447, 448-449, 452	
142A	John Adrain	Assault and battery	8 Nov 1862		E: 406	
143	William Taylor	Rape			E: 394, 399, 406	
144	Samuel J. Finley	Assault and battery	9 Aug 1862		E: 374, 395, 400	
145	Lancaster Clyman	Keeping stallions to be used for propagation for hire and profit without a license/violation of the Revenue Act	8 Nov 1862		E: 406, 441, 451	
146	The five documents in this case file consist of: 1.) an affidavit by William Wilks, District Attorney, dated 20 Nov 1862, accusing J. B. Gossage, a trial juror in the case of the People v. A. Skaggs et al. (case file # 158), of breaking away from the officer in charge of the jury and going to a drinking saloon when the jury was supposed to considering their verdict, 2.) a capias issued by the Court of Sessions dated 20 Nov 1862 commanding the Sheriff of Sonoma County to bring J. B. Gossage before the Court forthwith to show cause why he should not be punished for contempt, 3.) a copy of the judgment against J. B. Gossage for contempt dated 20 Nov 1862 fining him $100 and ordering him imprisoned in the County Jail of Sonoma County for the term of two days, 4.) a judgment copy title page noting J. B. Gossage had been committed on 20 Nov 1862 and discharged on 22 Nov 1862, and 5.) an execution issued by the Court of Sessions dated 25 Nov 1862 directing the Sheriff of Sonoma County to collect the $100 fine imposed on J. B. Gossage on 20 Nov 1862 and $5.40 in accruing costs out of Gossage's personal and real property. The Sheriff, J. M. Bowles, returned the execution satisfied in full on 10 Dec 1862.[126]					
147	J. W. Henderson	Violation of section 79 of the Revenue Act of 1861	7 Nov 1861	205	E: 301, 323-324, 326, 328, 336	
148	Budd Gann	Assault with a deadly weapon with intent to inflict bodily injury	8 Nov 1862		E: 406	
149	Hiram N. Green (indicted as H. N. Green)	Assault with a deadly weapon with intent to commit murder	3 Feb 1863		E: 440, 443, 444, 450, 458-459	
150	William Hendrickson	Assault with a deadly weapon with intent to inflict bodily injury	8 May 1862		E: 355	
151	H. H. Cooper	Vending and selling by retail spiritous, malt, vinous, and distilled liquors without a license	7 Feb 1862		E: 334, 346, 348, 350, 362	
152	This case file consists of two documents: 1.) an affidavit of William Wilks, District Attorney, dated 20 Nov 1862 accusing L. C. Lewis, the County officer [Coroner] in charge of the jury in the case of the People v. Wareham Easley et al. (case file # 158), of permitting the trial jurors in that case while they were considering their verdict to separate and of taking one of the trial jurors [J. B. Gossage] to a drinking saloon for the purpose of drinking spiritous liquors, and 2.) a capias issued by the Court of Sessions dated 20 Nov 1862 commanding the Sheriff of Sonoma County to bring L. C. Lewis, the Coroner of Sonoma County, before the Court forthwith to show cause why he should not be punished for contempt for not obeying the order of the Court. The Sheriff, J. M. Bowles, arrested Lewis on 20 Nov 1862 and brought him before the Court. He was discharged from the attachment after examination.[127]					

---

[126] Sonoma County, California, Court of Sessions, Minute Book E: 428–429, The People v. J. B. Gossage, judgment for contempt, 20 November 1862; Sonoma County Archives, Santa Rosa.
[127] Sonoma County, California, Court of Sessions, Minute Book E: 429, The People v. L. C. Lewis, court order to issue an attachment for the arrest of L. C. Lewis, 20 November 1862; Sonoma County Archives, Santa Rosa.

State Archives Case File #	Defendants	Charges	Date Indictment or Presentment Filed	Register Page(s)	Minute Book Volume: Page(s)	Judgment Book Page
152A	This case file consists of only one document, a capias issued by the Court of Sessions dated 7 May 1862 commanding the Sheriff of Sonoma County to bring W. P. Mahoney and Jake Peavey, witnesses for the People in the case the People v. William Rodgers (case file # 152I), before the Court forthwith to show cause why they should not be punished for contempt in not obeying the process of the Court. Mahoney and Peavey were arrested on 7 May 1862 and brought before the Court. They were discharged from the attachment after giving good and sufficient excuses to the satisfaction of the Court.[128]					
152B	Edward S. Emerson	Assault and battery	6 Aug 1861	193, 195	E: 260, 265-266, 274, 278	
152C	N. R. Ellis	Grand larceny	6 May 1862		E: 345-346, 347, 350, 351, 360	
152D	Henry P. Ferguson (indicted as H. P. Fergurson)	Assault with a deadly weapon with intent to inflict a bodily injury	7 May 1862		E: 345, 352, 355, 359, 360-361	
152E	John McCune (indicted as Jack Murray)	Assault with a deadly weapon with intent to inflict bodily injury	6 Feb 1862		E: 323, 325, 332, 333, 337-338, 340	
152F	This case file consists of five documents concerning William J. Harrison's failure to appear as a Grand Jury witness on 6 Aug 1862: 1.) a subpoena dated 5 Aug 1862 issued by William Wilks, Sonoma County District Attorney, commanding Joseph Binns and [William J.] Harrison to appear and testify before the Grand Jury forthwith, 2.) a capias issued by the Court of Sessions dated 6 Aug 1862 commanding the Sheriff of Sonoma County to bring [William J.] Harrison before the Court forthwith to show cause why he should not be punished for contempt in not obeying a process issued by the District Attorney requiring him to attend as a witness before the Grand Jury, 3.) a statement by the Sheriff, J. M. Bowles, by his Deputy, J. D. Binns, that on 9 Aug 1862 he had served the capias and arrested Harrison, who gave bail, 4.) a bond for appearance for $200 dated 9 Aug 1862 in which W. J. Harrison and E. T. Farmer undertake that W. J. Harrison will appear before the Court of Sessions on 11 Aug 1862 to show cause why he should not be punished for contempt of the Court in not appearing before the Grand Jury, and 5.) W. J. Harrison's answer to the attachment dated 11 Aug 1862.[129]					
152G	John Wood	Assault with a deadly weapon with intent to inflict a bodily injury	6 Nov 1862		E: 393B, 401	
152H	George Pitts	Petit larceny	9 Aug 1862		E: 374, 394, 409	
152I	William Rodgers	Resisting an officer in the discharge of his duty	9 Nov 1861		E: 304, 339, 341, 349-350, 351, 357	
152I	William Rodgers	Unlawful assemblage	9 Nov 1861		E: 304, 339, 341, 349-350, 351, 353	
152J	John Scanlon	Drawing and exhibiting a gun in an angry and threatening manner	6 Nov 1862		E: 394, 401, 404, 411, 413	
152K	This case file consists of only one document, an execution dated 25 Nov 1862 issued by the Court of Sessions requiring the Sheriff of Sonoma County to collect the $10 fine imposed on Martin Bunch on 19 Nov 1862 and accruing costs of $1.35 for contempt of Court for failing to appear and answer when called as a witness in the case of the People vs. Alexander Skaggs et al. out of Bunch's personal and real property.[130] The Sheriff, J. M. Bowles, returned the execution noting that he had found no property.					

---

[128] Sonoma County, California, Court of Sessions, Minute Book E: 349–350 and 351, The People v. William Rodgers, court order for attachment as to J. Peavey and W. P. Mahoney and discharge from attachment, 7 May 1862; Sonoma County Archives, Santa Rosa.

[129] Sonoma County, California, Court of Sessions, Minute Book E: 370 and 376–377, court order to issue an attachment for W. J. Harrison, 6 August 1862, and discharge from attachment, 11 August 1862, Sonoma County Archives, Santa Rosa.

[130] Sonoma County, California, Court of Sessions, Minute Book E: 422 and 426, The People v. Alexander Skaggs et al., court order to issue an attachment for the arrest of Martin Bunch, George Greenwood, and L. D. Latimer, 18 November 1862, and discharge from attachment, 19 November 1862; Sonoma County Archives, Santa Rosa.

State Archives Case File #	Defendants	Charges	Date Indictment or Presentment Filed	Register Page(s)	Minute Book Volume: Page(s)	Judgment Book Page
152L*						
152M	This case file consists of only one document, an execution dated 31 May 1862 issued by the Court of Sessions requiring the Sheriff of Sonoma County to collect the $2.40 fine imposed on William Breitlauch on 9 May 1862 for contempt of Court for failing to appear and answer when called as a trial juror and accruing costs of $1.75 out of Breitlauch's personal and real property.[131] The Sheriff, J. M. Bowles, by his Deputy, G. W. Harrington, returned the execution fully satisfied on 31 May 1862.					
152N	This case file consists of only one document, an execution dated 25 Nov 1862 issued by the Court of Sessions requiring the Sheriff of Sonoma County to collect the $50 fine imposed on Thomas J. Lamb on 5 Nov 1862 for contempt of Court for failing to appear and answer when called as a trial juror at the November term 1862 of the Court of Sessions and accruing costs of $2.05 out of Lamb's personal and real property.[132] The Sheriff, J. M. Bowles, found no property.					
153	James R. Glasscock	Assault with intent to commit murder	6 Nov 1862		E: 393A-393B, 401, 403, 447-448, 449-450, 452-453	
153	William Eller	Murder	8 May 1863		E: 469, 470	
153	Robert G. Meeks, Adam A. Bushnell, John B. Stamps, Winslow H. Bowen, and Benjamin Williams	Malicious mischief	7 Feb 1863		E: 457, 459	
154	Mathew Dillon	Grand larceny				
155	J. W. Barton (indicted as J. W. Barker)	Grand larceny	5 Nov 1863		E: 488, 489, 493, 494, 495, 496, 499	
156	Henry Hegeler	Trespassing	8 May 1863		E: 469, 493, 498	
157	Frederick T. Hedges	Carrying a concealed weapon	5 Nov 1863		E: 494, 495, 499	
157	Frederick T. Hedges	Assault with a deadly weapon with intent to commit murder			E: 488, 489, 500	
158	Warham Easley, Sylvester Prouse (var. Prowse), I. N. Stapp, James Miller, George Young (indicted as Gip Young), Isaac Miller, Joseph Baugh, B. W. Scott, Elisha Givens, A. M. Green, [?] Phipps, S. B. Martin, Joseph Derrick, Walker Wilson, William Freshour, George Lawrence, William Garrison, Peter T. Archambeau, Alexander Skaggs, John Hatfield, Franklin Burk, and C. C. Freshour	Unlawful assembly	8 Nov 1862		E: 406, 410, 412, 416-417, 418, 419-420, 425, 432, 433-435, 436-437, 442, 455-456	

---

[131] Sonoma County, California, Court of Sessions, Minute Book E: 358, court order to issue attachments for B. Hoen, S. Hinkston, William Breitlau [sic], and C. O. Grantham, and discharge from attachments, 9 May 1862; Sonoma County Archives, Santa Rosa.

[132] Sonoma County, California, Court of Sessions, Minute Book E: 398, court order to issue execution against Thomas J. Lamb, 5 November 1862; Sonoma County Archives, Santa Rosa.

State Archives Case File #	Defendants	Charges	Date Indictment or Presentment Filed	Register Page(s)	Minute Book Volume: Page(s)	Judgment Book Page
158	Warham Easley, Sylvester Prouse (var. Prowse), I. N. Stapp, James Miller, George Young (indicted as Gip Young), Isaac Miller, Joseph Baugh, B. W. Scott, Elisha Givens, A. M. Green, [?] Phipps, S. B. Martin, Joseph Derrick, Walker Wilson, William Freshour, George Lawrence, William Garrison, Peter T. Archambeau, Alexander Skaggs, John Hatfield, Franklin Burk, and C. C. Freshour	Resisting an officer in the discharge of his duty	8 Nov 1862		E: 406, 409-410, 413, 415-416, 418, 419-420, 422-423, 426, 427-429, 430, 441, 454-455	
158A	Brede Brady	Grand larceny	5 May 1863		E: 463, 464, 465, 471, 473-474, 475, 476-477	
158B	J. M. Hooper	Assault with intent to commit murder			E: 440, 443	
158C	The two documents in this case file consist of: 1.) a criminal complaint by Luke Fallen of Tomales, Marin County, filed in the Justice's Court of Bodega Township and dated 23 Jun 1863 accusing Robert Henry Duke, a resident of Petaluma, of stealing a mare of C. Hardin's of Petaluma (value $200), taking the mare to Tomales, Marin County, and selling him (Fallen) the mare on or about 19 Jun 1863, and 2.) an order issued by the Hon. G. Henckell, a Justice of the Peace of Bodega Township, dated 23 Jun 1863 directing that the defendant, Robert Henry Duke, should be held to answer to the charge before the Court of Sessions. The defendant escaped from the County Jail of Sonoma County on 4 Jul 1863.[133]					
158D*						
158E	Oliver Williams	Assault with intent to commit murder	7 Feb 1863		E: 457	
158F	This case file consists of one document, an execution issued by the Court of Sessions dated 25 Nov 1862 requiring the Sheriff of Sonoma County to collect the $25 fine imposed on William Wilks on 19 Nov 1862 for "using rude, violent, and contemptuous language in the presence of the Court" and accruing costs of $1.35.[134] The Sheriff, J. M. Bowles, by his Under Sheriff, O. T. Baldwin, returned the execution unsatisfied on 26 Jan 1863, not finding any property of Wilks's in Sonoma County.					
158G	This case file consists of one document, an execution issued by the Court of Sessions dated 25 Nov 1862 requiring the Sheriff of Sonoma County to collect the $25 fine imposed on William Ross on 19 Nov 1862 for "using rude, violent, and contemptuous language in the presence of the Court" and accruing costs of $1.35.[135] The Sheriff, J. M. Bowles, by his Under Sheriff, O. T. Baldwin, returned the execution unsatisfied on 26 Jan 1863, not finding any property of Ross's in Sonoma County.					
158H	This case file consists of one document, an execution issued by the Court of Sessions dated 25 Nov 1862 requiring the Sheriff of Sonoma County to collect the $50 fine imposed on John Ingram for failing to appear and answer when called as a trial juror at the November term 1862 of the Court of Sessions and accruing costs of $2.05 out of John Ingram's personal and real property.[136] The Sheriff, J. M. Bowles, by his Under Sheriff, O. T. Baldwin, returned the execution unsatisfied on 26 Jan 1863, not finding any property of Ingram's in Sonoma County.					
159	Eucebio Alvarado and John Vanderlieth	Illegal voting	7 Nov 1863		E: 497	

[133] "Broke Jail," *The Sonoma County Democrat* (Santa Rosa, California), 11 July 1863, p. 2, col. 4.

[134] Sonoma County, California, Court of Sessions, Minute Book E: 426, The People v. William Wilks and William Ross, court order fining William Wilks and William Ross $25 each for contempt of court, 19 November 1862; Sonoma County Archives, Santa Rosa.

[135] Ibid.

[136] Sonoma County, California, Court of Sessions, Minute Book E: 398, court order to issue execution against J. Ingram, 5 November 1862; Sonoma County Archives, Santa Rosa.

State Archives Case File #	Defendants	Charges	Date Indictment or Presentment Filed	Register Page(s)	Minute Book Volume: Page(s)	Judgment Book Page
159A	This case file consists of one document, a capias issued by the Court of Sessions dated 13 Aug 1861 commanding the Sheriff of Sonoma County to take T. B. Carey into custody forthwith so that he may appear before the Court of Sessions to show cause why he should not be punished for contempt for not appearing as a trial juror in the case of the People v. Fenwick Fisher when called.[137] The Sheriff, John J. Ellis, by his Deputy, John Ingram, certified that he had served the capias on Carey and had him before the Court on 14 Aug 1861. After an examination by the Court on 14 Aug 1861, Carey was discharged from the attachment.[138]					
160	This case file, erroneously filed among the Court of Sessions case files, contains two County Court of Sonoma County documents pertaining to County Court case # 248 (NS), People v. James Brown: 1.) a copy of the indictment presented and filed on 5 May 1864 in the County Court accusing James Brown of setting fire to and burning down the dwelling house of C. Clark on 9 Mar 1863, and 2.) a bench warrant issued by the County Court dated 23 Jan 1865 for the arrest of James Brown.					
160A	This case file, erroneously filed among the Court of Sessions case files, consists of one document, an undated $100 bail bond for Thomas Sunderland undertaken by his sureties G. A. Sensibaugh and R. S. Hanson which refers to a Court order by E. Brookshire, a Justice of the Peace [of St. Helena Township], dated 6 Mar 1865, holding Thomas Sunderland to answer to the charge of grand larceny and admitting him to bail.					
	David M. Graham	Manslaughter	10 Oct 1856			
	Amos B. Ingram, Benjamin F. McCardie, George W. Baylor, and O. H. P. Coleman	Murder	13 Oct 1856			
	A. B. Ingram, Benjamin F. McCardie, George W. Baylor, and O. H. P. Coleman	Murder	14 Oct 1856			
	Amos B. Ingram, Benjamin F. McCardie, George W. Baylor, and O. H. P. Coleman	Murder	16 Oct 1856			
	A. B. Ingram, Benjamin F. McCardie, George W. Baylor, and O. H. P. Coleman	Murder	16 Oct 1856			
	Christian Brunner and Peter Peterson	Murder	9 Oct 1857	60	D: 7, 24, 25, 29-30	
	Christian Brunner	Murder	5 Jan 1858	68	D: 31, 37, 42	
	T. M. Leavenworth	Grand larceny (no. 2)	13 Apr 1858	119	D: 76, 78, 83, 85, 87, 89, 90, 105, 107, 112, 113	
	John J. Domes	Manslaughter	10 Jan 1859		D: 38, 145, 152	
	James S. Oldham (indicted as Sim Oldham)	Murder in the 2nd degree	8 Apr 1859	126	D: 177, 178	
	Richard Wood	Murder	6 Feb 1860		E: 28, 37	
	Amariah Kibbee	Murder	9 May 1860		E: 86, 92	
	Richard (var. R. D.) Wilson	Grand larceny	10 Nov 1860	165	E: 166	
	George Edgar	Arson	15 Nov 1860	144	E: 162, 163	
	Thomas Stewart, James Stewart, and Samuel Stewart	Murder	9 Feb 1861	175	E: 172, 187	
	Ira Berry	Grand larceny	8 May 1861	190	E: 172, 207	
	Edmond T. Pepper	Murder	8 May 1861	145	E: 237, 243	

---

[137] Sonoma County, California, Court of Sessions, Minute Book E: 282, The People v. Fenwick Fisher, court order to issue an attachment against T. B. Carey, 13 August 1861; Sonoma County Archives, Santa Rosa.
[138] Sonoma County, California, Court of Sessions, Minute Book E: 286, The People v. Fenwick Fisher, court order discharging Thomas B. Carey from attachment, 14 August 1861; Sonoma County Archives, Santa Rosa.

State Archives Case File #	Defendants	Charges	Date Indictment or Presentment Filed	Register Page(s)	Minute Book Volume: Page(s)	Judgment Book Page
	George Edgar	Arson	9 May 1861	144	E: 244, 248	
	James B. Boggs	Murder	7 Aug 1861	194	E: 261, 266	
	D. M. Graham	Assault with intent to commit a rape	5 Aug 1862		E: 365, 367, 368, 371, 377, 379, 380, 381, 382-384, 385, 386, 387, 388, 465, 482	
	Alexander Lockwood	Perjury	7 Feb 1863		E: 457	
	Neville Lewis and Oliver H. Lewis	Grand larceny	6 May 1863		E: 463, 465, 466, 467, 471-472	
	Neville Lewis	Grand larceny	6 May 1863		E: 475	
	Oliver H. Lewis	Grand larceny	6 May 1863		E: 475	
	Nicholas Fortis	Grand larceny		61	D: 7, 24	
	George W. Bigelow	Assault with a deadly weapon		62	D: 7, 15	
	Andrew Arthur				D: 33	
	Peter Peterson	Murder		67	D: 36	
	Cardelia and Laventina (Indians)			121	D: 110, 114, 122	
	Nathaniel Brown (a colored man)				D: 137, 150	
	John Doe (Spaniard)				D: 165	
	Daniel Brown	Mayhem			D: 165, 178	
	John Smith and John N. Steele (var. Steel)	Grand larceny			D: 230	
	Nathaniel Brown	Assault with intent to inflict bodily injury		141	E: 7, 9, 10, 11, 15, 19	
	Uriah Miller	Assault with intent to commit murder			E: 26, 43	
	Thomas Haley	Murder			E: 28, 32	
	Joseph Madrad	Assault with intent to kill			E: 87, 91	
	William Manion	Assault with intent to inflict bodily injury			E: 172, 178	
	James Holivan	Vending liquors without a license			E: 202	
	Albert Hoffman Unger			143	E: 243, 255	
	F. W. Hudson	Murder			E: 261, 268	
	A. Myers	Assault with intent to kill			E: 365, 367	
	Catherine Waters	Perjury			E: 393A, 398	
	John Kelly	Grand larceny			E: 393B, 398	
	Arnold Stump and Lewis W. Stump	Illegal voting			E: 395, 402	
	M. Nathanson	Grand larceny			E: 439, 453	
	John Mann	Grand larceny			E: 439, 456	
	Jacob Weingartner	Assault with a deadly weapon with intent to inflict a bodily injury			E: 440, 443	

State Archives Case File #	Defendants	Charges	Date Indictment or Presentment Filed	Register Page(s)	Minute Book Volume: Page(s)	Judgment Book Page
	John Brotts	Grand larceny			E: 481, 482, 483	
	William Clark	Highway robbery			E: 481, 482, 483	
	Harrison Meacham	Murder			E: 487, 488, 492	
	J. William Fossett	Grand larceny			E: 488, 489, 491	
	B. C. Westfall			79		
	John Gouldin			92		

Court of Sessions Terms

September term 1850

Hon. Henry A. Green, County Judge
Hon. Charles Hudspeth, Associate Justice
Hon. Peter Campbell, Associate Justice
J. E. Brackett, Acting District Attorney
R. B. Butler, Clerk
L. W. Boggs, Grand Jury foreman

Veritas, the Sonoma correspondent to the *Daily Alta California*, reported in a letter on 10 Sep 1850 that the Sonoma County Grand Jury had recently "assembled at the district Court" and gave an account of its "strange and marvelous" doings.

> They sat two days and found or presented four bills. 1. Presented Mr. Joseph Maille, the county assessor, as not having a legal appointment and consequently no taxation could be collected this year if his appointment was illegal. 2. They ordered a Court house and Jail to be built by taxation – curious coincidence. 3. They presented a Bill representing one Peter Campbell as having exercised the office of Justice of the Peace and other offices, and he said to be an alien, and lastly, they ordered that the City Council should build a church and school house out of the city funds without subscription or taxation – but more singular they have failed in all four presentments.[139]

People v. Peter Campbell
Illegally holding and exercising the office of Justice of the Peace
The presentment erroneously dated 4 Aug 1850 and filed on 5 Sep 1850 states:

> The Grand Jury have reason to believe that Peter Campbell of this County now holding several important offices is not a citizen of the United States of America. The Grand Jury therefore recommend to the Court that the District Attorney of the district be directed to cause the proper steps to be taken as soon as possible to ascertain whether the said Peter Campbell is a citizen of the United States or not and that the said Peter Campbell be suspended from the exercise of any of the functions of his several offices until it is decided by the proper authority whether he holds the said offices in opposition to the Laws of the Land or not.[140]

The Hon. Robert Hopkins, Sonoma County District Court judge, summoned the defendant to appear before the District Court forthwith to show cause why he should not be removed from exercising the office of Justice of the Peace in and for the County of Sonoma on 9 Sep 1850.

---

[139] Veritas, "Sonoma Correspondence," *Daily Alta California* (San Francisco, California), 28 September 1850, p. 2, col. 3.

[140] Sonoma County, California, Justice's Court case files, case file # 21, People v. Peter Campbell, Grand Jury presentment, 4 August 1850, filed 5 September 1850; County Records, Sonoma County, Court Records, Justice's Court case files; California State Archives, Sacramento. The date of this presentment is most likely in error. It should be 4 September 1850, not 4 August 1850.

Presentment in relation to the present Court house
The presentment dated 4 Sep 1850 and filed on 5 Sep 1850 states:

> The Grand Jury for the body of the County of Sonoma have had under consideration the subject of the fitness of the present building occupied as a Court house and Clerk's and Recorder's offices and the manner in which it was procured. They are of [the] opinion that [the] said building is insufficient for the purposes intended, and that it has not been rented by the proper authority or not legally rented, and they recommend that the Sheriff be directed to procure a suitable building for the aforesaid purposes until a permanent Court house be erected.[141]

Presentment in relation to the Erection of a Court House and Jail
The undated presentment filed on 5 Sep 1850 states:

> The Grand Jury for the body of the County of Sonoma within said [7th Judicial] District make the following presentment to the Court, to wit, they have had under consideration the subject of providing by erection in the City of Sonoma the seat of justice of the County of Sonoma a suitable Court house and Jail for said County. The Grand Jury have given the subject that attention which the importance and necessity of such buildings for the convenience and safety of the people of this County so urgently require. The Grand Jury therefore recommend that the Court of Sessions or County Court of this County do proceed immediately to provide for the erection of a Court House and Jail in the City of Sonoma. That the said building should be at least sixty feet square, the lower apartments or first story to be of brick or stone suitable for a prison and the second story to be of frame suitably arranged for Court rooms and offices. That said building to be erected on the public square in the City of Sonoma. The Grand Jury further recommend that a County tax of one-fourth of one percent be levied on all objects of taxation in said County. Said tax to be applied solely to the purpose of erecting said building.[142]

Presentment in relation to the Erection of a House Adapted to Educational Purposes
The presentment erroneously dated November term 1850 and filed on 5 Sep 1850 states:

> Presentment of the Grand Jury of the Body of the County of Sonoma in relation to the subject of providing a suitable building for the purposes of Education within the City of Sonoma.
>
> The Grand Jury having had the above presentment under consideration, respectfully present to the Court that they deem it their duty to recommend to those who are in authority any matter which may tend to the general welfare of the whole or any portion of the people whom they represent. The Grand Jury therefore recommend that the Mayor

---

[141] Sonoma County, California, Court of Sessions, Grand Jury presentment "In relation to the present Court house," 4 September 1850; County Records, Sonoma County, Court Records, Miscellaneous Unprocessed Records, folder "District Court papers to be interfiled when District Court is indexed"; California State Archives, Sacramento.

[142] Sonoma County, California, Court of Sessions, Grand Jury presentment "In relation to the erection of a Court house and Jail," undated, filed 5 September 1850; County Records, Sonoma County, Court Records, Miscellaneous Unprocessed Records, folder "District Court papers to be interfiled when District Court is indexed"; California State Archives, Sacramento.

and Board of Aldermen of the City of Sonoma would meet the wishes of the people of this city and its vicinity, and would confer a great blessing on their constuents [constituents?] and add greatly to the prosperity and embellishment of the City and County, by providing forthwith for the erection of a suitable building to be located in the City of Sonoma, adapted to the purposes of Education, to be constructed so that an apartment in the same may be used as a place of public worship, by any or all religious denominations. Said building to be paid for out of the funds that have or may accrue to the City from the sale of the City Lands.

The necessity and importance to the using generation from the erection of such building and the advantages the City will derive from its location in enhancing the value of property and increasing its population is too evident to need further illustration. The Grand Jury would most respectfully ask of the Court to cause a copy of this presentment to be communicated to the City authorities of Sonoma.

L. W. Boggs, Foreman.[143]

August term 1851

Hon. William O. King, County Judge
John Hendley, Clerk
Israel Brockman, Sheriff
C. R. Jackson, Deputy Sheriff
George Pearce, Grand Jury foreman

People v. Samuel R. Church
Grand larceny

The indictment filed on 19 Aug 1851 accused the defendant, "late of the United States service and stationed at the City and County of Sonoma," of stealing one light grey horse (value $350), the property of Lt. George H. Derby, U. S. Army, at the soldier's garrison in the City of Sonoma on 9 Jun 1851.[144] Sergeant Mann appeared as a witness before the Grand Jury. The defendant, Samuel Church (alias James Gordon), a 23-year-old, red-headed cooper from New York missing his two front teeth, was convicted of grand larceny and sentenced to one year's imprisonment in the State Prison.[145] The State Prison received him on 22 Aug 1851, and he was discharged on 22 Aug 1852 after serving his full sentence.

---

[143] Sonoma County, California, Court of Sessions, Presentment of the Grand Jury of Sonoma County, Sept. Term 1850, in relation to the Erection of a House Adapted to Educational Purposes, November term 1850 [sic], filed 5 September 1850; County Records, Sonoma County, Court records, Miscellaneous Unprocessed Records, folder "Miscellaneous"; California State Archives, Sacramento.

[144] Sonoma County, California, Justice's Court case files, case file # 92, People v. Samuel Church, indictment, filed 19 August 1851; County Records, Sonoma County, Court Records, Justice's Court case files; California State Archives, Sacramento. George Horatio Derby served as a lieutenant in the U. S. Army Corps of Topographical Engineers and was an early California humorist, writing under the pseudonyms of "John Phoenix" and "Squibob." See, *Wikipedia* (https://en.wikipedia.org/wiki/George_Derby), "George Derby," rev. 13:23, 24 September 2019.

[145] California, State Prison Register (1851–1867), Executive Department, entry no. 22, Samuel Church (alias James Gordon), p. 2, received 22 August 1851; California State Archives, Sacramento.

People v. George H. Derby, Thomas Grady, and Daniel Gile
Setting at liberty a person charged with a crime punishable in the State Prison

The indictment dated August term 1851 accused the defendants of setting at liberty by force and arms Samuel Church, a prisoner under guard at the house of Joseph Hooker in the City of Sonoma, on the night of 16 Jul 1851.[146] Henry P. Mollison, Richard B. Butler, and Israel Brockman appeared as witnesses before the Grand Jury. The Grand Jury found no true bill.

People v. James Thompson
Grand larceny

The indictment dated August term 1851 accused the defendant of stealing a horse and buggy (value $300), the goods and chattel of Robert Anderson, at the City of Sonoma on or about 5 Aug 1851.[147] Robert Anderson and Patrick Sheridan appeared as witnesses before the Grand Jury. The Grand Jury found no true bill.

February term 1852

Hon. Charles P. Wilkins, County Judge
John E. McNair, District Attorney
James G. Spratt, District Attorney designated by order of the Court of Sessions
John Hendley, Clerk
Joseph E. Brockman, Grand Jury foreman
William A. Hereford, Grand Jury foreman, special term

Report of [the] Grand Jury in Relation [to the] Jaol and Prisoners[148]

We, the Grand Jury empaneled and sworn, do present the fact to be that one James O'Brian, a prisoner now under confinement in the County Jail of this County by a commitment from John A. Brewster, a Justice of the Peace within and for said County and State, charging that a jury of this County had rendered a verdict against said prisoner for the sum of twenty-five dollars and committed until the sum be paid.

We, the Grand Jury as aforesaid, do present the said John A. Brewster, Justice as aforesaid, for having illegally ordered and required by said commitment the imprisonment of said John O'Brian for the non-payment of said verdict, that he has made and issued his said commitment without date nor does it show upon its face that said O'Brien has been guilty of any offense for which he should be imprisoned. We do further now present the facts to be that we have

---

[146] Sonoma County, California, Justice's Court case files, case file # 110, People v. George H. Derby, Thomas Gready, and Daniel Gile, indictment, August term 1851; County Records, Sonoma County, Court Records, Justice's Court case files; California State Archives, Sacramento.

[147] Sonoma County, California, Justice's Court case files, case file # 159, People v. James Thompson, indictment, August term 1851; County Records, Sonoma County, Court Records, Justice's Court case files; California State Archives, Sacramento. This case file is erroneously labeled "Robert Anderson vs. James Thompson."

[148] Sonoma County, California, Court of Sessions, Report of Grand Jury in Relation Jaol and Prisoners, 24 February 1852; County Records, Sonoma County, Court Records, Miscellaneous Unprocessed Records, folder "Grand Jury Reports, 1852–1875"; California State Archives, Sacramento.

examined into the cause of the imprisonment of said O'Brien and do find that he has been guilty of no offence that deserves imprisonment.

We further now present the Sheriff of this County for carelessness in the discharge of the duties of his office as Jaoler as afores[aid] for receiving said prisoner into the Jaol of said County upon a commitment irregular, informal, and defective upon the face of it, and that the Court of Sessions be required or requested to release said prisoner from his imprisonment, and that the said Sheriff and Justice pay all expenses that this County may be at in supporting said prisoner whilst in Jaol.

Grand Jurors: William A. Hereford, Jr., Edward Marsh, Saml. D. Lonel [Lowell?], John G. Ray, Ed Gllen, J. C. Monel, J. C. McCracken, Joseph Noris, Henry Tyler, J. C. Blakesly, Benj. Mitchell, Wm. Potter, Joseph Wardlow, James A. Hardin, M. Coleman, Daniel Grayson, and J. M. Bennt

People v. John S. Hittle (var. Hittell)
Petit larceny (case file # 0C)
The indictment filed during the February term 1852 accused the defendant of stealing one hog (value $30), property of William M. Boggs, on or about the latter part of the year 1851. William M. Boggs and Josiah Ferguson appeared as witnesses before the Grand Jury.

People v. George B. Farrar
Assault with intent to kill (case file # 0B)
The indictment filed on 24 Feb 1852 accused the defendant of assaulting George Nugent (var. Newgent) on the head, arms, and other parts of his body with an ax and also assaulting him with a gun on 22 Feb 1852. The trial jury found the defendant not guilty April term 1852. George Nugnent [sic], William Hereford, and Samuel D. Lonel [Lowell?] appeared as witnesses before the Grand Jury.

People v. Gustave Sarrebourse D'Audeville (indicted as Gustave Sarbous De Autville)
Murder
The indictment filed on 24 Feb 1852 accused the defendant of: 1.) assaulting Lewis Legendre with a pistol, shooting him in the front part of the head, giving him one mortal wound of which he instantly died on or about 1 Feb 1852 at Legendre's house in Russian River Township, 2.) assaulting Lewis Legendre with a knife, giving him one mortal wound upon his head of which he instantly died on or about 1 Feb 1852 at Legendre's house in Russian River Township, 3.) assaulting Lewis Legendre with a club, giving him by diverse blows upon his head one mortal wound of which he instantly died on or about 1 Feb 1852 at Legendre's house in Russian River Township, and 4.) assaulting Lewis Legendre with a gun, shooting him in the right side and breast, giving him diverse mortal wounds of which he instantly died on or about 1 Feb 1852 at Legendre's house in Russian River Township.[149] Joseph Lebret, William Potter, and Oliver Bolio were examined before the Grand Jury. Legendre, a Frenchman, was one of the first settlers of the

---

[149] Sonoma County, California, Court of Sessions, The People v. Gustave Sarbous De Autville, indictment, 23 February 1852, filed 24 February 1862; County Records, Sonoma County, Court Records, Miscellaneous Unprocessed Records, folder "Miscellaneous to be interfiled – District (1)"; California State Archives, Sacramento.

Russian River Township and, along with Lindsay Carson, one of the "first considerable growers of wheat."[150]

Mangling the defendant's name, the *Daily Union* reported the murder of Legendre on 16 Feb 1852 as:

> We learn through Dr. Hurd, that a most horrible and revolting murder was perpetrated on the first Sunday of this month [1 Feb 1852] at Russian river, about 30 miles from Sonoma. The name of the murdered man was Louis Legendre. He was highly esteemed in that neighborhood. His body which was recently found, bore the marks of a ball wound in the right breast, a saber wound across the left temple, and [the] forepart of the skull broke in as if struck with an axe. Four men in the neighborhood were arrested upon suspicion; among whom was a vaquero, who was a great favorite of Gustavo Sabronsa Deaulorble, (one of the parties arrested), and who this vaquero declared had murdered Legendre. From his statement of the facts, this Deaulorble after the murder was committed, called upon the vaquero to assist him in disposing of the body. The murderer tied one end of a lariat into the cravat of the murdered man, and the vaquero fixing the other to his saddle, dragged the corpse about a mile from the place of murder, and there buried it. This Deaulorble, acknowledged that he killed the man, but said he did it in self-defense. He was committed.[151]

The case was transferred to the Sonoma County District Court on 24 Feb 1852. At the end of April 1852, the Hon. Robert Hopkins presided over the week-long trial of Sarrebourse D'Audeville, a Frenchman, in the Sonoma County District Court, which "drew together most of the citizens of the county."[152] The District Court trial jury deliberated for sixteen hours and returned a verdict of "guilty" on 1 May 1852. Judge Hopkins sentenced Sarrebourse D'Audeville to be hung on 11 June 1852. While awaiting his fate, however, Sarrebourse D'Audeville escaped from jail on 1 June 1852 despite having two guards in the same room with him and iron shackles on both his wrists and ankles.[153] Veritas, the Sonoma correspondent to the *Daily Alta California*, noted that Sarrebourse D'Audeville's escape was the third such escape of a convicted murderer from Sonoma's jail and wryly posed the question "Who says that Judge Lynch is not sometimes useful?"[154]

---

[150] Munro-Fraser, *History of Sonoma County*, 358–359.

[151] "Horrible Murder in Sonoma Valley," *The Daily Union* (Sacramento, California), 16 February 1852, p. 2, col. 1.

[152] "Convicted," *Daily Alta California* (San Francisco, California), 5 May 1852, p. 2, col. 2.

[153] "Escape of a Prisoner From the Jail at Sonoma," *Daily Alta California* (San Francisco, California), 3 June 1852, p. 2, col. 1.

[154] Veritas, "Fatal Accident – Escape of a Culprit," *Daily Alta California* (San Francisco, California), 12 June 1852, p. 2, col. 2.

June term 1852

Hon. Charles P. Wilkins, County Judge
John E. McNair, District Attorney
John Hendley, Clerk
J. A. Brewster, Deputy Clerk
John Cameron, Grand Jury foreman

People v. Thomas H. Pyatt
Assault with intent to commit murder (case file # 0D)
   The indictment filed on 9 Jun 1852 accused the defendant of assaulting Lewis D. Watkins in the City of Sonoma by shooting him in the face with a pistol on 9 Jun 1852. John M. Boggs, Guillermo Fitch, Hanson Olmstead, Edward Bodger, Theodore Boggs, John Hendley, J. P. Wilbur, and John A. Brewster appeared as witnesses before the Grand Jury. The trial jury found the defendant not guilty on 5 Oct 1852.

People v. James N. Cook
Assault with intent to commit murder (case file # 0A)
   The indictment filed on 10 Jun 1852 accused the defendant of assaulting William Walker by shooting him with a pistol with the intent of killing him on 11 Apr 1852. James W. Jameson appeared as a witness before the Grand Jury.

People v. William Hudson, A. Elliot, Benjamin Duel (var. Dewell), [?] Kearney, [?] White, and David O. Shattuck
Obstructing public highways of Sonoma County and public streets of the City of Sonoma
   The presentment filed on 10 Jun 1852 accused the defendants of obstructing various county roads so that they were inconvenient and dangerous to pass.[155]

   In his 1880 *History of Sonoma County* Munro-Fraser related that he had found "the first record of proceedings of the Court of Sessions extant among the county archives" dated 8 July 1852 in which the Hon. C. P. Wilkins and his Associate Justices, the Hon. Peter Campbell and the Hon. J. M. Miller, along with J. Hendley, Clerk, and J. A. Reynolds, Under Sheriff, "assembled to impanel a Grand Jury."[156] He then named the Grand Jurors: W. D. Kent, J. D. George, Alexander Spect, Samuel Havens, H. N. Ryder, Josiah Wilkins, James Crenshaw, J. P. Thrasher, A. C. Hollingshead, J. W. Davis, George Smith, Arnold Hutton, Edward Beasley, George Edgerton, John Smith, Benjamin Mitchell, H. L. Kamp, J. M. Gilliland, Robert Anderson, George B. Farrar, Hosea Norris, and Leonard Dodge. If the date of this record is correct then this must have been a special term of the Court of Sessions. No documents from this special term have been found.

---

[155] Sonoma County, California, Court of Sessions, People v. William Hudson, A. Elliot, Benjamin Duel, [?] Kearney, [?] White, and David O. Shattuck, Grand Jury presentment, 10 June 1852; County Records, Sonoma County, Court Records, Miscellaneous Unprocessed Records, folder "Grand Jury Reports, 1852–1875"; California State Archives, Sacramento.

[156] Munro-Fraser, *History of Sonoma County*, 143. This record can no longer be found in the Sonoma County Archives.

August term 1852

Hon. Charles P. Wilkins, County Judge
John E. McNair, District Attorney
John Hendley, Clerk
J. A. Brewster, Deputy Clerk
James H. McCord, Grand Jury foreman

People v. H. L. Lidstrom, C. H. Bartlett, Joseph Leprince, Oliver Bolio, [?] Blachier, and M. Rickman (var. Ryckman)
Violating the license law (case file # 0D)
    The presentment filed on 2 Aug 1852 accused the defendants of violating the license law.

People v. Alexander C. McDonald
As County Treasurer using State funds for himself (case file # 7D)
    The indictment filed on 3 Aug 1852 accused the defendant of using funds belonging to the State of California for his own use by betting at cards and losing while County Treasurer at the City of Sonoma during the latter part of 1851. George W. Miller and Israel Brockman appeared as witnesses before the Grand Jury.

October term 1852

Hon. Charles P. Wilkins, County Judge
Hon. Phil R. Thompson, Associate Justice[157]
Hon. A. C. Godwin, Associate Justice

February term 1853

Hon. Charles P. Wilkins, County Judge
Hon. Frank W. Shattuck, Associate Justice
Hon. Isaac N. Randolph, Associate Justice
John E. McNair, District Attorney
John Hendley, Clerk
J. A. Brewster, Deputy Clerk
B. B. Munday, Grand Jury foreman
John B. Scott, Grand Jury foreman, special session

---

[157] Munro-Fraser, *History of Sonoma County*, 143. Phil. R. Thompson and A. C. Godwin were elected as Associate Justices on 3 October 1852 in place of Peter Campbell and J. M. Miller, whose terms had expired. Robert A. Thompson gives the outgoing Associate Justices' names as Peter Campbell and J. M. Terrill. See, Thompson, *Historical and Descriptive Sketch of Sonoma County, California*, 47.

Grand Jurors: B. B. Munday, foreman, Daniel Grayson, John Andres, W. C. Goodman, William Ed. Taylor, Joseph Patton, Coleman Asbury, S. D. Lowell, Charles Owins, H. L. Johns, Alex Dunbar, L. G. Finley, Franklin Sears, W. M. Boggs, Robert McAllen, H. L. Kamp, and Richard Marshal.[158]

Report of the Grand Jury relative to the Court House[159]

We, the undersigned Grand Jury, state that after examining the Court House, beg leave to report that the same is in a dilapidated condition and altogether unfit for the use for which the County intended it. We further believe that it would be judicious to dispose of the same to the highest bidder and apply the proceeds of the sale to the erection of a more suitable building. Believing that such a report will meet the approbation of the citizens at large , we pray that the attention of the Board of Supervisors may be directed to this matter as early as practicable and we further believe that the new Court House should be erected in the center of the Public Square of Sonoma.

B. B. Munday, Foreman.

Report of [the] Grand Jury[160]

The Grand Jury for the County of Sonoma—in concluding their special session would represent that the circumstances under which the Shff. [Sheriff] of the County is required to act in summoning Grand Jurors exposes delinquency or neglect of duty on the part of some County Officers which deserves in their judgment reprehension. At present it seems the Shff. does not summon a Grand Jury according to Law.

The Grand Jury would further represent that the Corporation of the City of Sonoma have made no provision for the security of the citizens of the County against the spread of the small pox now raging in the city.

This neglect involves a risk of the spread of this terrible disease, which, during the ensuing warm weather, may depopulate the city and county. They recommend that the proper authority interfere and that the prosecuting attorney be directed to proceed according to Law to remedy the Evil.

The Grand Jury for the County of Sonoma would further unanimously present the Public road from the Embarcadero through the City limits and thence up the valley of Sonoma is a public nuisance. Its location and condition render it impassable during the rainy season. They therefore recommend that legal steps be taken to secure a better location of some parts through the valley

---

[158] This list of Grand Jurors for the February term 1853 appears amended to the Wilkins presentment. See, Sonoma County, California, Court of Sessions, The People v. the Hon. Charles P. Wilkins, presentment, February term 1853, filed 9 Feb 1853; County Records, Sonoma County, Court Records, Miscellaneous Unprocessed Records, folder "Miscellaneous to be interfiled – District (1)"; California State Archives, Sacramento.

[159] Sonoma County, California, Court of Sessions, Report of the Grand Jury relative to the Court House, filed 8 February 1853; County Records, Sonoma County, Court Records, Miscellaneous Unprocessed Records, folder "Grand Jury Reports, 1852–1875"; California State Archives, Sacramento.

[160] Sonoma County, California, Court of Sessions, Report of Grand Jury, filed 12 February 1853; County Records, Sonoma County, Court Records, Miscellaneous Unprocessed Records, folder "Grand Jury Reports, 1852–1875"; California State Archives, Sacramento.

and the working the same in a suitable manner. They would call the attention of the proper authorities to the importance of constructing bridges over several creeks in the valley before the rainy season. The expense of which will be light, and the working of the road and bridges, they have reason to believe, will be done forthwith in reliance upon the County for such payment as it thinks just.

The above resolutions were all passed unanimously.

Signed by the Foreman, John B. Scott

Attest, J. B. Boggs, Sec.

People v. Adolph Blachen (var. Blashen) (indicted as John Doe)
Selling intoxicating liquor to an Indian (case file # 5)

The indictment filed on 8 Feb 1853 accused the defendant of selling an Indian a glass of intoxicating liquor for 25 cents at his store in the City of Sonoma on 1 Jan 1853. Joseph Patten appeared as a witness before the Grand Jury.

People v. G. T. Pauli and F. Schultz
Retailing dry goods and spiritous liquors without a license (case file # 7C)

The indictment filed on 8 Feb 1853 accused the defendants of retailing dry goods and spiritous liquors without a license in Sonoma Township for a long time before the finding of the indictment. Daniel Grayson appeared as a witness before the Grand Jury.

People v. [?] Metcham
Retailing dry goods and spiritous liquors without a license (case file # 7E)

The indictment filed on 8 Feb 1853 accused the defendant of retailing dry goods and spiritous liquors without a license in Santa Rosa Township during the year of 1852. S. J. Finley and Woodson Manion appeared as witnesses before the Grand Jury.

People v. Richard Fowler and [?] Harris
Retailing spiritous liquors without a license (case file # 7O)

The indictment filed on 8 Feb 1853 accused the defendants of retailing spiritous liquors without a license in Sonoma Township for a long time past before the finding of the indictment. Jason Smith and William Goodman appeared as witnesses before the Grand Jury.

People v. Lewis Adler
Retailing dry goods and spiritous liquors without a license (case file # 7R)

The indictment filed on 8 Feb 1853 accused the defendant of retailing dry goods and spiritous liquors without a license in Sonoma Township for a long time past before the finding of the indictment. Daniel Grayson and H. L. Johns appeared as witnesses before the Grand Jury.

People v. Thomas Baylis and [?] Flogdell
Retailing dry goods and spiritous liquors without a license (case file # 7U)

The indictment filed on 8 Feb 1853 accused the defendants of retailing dry goods and spiritous liquors without a license at Petaluma Township for a long time past before the finding of the indictment. S. J. Finley appeared as a witness before the Grand Jury.

People v. [?] Blachen and [?] Ducollet
Retailing dry goods and spiritous liquors without a license (case file # 7W)

The indictment filed on 8 Feb 1853 accused the defendants of retailing dry goods and spiritous liquors without a license at Sonoma Township for a long time past before the finding of the indictment. Joseph Patton, William Taylor, and John Andrews appeared as witnesses before the Grand Jury.

People v. the Hon. Charles P. Wilkins, County Judge
Wilful misconduct in office

The presentment filed on 9 Feb 1853 accused the defendant of becoming so intoxicated on 5 Oct 1852 during the Court of Sessions trial of the case entitled People v. Thomas H. Pyatt in which the defendant was the presiding judge that he was unfit to discharge the duties of his office and unable to charge the jury in an understandable manner.[161] District Attorney John E. McNair subpoenaed William M. Boggs, Nicholas Long, and Joseph Patten on 21 Feb 1853 to appear in Sonoma County District Court on 22 Feb 1853 as witnesses in the case. No District Court case file number was assigned to this case, the appropriate District Court minute book is missing, and no newspaper accounts of a trial could be found. There are, however, several documents for the case among the unprocessed Sonoma County court records at the State Archives.

People v. Francisco Caseres (alias Pancho, indicted as Francisco Carceras)
Petit larceny (case file # 3)

The indictment filed on 12 Feb 1853 accused the defendant of stealing lumber from the mill of Hender and Duncan (value $49.75), property of Charles M. Hudspeth, which the defendant converted to his own use sometime during the year of 1852. Charles M. Hudspeth, Samuel M. Duncan, and [?] Hubbard appeared as witnesses before the Grand Jury.

April term 1853

Hon. Charles P. Wilkins, County Judge
John E. McNair, District Attorney
John Hendley, Clerk
John A. Brewster, Deputy Clerk
Henry P. Heintzelman, Grand Jury foreman

Report of the Grand Jury[162]

To the Honorable the Court of Sessions of Sonoma County,

---

[161] Sonoma County, California, Court of Sessions, The People v. the Hon. Charles P. Wilkins, presentment, February term 1853, filed 9 Feb 1853; County Records, Sonoma County, Court Records, Miscellaneous Unprocessed Records, folder "Miscellaneous to be interfiled – District (1)"; California State Archives, Sacramento.

[162] Sonoma County, California, Court of Sessions, Grand Jury report for April term 1853, filed 14 April 1853; County Records, Sonoma County, Court Records, Miscellaneous Unprocessed Records, folder "Grand Jury Reports, 1852–1875"; California State Archives, Sacramento.

The Grand Jury enquiring for the County of Sonoma respectfully report to this Court at the empaneling of the Grand Jury we were congratulated by the Court on the small amount of crime that had been committed in the County. We regret after the termination of our labours that the expectations of the Court and Jury were not realized. We are happy, however, to state that the aggravated crimes which we have found to have been committed have occurred beyond the limits of this valley in the remote portions of the County, and they of the most aggravated character have been truly alarming. The following list of true bills have been found: grand larceny, 9; petit larceny, 3; perjury, 11; accessories, 5; misdemeanors, 14.

The Grand Jury are fully impressed that an organized band of horse and cattle thieves exist in our midst, their ramifications extending throughout our County and connecting at Clear Lake with another band who drive the stolen horses to the northern mines and Sacramento, and so perfect are their organization that all efforts made by us to procure testimony against them have signally failed (two instances excepted) either from fear or connection with the band.

We find upon examination of the books of the Treasurer and Auditor that there are sufficient funds in the treasury to meet all the outstanding warrants of the old series and up to the twenty-third of March 1853 there had been issued of the new series $5,000, the full amount of the just debt of the County to that date.

Also an alleged debt, due by the County for the purchase of the so-called Court House and Jail of $5,500 bearing interest at the rate of 2½ percent [per] month that there has been paid on account $3,000 and the balance still due $5,000. We say alleged from the fact that said building was at the time of purchase the property of the then County judge and that the trustees were creditors of the said County judge.

We find the books of the Auditor and County Treasurer well and regularly kept and the officers faithful and efficient.

We would call the attention of the Court to the fact that a large number [of] persons are doing business in the County without license to the great injury of the law-abiding merchant[s] as well as to the detriment of the revenue of the County.

The public roads have been much neglected and are in bad condition, in many places so fenced off as to compel [a] person to go a considerable distance out of their way, and [we] would recommend that strenuous measures be taken for the purpose of removing said obstructions and repairing the aforesaid highways in which not only the farming community, but the travelling public, are so greatly interested.

Upon enquiry made we are led to believe that if the assessment of the County now going on is properly done and we have full confidence in the officer entrusted with that duty, the income of the County for the present fiscal year will amount to $24,000 at the lowest estimate and will be sufficient under the economical administration of the present board of supervisors to meet all liabilities of the County.

The course heretofore pursued in making the assessments of the County we believe [is] injudicious and detrimental to the revenue of the County, viz., permitting the holders of large ranches to return their own estimate of the value of their real property. We find that in no instance have they returned a higher valuation than $1 per acre while their selling price is from $10 to $20. While on the owner of small tract of land is assessed at its full value.

Our attention was called more particularly to [the] County building and to the repairs needed. Upon examination, we find that the building at present used as a Court House and Jail are unworthy of the name and totally unfit for the uses intended and to expend any money in repair upon it would be injudicious and an extravagant waste of the public monies, and [we] would recommend that if the building belongs to the County it be sold and the proceeds appropriated to the erection of suitable building for County purposes.

To the Court, District Attorney, and Sheriff we tender our thanks for their prompt attention to us while in session.

All of which we respectfully submit, H. P. Heintzelman, Foreman.

People v. John Hollingsworth
Rendering aid and assistance to a prisoner enabling his escape (case file # 1)

The indictment filed on 5 Apr 1853 accused the defendant of furnishing aid and assistance to S. R. McDonald, a prisoner in the custody of Benjamin A. Snoddy in the Common Jail Room in the City of Sonoma, by removing his irons and providing other assistance on 29 Mar 1853. William H. Conklin, James E. Smith, and Harriet Anderson appeared as witnesses before the Grand Jury. The jury found the defendant not guilty. For related cases, see also case file #s 4, 7, and 7Q.

People v. William H. Conklin
Rendering aid and assistance to a prisoner his enabling escape (case file # 4)

The indictment filed on 5 Apr 1853 accused the defendant of furnishing aid and assistance to S. R. McDonald, a prisoner in the custody of Benjamin A. Snoddy in the Common Jail Room in the City of Sonoma, by removing his irons and providing other assistance on 29 Mar 1853. John Hollingsworth, James E. Smith, and Nancy Ann Gwinett appeared as witnesses before the Grand Jury. For related cases, see also case file #s 1, 7, and 7Q.

People v. John McCurdy
Perjury (case file # 7G)

The indictment filed on 5 Apr 1853 accused the defendant of giving false testimony concerning putting up or assisting in putting stakes on the line in the valley between himself and Joseph Antonio Vandernoot in the case of the People v. Joseph Antonio Vandernoot on or about 15 Feb 1853. M. G. Lewis and Joseph Antonio Vandernoot appeared as witnesses before the Grand Jury.

People v. Jesse Beasley, Mrs. Mark West, James Prewitt, and [?] Lee
Obstructing public highways

The presentment filed on 6 Apr 1853 accused the defendants of obstructing various county roads by constructing fencing across them. Joseph G. Dow, Hugh Patton, and James Boggs appeared as witnesses before the Grand Jury.[163]

---

[163] Sonoma County, California, Court of Sessions, People v. Jesse Beasley, Mrs. Mark West, James Prewitt, and [?] Lee, Grand Jury presentment, filed 6 April 1853; County Records, Sonoma County, Court Records, Miscellaneous Unprocessed Records, folder "Grand Jury Reports, 1852–1875"; California State Archives, Sacramento.

People v. John Casey, [?] Beans, and [?] Beans
Obstructing a public highway

The undated presentment accused the defendants of obstructing the public highway leading from Petaluma to the port of Bodega.[164]

People v. DeWitt C. Thompson
Grand larceny (case file # 7B)

The indictment filed on 6 Apr 1853 accused the defendant of stealing, killing, and carrying away one cow (value $100), property of Nancy Jane Guinett, on 15 Nov 1852. Howard Clark and Capt. Guinett appeared as witnesses before the Grand Jury.

People v. Nicholas J. T. Long and Norman Galusha
Petit larceny (case file # 7J)

The indictment filed on 6 Apr 1853 accused the defendants of stealing, killing, and carrying away one cow (value $25), property of M. G. Vallejo, in or near the tule marsh or swamp situated below the Embarcadero of St. Louis in Sonoma Township on 20 Mar 1853. Martin E. Cooke and Israel Brockman appeared as witnesses before the Grand Jury.

People v. S. R. McDonald, Nancy Jane Gwinnette, John Smith, James J. Smith, and William H. Conklin
Rendering aid and assistance to a prisoner enabling his escape (case file # 7)

The indictment filed on 7 Apr 1853 accused the defendant S. R. McDonald of stealing one horse (value $50), property of W. P. Ewing, from the ranch in Sonoma Township owned and occupied by George Smith, now deceased, on 15 Nov 1852 and accused the defendants Nancy Jane Gwinnette, John Smith, James J. Smith, and William H. Conklin of protecting and harboring S. R. McDonald in the City of Sonoma at the house of Nancy Jane Gwinnette knowing he had committed grand larceny on or about 28 Mar 1853. John Hollingsworth and Harriet Anderson appeared as witnesses before the Grand Jury. For related cases, see also case file #s 1, 4, and 7Q.

People v. J. B. Scott
Selling spiritous liquors at retail without a license (case file # 7A)

The indictment filed on 7 Apr 1853 accused the defendant of selling spiritous liquors at retail without a license in Sonoma Township on 27 Mar 1853. Gibbs Randall appeared as a witness before the Grand Jury.

People v. Donald McDonald
Selling goods, wares, and merchandise without a license (case file # 7F)

The indictment filed on 7 Apr 1853 accused the defendant of selling goods, wares, and merchandise without a license in Bodega Township on 2 Apr 1853. George Edgerton appeared as a witness before the Grand Jury.

---

[164] Sonoma County, California, Court of Sessions, People v. John Casey, [?] Beans, and [?] Beans, Grand Jury presentment, April term 1853; County Records, Sonoma County, Court Records, Miscellaneous Unprocessed Records, folder "Grand Jury Reports, 1852–1875"; California State Archives, Sacramento.

People v. [?] McCallister
Selling spiritous liquors without a license (case file # 7H)

The indictment filed on 7 Apr 1853 accused the defendant of selling spiritous liquors without a license on the Petaluma and Bodega road on or about the month of March 1853. John Griffith appeared as a witness before the Grand Jury.

People v. [?] Lille and [?] Godwin
Selling liquor and vending goods, wares, and merchandise without a license (case file # 7K)

The indictment filed on 7 Apr 1853 accused the defendants of selling liquor by retail and vending goods, wares, and merchandise without a license in Mendocino County during the winter of 1852. Edmond Bodger appeared as a witness before the Grand Jury.

People v. Thomas Hogan
Grand larceny (case file # 7P)

The indictment filed on 7 Apr 1853 accused the defendant of stealing a horse (value $300), property of Leonard Dodge, at or near the House known as the California House in the City of Sonoma on 15 Feb 1853. Leonard Dodge appeared as a witness before the Grand Jury.

People v. Nancy Jane Gwinett
Perjury (case file # 7Q)

The indictment filed on 7 Apr 1853 accused the defendant of lying under oath as a witness before the Grand Jury concerning whether she knew of the concealment of S. R. McDonald in her house on 6 Apr 1853. S. R. McDonald, John Hollingsworth, and William H. Conklin appeared as witnesses before the Grand Jury. For related cases, see also case file #s 1, 4, and 7.

People v. Juan Beronda
Grand larceny (case file # 7S)

The indictment filed on 7 Apr 1853 accused the defendant of stealing one horse (value $100), property of William Beeler [William Bihler], in Bodega Township on 20 Nov 1852. Leonard Dodge and F. G. Blume appeared as witnesses before the Grand Jury.

People v. [?] Bugner
Selling, giving, or furnishing spiritous liquors to an Indian (case file # 7V)

The indictment filed on 7 Apr 1853 accused the defendant of selling, giving, or furnishing spiritous liquors to an Indian in the City of Sonoma on 12 Mar 1853. Daniel Davidson and John Griffeth appeared as witnesses before the Grand Jury.

People v. [?] Blachen and [?] Ducollet
Selling goods, wares, and merchandise without a license (case file # 7W)

The indictment filed on 7 Apr 1853 accused the defendants of selling goods, wares, and merchandise without a license at the City of Sonoma on 5 Apr 1853. Isaac Randolph appeared as a witness before the Grand Jury.

People v. [?] Cousins
Selling goods, wares, and merchandise contrary to the laws of the State (case file # 7Y)

The indictment filed on 7 Apr 1853 accused the defendant of selling goods, wares, and merchandise contrary to the laws of the State in Mendocino County for a long time past before the finding of the indictment. Edward Bodger appeared as a witness before the Grand Jury.

People v. [?] Breckenbridge
Selling spiritous liquors without a license (case file # 7GG)

The indictment filed on 7 Apr 1853 accused the defendant of selling spiritous liquors without a license in Petaluma Township on or about 10 Feb 1853. M. G. Lewis and William Zartman appeared as witnesses before the Grand Jury.

People v. [?] Nathanson
Selling spiritous liquors at retail by the glass without a license (case file # 7HH)

The indictment filed on 7 Apr 1853 accused the defendant of selling spiritous liquors at retail by the glass without a license in Sonoma Township on or about 20 Jan 1853. P. J. Vasques and Joseph Pellicee appeared as witnesses before the Grand Jury. The Court sustained the defendant's demurrer and ordered the defendant discharged from his recognizance on 13 Apr 1853.

People v. [?] Pierce and [?] Randolph
Selling spiritous liquors without a license (case file # 11G)

The indictment filed on 7 Apr 1853 accused the defendants of selling spiritous liquors without a license in the City of Sonoma on or about the month of March 1853. Franklin Cooke and Thomas Williamson appeared as witnesses before the Grand Jury.

People v. Harmon Heald
Selling liquor, merchandise, and wares without a license (case file # 7N)

The indictment filed on 8 Apr 1853 accused the defendant of selling liquor, merchandise, and wares without a license in Mendocino County in or about the month of January 1853. J. G. Dow appeared as a witness before the Grand Jury.

People v. Raphael Celia
Petit larceny (case file # 7BB)

The indictment filed on 8 Apr 1853 accused the defendant of stealing one of Josepha C. Fitch's calves (value $25) at or near the Sotoyoma Rancho in Russian River Township on or about the month of February 1853. Henry Fitch, Frederick Fitch, and Jose Vevianco appeared as witnesses before the Grand Jury.

People v. Antonio Piña (var. Peña)
Grand larceny (case file # 11H)

The indictment filed on 8 Apr 1853 accused the defendant of stealing one steer (value $60), property of Mrs. Josepha C. Fitch, on or near her Sotoyoma Ranch in the Russian River Township on or about the middle of the month of February 1853. Henry Fitch, Frederick Fitch, and Jose

Vivecina appeared as witnesses before the Grand Jury. Israel Brockman, the Sheriff of Sonoma County, returned the bench warrant for the defendant issued by the Court on 8 Apr 1853 not served on 16 Apr 1853 as the defendant had died.

People v. S. R. McDonald
Grand larceny (case file # 7)
    The indictment filed on 9 Apr 1853 accused the defendant of stealing one grey horse (value $50), property of W. P. Ewing, from the ranch in Sonoma Township owned and occupied by George Smith, now deceased, on 15 Nov 1852. R. D. Foster, Frank Burrus, Edward Bodger, and George Spence appeared as witnesses before the Grand Jury.

People v. James Jackson, John Jackson, John Doe, Richard Roe, and Hiram Smith
Grand larceny (case file # 7M)
    The indictment filed on 9 Apr 1853 accused the defendants of stealing a heifer (value $60), property of William Howard, at Bodega Township on 20 Mar 1853. Jasper O'Farrell and F. G. Blume appeared as witnesses before the Grand Jury. For a related case, see also case file # 7DD.

People v. Nancy Jane Gwinett, John Smith, James J. Smith, and William H. Conklin
Accessories after the fact in the commission of the crime of grand larceny (case file # 7Q)
    The indictment filed on 9 Apr 1853 accused the defendants of protecting and harboring S. R. McDonald at Nancy Jane Gwinett's house in the City of Sonoma knowing that he had committed grand larceny on or about 28 Mar 1853 or between the middle of the month of March 1853 and the finding of the indictment. John Hollingsworth, Harriet Anderson, William H. Conklin, and S. R. McDonald appeared as witnesses before the Grand Jury. For related cases, see also case file #s 1, 4, and 7.

People v. Isaac N. Randolph
Keeping a billiard table for pay at $1 a game without a license (case file # 11F)
    The indictment filed on 9 Apr 1853 accused the defendant of keeping a billiard table for pay at $1 a game at his hotel in the City of Sonoma without a license on or about the month of January 1853. Thomas D. Williamson and Thomas H. Pyatt appeared as witnesses before the Grand Jury.

People v. J. B. Scott
Furnishing intoxicating liquor to an Indian (case file # 7A)
    The indictment filed on 14 Apr 1853 accused the defendant of furnishing intoxicating liquor to an Indian in Sonoma township on 15 Mar 1853. S. R. McDonald appeared as a witness before the Grand Jury.

People v. Christian Mertin
Furnishing intoxicating liquor to an Indian (case file # 7I)
    The indictment filed on 14 Apr 1853 accused the defendant of furnishing intoxicating liquor to an Indian at Sonoma Township on 1 Mar 1853. W. R. Concklin appeared as a witness before the Grand Jury.

People v. Christian Mertin
Furnishing intoxicating liquor to an Indian (case file # 7I)

The indictment filed on 14 Apr 1853 accused the defendant of furnishing intoxicating liquor to an Indian at Sonoma Township on 8 Mar 1853. W. R. Concklin appeared as a witness before the Grand Jury.

People v. William Fraseir (var. Frazer)
Assault with intent to commit murder (case file # 7X)

The presentment filed on 14 Apr 1853 accused the defendant of assault with intent to commit murder in Russian River Township. While the presentment uncharacteristically does not provide any details of the assault, the *Sacramento Daily Union* quoting the *Sonoma Bulletin* of 16 Apr 1853 does:

> We have learned that Antonio Pena, a native Californian, and long residing in Mendocino County, was shot on Saturday last [9 Apr 1853] by William Frazer. From what little information we have of the affair, it appears that the wild stock belonging to the Pena ranch had trampled and otherwise injured crops of the settlers on the ranch, and that some horses were in consequence killed by them. Pena hearing of this, remonstrated against this injustice, when he was himself shot. When it is considered that these settlers are located on the land claimed by the Penas, and that some of their fields are unfenced, the case presents itself as one of the grossest outrage. Pena lingered in agony till Thursday [14 Apr 1853], when he died. He was at a distance of a hundred yards when shot, the ball entering the back, passing through the right lung. Frazer has not yet been arrested.[165]

Frazer was apparently still at large in October of 1853 when Frederick Fitch informed the *Sonoma Bulletin* that Frazer was "prowling about the neighborhood of Russian River."[166]

People v. Walter Comstock (indicted as William G. Comstock)
Petit larceny (case file # 7Z)

The indictment filed on 14 Apr 1853 accused the defendant of stealing a Bowie or dirk knife (value $5), property of Kent and Co., from the store of Kent and Co. in Petaluma on 11 Apr 1853. S. N. Terrill and [?] Van Ryper appeared as witnesses before the Grand Jury.

People v. Walter Comstock (indicted as William G. Comstock)
Grand larceny (case file # 7AA)

The indictment filed on 14 Apr 1853 accused the defendant of stealing a gold breast pin, two gold specimens, a specimen gold pin, 13 American gold dollars, 1 gold 50 cent piece, and 3 silver dollars (total value $82.50), property of Samuel N. Terrell, Esq., from Terrell's house in Petaluma Township on or about 12 Apr 1853. S. N. Terrel and [?] Van Ryper appeared as witnesses before the Grand Jury. The defendant was apparently convicted of grand larceny. The Court sentenced

---

[165] "Shooting of Antonio Pena," *Sacramento (California) Daily Union*, 19 April 1853, p. 3, col. 1.
[166] "From Russian River," *Sacramento (California) Daily Union*, 31 October 1853, p. 3, col. 1.

him to one year's imprisonment in the State Prison on 20 Apr 1853.[167] The State Prison received him on 26 Apr 1853.[168] His date of discharge was not recorded in the State Prison register.

People v. Raphael Celia
Grand larceny (case file # 7CC)

The indictment filed on 14 Apr 1853 accused the defendant of stealing one of Antonio Maso's horses (value $200) in the Russian River Township on or about 1 Mar 1853. Jose Zeriano, Antonia Mesa, Henry Fitch, and Frederick Fitch appeared as witnesses before the Grand Jury.

People v. Robert G. Bynum, Hiram Smith, and James Jackson
Receiving stolen property (case file # 7DD)

The indictment filed during the April term 1853 accused the defendants of receiving, partaking of, and using for their own gain a stolen heifer, knowing it to be stolen, on 21 Mar 1853. The heifer (value $60), property of William Howard, had been stolen by William Jackson and John Major at Bodega Township on 20 Mar 1853. Jasper O'Farrell, F. G. Blume, William Howard, and C. M. Hudspeth appeared as witnesses before the Grand Jury. For a related case, see also case file # 7M.

June term 1853

There were apparently two Grand Juries this term.

Hon. Charles P. Wilkins, County Judge
John E. McNair, District Attorney
John Hendley, Clerk
J. A. Brewster, Deputy Clerk
Israel Brockman, Sheriff
S. H. Boake, Grand Jury foreman
J. N. Nevill, Grand Jury foreman

Report of the Committee appointed to examine the County Jail by order of the Grand Jury[169]

The committee to whom was assigned the duty of inspecting the County prison beg leave to report as follows: They visited the chamber set apart as a prison and find the same (as every Grand Jury has heretofore done) entirely unfit for the purpose, there being no security for the safe keeping of the prisoners except the continuing vigilance of the Sheriff or the prisoner's disinclination to change his quarters, being well provided for in food and lodging. Additional irons are much wanted for the better security of prisoners, and as affording some relief to those having

---

[167] "Criminal Record," *The Sonoma County Journal* (Petaluma, California), 13 May 1859, p. 2, col. 3.

[168] California, State Prison Register (1851–1867), Executive Department, entry no. 205, Walter Comstock, p. 14, received 26 April 1853; California State Archives, Sacramento.

[169] Sonoma County, California, Court of Sessions, Report of the Committee appointed to examine the County Jail by order of the Grand Jury, filed 14 June 1853; County Records, Sonoma County, Court Records, Miscellaneous Unprocessed Records, folder "Grand Jury Reports, 1852–1875"; California State Archives, Sacramento.

them in charge. The committee deem it unnecessary to urge the expenditure of any money on the present prison as we would deem any outlay on the present House occupied as a prison to be a useless expenditure of money.

G. W. Ryder
J. H. Jenkins
Milton Brockman
Wiley Sneed
Sonoma, June 14th, 1853
Report unanimously accepted
Jos. N. Nevill, forema[n], Grand Ju[ry]

People v. Robert Graham
Obstructing the navigation of the Sonoma river (case file # 6)

The indictment filed on 7 Jun 1853 accused the defendant of obstructing the navigation of the Sonoma river with a large brig, ship, or vessel on 1 Mar 1853. William F. Bond, William Green, Jason Smith, M. S. Prime, Willis Goodman, Wylie (var. Wiley) Sneed, and Samuel Orr appeared as witnesses before the Grand Jury.

People v. Peter Bean
Fencing up and obstructing a public road or highway

In a complaint subscribed and sworn to before the Hon. Samuel N. Terrill, a Justice of the Peace for Petaluma Township, on 23 May 1853, J. S. Field accused the defendant of obstructing the public road or highway leading from Bodega to Petaluma by building a fence across it on or about 19 May 1853. The Grand Jury dismissed the charge.

People v. Basil Barratt
Grand larceny (case file # 7T)

The indictment filed on 13 Jun 1853 accused the defendant of stealing a horse (value $250), property of Frederick Taylor, in or near the Petaluma Valley on 8 Jun 1853. J. McGimsey, George W. Ryder, and Frederick Taylor appeared as witnesses before the Grand Jury.

People v. Benjamin L. Moore
Murder (case file # 2)

The indictment filed on 14 Jun 1853 accused the defendant of killing Captain Samuel A. Boak at his house near the Embarcadero San Louis in Sonoma Township by shooting him with a pistol in the lower part of the breast giving him one mortal wound on 10 Jun 1853. Leonard Dodge, Willis Goodman, Daniel D. Davidson, R. S. Vail, R. G. Turner, Bruno Conrad, C. W. Victor, and T. E. L. Andrews appeared as witnesses before the Grand Jury.

August term 1853

Hon. Charles P. Wilkins, County Judge
John E. McNair, District Attorney
John Hendley, Clerk
John A. Brewster, Deputy Clerk
J. B. Boggs, Deputy Clerk
James Clyman, Grand Jury foreman

People v. William Bihler
Assault and battery (case file #s 7EE and 7FF)

The indictment filed on 10 Aug 1853 accused the defendant of assaulting Emuel [Emil?] Lubeck by beating, striking, and ill-treating him at the Embarcadero of Sonoma in Sonoma Township on 10 Aug 1853. Emuel [Emil?] Lubeck and Willis Goodman appeared as witnesses before the Grand Jury.

People v. John Leary (alias Jack Leary)
Petit larceny (case file # 7L)

The indictment filed on 12 Aug 1853 accused the defendant of stealing $18 of gold and silver coins, property of Seraphine Bruggeman, at her store in Annally Township on 15 May 1853. Seraphine Bruggeman appeared as a witness before the Grand Jury.

February term 1854

Hon. Frank W. Shattuck, County Judge
A. Clark (var. Clarke), District Attorney
N. McC. Menefee, Clerk
J. A. Reynolds, Deputy Clerk
Robert Beck, Grand Jury foreman

People v. John Williams
Grand larceny (case file # 8)

The indictment filed on 9 Feb 1854 accused the defendant of stealing the sum of $120 or thereabouts in gold or silver coin from James Richardson in the City of Sonoma on or about 10 Dec 1853. James Richardson, John Henderson, Joseph N. Nevill, P. J. Vasques, William Bond, Barbara Biles, J. C. Blakely, and James Morrow appeared as witnesses before the Grand Jury. The *Sacramento Daily Union* reported on 20 March 1854 that the defendant had escaped from the Sonoma County Jail on 15 March 1854 and quoted the *Sonoma Bulletin* as saying of the escape: "Assuredly no one will attach blame to the jailor, for every man in the county is aware of the wretched, rickety condition of the so-called prison. The only surprise is that he had not bid us adieu two months ago. Our prison should be hereafter be styled 'Bastille de Sonoma'."[170]

---

[170] "Escaped," *Sacramento (California) Daily Union*, 20 March 1854, p. 3, col. 1.

People v. John Williams
Petit larceny (case file # 8)

The indictment filed on 9 Feb 1854 accused the defendant of stealing the sum of $30, $35, or $40 in gold or silver coin from Mr. Snody in the City of Sonoma on or about 4 Jan 1854. Mr. Snody appeared as a witness before the Grand Jury.

People v. William Norman
Obtaining money or a draft or an order for money by false pretenses (case file # 11E)

The indictment filed on 9 Feb 1854 accused the defendant of obtaining money or a draft or an order for money by false pretenses by pretending and representing to Thomas B. Wade that he (Norman) was the owner of a large amount of property in the counties of Napa and Sonoma and obtaining from Wade an order or draft for $40 or thereabouts drawn by Wade on George W. Miller who honored and paid the money to Norman on or about 31 Jan 1854. Thomas Wade, Robert Fowler, George W. Miller, and Tyler Curtis appeared as witnesses before the Grand Jury.

April term 1854

Hon. Frank W. Shattuck, County Judge
N. McC. Menefee, Clerk
B. B. Munday, Grand Jury foreman

Grand Jurors' Report April term 1854[171]

We the undersigned Grand Jurors for the County of Sonoma beg leave to report that the business before the Jury has been very limited owing to the small amount of crime which has been committed within the limits of our County which circumstance we propose to congratulate your Honor and the people generally of the County upon. It argues well for the morals of our people and the growing observance of the laws of the land. We were immediately after being impaneled informed by the District Attorney that he had but little business to present for our consideration, perhaps but one or two cases, one of which a man by the name of Davis charged with grand larceny sent up from the Court below. We failed to find a bill.

The othe[r], a man by the name of Williams, which we also failed to find a bill in believing that the circumstances and the evidence did not warrant us in doing so. The latter having been confined in gaol for the action of this Grand Jury owing to insufficiency of the gaol, broke out and has cleared himself which circumstance we think is fortunate for the County. Having no other business before us we have failed to find any bills at all.

One other cause, perhaps, of the limited amount of business before the Grand Jury is that almost all the members are within or near the limits of this City, therefore not having an opportunity to know or hear what was or what might be going on in other parts of the County. We have been compelled to confine our investigations principally to this end of the County.

---

[171] Sonoma County, California, Court of Sessions, Grand Jurors' Report, April term 1854, filed 4 April 1854; County Records, Sonoma County, Court Records, Miscellaneous Unprocessed Records, folder "Grand Jury Reports, 1852–1875"; California State Archives, Sacramento.

Having, as ordered by your Honor, examined the Court House and Gaol of the County, [we] would beg leave to say that we deem them unworthy [of] the name they bear, altogether unfit for the purposes intended, and [we] would recommend that they be sold to the best bidder, and the money, as far as it will go, [be] appropriated to the building of a more suitable one.

E. T. Peobode [Peabody?] and Hobart Smith failed to atten[d] this morning according to appointment. Having no other business before the Jury we ask to be discharged.

B. B. Munday, Foreman.

June term 1854

Hon. Frank W. Shattuck, County Judge
A. Clarke, District Attorney
N. McC. Menefee, Clerk
Joel Miller, Deputy Clerk
S. B. Bright, Grand Jury foreman

People v. Alejandro (an Indian)
Murder (case file # 11D)

The indictment filed on 8 Jun 1854 accused the defendant of murdering Hammond Warfield on or about 20 May 1854. John G. Ray, Edward Bodger, and William Ray appeared as witnesses before the Grand Jury. The case was transferred to the Sonoma County District Court on 17 Apr 1855. For a related case, see Sonoma County District Court case # 88 (OS) and Court of Sessions case file # 20. The *Daily Alta California* reported that Capt. Hammond Warfield, born in Baltimore and about 35 years of age, was a Deputy Sheriff of Marin County who had been "in pursuit of an Indian who had committed a murder in Marin County and some escaped convicts, who were supposed to have fled beyond the Russian River."[172]

People v. William M. Ormsby
Grand larceny (case file # 23I)

The indictment filed on 8 Jun 1854 accused the defendant of stealing three of widow Fitch's horses (value $250) on 15 Apr 1854. Samuel F. Cowan appeared as a witness before the Grand Jury.

People v. William M. Ormsby
Grand larceny (case file # 23I)

The indictment filed on 8 Jun 1854 accused the defendant of stealing eight of widow West's horses (value $250) on 15 Apr 1854. Samuel F. Cowan appeared as a witness before the Grand Jury.

---

[172] "Murder of the Deputy Sheriff of Marin," *Daily Alta California* (San Francisco, California), 8 June 1854, p. 2, col. 3.

People v. Pitt Van
Performing an unlawful marriage

The indictment filed on 8 Jun 1854 accused the defendant of unlawfully joining in marriage Mary Ann Sansburry, a female under the age of eighteen years, to Henry Beason, on 15 Feb 1854 without the consent of her parents with whom she was residing.[173] W. H. Sansburry appeared as a witness before the Grand Jury.

August term 1854

Hon. Frank W. Shattuck, County Judge
John E. McNair, District Attorney
N. McC. Menefee, Clerk
Thomas H. Pyatt, Deputy Clerk
Israel Brockman, Sheriff
W. B. Hagans, Grand Jury foreman

Grand Jury Report[174]

To the Honorable Court of Sessions, may it please the Court,

The Grand Jury having concluded their labors for the present term of this Court beg leave to submit the following report:

They have visited the County Jail and found it kept clean, but a very insecure place for the safekeeping of prisoners and recommend that a safer place be provided for the confinement of prisoners charged with the commissions of crimes within the county and that the Board of Supervisors take early steps in this behalf.

The insecurity of the Jail Room of Sonoma County has been a cause of complaint on the pa[rt] of the citizens for a long time and many previo[us] Grand Juries have reported the same insecure. The Grand Jury believe that the escape of prisoners heretofore has resulted chiefly from this fact. They find that the safekeeping of prisoners is wholly confided to the care of guards employed by the Sheriff of Sonoma County. The recent escape of the prisoners from the Jail was owing partly to the negligence and mismanagement of the guard employed. They therefore recommend that the guard on duty at that time and now in the employ of the Sheriff be discharged without compensation and that other and more trust[ed] persons be employed to perform that duty.

The Grand Jury in accordance with a charge of his honor the judge have investigated the conduct of the public officers of this county, and much complaint has been made to them of the inability of the County Clerk in the discharge of his official duty, and upon investigation of the affairs of the Clerk's Office, the Grand Jury are of [the] opinion that the best interests of the people of this County demand that the County Clerk employ a competent assistant to discharge

---

[173] Sonoma County, California, Justice's Court case files, case file # 237, People v. Pitt Van, indictment, 8 June 1854; County Records, Sonoma County, Court Records, Justice's Court case files; California State Archives, Sacramento.
[174] Sonoma County, California, Court of Sessions, Report of the Grand Jury, filed 11 August 1854; County Records, Sonoma County, Court Records, Miscellaneous Unprocessed Records, folder "Grand Jury Reports, 1852–1875"; California State Archives, Sacramento.

the duties of the office or resign his position, the Grand Jury believing him incompetent to discharge the duties properly.

There is much cause of complaint on a/c [account?] of the drunkenness of Indians, but the Grand Jury have been unable to discover that any person has been guilty of either giving or selling liquor to Indians.

The Grand Jury return four bills against parties for misdemeanor and have ignored one bill against Jose Antonio and Surdo, two Indians charged with the crime of murder, the evidence against them being of such a contradictory character as to be insufficient in their opinion to warrant a conviction before a trial jury.

W. B. Hagans, Foreman.

Adopted unanimously.

People v. Peter Campbell
Offering a bribe to an Officer (case file # 9)
The indictment filed on 9 Aug 1854 accused the defendant of offering a bribe of $3.50 to John Sharkey, a Constable of Sonoma Township, so that he not execute a writ of attachment for $25 plus the costs of the suit against Samuel Kelsey to satisfy the demand of John Luman at the City of Sonoma on 28 Jun 1854. John Sharkey and James B. Boggs appeared as witnesses before the Grand Jury. The case was transferred to the Sonoma County District Court because the defendant was a Justice of the Peace.

People v. Elisha Ely
Intentionally defacing, obliterating, tearing down, and destroying an advertisement for the sale of certain property to pay taxes (case file # 11C)
The indictment filed on 9 Aug 1854 accused the defendant of intentionally defacing, obliterating, tearing down, and destroying an advertisement set up by William Ellis, a Deputy Sheriff of Sonoma County, on 13 or 14 Jul 1854 in Mendocino County for the sale of certain property to pay taxes the defendant owed on or about 22, 23, or 24 Jul 1854. William Ellis appeared as a witness before the Grand Jury.

People v. T. M. Leavenworth, William Leavenworth, and M. M. Cummings
Petit larceny (case file # 11A)
The indictment filed on 11 Aug 1854 accused the defendants of stealing three hogs (value $30), property of Nancy Gwinnett, on 5 Jul 1854. Nancy Gwinnett, William Robinson, Israel Cooke, William Casey, and Fred Clarke appeared as witnesses before the Grand Jury.

People v. T. M. Leavenworth, William Leavenworth, and M. M. Cummings
Malicious mischief (case file # 11A)
The indictment filed on 11 Aug 1854 accused the defendants of wantonly, maliciously, and mischievously killing the three hogs (value $30) the defendants had stolen from Nancy Gwinnett on 5 Jul 1854. Nancy Gwinnett, William Robinson, Israel Cooke, William Casey, and Fred Clarke appeared as witnesses before the Grand Jury.

People v. Jose Antonio and Surdo (Indians)
Murder

The Grand Jury ignored the bill against the defendants August term 1854. The defendants, however, were indicted April term 1855. See case file # 20. The *Sacramento Daily Union* quoting the *Sonoma Bulletin* reported that the two Indian defendants had escaped from the Sonoma County Jail on 29 July 1854:

> About midnight, the jailor being sound asleep, they rose leisurely and quietly, took the key of the prison, which was lying upon a bench in the room, unlocked the door and stepped out. One of them, Antonio, in his hurry, jumped off the verandah, spraining his ankle and otherwise bruising himself severely. He proceeded some three or four miles up the valley, when becoming entirely crippled and unable to go on, he delivered himself up – still handcuffed. The other prisoner is still at large. Well, if they had not escaped thus, they would have got off in some other way. All our prisoners break jail. Indeed, we see no reason why they should stay in the prison unless they are so disposed. Our county bought the structure which we use as a jail on account of its cheapness; it only cost $6,000, and, notwithstanding the great depreciation in value of real estate, it would, if brought to the hammer tomorrow, bring $600. With such facilities as these for securing prisoners, how wonderful that we should have midnight lynch trials and torch-light executions in Sonoma?[175]

October term 1854

Hon. Frank W. Shattuck, County Judge
John E. McNair, District Attorney
N. McC. Menefee, Clerk
Joseph Hooker, Grand Jury foreman

Report of the Grand Jury[176]

To the Honorable Court of Sessions of the County of Sonoma: The Grand Jury of the County of Sonoma beg leave to report that they have given the subject to which the Court called their attention a careful consideration. They are satisfied that the building now used for [the] County Jail is inconvenient, insecure, and totally unfit for the use to which it is applied. They have also considered the present state of the County Treasury, and in view of all of these matters, the Grand Jury earnestly recommends that immediate provision be made for the erection of a building for a County Jail to be built on a scale sufficiently large to meet with all of the wants of the County.

The Grand Jury also report [illegible] true bills which herewith accompanies their report. They have no further business before them.

Jos. Hooker, Foreman, Santa Rosa, October 3, 1854

---

[175] "Jail Delivery," *Sacramento (California) Daily Union*, 1 August 1854, p. 3, col. 1.
[176] Sonoma County, California, Court of Sessions, Report of the Grand Jury, 3 October 1854; County Records, Sonoma County, Court Records, Miscellaneous Unprocessed Records, folder "Grand Jury Reports, 1852–1875"; California State Archives, Sacramento.

People v. [?] Hunter
Disquieting and disturbing a congregation by talking, cursing, and swearing with a loud voice (case file # 11B)

The indictment filed on 3 Oct 1854 accused the defendant of disquieting and disturbing a congregation of Methodists, Presbyterians, Baptists, Christians, and others by talking, cursing, and swearing with a loud voice during divine service at or near the store of Miller and Walker in Anally Township on 1 Oct 1854. John Walker, John Dougherty, and W. C. Irwin appeared as witnesses before the Grand Jury.

April term 1855

Hon. John E. McNair, County Judge
William Ross, District Attorney
Charles M. Hudspeth, Grand Jury foreman
Jacob Smith, Grand Jury foreman

People v. Alexander Shaw
Murder (case file # 23C)

The indictment filed on 4 Apr 1855 accused the defendant of murdering Angelo Capolo at the port of Bodega by shooting him in the head with a shot gun on 18 Mar 1855. William Elson, Peter O'Neal, Donald McDonald, William Danforth, and James Billett appeared as witnesses before the Grand Jury. The case was transferred to the Sonoma County District Court on 17 May 1855. See Sonoma County District Court case # 87 (OS).

People v. Alexander Shaw and John Campbell
Murder (case file # 23C)

The indictment filed on 4 Apr 1855 accused the defendant Alexander Shaw of murdering Angelo Capolo at the port of Bodega by shooting him in the head with a shot gun by the counsel, order, and advice of the defendant John Campbell on 18 Mar 1855. William Elson, Peter O'Neal, Donald McDonald, William Danforth, and James Billett appeared as witnesses before the Grand Jury. The case was transferred to the Sonoma County District Court on 17 May 1855. See Sonoma County District Court case # 87 (OS).

People v. John Campbell
Accessory to murder (case file # 23D)

The indictment filed on 4 Apr 1855 accused the defendant of being an accessory in the murder of Angelo Capolo at the port of Bodega on 18 Mar 1855. William Elson, Peter O'Neal, Donald McDonald, William Danforth, and James Billett appeared as witnesses before the Grand Jury. The case was transferred to the Sonoma County District Court on 17 May 1855. See Sonoma County District Court case # 87 (OS).

People v. Jose Antonio and Surdo (Indians)
Murder (case file # 20)

The indictment filed on 26 Apr 1855 accused the defendants of murdering [Hammond] Warfield by shooting him with a shot gun, shooting him with a bow and arrow, and beating him with their hands and a club in Mendocino County on 8 May 1854. Alexander [Alejandro] (an Indian) appeared as a witness before the Grand Jury. The case was transferred to the Sonoma County District Court. The District Court jury found the defendants not guilty on 24 May 1855. See Sonoma County District Court case # 88 (OS). For a related case, see Court of Sessions case file # 11D. The *Daily Alta California* reported on 8 Jun 1854 that Capt. Hammond Warfield, born in Baltimore and about 35 years of age, was a Deputy Sheriff of Marin County who had been "in pursuit of an Indian who had committed a murder in Marin County and some escaped convicts, who were supposed to have fled beyond the Russian River."[177]

People v. C. P. Vores (var. Vorse, Vorce)
Grand larceny (case file # 21)

The indictment filed on 26 Apr 1855 accused the defendant of stealing six American steers or work oxen (value $400), the property of Harrison J. Williams, on 3 Apr 1855. H. J. Williams and Milroy Powell appeared as witnesses before the Grand Jury. The defendant was convicted of the crime of grand larceny on 5 May 1855 and sentenced to 23 months' imprisonment in the State Penitentiary.[178] Vores was received by San Quentin on 9 May 1855.[179] Governor John Bigler pardoned him on 13 Nov 1855, and Vores was discharged three days later.[180]

June term 1855

Hon. John E. McNair, County Judge
Charles P. Wilkins, District Attorney
Robert Beck, Grand Jury foreman

People v. James Hendry, Charles Jefferson, R. C. Smith, and Milroy Powell
False imprisonment (case file # 13)

The indictment filed on 4 Jun 1855 accused the defendants of falsely imprisoning William Hoagland against his will and without any sufficient legal authority to do so at Vallejo Township on 7 May 1855. William Hoagland and Elijah Smith appeared as witnesses before the Grand Jury.

---

[177] "Murder of the Deputy Sheriff of Marin," *Daily Alta California* (San Francisco, California), 8 June 1854, p. 2, col. 3.

[178] Notice to John E. McNair, Judge, and William Ross, District Attorney of Sonoma County, by I. G. Wickersham, *The Petaluma (California) Weekly Journal and Sonoma County Advertiser*, 29 September 1855, p. 3, col. 4.

[179] California, State Prison Register (1851–1867), Executive Department, entry no. 617, C. P. Vores, p. 42, received 9 May 1855; California State Archives, Sacramento.

[180] *Journal of the Seventh Session of the Assembly of the State of California, Begun on [7 January 1856], and Ended on [21 April 1856] at the City of Sacramento* (Sacramento: James Allen, State Printer, 1856), p. 60 and p. 64. These dates are given in the appendix to the annual message of the Governor to the Senate and Assembly dated January 1856. C. P. Vores's name is variously given as C. P. Vries and C. P. Vose.

People v. James Hendry, Charles Jefferson, R. C. Smith, and Milroy Powell
False imprisonment (case file # 13)

The indictment filed on 4 Jun 1855 accused the defendants of falsely imprisoning Elijah Smith against his will and without any sufficient legal authority to do so at Vallejo Township on 7 May 1855. William Hoagland and Elijah Smith appeared as witnesses before the Grand Jury.

People v. James Hendry, Charles Jefferson, R. C. Smith, and Milroy Powell
False imprisonment (case file # 13)

The indictment filed on 4 Jun 1855 accused the defendants of falsely imprisoning William Hoagland and Elijah Smith against their wills and without any sufficient legal authority to do so at Vallejo Township on 7 May 1855. William Hoagland and Elijah Smith appeared as witnesses before the Grand Jury.

People v. Francisco Esparsa (alias Chihuahua)
Grand larceny (case file # 18)

The indictment filed on 4 Jun 1855 accused the defendant of stealing Dr. John Hendley's horse (value $150) in the City of Sonoma on 14 Nov 1854. Dr. John Hendley, John W. Bones, James C. Bones, and John Campbell appeared as witnesses before the Grand Jury. The defendant was found guilty and sentenced to two years in the State Prison.[181] He was received at San Quentin on 15 Jun 1855 and discharged on 15 Jun 1857 after serving his full term.

People v. Charles M. Hudspeth
Assault and battery (case file # 23F)

The indictment filed on 4 Jun 1855 accused the defendant of assaulting Henry M. Taylor at Analy Township on 1 Jun 1855. Henry M. Taylor and Josiah Moran appeared as witnesses before the Grand Jury.

On 24 November 1855, notice was given to the Justices of the Peace of Sonoma County to assemble in convention at the Court House on 3 December 1855 for the purpose of electing two Associate Justices of the Court of Sessions.[182]

December term 1855

Hon. William Churchman, County Judge
Hon. Ive D. Long, Associate Justice[183]
I. G. Wickersham, District Attorney
Charles Patton, Grand Jury foreman

---

[181] California, State Prison Register (1851–1867), Executive Department, entry no. 639, Francisco Esparsa, p. 44, received 15 June 1855; California State Archives, Sacramento.
[182] "To Justices of the Peace," The Petaluma (California) Weekly Journal and Sonoma County Advertiser, 24 November 1855, p. 3, col. 2.
[183] Sonoma County, California, oath of office for Ive D. Long as an Associate Justice of the Court of Sessions, 3 December 1855; Sonoma County Archives, Santa Rosa.

Grand Jurors: J. F. Read, C. I. Robinson, A. B. Nally, James W. Neal, George Ragle, T. B. Patton, M. W. Nelson, A. Peoples, Samuel Orr, M. Quesenbery, Aug. Peterson, Calvin Rohrer, Jordan Peter, W. R. O'Howell, Henry Nelson, J. Seward, John R. Peck, Charles Patton, and Stephen Payran. Charles Patton was Grand Jury foreman.

Grand Jury Report[184]

The Grand Jurors in and for the County of Sonoma, in the State of California, met at Santa Rosa on the 3rd day of Dec., A. D. 1855, and transacted the following business:

The following True bills were found, to wit – two bills for Grand Larceny; one for Assault and Battery on officer; one for Rescuing Prisoner; one for Misdemeanor, and two for Gambling Houses.

The Grand Jurors very carefully and with much patience, examined the documentary testimony in the late explosion of the boiler of the steamer *Georgina*, at the town of Petaluma, by which awful calamity two of our fellow beings met their death, and others were injured, by which testimony it is apparent that said accident happened by the carelessness of Captain Thompson, (who had charge of the boat,) as well as of the owners, and duly present the said parties as being amenable to the laws, and would strongly recommend that some measures be adopted by which security may be attained in traveling on steamers navigating our creeks and bays, and would recommend to our fellow citizens not to patronize or travel on any steam vessel without first knowing that it sails under a proper certificate, and under care of proper officers.[185]

The Grand Jurors would also call the attention of the County Supervisors to the state of the roads and bridges in our county, it appearing on information that no money has really been expended according to the intent and meaning of the statute, although ample means are provided under the law, if the duties therein prescribed were fully carried out. We conceive it to be the duty of our Supervisors, to see that the Overseers of districts discharge their duty, and make a report. We would also call their attention to the obstructions on the old road granted by M. G. Vallejo, running east and west through the Petaluma Ranch, said road being the connecting link between the Bay, Sonoma and up country, the present obstructions on said road inconvenience public travel and retard intercourse.

We much deprecate the disposition to resist public officers in the discharge of their duties, and would in all cases present such for punishment.

Vice and Immorality have also met with attention on our part, and so far as it has laid in our part, we have adopted measures for its suppression, trusting the few examples made by us, may cure the evil. – We are happy to say that our county is in general quite free.

The Grand Jurors would call the attention of the District Attorney to the matter of licenses, it appearing clearly that much business is done by persons who may not have a knowledge of the

---

[184] "Report of the Grand Jury," *The Petaluma (California) Weekly Journal and Sonoma County Advertiser*, 8 December 1855, p. 2, cols. 2–3.

[185] The boiler of the steamer *Georgina* exploded while the boat was taking on passengers and freight at its landing in Petaluma on the morning of 23 November 1855 killing George Funk, proprietor of the Oak Grove House, and John Flood, a fireman on board the *Georgina*. See, "Steamboat Disaster," *The Petaluma (California) Weekly Journal and Sonoma County Advertiser*, 24 November 1855, p. 2, col. 1. "Died," *The Petaluma (California) Weekly Journal and Sonoma County Advertiser*, 1 December 1855, p. 3, col. 3.

necessity of first having obtained such license. We recommend that he appoint the Constables of each Township to call on all persons doing business in his respective Township, ask for an exhibit of license, and render to the District Attorney the name, date of license, and time paid for, and that the same be classed according to Townships and alphabetically arranged, by which means much labor will be saved to future Grand Jurors in investigating the affairs of Revenue arising therefrom.

We would also call the attention of the Court to the fact that there is a large amount of taxes for the year ending March 1855 remaining unpaid, and earnestly hope that the present officers will use strenuous efforts to collect the same, and that the taxes for 1855 and 1856, may be collected by the time of expiration for the payment of the same.

J. F. Read, C. I. Robinson, A. B. Nally, Jas. W. Neal, Geo. Ragle, T. B. Patton, M. W. Nelson, A. Peoples, Samuel Orr, M. Quesenbery, Aug. Peterson, Calvin Rohrer, Jordan Peter, W. R. O'Howell, Henry Nelson, J. Seward, John R. Peck, Chas. Patton, Foreman. Stephen Payran, Secretary.

People v. Robert Patton
Grand larceny (case file # 27)

The indictment filed on 4 Dec 1855 accused the defendant of stealing William Greening's horse (value $100) on 29 Sep 1855. Reuben Lunceford, William Greening, Horace Nutting, and Hiram Nutting appeared as witnesses before the Grand Jury. The defendant was convicted of the crime of grand larceny on 8 February 1856 and sentenced to one year's imprisonment in the State Prison. Charles P. Wilkins gave notice on 14 June 1856 that an application for pardon would be made to J. N. Johnson, Governor of California.[186] This application, if made, was apparently unsuccessful as Patton was discharged from the State Prison on 10 Feb 1857 after serving his full sentence.[187]

People v. Alfred Davenport (var. Deavenport)
Grand larceny (case file # 15)

The indictment filed on 4 Dec 1855 accused the defendant of stealing one horse and one mare (total value $150), the property of A. J. Bayer, on 17 Sep 1855. John Moffatt, Frank Mayfield, and A. J. Bayer appeared as witnesses before the Grand Jury. The defendant pleaded guilty to the charge of grand larceny for stealing two horses from Vallejo Township. The Court was to sentence him on 7 December 1855, but he escaped that morning from the custody of the officers in the town of Santa Rosa, and Sheriff A. C. Bledsoe offered a $50 reward if he were taken within the county and $100 if taken out of the county and delivered into his possession.[188]

---

[186] "Notice of Application for Pardon," *The Petaluma (California) Weekly Journal and Sonoma County Advertiser*, 28 June 1856, p. 4, col. 1.

[187] California, State Prison Register (1851–1867), Executive Department, entry no. 827, Robert Patten, p. 57, discharged 10 February 1857; California State Archives, Sacramento.

[188] "Court of Sessions," *The Petaluma (California) Weekly Journal and Sonoma County Advertiser*, 8 December 1855, p. 2, col. 1. "$100 Reward!," *The Petaluma (California) Weekly Journal and Sonoma County Advertiser* (Petaluma, California), 8 December 1855, p. 3, col. 3.

People v. B. B. Bonham
Performing an unlawful marriage (case file # 12)

The indictment filed on 5 Dec 1855 accused the defendant of marrying Nancy Ann Bray, a minor under the age of eighteen years, to Fulmer More [Moore] without the consent of her parents with whom she resided on 28 Oct 1855. Harrel Bray and Robert More appeared as witnesses before the Grand Jury. Reverend Bonham pleaded guilty and was fined $375 during the February term 1856 of the Court of Sessions. After receiving a petition signed by numerous Sonoma County residents, Governor J. Neely Johnson ordered the remission of the fine on 20 Mar 1856 "on [the] condition that the defendant pay all the costs of the prosecution legally taxed and charged in said case."[189]

People v. Scotch Smith
Rescue of a prisoner from the custody of an officer (case file # 23A)

The indictment filed on 5 Dec 1855 accused the defendant of rescuing the prisoner Samuel Smith from the custody of Constable J. S. Field on 28 Oct 1855. J. S. Field and Woodson Beasly appeared as witnesses before the Grand jury.

People v. Samuel Smith
Assaulting a peace officer (case file # 23B)

The indictment filed on 5 Dec 1855 accused the defendant of assaulting Constable J. S. Field on 28 Oct 1855. J. S. Field and Woodson Beasly appeared as witnesses before the Grand Jury.

People v. Joseph H. P. Morris
Gaming house (case file # 23E)

The indictment filed on 5 Dec 1855 accused the defendant of being the occupant of a house where money had been lost by gaming on 1 Oct 1855. Andrew Fife and John Dougherty appeared as witnesses before the Grand Jury.

People v. King Emerson and Charles Smith
Gaming house (case file #23H)

The indictment filed on 5 Dec 1855 accused the defendants of keeping a gaming house in Santa Rosa on 1 Nov 1855. I. C. Morehouse, Adam Shane, William R. Smith, and James E. Neal appeared as witnesses before the Grand Jury.

---

[189] California, Pardon Applications, pardon application file # 856, B. B. Bonham, J. Neely Johnson, Governor of California, to General D. H. Douglass, Secretary of State of California, Governor's order to remit fine of B. B. Bonham for marrying a female under age, 20 March 1856; Governor's Office records, Applications for Pardon, Historical Case Files (1850–ca. 1935); California State Archives, Sacramento.

February term 1856

Hon. William Churchman, County Judge
I. G. Wickersham, District Attorney
N. McC. Menefee, Clerk
George Campbell, Grand Jury foreman

People v. Samuel Finley
Furnishing intoxicating liquors to Indians (case file # 24)
    The indictment filed on 6 Feb 1856 accused the defendant of furnishing intoxicating liquors to Indians on 1 Jan 1856. Jared Hoag and Henry Emerson appeared as witnesses before the Grand Jury.

People v. Samuel Finley
Keeping a gaming house (case file # 32B)
    The indictment filed on 6 Feb 1856 accused the defendant of opening a game of chance (the game of 21) on 15 Jan 1856. Henry Emerson and William Stephenson appeared as witnesses before the Grand Jury.

People v. Samuel Finley
Assault and battery (case file # 32C)
    The indictment filed on 6 Feb 1856 accused the defendant of assaulting George Campbell on 25 Jan 1856. Joshua Adams, Jr., William Bryant, Sr., and Joshua Adams, Sr. appeared as witnesses before the Grand Jury.

People v. Moses C. Briggs
Assault with a deadly weapon (case file #28)
    The indictment filed on 6 Feb 1856 accused the defendant of assaulting William D. Turner with a gun with the intent to commit bodily injury on 1 Dec 1855. George Brumfield, J. D. Thompson, and William R. Dodge appeared as witnesses before the Grand Jury.

July term 1856

Hon. William Churchman, County Judge
I. G. Wickersham, District Attorney
N. McC. Menefee, Clerk
John Brown, Deputy Clerk
William Elder, Grand Jury foreman

Report of the Grand Jury[190]

The Grand Jury of the county of Sonoma, for the July term of the Court of Sessions, respectfully beg leave to report: That in discharging the duties imposed upon them, state with great satisfaction that the morals of this county are, in the opinion of the Jury, much improved, if we may judge of the past by the history and report of other Grand Juries which have preceded us. We have found five bills of indictment.

We would respectfully call the attention of the Board of Supervisors to the fact, that the Jail of this county is insecure and so badly ventilated as to make it unfit, in its present condition, for the health and safe-keeping of prisoners, and cheerfully add, that no prisoners are at present confined therein.

The Jury would further report, that they have examined the various books presented to them, and have found the accounts correct so far as examined; but we feel bound to say, that they are not kept in that clear and business-like manner that would enable us at a glance, to ascertain the fiscal condition of the county; and we would recommend to the officers greater care, especially in the keeping of fee books.

We would further report, that we find many of the roads and bridges of the county in a very bad condition, and we would especially direct the attention of the Supervisors to this subject, and see that the Overseers do their duty.

All of which is respectfully submitted.

WM. ELDER, Foreman.

Santa Rosa, July 9, 1856.

People v. Baronet Barns, Reason Barns, and Jackson Estis
Assault with intent to commit murder (case file # 32)

The indictment filed on 8 Jul 1856 accused the defendants of assaulting O. H. P. Coleman by shooting at him at Mendocino County with the intent to murder him on 27 May 1856. James Lampkins, A. B. Ingram, William Prather, and O. H. P. Coleman appeared as witnesses before the Grand Jury. For related cases, see case file # 26 and Sonoma County District Court cases # 715 (OS) and # 813 (OS). The assault of Coleman was described in a long letter by an "Observer" to the *Petaluma Weekly Journal and Sonoma County Advertiser* dated Anderson Valley, Mendocino County, 27 May 1856, the date of the assault:

> On the morning of the 27th inst. [27 May 1856], Mr. O. H. P. Coleman, of this valley [Anderson Valley], in company with Messrs. Lamkin, Clark, and Rusk, started from this place with the intention of going out to Russian River, about thirty miles distant, and after proceeding about four miles on the way, Messrs. Lamkin and Rusk turned off the main road to go by a soda spring, Messrs. Coleman and Clark pursuing their course on the road. About the time that Lampkin and Rusk reached the spring, they heard the report of a rifle in the direction of the road, about four hundred yards distant, but supposed Coleman had shot at something with his pistol; it however proved a mistake. — Mr. Coleman had been shot by a man secreted in the willows, about ten yards from the road, on the bank of a

---

[190] "Report of the Grand Jury," *The Petaluma (California) Weekly Journal and Sonoma County Advertiser*, 12 July 1856, p. 2, col. 3.

little creek. But the villain failed to make a deadly shot. The ball struck the right arm near the elbow joint, in such a manner as to cause it to glance, entering the side and crossing the back, but so near the surface as not to injure the back bone, and lodging near the left side.[191]

After relating the details of the search for those responsible for the assault, the letter writer went on to say:

> Nearly all that are acquainted with the circumstances of the case, believe the villains who committed the deed are camped somewhere in the mountains or gulches, in the vicinity of the road leading from Russian River to Anderson Valley. Two of them were identified by the men who encountered them at the large rock, as being the Barnes' (two brothers), who are well-known to the three men and to the Indians who pursued and met them while secreted at the rock watching the road. The third individual was not satisfactorily identified, but strong suspicion rests upon an old ruffian by the name of Estis – generally known as Old Dad – who formerly resided in Oat Valley on R. River, but who of late has been rather associated with the Barnes' of this place.
>
> It is universally believed by all best acquainted with the affair, that the attempt to murder Mr. Coleman was not for the purpose of robbery, but that it was done by way of seeking revenge. Circumstances seem to warrant this supposition, as from the best information obtained, considerable enmity had existed between the Barnes' and Coleman, during more than a year past, in consequence of the Barnes' and others abusing some Indian women, which exasperated Coleman, upon which he denounced the conduct of such men, and thus they became much offended at Coleman. Thus matters continued until lately, when one of the Barnes' took a Mrs. Norton to his house, while her husband was in the mines, and was known to be living with her in a state of adultery, upon which, when her husband returned, a party gathered and inflicted upon Barnes a coating of tar and feathers. Barnes still lived with the woman, and blamed Coleman with having headed the party that tarred and feathered him. It is believed that this Mrs. Norton and others in the valley are and have been communicating with these men, while secreted, or lying in wait to kill Coleman. Circumstances seem to warrant this general supposition.

People v. Baronet Barns, Reason Barns, and Jackson Estis
Assault with intent to commit murder (case file # 32)

The indictment filed on 8 Jul 1856 accused the defendants of assaulting James Lampkins, A. B. Ingram, and William Prather by shooting at them with guns at Mendocino County with the intent to murder them on 27 May 1856. James Lampkins, A. B. Ingram, William Prather, and O. H. P. Coleman appeared as witnesses before the Grand Jury. For related cases, see case file # 26 and Sonoma County District Court case #s 715 (OS) and 813 (OS).

---

[191] Observer, "Attempt to Murder," *The Petaluma (California) Weekly Journal and Sonoma County Advertiser*, 14 June 1856, p. 2, col. 5.

People v. Joseph Finley and William Finley
Assault with a deadly weapon (case file # 24)

The indictment filed on 9 Jul 1856 accused the defendants of assaulting John Dougherty with pistols on 23 Apr 1856. Warham Easly (var. Easley), John Dougherty, Robert Dobson, and William Ealy appeared as witnesses before the Grand Jury.

People v. Joseph Finley and William Finley
False imprisonment (case file # 24)

The indictment filed on 9 Jul 1856 accused the defendants of falsely imprisoning Ramon Sanches at Analy Township on 19 Apr 1856. Robert Dobson, Joaquin Carrillo, Joel Walker, Sr., John Young, and William Ealy appeared as witnesses before the Grand Jury.

People v. Joseph Finley and William Finley
Exhibiting deadly weapons (case file # 24)

The indictment filed on 9 Jul 1856 accused the defendants of exhibiting deadly weapons (pistols) in the presence of Robert Dobson and Joaquin Carrillo on 23 Apr 1856. Robert Dobson and Joaquin Carrillo appeared as witnesses before the Grand Jury.

People v. Henry Eiles
Fraudulent and unlawful conveyance of property with intent to defraud a creditor

In a complaint filed in the Hon. Thomas A. Hylton's Justice's Court of Petaluma Township on 29 Mar 1856, Walter D. Kent accused the defendant of having been a party to a fraudulent contract and conveyance made with the intent to hinder and delay creditors of their just debts and demands against the defendant.[192] After hearing testimony from William Zartman and W. D. Kent, Justice Hylton held the defendant to appear and answer to the charge and admitted him to bail in the sum of $500. The Grand Jury ignored the charge.

October term 1856

Two Grand Juries were called this term. The first completed their business on the morning of 15 Oct 1856. That afternoon another Grand Jury was empaneled "to complete some unfinished business of a former Jury."[193]

Hon. William Churchman, County Judge
I. G. Wickersham, District Attorney
N. McC. Menefee, Clerk
Joel Miller, Deputy Clerk
John Brown, Deputy Clerk
A. C. Bledsoe, Sheriff

---

[192] Sonoma County, California, Justice's Court case files, case file # 31, People v. Henry Eiles, complaint of Walter D. Kent, 29 March 1856; County Records, Sonoma County, Court Records, Justice's Court Records; California State Archives, Sacramento.

[193] "The Grand Jury," *The Sonoma County Journal* (Petaluma, California), 17 October 1856, p. 2, col. 1.

E. L. Green, Under Sheriff
P. L. Maxey, first Grand Jury foreman
J. William Hartman, second Grand Jury foreman

People v. Raphael Selalla
Grand larceny (case file # 32A)

The indictment filed on 7 Oct 1856 accused the defendant of stealing one of William Fitch's horses (value $60) on 1 Aug 1856. Daniel Troy, Joseph Fitch, William Fitch, and Jesus Mendoza appeared as witnesses before the Grand Jury. The trial jury found the defendant guilty on 9 Oct 1856. He was sentenced to six years' imprisonment in the State Prison.[194] He was discharged from San Quentin on 20 Oct 1862 after serving his full term.[195]

People v. Charles Spurgen and Robert Fowler
Assault with a deadly weapon with intent to commit bodily injury (case file # 49)

The indictment filed on 8 Oct 1856 accused the defendants of assaulting William C. Gaines with a deadly weapon in Mendocino County on 23 Aug 1856. W. C. Gaines, E. H. Ewbanks, J. A. Stephenson, and William Crist appeared as witnesses before the Grand Jury. The defendants requested separate trials January term 1857. The trial jury found the defendant Charles Spurgen guilty of a simple assault on 6 Jan 1857. The defendant Robert Fowler was tried by three separate trial juries and apparently not convicted nor acquitted. In an application for dismissal of action filed 7 Apr 1857, District Attorney I. G. Wickersham asked the Court to discontinue further prosecution of this case and the related case of false imprisonment because of conflicting testimony and the unavailability of one of the witnesses for the People.

People v. Charles Spurgen and Robert Fowler
False imprisonment (case file # 49)

The indictment filed on 8 Oct 1856 accused the defendants of assaulting, then falsely imprisoning William C. Gaines in Mendocino County on 23 Aug 1856. William C. Gaines, E. H. Ewbanks, J. A. Stephenson, and William Crist appeared as witnesses before the Grand Jury. In an undated offer to compromise, William C. Gaines acknowledged that he had received satisfaction for the injury he had sustained and that the defendants offered to pay the costs of the suit incurred. In an application for dismissal of action filed 7 Apr 1857, District Attorney I. G. Wickersham asked the Court to discontinue further prosecution of this case and the related case of assault with a deadly weapon because of conflicting testimony and the unavailability of one of the witnesses for the People.

People v. Charles L. Lambert
Assault with intent to commit murder (case file # 50)

The indictment filed on 8 Oct 1856 accused the defendant of shooting at B. C. Soule with a gun with the intent to murder him on 23 Jul 1856. Daniel [sic] Miles, John Miles, and B. C. Soule

---

[194] "The Grand Jury," *The Sonoma County Journal* (Petaluma, California), 17 October 1856, p. 2, col. 1.
[195] California, State Prison Register (1851–1867), Executive Department, entry no. 1024, Rafael Selalla, p. 71, discharged 20 October 1862; California State Archives, Sacramento.

appeared as witnesses before the Grand Jury.[196] The trial jury found the defendant guilty of an assault and recommended him to the mercy of the Court, intending their verdict to be of the mildest form, October term 1856.

People v. Joshua Perkins
Assault with a deadly weapon (case file # 29A)

The indictment filed on 9 Oct 1856 accused the defendant of assaulting Washington Elias on 7 Oct 1856. Washington Elias appeared as a witness before the Grand Jury. The defendant was convicted and "sentenced to six months imprisonment in the County Jail."[197] The assault was described by the *Sonoma County Journal* on 10 Oct 1856 as:

> An affray occurred at Miller's Shaving Saloon last Tuesday evening [7 Oct 1856] between one of his workmen named Washington Ellis and another mulatto (an outsider) known as Joshua Perkins which resulted in Ellis being severely cut and Perkins getting a shocking bad pate and the loss of a large portion of his ebon locks. Perkins was the aggressor, having, in a fit of intoxication, broken into the shop and attacked Ellis with a razor, inflicting three severe wounds, two in the face and one in the side. Ellis, finding himself cut, and an evident desire manifested by Perkins to commit murder, seized a heavy club and commenced belaboring his enemy over the head and shoulders. The blows fell thick and fast, and in a few moments time Perkins's head presented more the appearance of an old pitch-mop than anything human. Drs. Hylton and Bradley administered medical aid, and both are now in a fair way of recovery.[198]

People v. Oliver Bolieu
Branding cattle not of his own property (case file # 30)

The indictment filed on 10 Oct 1856 accused the defendant of branding and marking a two-year-old heifer, the property of C. F. Elliott, with the intent to steal the heifer and prevent its identification on 1 Oct 1854. William More, Emsy [Emsley] Elliott, and J. Galager [Jacob Gallagher] appeared as witnesses before the Grand Jury. The trial jury found the defendant not guilty on 8 April 1857.

People v. David M. Graham
Manslaughter

The indictment filed on 10 Oct 1856 accused the defendant of killing James Cooper on 5 Sep 1856.[199] Thomas Nugent, T. H. Tate, and John B. Prater appeared as witnesses before the Grand Jury. The case was transferred to the Sonoma County District Court on 22 Oct 1856. See Sonoma County District Court case # 720 (OS). An article in the 12 Sep 1856 edition of the *Sonoma County Journal* described the circumstances of the homicide.

---

[196] All other documents in this case file give Daniel Miles's name as Andrew Miles.

[197] "The Grand Jury," *The Sonoma County Journal* (Petaluma, California), 17 October 1856, p. 2, col. 1.

[198] "Affray," *The Sonoma County Journal* (Petaluma, California), 10 October 1856, p. 2, col. 2.

[199] Sonoma County, California, District Court, case file # 720 (OS), People v. David M. Graham, indictment, filed 10 Oct 1856; County records, Sonoma County, Court Records, District Court case files; California State Archives, Sacramento.

Homicide at Sonoma. — One of these melancholy events transpired at Sonoma last Friday [5 Sep 1856], in which Mr. James Cooper of Sonoma was the victim, and a school teacher by the name of D. M. Graham, was the perpetrator. From the reports circulated we gather the following statement:

It appears that during the early part of the week, Mr. Cooper and Graham had had some difficulty relative to whipping in his school. On the following Friday, Mr. Cooper had a job of threshing at a Mr. Tate's, in the neighborhood, where Graham was boarding at the time. At dinner hour, they met, when Mr. Cooper addressed some remark to Graham, who, in turn, desired him to offer no further converse until he had retracted some offensive remark. To this Mr. Cooper replied in an irritable tone; when Graham passed into the open air, Mr. C. following him, but not in a threatening manner. A few words were here passed when suddenly Graham drew from his bosom several rocks which he hurled at Cooper, striking him in the breast. At this Cooper rushed upon Graham, with the evident intention of restraining him, when Graham drew a dirk knife and instantly inflicted three frightful wounds upon the person of Cooper, either of which would have proved fatal. Mr. C. expired almost instantly.

Graham fled, but was pursued and overtaken; he was taken to Sonoma, where the excitement was so intense that fears were entertained of his being lynched. Fortunately for the good name of our County, wiser counsels prevailed, and he is now lying in the County jail awaiting his trial for murder.

Deceased was one of our oldest and best citizens, and leaves a wife and six children and a large circle of friends to mourn his loss. He was a Scotchman by birth, and aged about forty years. His remains were consigned to mother earth on Saturday afternoon, with all the solemnity of the Masonic rites.[200]

The District Court trial jury found the defendant not guilty during the first week of Nov 1856.[201]

People v. Angus McDonald
Assault and battery (case file # 52)
The indictment filed on 11 Oct 1856 accused the defendant of assaulting David M. Graham on 1 Sep 1856. Robert Lennox, B. B. Munday, D. M. Graham, Thomas Nugent, and D. P. Shattuck appeared as witnesses before the Grand Jury.

People v. Joshua Lewis
Petit larceny (case file # 28A)
The indictment filed on 11 Oct 1856 accused the defendant of stealing one of Gustav Warner's steers (value $30) on 1 Feb 1856. G. Warner, E. L. N. King, T. B. Cary, and James Stuart appeared as witnesses before the Grand Jury.

---

[200] "Homicide at Sonoma," *The Sonoma County Journal* (Petaluma, California), 12 September 1856, p. 2, col. 1.
[201] "Acquitted," *The Sonoma County Journal* (Petaluma, California), 7 November 1856, p. 2, col. 2.

People v. Amos B. Ingram, Benjamin F. McCardie, George W. Baylor, and O. H. P. Coleman
Murder

The indictment filed on 13 Oct 1856 accused the defendants of murdering Peter Seilor at Mendocino County on 12 Aug 1856. Mary Ann Norton, Albert Brayton, and Mrs. Brayton appeared as witnesses before the Grand Jury. The defendants were reindicted on the same charge on 16 Oct 1856.

People v. Amos B. Ingram, Benjamin F. McCardie, George W. Baylor, and O. H. P. Coleman
Murder

The indictment filed on 14 Oct 1856 accused the defendants of murdering Baronett Barns at Mendocino County on 12 Aug 1856. Mary Ann Norton, Albert Brayton, and Mrs. Brayton appeared as witnesses before the Grand Jury. The defendants were reindicted on the same charge on 16 Oct 1856.

People v. George W. Baylor, Amos B. Ingram, Benjamin F. McCardie, [?] Buyes, and [?] Prather
Assault with intent to commit murder (case file # 26)

The indictment filed on 15 Oct 1856 accused the defendants of assaulting Baronett Barns and Reason Barns at Mendocino County by shooting at them with guns with the intent to murder them on 1 Aug 1856. John Rudisal and R. B. Markle appeared as witnesses before the Grand Jury. The Court dismissed the case January term 1857 because of insufficient evidence to obtain a conviction. For related cases, see also case file # 32 and Sonoma County District Court case #s 715 (OS) and 813 (OS).

People v. Amos B. Ingram, Benjamin F. McCardie, George W. Baylor, and O. H. P. Coleman
Murder

The indictment filed on 16 Oct 1856 accused the defendants of murdering Peter Seilor at Mendocino County on 12 Aug 1856. Mary Ann Norton, Albert Brayton, and Mrs. Brayton appeared as witnesses before the Grand Jury. The *Sonoma County Journal* described the homicide in its 22 Aug 1856 edition as:

> We have taken considerable pains to ascertain the facts connected with this affair, but the conflicting accounts given of the matter seem to render this almost impossible. The following statement we think, however, can be relied upon as substantially correct.
>
> It seems that after the two Barnes [Reason and Baronet Barns] and Estis [Jackson Estis] had been discharged by Justice Smith, as stated in our last issue, an ineffectual attempt was made to arrest them by the Sheriff of this County, and that subsequently they were indicted by the Grand Jury of Sonoma County, for the attempted assassination of Mr. Coleman [O. H. P. Coleman, see case file # 32]. Some of Mr. Coleman's friends, learning that they continued to lurk in the neighborhood, determined upon their arrest. Accordingly, on the morning of the 11th inst., a small party, consisting of a Mr. Ingram, Mr. McCarty, and a Mr. Baylor, proceeded to a small house, immediately adjoining the house of Mr. A. Brayton, and which was at that time occupied by Mrs. Norton, where it was supposed the parties were in the habit of visiting.
>
> As they rode up to the house, Mrs. Norton, and Peter Leiber [Peter Seilor] who happened to be at the house at the time, came out – the latter holding a rifle in his hands,

which he cocked and partly presented. The attacking party also presented their weapons, at the same time making known the object of their visit. They were told by Mr. Leiber that they could not take Barnes. At the same instant a shot was fired, as is alleged, from the house, which, striking the gun held by Mr. Baylor, caused its discharge. Its contents lodged in the person of Mr. Leiber, who was standing directly before him. Both parties immediately commenced firing. At this juncture Baronet Barnes, coming out of the house with a revolver in his hand, was shot down. Mr. Barnes and Mr. Leiber both expired almost immediately. Mr. Baylor received a severe wound in his hand, and Mr. Ingram's forehead was grazed by a bullet, without however doing any serious injury.

As soon as intelligence of the affair was received at Santa Rosa, Dr. Williams, the Coroner, repaired to Anderson Valley for the purpose of holding an inquest upon the bodies of the deceased. It appeared that each of the deceased had received three wounds, either of which would have proved fatal.

The Coroner proceeded to issue a warrant for the arrest of Messrs. Ingram, McCarty, and Baylor, who immediately came in and delivered themselves up to the authorities at Santa Rosa. At the date of our latest advices, they were undergoing a preliminary examination before Mr. Justice Coulter.

Mr. Baylor, we are told, is a young gentleman from San Francisco, who has been stopping for a short time in Anderson Valley on a visit. He was one of Mr. Tobin's party, which some of our readers will recollect passed through Petaluma a few weeks since on a hunting excursion to the Russian River Mountains.

The following is the verdict rendered by the Coroner's Jury, upon the body of Barnes. A similar verdict was rendered in the case of Leiber:

County of Mendocino, State of California, August 13th, 1856.

"We, the undersigned Jurors, summoned and sworn by J. S. Williams, the Coroner of said County, find that the deceased, Baronet Barnes, came to his death at the house of Mr. Brayton of Anderson Valley, in the county aforesaid, on the 11th day of the present month, from the effects of several wounds made by balls discharged from [a] gun or guns and pistols in the hands of and fired by one Benjamin McCarty, one Ingram, and one Baylor." – J. B. Lamar, foreman, B. McManus, J. D. Ball, James Garlich, Isaac Buson, J. H. Steelbam and Milton Maupin – Jurors.[202]

As to the events that led up to the homicide, an article in the 16 Aug 1856 edition of the *Petaluma Weekly Journal and Sonoma County Advertiser* sheds some light.

We learn that a shooting affray occurred at Anderson Valley, Mendocino county, last Sunday [10 Aug 1856], between the Barnes brothers and a party of the citizens of that locality, which resulted in the death of Rergan Barnes [Reason Barnes], and the wounding of one of the pursuers. It will be recollected that the Barnes brothers and an old man named Estis, were arrested at Union, Humboldt county, charged with an attempt to kill O. H. P. Coleman, of Anderson Valley; that on their arrival at Big River township, Justice Smith ordered their release, without even the form of an examination. Since that time their whereabouts has remained a secret until last Sunday, when it becoming known that the two Barnes' were in the neighborhood of their attempted murder, a party of citizens

[202] "The Anderson Valley Homicide," *The Sonoma County Journal* (Petaluma, California), 22 August 1856, p. 2, col. 2.

started in pursuit. Upon discovering that they were pursued, the Barnes' commenced firing upon their pursuers, severely wounding one of the party. The fire was returned, and Rergan Barnes fell dead, when his brother fled to the woods, and escaped. The origin of this protracted strife between the Barnes' and the citizens, was caused by one of the Barnes taking a Mrs. Norton to his house, and living with her in a state of adultery, while her husband was at the mines, for which offence the citizens administered to him a coat of tar and feathers.[203]

The case was transferred to the Sonoma County District Court on 22 Oct 1856. See Sonoma County District Court case # 715 (OS). The District Court trial jury found the defendant George W. Baylor not guilty on 6 Nov 1856.[204] The District Court trial jury found the defendant Amos B. Ingram not guilty two days later on 8 Nov 1856. The District Court dismissed the indictment against the defendants Benjamin F. McCardie and O. H. P. Coleman on 10 Nov 1856. For related cases, see also case file #s 32 and 26 and Sonoma County District Court case # 813 (OS).

People v. Amos B. Ingram, Benjamin F. McCardie, George W. Baylor, and O. H. P. Coleman
Murder
The indictment filed on 16 Oct 1856 accused the defendants of murdering Baronett Barns at Mendocino County on 12 Aug 1856. Mary Ann Norton, Albert Brayton, and Mrs. Brayton appeared as witnesses before the Grand Jury. The case was transferred to the Sonoma County District Court on 22 Oct 1856. See Sonoma County District Court case # 715 (OS). The District Court ordered a *nolle prosequi* entered for all the defendants on 10 Nov 1856. For related cases, see also case file #s 32 and 26 and Sonoma County District Court case # 813 (OS).

People v. George W. Baylor, A. B. Ingram, Benjamin F. McCardie, William Prather, and [?] Buyes
Assault with intent to commit murder (case file # 26)
The indictment filed on 16 Oct 1856 accused the defendants of assaulting Baronett Barns and Reason Barns at Mendocino County by shooting at them with guns with the intent to murder them on 1 Aug 1856. John Rudisal and Mr. and Mrs. Counts appeared as witnesses before the Grand Jury. The Court dismissed the case January term 1857 because of insufficient evidence to obtain a conviction. For related cases, see also case file # 32 and Sonoma County District Court case #s 715 (OS) and 813 (OS).

People v. William A. Buster
Using and loaning of money belonging to the State of California and the County of Sonoma for his use and benefit (case file # 25)
The indictment filed on 17 Oct 1856 accused the defendant as Treasurer of Sonoma County of using and loaning money belonging to the State of California and County of Sonoma for the use and benefit of himself, James E. Crane, and James M. Case on 1 Jan 1856. James E. Crane, Henry M. Branstetter, A. C. Bledsoe, Richard Fulkerson, J. F. Boyce, A. B. Nalley, D. P. V. Ogan, Donald McDonald, Thomas H. Pyatt, B. Hoen, Preston Tucker, N. McC. Menefee, John Capell, and

---

[203] "Shooting Affray," *The Petaluma (California) Weekly Journal and Sonoma County Advertiser*, 16 August 1856, p. 2, col. 2.
[204] "District Court," *The Sonoma County Journal* (Petaluma, California), 7 November 1856, p. 2, col. 2.

Madison B. Cummins appeared as witnesses before the Grand Jury. The defendant was reindicted April term 1857.

On 15 December 1856, the Hon. William Churchman, County Judge of Sonoma County, gave notice to the Justices of the Peace of Sonoma County that they would meet in convention on 5 January 1857 to elect two Associate Justices of the Court of Sessions from their own number.[205]

January term 1857

Hon. William Churchman, County Judge
Hon. W. H. Crowell, Associate Justice
Hon. S. J. Coulter, Associate Justice[206]
N. McC. Menefee, Clerk
I. G. Wickersham, District Attorney
Thomas H. Pyatt, Grand Jury foreman

People v. William Townsend
Burglary (case file # 48)
    The indictment filed on 6 Jan 1857 accused the defendant of burgling one cloth Talmer cloak, one gold specimen, and silver coin (total value $50) from the store house of J. M. Miller in Anally Township on 20 Dec 1856 about eleven o'clock at night. John Walker, J. M. Miller, N. Nuckolls, C. J. Pickle, and J. S. Field appeared as witnesses before the Grand Jury. The trial jury found the defendant guilty on 9 Jan 1857, and the Court sentenced him to 3 years' imprisonment in the State Prison.[207] He was received at San Quentin on 14 Jan 1857, served his full sentence, and was discharged on 10 Jan 1860.[208]

April term 1857

Hon. William Churchman, County Judge
Hon. W. H. Crowell, Associate Justice
Hon. J. C. Coulter, Associate Justice[209]
I. G. Wickersham, District Attorney
Stephen L. Fowler, Grand Jury foreman

    The Court of Sessions convened at Santa Rosa on Monday, 5 Apr 1857, with the Hon. W. Churchman, Judge, and the Hon. W. H. Crowell and the Hon. J. C. Coulter, Associate Justices. The

[205] "To Justices of the Peace," *The Sonoma County Journal* (Petaluma, California), 19 December 1856, p. 3, col. 1.
[206] Most likely this was the Hon. Sterling T. Coulter, Justice of the Peace for Santa Rosa Township, elected on 4 November 1856.
[207] "Sentenced," *The Sonoma County Journal* (Petaluma, California), 16 January 1857, p. 2, col. 1.
[208] California, State Prison Register (1851–1867), Executive Department, entry no. 1073, Wm. Townsend, p. 74, received 14 January 1857; California State Archives, Sacramento.
[209] Most likely this was the Hon. Sterling T. Coulter, Justice of the Peace for Santa Rosa Township, elected on 4 November 1856.

following are the names of the Grand Jurors empaneled: C. Arthur, H. Bassett, J. Brown, J. Andrews, D. S. Bowman, C. C. Carlton, Robert Cunningham, C. Bice, C. H. Barnes, J. Abbay, William Bidwell, S. L. Fowler, T. Blackwell, J. Devick, H. Beaver, J. Morehouse, J. C. Russell, J. Smith, D. Vaughn, G. R. Bell, and F. Fisher. The Court appointed S. L. Fowler Grand Jury foreman. On 8 Apr 1857, the Grand Jury came into Court with eight bills of indictment and was discharged.[210]

Report of the Grand Jury[211]

We, the undersigned members of the Grand Jury for the April term of the Court of Sessions for the year A. D. 1857, beg leave to submit the following report:

We examined into the condition of the Jail and find it conducted in a proper manner. The prisoners are as well cared for as the circumstances will admit. We would recommend that iron grating be securely place[d] in the wall where the circular windows are for the purpose of ventilation and making the Jail more secure. Upon examination of the Treasurer's books we find a balance in favor of County Gen. Fund of [$]1200, indigent sick fund of [$]95.27, County special fund of $468.10, and the books kept in a business-like manner.

The most of the roads in the County are in bad condition, and we would earnestly recommend that those in authority would as early as practical have them repaved and enforce the law against delinquents.

The morals of our County, judging from the number of indictments found by our former Grand Jury and the business that has been before us, we are happy to state are improving.

We have found eight true bills. Stephen L. Fowler, Foreman.

People v. Vincent Lambert
Manslaughter (case file # 50A)

The charge of killing Thomas O'Brien on 19 Jan 1857 was ignored by the Grand Jury, and the defendant was discharged by the Court 6 Apr 1857.[212] The affair was reported by the *Sonoma County Journal* on 23 Jan 1857 as:

> About 3 o'clock last Monday morning, our town [Petaluma] was the scene of a bloody tragedy. The victim named Thomas O'Brien, and the perpetrator of the act, Vincent Lambert, keeper of a Burton Ale Saloon in this place.
>
> The facts of the case, so far as we have learned them, are these: O'Brien had been in Lambert's employ in the capacity of a waterman, in consequence of his drunken and worthless character, had been discharged. During his stop with [illegible] O'Brien had become aware that one of the front doors to L.'s Saloon was fastened at night by placing a prop against it on the inside, instead of securing it by a lock, and that by reaching through a broken pane of glass, he could remove the fastening, and then effect an entrance. On [illegible], [illegible] certain indications, Mr. Lambert had become satisfied

---

[210] "Legal Intelligence," *The Sonoma County Journal* (Petaluma, California), 10 April 1857, p. 2, col. 3.

[211] Sonoma County, California, Court of Sessions, Report of the Grand Jury, 8 April 1857; County Records, Sonoma County, Court Records, Miscellaneous Unprocessed Records, folder "County Records – Sonoma County – Court of Sessions – Reports of the Grand Jury"; California State Archives, Sacramento.

[212] "Legal Intelligence," *The Sonoma County Journal* (Petaluma, California), 10 April 1857, p. 2, col. 3.

that some person or persons had entered his Saloon during the night previous, and as his sleeping apartment was in the rear of the Saloon, he determined to detect the thief.

He accordingly borrowed a gun and charged it with powder and shot – using a very small-sized shot (No. 8) with the intention, as he then avowed, of simply "frightening the rascal." Toward morning he was aroused from his sleep by a noise in the front room. Springing from his bed he seized his gun and entered the Saloon, just as the thief was backing out of the door. Hastily raising the gun, L. fired, after which he proceeded to the door, and beheld O'Brien supporting himself by a post. His only remark was, "You have shot me in the thigh." Finding that the wounded man was bleeding profusely, and evidently sinking, Mr. Lambert placed him in charge of two gentlemen, whom the report of the gun had summoned to the spot, and hastened for Dr. Hylton, but to no avail, as O'Brien was a corpse before medical aid could be rendered. The charge entered the thigh and groin, severing the femoral artery, and the miserable man survived but about forty minutes after receiving the wound.

Lambert, who had voluntarily surrendered himself into the hands of justice, underwent an examination before Justice Shattuck, last Wednesday, and has been held to bail in the sum of $2,000 for his appearance at Court next April to answer to the charge of manslaughter.[213]

People v. William A. Buster
Using and loaning money belonging to the County of Sonoma (case file # 25)

The indictment filed on 7 Apr 1857 accused the defendant as Treasurer of Sonoma County of using and loaning of money belonging to the County of Sonoma on 1 Jan 1857. James E. Crane, A. C. Bledsoe, John Brown, N. McC. Menefee, J. F. Boyce, and John Powell appeared as witnesses before the Grand Jury. A trial jury found the defendant guilty, and the Court ordered him imprisoned in the State Prison for the term of 30 months.[214] San Quentin received the defendant on 6 May 1857.[215] Governor John G. Downey pardoned Buster on 11 Oct 1860, citing "his excellent conduct during his long imprisonment, as testified to by the officers of the prison" and thinking him "having been punished sufficiently."[216]

People v. William A. Buster
Using and loaning money belonging to the State of California (case file # 25)

The indictment filed on 7 Apr 1857 accused the defendant as Treasurer of Sonoma County of using and loaning money belonging to the State of California for the use and benefit of himself, James E. Crane, and James M. Case on 17 Oct 1856. James E. Crane, A. C. Bledsoe, John Brown, N. McC. Menefee, J. F. Boyce, and John Powell appeared as witnesses before the Grand Jury. A

---

[213] "Homicide," *The Sonoma County Journal* (Petaluma, California), 23 January 1857, p. 2, cols. 1–2.

[214] "The People vs. Wm. A. Buster," *The Sonoma County Journal (Petaluma, California)*, 8 May 1857, p. 2, cols. 4–5.

[215] California, State Prison Register (1851–1867), Executive Department, entry no. 1142, William A. Buster, p. 79, received 6 May 1857; California State Archives, Sacramento.

[216] *Journal of the House of Assembly of California, at the Twelfth Session of the Legislature, Begun on [7 January 1861], and Ended on [20 May 1861], at the City of Sacramento* (Sacramento: C. T. Botts, State Printer, 1861), 114 (hereafter cited as *Journal of the House of Assembly of California, Twelfth Session*). Buster's pardon is enumerated among the list of pardons in the appendix to the Governor's message to the Senate and Assembly dated 7 January 1861.

trial jury found the defendant guilty on 22 Apr 1857.[217] The Court ordered him imprisoned in the State Prison for the term of 30 months on 29 Apr 1857.[218] San Quentin received the defendant on 6 May 1857.[219] Governor John G. Downey pardoned Buster on 11 Oct 1860, citing "his excellent conduct during his long imprisonment, as testified to by the officers of the prison" and thinking him "having been punished sufficiently."[220]

People v. A. C. Freeland and William Freeland
Branding cattle not their own property (case file # 34)
   The indictment filed on 8 Apr 1857 accused the defendants of branding and marking three head of Thomas H. Pyatt's cattle with the intent of stealing them and preventing their identification on 4 Apr 1857. Thomas Pyatt and Jacob Harris appeared as witnesses before the Grand Jury. A trial jury found the defendant William Freeland not guilty July term 1857.[221]

People v. James (var. John R.) Shaw
Keeping a gaming house (case file #s 36 and 44)
   The indictment filed on 8 Apr 1857 accused the defendant of permitting gaming in which money was lost in a house of which he was an occupant on 2 Mar 1857. John Lamb, Joshua Lamb, Frank M. Prouse, and Reese Singley appeared as witnesses before the Grand Jury. The case was dismissed by the District Attorney for want of evidence July term 1857.[222]

People v. Davenport Cousins (var. Cousens)
Keeping a gaming house (case file # 37)
   The indictment filed on 8 Apr 1857 accused the defendant of having been the occupant of a house in which money was lost by gaming on 2 Mar 1857. F. M. Prouse appeared as a witness before the Grand Jury. The case was dismissed by the prosecution for want of evidence July term 1857.[223]

People v. William Leary (var. Larry)
Assault with a deadly weapon (case file # 51)
   The indictment filed on 8 Apr 1857 accused the defendant of assaulting Daniel Madison with a knife on 26 Feb 1857. William Webb, F. W. Shattuck, and William B. Barnett appeared as witnesses before the Grand Jury. A trial jury found the defendant guilty July term 1857, and the Court granted the defendant a new trial.[224] The second trial jury found the defendant not guilty on 6 Oct 1857.

---

[217] "Court of Sessions," *The Sonoma County Journal (Petaluma, California)*, 24 Apr 1857, p. 2, col. 1.

[218] "Buster Sentenced," *The Sonoma County Journal (Petaluma, California)*, 1 May 1857, p. 2, col. 1.

[219] California, State Prison Register (1851–1867), Executive Department, entry no. 1142, William A. Buster, p. 79, received 6 May 1857; California State Archives, Sacramento.

[220] *Journal of the House of Assembly of California, Twelfth Session*, 114. Buster's pardon is enumerated among the list of pardons in the appendix to the Governor's message to the Senate and Assembly dated 7 January 1861.

[221] "Legal Intelligence," *The Sonoma County Journal* (Petaluma, California), 17 July 1857, p. 2, col. 6.

[222] Ibid.

[223] Ibid.

[224] Ibid.

People v. William A. Buster
Keeping a gaming house (case file #25)

The indictment filed on 8 Apr 1857 accused the defendant of permitting gaming in a house in which he was an occupant on 15 Feb 1857. Preston Tucker, [?] Russell, and F. Fisher appeared as witnesses before the Grand Jury. The defendant pleaded guilty, and the Court ordered him to pay a fine of $300.[225]

People v. William A. Buster
Embezzlement (case file # 25)

The indictment filed on 8 Apr 1857 accused the defendant as Treasurer of Sonoma County of embezzling money belonging to the County of Sonoma on 4 Feb 1857 and money belonging to the School Fund of the County of Sonoma on 5 Feb 1857 for his own use. B. B. Berry and James Prewett appeared as witnesses before the Grand Jury. The defendant pleaded guilty, and the Court ordered him imprisoned in the State Prison for the term of three years.[226] San Quentin received the defendant on 6 May 1857.[227] Governor John G. Downey pardoned Buster on 11 Oct 1860, citing "his excellent conduct during his long imprisonment, as testified to by the officers of the prison" and thinking him "having been punished sufficiently."[228]

July term 1857

The Court of Sessions first met this term on 6 Jul 1857 at Santa Rosa and adjourned on 13 Jul 1857. The Grand Jury was in session for four days and brought in seven indictments.[229]

Hon. William Churchman, County Judge
I. G. Wickersham, District Attorney
J. A. Campbell, Grand Jury foreman

People v. Jose Remeris and Fernando Remeris
Grand larceny (case file # 39)

The indictment filed on 7 Jul 1857 accused the defendants of stealing a horse about two years old worth $75 from an Indian named Conuto on 1 Apr 1857. William B. Hagans, Wallace M. Hagans, Charles McCauley, and William Travis appeared as witnesses before the Grand Jury. The defendant Jose Remeris was found guilty of petit larceny and sentenced to 30 days imprisonment in the County Jail of Sonoma County and fined $100 July term 1857.[230] The defendant Fernando Remeris was found guilty of grand larceny and sentenced to two years' imprisonment in the State

---

[225] "Court of Sessions," *The Sonoma County Journal* (Petaluma, California), 24 Apr 1857, p. 2, col. 1.

[226] "The People vs. Wm. A. Buster," *The Sonoma County Journal* (Petaluma, California), 8 May 1857, p. 2, cols. 4–5.

[227] California, State Prison Register (1851–1867), Executive Department, entry no. 1142, William A. Buster, p. 79, received 6 May 1857; California State Archives, Sacramento.

[228] *Journal of the House of Assembly of California, Twelfth Session*, 114. Buster's pardon is enumerated among the list of pardons in the appendix to the Governor's message to the Senate and Assembly dated 7 January 1861.

[229] "Legal Intelligence," *The Sonoma County Journal* (Petaluma, California), 17 July 1857, p. 2, col. 6.

[230] Ibid.

Prison July term 1857.[231] He was received by San Quentin on 14 Jul 1857 and discharged 13 Jul 1859 after serving his full term.[232]

People v. J. S. Ormsby
Assault and battery (case file # 42)

The indictment filed on 8 Jul 1857 accused the defendant of assaulting G. Treadway on 8 May 1857. G. Treadway and B. Hoen appeared as witnesses before the Grand Jury. The Court dismissed the indictment on 6 Oct 1857 because the defendant had already been tried and convicted of the offense charged in the indictment in the Hon. William H. Crowell's Justice's Court.

People v. Condy Coneghan
Grand larceny (case file # 43)

The indictment filed on 8 Jul 1857 accused the defendant of stealing William Miles's cow (value $80) on 4 Jul 1857. William Miles, E. F. Clark, W. K. Ruffner, and William White appeared as witnesses before the Grand Jury. The defendant was apparently found guilty of the offense because the Court ordered him imprisoned in the State Prison for the term of two years July term 1857.[233] He was received by San Quentin on 14 Jul 1857 and discharged on 13 Jul 1859 after serving his full term.[234]

People v. Byrd Brumfield
Assault with a deadly weapon (case file # 38)

The indictment filed on 9 Jul 1857 accused the defendant of assaulting Amariah Kibbe with a knife on 28 Jun 1857. James Hollis, Amariah Kibbe, and A. Somsburry appeared as witnesses before the Grand Jury. At trial on 7 Oct 1857, the District Attorney could produce no witnesses for the prosecution, and the Court ordered the trial jurors to bring in a verdict of not guilty, which they did.

People v. Jack (var. A. J.) Forrester (var. Forrister)
Keeping a gaming house (case file # 40)

The indictment filed on 9 Jul 1857 accused the defendant of being an occupant of a house in which money was lost by gaming on 4 Jul 1857. Amariah Kibbe, S. McCune, William Powell, and George Chamberlain appeared as witnesses before the Grand Jury. The Court sustained the defendant's demurrer and discharged the defendant on 6 Oct 1857.

---

[231] Ibid.

[232] California, State Prison Register (1851–1867), Executive Department, entry no. 1188, Fernando Ramirez, p. 82, received 14 July 1857; California State Archives, Sacramento.

[233] "Legal Intelligence," *The Sonoma County Journal* (Petaluma, California), 17 July 1857, p. 2, col. 6.

[234] California, State Prison Register (1851–1867), Executive Department, entry no. 1187, Condy Canegham [*sic*], p. 82, received 14 July 1857; California State Archives, Sacramento.

People v. Charles Spurgen and James Stephens
Setting a spring gun (case file # 41)

The indictment filed on 9 Jul 1857 accused the defendants of setting a spring gun with the intent of inflicting grievous bodily harm to Walter S. Jarbo or another person on 26 Jun 1857. W. S. Jarboe, [?] McDowell, Joseph McCormick, E. H. Eubanks, W. H. Levalley, J. B. Price, Jr., and D. P. Murry appeared as witnesses before the Grand Jury. See also case file # 49 for a few documents related to this case regarding Charles Spurgen.

People v. Charles Spurgen and James Stephens
Assault with intent to commit murder (case file # 41)

The indictment filed on 9 Jul 1857 accused the defendants of assaulting Walter S. Jarbo with a gun with the intent of murdering him on 26 Jun 1857. W. S. Jarbo, [?] McDowell, Joseph McCormick, E. H. Eubanks, W. H. Levalley, J. B. Price, Jr., and D. P. Murry appeared as witnesses before the Grand Jury. The Court directed the trial jurors to bring in a verdict of not guilty for the defendant Charles Spurgen for want of evidence, and they did so on 9 Oct 1857. The Court ordered a *nolle prosequi* entered for the defendant James Stephens on 9 Oct 1857. See also case file # 49 for a few documents related to this case regarding Charles Spurgen.

October term 1857

The Court of Sessions met for five days this term, 5–9 October 1857.[235]

Hon. William Churchman, County Judge
Hon. Thomas H. Pyatt, Associate Justice
Hon. L. D. Cockrill, Associate Justice
William G. Gordon, District Attorney
William H. Crowell, Clerk
A. C. Bledsoe, Sheriff
Jacob M. Gallagher, Deputy Sheriff
James A. Reynolds, Deputy Sheriff
I. A. Holman, Grand Jury foreman

At a convention of the Justices of the Peace of Sonoma County held on 5 Oct 1857 Thomas H. Pyatt, Esq., and L. D. Cockrill, Esq., were elected as Associate Justices of the Court of Sessions for the next ensuing year.

Persons called as Grand Jurors but not empaneled: James Haywood (gave a satisfactory excuse), George Hinkle (failed to answer when his name was called), and S. C. Haydon (a member of the Petaluma Guards).

---

[235] Sonoma County, California, Court of Sessions, Minute Book D: 1–25, October term 1857 proceedings; Sonoma County Archives, Santa Rosa.

Grand Jurors sworn and empaneled on 5 Oct 1857: John Hopper, C. P. Hatch, David Hotel, Isaac Holman, W. J. Hardin, E. L. Reed, John Huffman, A. B. Ingram, William Hood, Smith Davidson, J. B. Holloway, Vernon Downs, Miles Hinman, H. P. Larrabee, J. B. Hogle, Colman Talbott, O. Hubble, D. P. V. Ogan, Alfred Herrick, and C. McGuire.

Report of the Grand Jury[236]

The Grand Jurors of the County of Sonoma, State of California, for the October term of the Court of Sessions, A. D. 1857, present to the Honorable Court the following report:

We have during our session found five bills of indictment. We find on an examination of the County Jail that it is well-kept and in a cleanly condition, but that a part of the jail building is in a dilapidated and unsafe state, requiring both ventilation and repairs, and we would respectfully but earnestly call the immediate attention of the Board of Supervisors to these facts. We also ask the attention of the Board of Supervisors to the necessity of an examination into and the provision of some means for the greater preservation of County Records and papers.

We, finally, present the necessity of instructing the Justices of the Peace as to their official acts, and of reminding delinquents of their duty, particularly as to the transmission of all necessary papers to the Court, inasmuch as we have on examination found prisoners in jail without any sort of evidence against them. All of which is respectfully submitted.

J. A. HOLMAN, Foreman.

People v. George Johnson (indicted as George A. Johnson)
Assault with intent to commit rape (case file # 35)

The indictment filed on 7 Oct 1857 accused the defendant of assaulting Charlotte R. Williams by beating and ill-treating her with the intent to ravish and carnally know her on 16 Jul 1857. Charlotte R. Williams and Nathaniel Bennett appeared as witnesses before the Grand Jury. Johnson, a dentist, was tarred and feathered by the populace of Petaluma on the evening of 16 Jul 1857.[237] The trial jury found the defendant not guilty on 8 Oct 1857. For a related case, see case file # 62.

People v. George Powell
Petit larceny (case file # 46)

The indictment filed on 7 Oct 1857 accused the defendant of stealing 600 of Elmsley [Emsley] Elliott's wooden rails (value $25) on 1 Sep 1857. Elmsley [Emsley] Elliott and H. P. Larrabee appeared as witnesses before the Grand Jury.

---

[236] "Report of the Grand Jury of Sonoma County," The Sonoma Democrat (Santa Rosa, California), 22 October 1857, p. 2, col. 4. The newspaper transcriber misread the "I" of I. A. Holman as a "J." This is a more well-written version of the original Report of the Grand Jury. See Sonoma County, California, Court of Sessions, Report of the Grand Jury, filed 12 October 1857; County Records, Sonoma County, Court Records, Miscellaneous Unprocessed Records, folder "County Records – Sonoma County – Court of Sessions – Reports of the Grand Jury"; California State Archives, Sacramento.

[237] "Lynched," The Sonoma County Journal (Petaluma, California), 17 July 1857, p. 2, col. 2.

People v. Amos Merrifield (var. Merryfield, alias Cheap John)
Selling spiritous liquors less than one mile from a camp meeting (case file # 33)

The Grand Jury dismissed the charge of selling spiritous liquors less than one mile from a camp meeting engaged in religious worship near Sebastopol on 6 Sep 1857 for want of sufficient evidence on 7 Oct 1857.

People v. George W. Bigelow
Assault with a deadly weapon

The Grand Jury dismissed the charge for want of sufficient evidence on 7 Oct 1857.

People v. Lorenzo Failis
Grand larceny (case file # 45)

The indictment filed on 8 Oct 1857 accused the defendant of stealing one mare and two colts of N. McC. Menefee's (value $100) on 1 Oct 1856. N. McC. Menefee and Thomas Carson appeared as witnesses before the Grand Jury.

People v. Israel M. Malay
Petit larceny (case file # 47)

The indictment filed on 9 Oct 1857 accused the defendant of stealing 100 of Wallace Waldron's rails (value $4) on 1 Feb 1857. Wallace Waldron, George Backman, and Isaac Gum appeared as witnesses before the Grand Jury. The trial jury found the defendant not guilty on 7 Jan 1858.

People v. Israel M. Malay
Malicious mischief (case file # 47)

The indictment filed on 9 Oct 1857 accused the defendant of setting fire to a large quantity of Wallace Waldron's rails on 1 Feb 1857. Wallace Waldron, George Backman, and Isaac Gum appeared as witnesses before the Grand Jury. The trial jury found the defendant not guilty by the instruction of the Court on 7 Jan 1858.

People v. Christian Brunner and Peter Peterson
Murder

The indictment filed on 9 Oct 1857 accused the defendants of killing Anton Dellebach on 9 Sep 1857.[238] Doctor Van Guilden [Dr. Charles Van Geldern], Peter Petersen [Peterson], John Hoffman [Huffman], and John Mann appeared as witnesses before the Grand Jury. An article in the *Sonoma County Journal* of 18 Sep 1857 gave the details of the shooting as:

> Intelligence was received in this town [Petaluma], last Friday [11 Sep 1857], that Christian Brunner, an old resident of Sonoma, had, on the night previous [9 Sep 1857], killed a young man by shooting him while in bed. From persons residing in Sonoma, we learn that the young man was a nephew of Mr. B.'s, that he had been a resident of the

---

[238] Sonoma County, California, District Court, case file # 109 (OS), The People v. Christian Brunner and Peter Peterson, indictment, filed 9 October 1857; County Records, Sonoma County, Court Records, District Court, Old Series cases files; California State Archives, Sacramento.

State but a few months, and that he came from Germany to California by the request and at the expense of Mr. Brunner. Since his arrival in Sonoma, Mrs. Brunner, it appears, has declared her determination to leave her husband and to apply to the court for a divorce and for a partition of the property. In her course she seems to have been counseled by the deceased; at least she had appointed him her agent, she having found it necessary to go to San Francisco to live alleging as a reason that Brunner had threatened her life. At the time of the murder, the only person present was a Mr. Peterson, a man in Brunner's employ—who says that Mr. B. found the young man in his (Brunner's) bed, and on ordering him to get up he refused, saying that he had as good a right in it as had Brunner; that he further attempted to strike Mr. B., when Mr. B. presented a pistol and fired. The young man survived but a few minutes. On Friday Brunner had an examination and was committed to jail to await his trial for murder, as was also the man Peterson, as an accomplice. Mr. Brunner has been addicted to hard drinking for a number of years, and to this habit is to be traced this deed of blood.[239]

The case was transferred to the Sonoma County District Court on 9 Oct 1857. See Sonoma County District Court case # 109 (OS). The District Court granted the defendants separate trials on 27 Oct 1857.[240] The District Court trial jury was empaneled in the case of the People v. Christian Brunner on the same day, but the Court dismissed the indictment and discharged the trial jury, reasoning that the indictment did not "contain a sufficient statement of facts to constitute a public offence or to authorize the introduction of testimony or to found a judgment upon."[241] The Court further ordered that the case be resubmitted to the next Grand Jury. A *nolle prosequi* was entered in the case of the defendant Peter Peterson, and the Court ordered that his case be resubmitted to the next Grand Jury as well.

People v. Nicholas Fortis
Grand larceny
The Grand Jury dismissed the charge for want of sufficient evidence on 9 Oct 1857.

January term 1858

The Court of Sessions met for ten days this term, 4–9 and 11–14 January 1858.[242]

Hon. William Churchman, County Judge
Hon. Thomas H. Pyatt, Associate Justice
Hon. L. D. Cockrill, Associate Justice
William G. Gordon, District Attorney

---

[239] "Homicide in Sonoma," *The Sonoma County Journal* (Petaluma, California), 18 September 1857, p. 2, col. 1.
[240] Sonoma County, California, District Court, Minute Book B: 2, The People v. Christian Brunner and Peter Peterson, court order granting the defendants separate trials, 27 October 1857; Sonoma County Archives, Santa Rosa.
[241] Sonoma County, California, District Court, Minute Book B: 8, The People v. Christian Brunner, court order dismissing case, 28 October 1857; Sonoma County Archives, Santa Rosa.
[242] Sonoma County, California, Court of Sessions, Minute Book D: 27–43, January term 1858 proceedings; Sonoma County Archives, Santa Rosa.

William H. Crowell, Clerk
F. Fitch, Deputy Clerk
E. L. Green, Sheriff
A. B. Nally, Under Sheriff
J. J. Ellis, Deputy Sheriff
S. T. Coulter, Grand Jury foreman

Persons summoned as Grand Jurors but not empaneled: S. D. Lowell, G. P. Kellogg, John Kalkman, Thomas Murry, R. B. Markle, J. R. Short, G. W. Moody, and Matthew Cummons.

The *Sonoma Democrat* on 18 Feb 1858 gave the following names of Grand Jurors duly sworn and empaneled for the January term 1858: S. T. Coulter, James Kennedy, W. D. Kent, George Kline, H. P. Holmes, P. Maddox, Robert B. Lyons, Albert G. Lyons, H. H. Lewis, B. P. McPherson [C. P. McPherson], Hiram Lewis, J. C. Laymance, J. G. Cook, Sherman Bill [Sherman Bills], G. P. Sanders, H. P. Mullison, D. P. V. Ogan, Thomas Hudson, and J. S. Taylor.[243]

Thomas Hudson was discharged as a Grand Juror on account of a sickness in his family on 7 Jan 1858. J. S. Taylor was sworn and empaneled as a Grand Juror to replace Hudson the same day.

Report of the Grand Jury[244]

To the Honorable Court of Sessions of the County of Sonoma, January Term, 1858.

The Grand Jury of the County of Sonoma most respectfully report, that during a session of ten days, they have found twenty-two indictments and two presentments.

Much complaint is made and great dissatisfaction is felt because of the fact that the roads of the county are constantly changed by private individuals, from their original places and direction.

They further report that they have visited the jail and found therein two prisoners. The jail is well-kept and clean, but stands greatly in need of better ventilation, which, in the opinion of the jury, might be effected at a trifling expense by making an opening near the ceiling in each cell to the hall, and placing a grating in the ceiling of the hall. The windows should also be protected by iron Venetian blinds on the outside of the grating, in order that prisoners may be precluded from any communication with persons outside. In its present condition means of escape might be easily afforded those in confinement.

We respectfully and earnestly invite attention to the insecure state of the Clerk's and Recorder's offices, and recommend that they be provided with shutters on the inside, and that better locks be furnished.

They further recommend that drugget be laid down in the hall of the court-room, and also in the bar, that proceedings may not be interrupted as now by the noise unavoidably made in walking about the room; and that the doors leading to the court-room be immediately

---

[243] "Accounts Allowed," *The Sonoma Democrat* (Santa Rosa, California), 18 February 1858, p. 2, col. 4.
[244] "Report of the Grand Jury," *The Sonoma Democrat* (Santa Rosa, California), 21 January 1858, p. 2, col. 6.

repaired.[245] They also recommend that the roof of the court house be repaired at once, as the leakage is causing the plastering of the jury rooms to fall off.

As a matter of vital importance, we most earnestly urge that our Representatives should use their influence in the procuring of an enactment prohibiting all games played with cards for money or other valuables. All of which is respectfully submitted.

S. T. Coulter, Foreman. W. D. Kent, Cl'k.

Santa Rosa, Jan'y 14th, 1858

People v. Christian Brunner
Murder

The indictment filed on 6 Jan 1858 accused the defendant of shooting Antone Dellebach in the right breast with a pistol giving him one mortal wound and killing him instantly on or about 9 Sep 1857.[246] Peter Petersen [Peterson], John Mann, Charles Van Guelden [Charles Van Geldern], John Hoffman [Huffman], and Sidney Harris appeared as witnesses before the Grand Jury. The case was transferred to the Sonoma County District Court on 14 Jan 1858. See Sonoma County District Court case # 729 (OS). On 6 Feb 1858, the District Court trial jury found Brunner guilty of murder in the 2nd degree "after a deliberation of about seven hours."[247] District Court Judge E. W. McKinstry sentenced Brunner to eleven years' imprisonment in the State Prison on 8 Feb 1858.[248] The next day, San Quentin received the defendant.[249] Governor John G. Downey pardoned Brunner on 20 Mar 1861, citing Brunner's "uniform good conduct prior to the commission of the rash deed for which he was sentenced, his great age, and the exemplary manner in which he has conducted himself since his imprisonment."[250]

People v. Moses C. Briggs
Assault with intent to commit murder (case file # 28)

The indictment filed on 6 Jan 1858 accused the defendant of assaulting Stephen F. Rossell by shooting at him with a pistol and striking him on the nose and arm with the pistol at Mendocino County with the intent to murder him on 30 Sep 1857. Stephen F. Rossel appeared as a witness before the Grand Jury. The trial jury found the defendant not guilty on 6 Jul 1858.

---

[245] Drugget is defined as "a coarse durable cloth used chiefly as a floor covering" and "a rug having a cotton warp and a wool filling." See, *Merriam-Webster Online Dictionary* (http://www.merriam-webster.com : accessed 14 October 2018), "drugget."

[246] Sonoma County, California, District Court, case file # 729 (OS), People v. Christian Brunner, indictment, 6 January 1858; California State Archives, Sacramento.

[247] "The Case of Brunner," *The Sonoma Democrat* (Santa Rosa, California), 11 February 1858, p. 2, cols. 3–4.

[248] Sonoma County, California, District Court, Minute Book B: 52, The People v. Christian Brunner, sentence of defendant, 8 February 1858; Sonoma County Archives, Santa Rosa.

[249] California, State Prison Register (1851–1867), Executive Department, entry no. 1332, Christian Brunner, p. 93, received 9 February 1858; California State Archives, Sacramento.

[250] *The Journal of the Assembly, During the Thirteenth Session of the Legislature of the State of California: 1862. Begun on Monday, [6 January 1862], and Ended on Thursday, [15 May 1862]* (Sacramento: Benj. P. Avery, State Printer, 1862), 58 (hereafter cited as *The Journal of the Assembly, Thirteenth Session*). Brunner's pardon is enumerated in the list of pardons contained in the appendix to the Governor's annual message to the Senate and Assembly dated 8 January 1862.

People v. Andrew Arthur

Obstructing an officer in the discharge of his duty

In a complaint dated 20 Nov 1857 and sworn to and subscribed before the Hon. S. M. Martin, a Justice of the Peace for Petaluma Township, Nathaniel Nuckolls, the Sonoma County Assessor, accused the defendant of obstructing, resisting, and opposing him in the performance of his duties as Assessor by refusing to allow him to take property to satisfy the defendant's poll tax on or about 19 Nov 1857. The Grand Jury ignored the bill against the defendant on 6 Jan 1858.

People v. Peter Peterson

Murder

The Grand Jury ignored the bill against the defendant on 7 Jan 1858.

People v. Thomas Burns

Grand larceny (case file # 53)

The indictment filed on 8 Jan 1858 accused the defendant of stealing eight hogs and fourteen pigs, the property of George Rouschart (var. Rauschert) (value $50), on 15 Sep 1857. T. C. Bishop, George Rouschart (var. Rauschert), and Nick Long appeared as witnesses before the Grand Jury. The Court sustained the defendant's demurrer and ordered the indictment be resubmitted to the Grand Jury on 6 Apr 1858. The Grand Jury dismissed the indictment and charge on 10 Apr 1858.

People v. Walter S. Jarboe

Assault with intent to commit bodily injury (case file # 58)

The indictment filed on 9 Jan 1858 accused the defendant of assaulting Amos Merryfield with a large knife on 5 Dec 1857. Henry Ellis and Amos Merryfield appeared as witnesses before the Grand Jury. The trial jury returned a verdict of not guilty on 6 Jul 1858.

People v. James Davis

Raffling (case file # 61)

The indictment filed on 9 Jan 1858 accused the defendant of unlawfully disposing of one watch (value $60) by the throwing and counting of dice on 24 Dec 1857. M. Rosenberg and W. R. Smith appeared as witnesses before the Grand Jury. The Court sustained the defendant's demurrer and discharged the defendant on 6 Jul 1858.

People v. John J. Domes

Manslaughter

The Grand Jury ignored the bill against the defendant on 9 Jan 1858. The case was resubmitted to the Grand Jury on 6 Jan 1859.

People v. George W. M. Cowles

Raffling (case file # 60)

The indictment filed on 13 Jan 1858 accused the defendant of unlawfully disposing of millinery goods (value $100) by the throwing and counting of dice on 30 Dec 1857. B. Palmer and

S. May appeared as witnesses before the Grand Jury. The Court sustained the defendant's demurrer and discharged the defendant on 6 Apr 1858.

People v. [?] King and [?] Harrington
Raffling (case file # 63)

The indictment filed on 13 Jan 1858 accused the defendants of aiding and assisting in a raffle conducted by [?] McVicar of goods and chattels (value $100) disposed of by the throwing and counting of dice on 20 Dec 1857. J. J. Ellis, B. Palmer, and S. May appeared as witnesses before the Grand Jury. The Court sustained the defendants' demurrer, and the defendants were discharged on 6 Apr 1858.

People v. Smith D. Towne
Raffling (case file # 68)

The indictment filed on 13 Jan 1858 accused the defendant of unlawfully disposing of one watch (value $100) by the throwing and counting of dice on 1 Dec 1857. Jesse Jackson and S. May appeared as witnesses before the Grand Jury. The Court sustained the defendant's demurrer and discharged the defendant on 6 Apr 1858.

People v. C. M. C. McVicar
Raffling (case file #75)

The indictment filed on 13 Jan 1858 accused the defendant of disposing of one watch (value $100) by the throwing and counting of dice on 30 Dec 1857. John Ellis, S. May, and Jesse Jackson appeared as witnesses before the Grand Jury. The Court sustained the defendant's demurrer and discharged the defendant on 6 Apr 1858.

People v. B. Newman
Raffling (case file # 76)

The indictment filed on 13 Jan 1858 accused the defendant of unlawfully disposing of three cloaks (value $100) by the throwing and counting of dice on 9 Jan 1858. B. Palmer, S. May, and J. J. Pennypacker appeared as witnesses before the Grand Jury. The Court sustained the defendant's demurrer and discharged the defendant on 6 Apr 1858.

People v. H. L. Weston
Raffling (case file # 77)

The indictment filed on 13 Jan 1858 accused the defendant of unlawfully aiding and assisting in a raffle by the printing of tickets and posters for the raffle conducted by [?] McVicar of goods and chattels (value $100) disposed of by the throwing and counting of dice on 20 Dec 1857. J. J. Pennypacker appeared as a witness before the Grand Jury. The Court sustained the defendant's demurrer and discharged the defendant on 6 Apr 1858. Henry L. Weston was the owner and proprietor of the *Sonoma County Journal* at the time he was indicted. On 29 Jan 1858, this newspaper reported on the indictments brought by the January term 1858 Grand Jury and sarcastically described Weston's alleged offence.

Among the number thus indicted by the Grand Jury, for the atrocious crime of "misdemeanor," is the proprietor of this paper, his bonds being fixed at the moderate sum of $800; and he being of that class who are disposed to choose their company, we accordingly called upon two friends, whom we found hazardous enough to become our sureties; probably from the fact, that they well knew our inability to raise enough of the *plata* to "absquatulate to parts unknown."

We are told that our crime consists in the printing, upon pieces of paper, cards, pasteboard, parchment, sheep or goat skin, and what-not, of certain cards, bills or documents, the same having been by second, third, or fourth parties, used for, and applied to the object of distributing among the great unwashed of these benighted regions – the weaker sex included – of sundry articles of female apparel and ornaments, vulgarly denominated bonnets, capes, crinolines, garters, &c. Serious the charge, and grave the offence. Angels of mercy, deliver us![251]

People v. Fred Johnson
Raffling (case file # 78)

The indictment filed on 13 Jan 1858 accused the defendant of aiding and assisting in a raffle of goods and chattels (value $100) disposed of by the throwing and counting of dice conducted by B. Newman by allowing him to conduct the raffle in the house the defendant was occupying on or about 1 Jan 1858. S. May and B. Palmer appeared as witnesses before the Grand Jury. The Court sustained the defendant's demurrer and discharged the defendant on 6 Apr 1858.

People v. Thomas D. Williamson
Raffling (case file # 81)

The indictment filed on 13 Jan 1858 accused the defendant of aiding and assisting in a raffle of a watch (value $50) conducted by J. Davis disposed of by the throwing and counting of dice by allowing Davis to conduct the raffle in a house occupied by the defendant on 24 Dec 1857. W. R. Smith and [?] Rosenberg appeared as witnesses before the Grand Jury. The Court sustained the defendant's demurrer and discharged the defendant on 6 Apr 1858.

People v. Moses C. Briggs
Assault with a deadly weapon (case file # 28)

The presentment filed on 14 Jan 1858 accused the defendant of assaulting [?] Bryant by cutting and stabbing him on or about 1 Sep 1858. S. F. Rossell appeared as a witness before the Grand Jury.

People v. Thomas Burns
Altering marks and brands (case file # 53)

The indictment filed on 14 Jan 1858 accused the defendant of altering and defacing marks on two of George Rouschart's (var. Rauschert's) hogs (value $30) with the intent of stealing them and preventing their identification on 10 Sep 1857. T. C. Bishop, George Rouschart (var. Rauschert), and Nick Long appeared as witnesses before the Grand Jury. By the direction of the Court the trial jury found the defendant not guilty on 6 Apr 1858.

---

[251] "Indictments," *The Sonoma County Journal* (Petaluma, California), 29 January 1858, p. 2, col. 1.

People v. Thomas Burns
Grand larceny (case file # 53)

The presentment filed on 14 Jan 1858 accused the defendant of stealing one yearling steer (value $30) and one yearling heifer (value $30) of Smith's on 1 Oct 1857. A. L. Boggs, John Gardner, Alexander Dunbar, W. J. Smith, and Manuel Spindola appeared as witnesses before the Grand Jury.

People v. O. P. Cash
Malicious mischief (case file # 59)

The indictment filed on 14 Jan 1858 accused the defendant of shooting and killing one of Patrick Roach's cows (value $50) on 10 May 1857. Patrick Roach, David Pierson, and J. Loyd appeared as witnesses before the Grand Jury. The trial jury found the defendant not guilty on 7 Apr 1858.

People v. M. Doyle, James Knowles, John H. Richardson, C. I. Robinson, and Samuel Kern
Assault and battery (case file # 62)

The indictment filed on 14 Jan 1858 accused the defendants of assaulting G. A. Johnson by beating him, dragging him on the ground by a rope, and besmearing him with tar on 16 Jul 1857. J. S. Field, James Crofts, and George A. Johnson appeared as witnesses before the Grand Jury. The trial jury found James Knowles guilty of an assault and the other defendants not guilty on 6 Apr 1858. The Court ordered the defendant James Knowles to pay a fine of $60 and stand committed for 30 days or until the fine was paid on 8 Apr 1858. For a related case, see case file # 35.

People v. M. Doyle, James Knowles, John H. Richardson, C. I. Robinson, and Samuel Kern
Rescue (case file # 62)

The indictment filed on 14 Jan 1858 accused the defendants of unlawfully and forcibly rescuing G. A. Johnson, charged with assault with intent to commit rape in the custody of Constable J. S. Field, on 16 Jul 1857. J. S. Field, James Crofts, and George A. Johnson appeared as witnesses before the Grand Jury. The Court sustained the defendants' demurrer and discharged the defendants on 6 Apr 1858. For a related case, see case file # 35.

People v. T. M. Leavenworth
Grand larceny (case file # 64)

The indictment filed on 14 Jan 1858 accused the defendant of stealing three of John Kendall's heifers (value $90) on 1 May 1856. John Kendall and John Morris appeared as witnesses before the Grand Jury. The Court sustained the defendant's demurrer and ordered that the indictment be resubmitted to the Grand Jury on 7 Apr 1858. The case was transmitted to the Court of Sessions of San Francisco County for trial on 6 Oct 1858.

People v. T. M. Leavenworth
Altering marks and brands (case file # 64)

The indictment filed on 14 Jan 1858 accused the defendant of altering and defacing the marks and brands on one of John Kendall's heifers (value $30) on 10 Oct 1856. J. Morris, J. Kendall, and

C. A. Johnson appeared as witnesses before the Grand Jury. The Court sustained the defendant's demurrer, and the indictment was resubmitted to the Grand Jury on 7 Apr 1858.

People v. T. M. Leavenworth
Petit larceny (case file # 64)
The indictment filed on 14 Jan 1858 accused the defendant of stealing one of C. A. Johnson's heifer calves (value $30) on 1 Oct 1856. J. Morris and C. A. Johnson appeared as witnesses before the Grand Jury. The Court sustained the defendant's demurrer, and the indictment was resubmitted to the Grand Jury on 7 Apr 1858.

People v. [?] Badger
Petit larceny (case file # 79)
The indictment filed on 14 Jan 1858 accused the defendant of stealing two coats, one pair of boots, one pair of gaiter shoes, and one vest (total value $40) belonging to J. V. Caldwell on or about 15 Jul 1857. J. V. Caldwell and J. R. Shaw appeared as witnesses before the Grand Jury.

People v. Jacob B. Palmer
Raffling (case file # 80)
The indictment filed on 14 Jan 1858 accused the defendant of unlawfully disposing of six cakes (value $60) by the throwing and counting of dice on or about 30 Dec 1857. S. May and B. Palmer appeared as witnesses before the Grand Jury. The Court sustained the defendant's demurrer and discharged the defendant on 6 Apr 1858.

April term 1858

The Court of Sessions met for nine days this term, 5–10 and 12–14 Apr 1858.[252]

Hon. William Churchman, County Judge
Hon. Thomas H. Pyatt, Associate Justice
Hon. L. D. Cockrill, Associate Justice
William G. Gordon, District Attorney
George Pearce, Acting District Attorney (appointed 9 Apr 1858)
William H. Crowell, Clerk
A. D. Merrifield, Deputy Clerk
E. L. Green, Sheriff
A. B. Nally, Under Sheriff
Daniel Rice, Deputy Sheriff
James N. Bennett, Grand Jury foreman

Persons summoned as Grand Jurors but not empaneled: A. G. Oakes (his official duties as mayor of Sonoma City compelling him to be absent), Archer Patterson (not a United States citizen),

---

[252] Sonoma County, California, Court of Sessions, Minute Book D: 45–78, April term 1858 proceedings; Sonoma County Archives, Santa Rosa.

James Nowland (his duties as constable compelling him to be absent), Robert Neeley (ill health), L. W. Olmsted (absent), William Philips (absent), B. M. Pearce (absent), and A. O. Olmstead (absent).

Grand Jurors duly sworn and empaneled on 5 Apr 1858: J. N. Bennett, J. W. Neal, W. R. O'Howell, A. S. Patterson, A. T. Perkins, J. D. Patton, J. P. Pugh, J. R. Short, G. W. Petra, John Ney, William O'Keoff, B. Newman, F. A. Parker, G. R. Perkins, Jeptha Osborn, John Barry, Merril Mise, W. M. Williamson, John Huff, and Berthold Hoen. The Court appointed J. N. Bennett as Grand Jury foreman.

Report of the Grand Jury[253]

To the Honorable Court of Sessions of the County of Sonoma, April Term,

The Grand Jury of the County of Sonoma most respectfully report, that during a session of 6 days, they have found eight indictments and one accusation.

1. Much complaint is still being made about our public roads and highways. We find them in many instances almost impassable, notwithstanding the immense amount of money and work expended in their construction and repairs. In many instances our Road Supervisors are wholly unable to know where to expend the labor and money of the County, in consequence of the roads not being legalized by the Board of Supervisors. Therefore, we recommend that there be some measures taken as soon as possible to legalize and locate the different roads of the County so as to prevent further obstruction of them.

2. We have examined the Grand Jury rooms and find them entirely unfit for the purpose, the same being entirely too small without sufficient ventilation and recommend that a door and lock be put at the foot of the stairs leading to the same.

The County Clerk's and Auditor's rooms we find to be too small and in a very unsafe condition, their doors and windows being neither provided with fastenings nor shutters. We deem it therefore essentially necessary for the safety of the County records, that said rooms be provided with iron doors and shutters.

The Courtroom we find in tolerable good condition, with the exception of the ceiling which we consider too high, and is calculated to cause an echo and destroy the sound. We therefore recommend that a false ceiling be put in some six feet lower than the present.

The Sheriff's and Judge's room, we by no means consider safe, but if provided with locks and keys, will answer for the short time the building will stand.

The Jail we are happy to state is, at present, without any occupant. The cells are kept as neat and clean as circumstances will permit, but do not consider them safe on account of the bad condition of the ceiling. To particularize all the deficiencies existing in the whole building, would take up too much time and space, we consider it a "public nuisance." The roof in all its parts is leaky, the walls cracked to such an extent, that we do not only consider the same unsafe but dangerous.

---

[253] Sonoma County, California, Court of Sessions, Report of the Grand Jury, 12 April 1858; County Records, Sonoma County, Court Records, Miscellaneous Unprocessed Records, folder "County Records – Sonoma County – Court of Sessions – Reports of the Grand Jury"; California State Archives, Sacramento.

3. We have also examined the Sheriff's books and papers and believe them to be correct and kept in a proper manner. We find that he has collected during his term of office $54,072.71 and the unpaid taxes on the "Delinquent List" amounting to some twelve or fourteen thousand dollars which will be collected as soon as possible.

The Auditor's and Assessor's Book have been kept in rather a loose manner, thereby giving the Sheriff a great deal of unnecessary labor, and find that some of our taxpayers have not been assessed at all. We would therefore recommend that the Assessor and Auditor for the present year be more punctual in making out their books in accordance with the time prescribed by law, thereby giving the Sheriff more time to collect taxes in.

We have also examined the general condition of the County Treasury, and find that as regards the duties of the office are concerned, we take pleasure in reporting that the books and official documents of that officer are kept in a clear and businesslike manner, setting forth the financial condition of the County in a precise and intelligible manner.

The general condition of the County Treasury we do not find in as healthy a condition as we would wish to report. From the last quarterly report we find that from February 6th 1857 to February 3rd 1858 liabilities to the amount of $21,928.00 have been issued on the general fund of the County, against $11,365.00 redeemed, showing an accumulation of $10,563.00 of indebtedness during the year 1857. We also find that this indebtedness has been brought about in a great measure by the increased criminal business of the County. We have reason to believe that in many cases the sessions of [the] Grand Juries and the Court of Sessions have been prolonged by frivolous and malicious charges, by which the increased liabilities of the County, in a great measure, have been created.

One great revenue of the County is the License Tax, and as we have good reason to believe that a great many persons in the County carry on business without license we invite the attention of the proper officer for the strict enforcement of the law governing this source of revenue.

In conclusion we would state, that we believe the iron safe now in use by that officer is totally unfit for the protection of the funds, books, and documents of that office and recommend a good and efficient one be procured with a view to the increase of the business of that office.

The entire indebtedness of the County on the 3rd day of February 1858 we find to be the sum of $17,938.00.

We find that the present salaries of the County Judge and District Attorney insufficient, and would recommend that our Representatives and Senator procure the passage of a law increasing the salaries of said officers.

4. While we have endeavored to promote the best interests of the County under the most extraordinary circumstances, it has become our imperative and painful duty to exercise high prerogatives as a body, believing that the line of duty was plainly dictated and that the interests of the County required it, we have taken the responsibility.

All of which is respectfully submitted.

James N. Bennett, Foreman

William N. Williamson, Clerk

Santa Rosa, April 12, 1858

The *Sonoma Democrat* added a correction to the Report of the Grand Jury when it printed the report on 12 Apr 1858.

Correction. – From subsequent examination of the books of the County Treasurer, we are satisfied, that the statement in regard to the county finances is erroneous.

The following figures are the correct ones: Amount of orders paid from Feb. 6th, 1857 to Feb. 3d, 1858, $27,913.76; amount registered during the same time, $21,928.00; present indebtedness of county about $10,000.[254]

People v. Thomas Burns

Grand larceny (case file # 53)

The indictment originally filed on 8 Jan 1858 and resubmitted to the Grand Jury on 6 Apr 1858 accused the defendant of stealing eight hogs and fourteen pigs, the property of George Rouschart (var. Rauschert) (value $50), on 15 Sep 1857. T. C. Bishop, George Rouschart (var. Rauschert), and Nick Long appeared as witnesses before the Grand Jury. The Grand Jury dismissed the indictment and charge on 10 Apr 1858.

People v. James B. Boggs

Assault and battery (case file # 81C)

The indictment filed on 10 Apr 1858 accused the defendant of assaulting A. W. Russell by unlawfully beating, wounding, and ill-treating him on 7 Apr 1858. A. W. Russell, Jackson Temple, and James M. Ellis appeared as witnesses before the Grand Jury. The defendant entered a plea of guilty on 10 Apr 1858. The Court ordered the defendant to pay a fine of $50 or be imprisoned for 25 days until the fine was paid on 12 Apr 1858. Alpheus W. Russell, the proprietor of the *Sonoma Democrat* at the time of the assault, printed a lengthy personal note in the 15 Apr 1858 edition of his newspaper which laid out the circumstances which led up to the assault and described the assault itself.

Last week while standing in the store of Ellis & Bro., in this place [Santa Rosa], I was struck with a buggy whip by a fellow by the name of Jas. B. Boggs while he, Boggs, was drunk. I was standing with my back towards him at the time he struck me in conversation with a gentleman by the name of Stump, and did not see Boggs until I was struck.[255]

People v. James Morris

Resisting an officer in the discharge of his official duties (case file # 54)

The indictment filed on 12 Apr 1858 accused the defendant of obstructing, resisting, and opposing Sonoma County Deputy Sheriff Daniel Rice, attempting to arrest John Morris, with a pistol on 27 Feb 1858. Daniel Rice and N. J. T. Long appeared as witnesses before the Grand Jury. The trial jury found the defendant not guilty on 11 Oct 1858.

People v. John Morris

Resisting an officer in the discharge of his official duties (case file # 54)

The indictment filed on 12 Apr 1858 accused the defendant of obstructing, resisting, and opposing Sonoma County Deputy Sheriff Daniel Rice, attempting to arrest John Morris, with a

---

[254] "Report of the Grand Jury," *The Sonoma Democrat* (Santa Rosa, California), 15 April 1858, p. 2, col. 4.

[255] "Personal," *The Sonoma Democrat* (Santa Rosa, California), 15 April 1858, p. 2, col. 5.

pistol on 27 Feb 1858. Daniel Rice and N. J. T. Long appeared as witnesses before the Grand Jury. The trial jury found the defendant not guilty on 11 Oct 1858.

People v. Robert Mills and Simon Taylor
False imprisonment (case file # 69)
The indictment filed on 12 Apr 1858 accused the defendants of assaulting and falsely imprisoning John Romin (var. Romine) for 48 hours on 15 Jan 1858. John Romin (var. Romine), A. T. Perkins, and C. H. Veeder appeared as witnesses before the Grand Jury. The trial jury found the defendant Robert Mills not guilty on 10 Jan 1859.

People v. James Veeder
Selling liquor to an Indian (case file # 71)
The indictment filed on 12 Apr 1858 accused the defendant of selling an Indian a bottle of whiskey (value $1) in Mendocino County on 25 Dec 1857. Stephen Rosell appeared as a witness before the Grand Jury. The trial jury returned a verdict of not guilty on 6 Jul 1858.

People v. Samuel Means
Petit larceny (case file # 73)
The indictment filed on 12 Apr 1858 accused the defendant of stealing two of James Berry's white hogs (value $40) on 30 Mar 1858. James Berry, [?] Prier, and Isaac Miller appeared as witnesses before the Grand Jury. The trial jury returned a verdict of not guilty on 6 Jul 1858.

People v. T. M. Leavenworth
Grand larceny (no. 2)
The indictment was filed on 13 Apr 1858. The case was transmitted to the Court of Sessions of San Francisco County for trial on 6 Oct 1858.

July term 1858

The Court of Sessions met for seven days this term, 5–9 and 14–15 July 1858.[256]

Hon. William Churchman, County Judge
Hon. L. D. Cockrill, Associate Justice
Hon. Thomas H. Pyatt, Associate Justice
William G. Gordon, District Attorney
William H. Crowell, Clerk
W. H. Bond, Deputy Clerk
E. L. Green, Sheriff
B. B. Munday, Grand Jury foreman

---

[256] Sonoma County, California, Court of Sessions, Minute Book D: 81–99, July term 1858 proceedings; Sonoma County Archives, Santa Rosa.

Persons duly called as Grand Jurors but not empaneled: J. Smith (absent), Thomas Slusser (absent), L. A. Sackett (absent), F. G. Wentworth (absent), E. R. Stanley (absent), James Singley (absent), Samuel West (absent), John Sharon (excused for want of qualifications as Grand Juror), Marshal Steel (excused for want of qualifications as Grand Juror), Thomas Smith (excused for want of qualifications as Grand Juror), Stephen Soule (has practiced law in the Federal courts), J. W. Stanley, G. B. Williams, James Campbell, Charles Hunt, William Potter, Ephram Denman, J. Linn, and D. A. Sackett.

Grand Jurors duly sworn and empaneled on 6 Jul 1858: B. B. Munday, J. A. Sproule, J. D. Thompson, B. Sloan, Sol. Smith, Henry Stump, J. P. Smith, Irwin R. Morris, Job Cash, John Mock, J. M. Palmer, Ezekiel Denman, Charles Hopkins, William R. Wells, Thomas Gray, William K. Rufner, Stephen Soule, Fenwick Fisher, Mathew Henderson, George Davis, Leonard Boggs, and J. Q. Shirley. B. B. Munday was elected Grand Jury foreman.

Grand Jury Report[257]

To the Hon. the Court of Sessions of Sonoma County, State of California:

We, the Grand Jury for the July term of the Court, beg leave to make the following report:

That we have enquired into and duly considered all business that has come to our notice, and have found the following bills of indictment: Two for obtaining money under false pretenses, two for assault with intent to commit great bodily injury, and one for an assault with a deadly weapon, with intent to commit murder, and one for perjury.

We have also examined the books and papers of the several county offices, and the condition of the Court House and Jail. We find the books of the present incumbent of the Clerk's Office kept in a neat and businesslike manner.

We recommend for the greater convenience of this office that the Board of Supervisors, in accordance with act 210 of the last Legislature, order at their next sitting all the back records, which are defaced, mutilated or imperfect, be newly indexed in a plain and legible style, and that they order the construction of a standing desk, and the painting of the Secretary and lower part of [the] Book Case.[258]

We find the books of the Recorder kept correctly, so far as we were able to judge upon a short examination, but not in a businesslike manner, containing many erasures, blots and interlineations.

Owing to the great accumulation of business in this office, we find the furniture insufficient, and recommend that an additional desk and book case be procured.

Upon an examination of the Jail, we find it entirely insecure, and recommend that the hall in front of the cells be planked overhead, and the wall, which is cracked, be repaired.

Upon examination of the Treasury, we find on hand the following amounts, to wit:

---

[257] "Grand Jury Report," *The Sonoma Democrat* (Santa Rosa, California), 15 July 1858, p. 2, col. 2.

[258] The "act 210" to which the Grand Jury refers was "An Act to Legalize and Amend the County Records in the Counties of this State" approved by the California Legislature on 15 April 1858 which directed the Clerk or Recorder of each County (except Sacramento, Nevada, Sierra, and Placer Counties) upon the order of the County's Board of Supervisors to make new indexes of defective County records. See, *The Statutes of California, Ninth Session*, p. 171, Chap. CCX, "An Act to Legalize and Amend the County Records in the Counties of this State."

State Fund	$5,329.77
County Fund	$452.02
Indigent Sick Fund	$96.38
Swamp and Overflowed Lands	$39.75
County Special Fund	$142.55
	$6,070.87

County School Fund, not apportioned	$880.81
County School Fund, apportioned and balance due districts	$1,312.59
	$8,263.87[259]

All of which is respectfully submitted. Having no other business before us, we ask to be discharged.

B. B. Munday, Foreman.

People v. John Dayton
Perjury (case file # 55)

The indictment filed on 8 Jul 1858 accused the defendant of falsely swearing he had no taxable property on 15 May 1858. J. A. Huffman, [?] Smith, and N. Nuckels (Sonoma County Assessor) appeared as witnesses before the Grand Jury.

People v. Edward McLaughlin
Assault with intent to commit great bodily injury (case file # 56)

The indictment filed on 8 Jul 1858 accused the defendant of assaulting Frank Fox with a knife on 20 Mar 1858.[260] Frank Fox, S. W. Brown, and Richard Harris appeared as witnesses before the Grand Jury. The Court ordered the action dismissed, and the indictment was resubmitted to the Grand Jury on 5 Oct 1858.

People v. Robert E. Harrison
Assault with intent to commit murder (case file # 65)

The indictment filed on 8 Jul 1858 accused the defendant of cutting, beating, striking, wounding, and evil-treating Lewis Freeman with a large knife on 30 Jun 1858. Silas E. Gaskill and William Johnson appeared as witnesses before the Grand Jury. The trial jury found the defendant guilty on 14 Jul 1858. The Court ordered the defendant imprisoned in the County Jail of Sonoma County for the term of three months on 15 Jul 1858.

People v. Henry S. Gird
False representation (case file # 67)

The indictment filed on 8 Jul 1858 accused the defendant of falsely representing and pretending to be a regularly elected and qualified magistrate for Washington Township and

---

[259] The math here does not add up correctly.
[260] In subsequent Court papers and newspaper accounts Frank Fox is referred to as Patrick Fox.

charging, demanding, and receiving $10 from W. S. Jarboe as fees for his services on 1 Apr 1858. W. S. Jarboe, R. R. Singley, and Charles Macpherson (var. McPherson) appeared as witnesses before the Grand Jury. On the motion of acting District Attorney Wilks, the Court ordered the case dismissed and the indictment resubmitted to the next Grand Jury on 5 Oct 1858.

People v. George Canning Smith
False representation (case file # 70)

The indictment filed on 8 Jul 1858 accused the defendant of falsely representing and pretending to be a regularly elected and qualified Justice of the Peace in and for Mendocino City, Mendocino County and unlawfully imposing and collecting a $350 fine from Charles Fletcher on 10 Sep 1857. A. W. Macpherson, W. S. Jarboe, and Charles Fletcher appeared as witnesses before the Grand Jury. On the motion of acting District Attorney Wilks, the Court ordered the case dismissed and the indictment resubmitted to the next Grand Jury on 5 Oct 1858.

People v. Charles Broback
Assault with a deadly weapon with intent to commit bodily injury (case file # 81D)

The indictment filed on 8 Jul 1858 accused the defendant of assaulting Frank Howard by beating, striking, cutting, and wounding him with a large-sized Colt revolver on 3 Jun 1858. J. Edmondson, Thomas Edmondson, and Frank Howard appeared as witnesses before the Grand Jury. The trial jury found the defendant not guilty on 9 Jul 1858.

October term 1858

The Court of Sessions met for ten days this term, 4–9 and 11–14 October 1858.[261]

Hon. William Churchman, County Judge
Hon. Thomas H. Pyatt, Associate Justice
Hon. L. D. Cockrill, Associate Justice
William G. Gordon, District Attorney
William Wilks, Acting District Attorney
William H. Crowell, Clerk
W. H. Bond, Deputy Clerk
Edward L. Green, Sheriff
J. J. Ellis, Deputy Sheriff
N. L. Allen, Grand Jury foreman

At a convention of the Justices of the Peace for Sonoma County held on 4 Oct 1858, Thomas H. Pyatt and L. D. Cockrill were elected as Associate Justices of the Court of Sessions to serve for one year.

---

[261] Sonoma County, California, Court of Sessions, Minute Book D: 102–132, October term 1858 proceedings; Sonoma County Archives, Santa Rosa.

Persons called as Grand Jurors but not empaneled: G. P. Brumfield (excused), Moses Ames (excused), E. W. Anser (excused), William Allard (excused), Frederick Alberdine (excused), Jesse Adams (excused), John Bailhache (excused), Wesley Brown (excused), William B. Atterberry (failed to answer call), John Adams, S. N. Allen, W. L. Anderson, J. A. Abbey, and M. T. Allen.

Grand Jurors sworn and empaneled on 5 Oct 1858: Lewis Adler, N. L. Allen, Isaac Gregg, George W. Brewington (var. Bruington), John Farmer, Alexander Burk (var. Burke), Simon Branstetter, Sherman Bills, J. B. Fretwell, John Abbey, James Asher, J. F. Patrick, H. N. Tedford, F. Adams, G. W. Byrd (var. Bird), James E. Crane, S. Allen, Henry Fitch, John Bowman, A. W. Russell, and G. S. Alford. The Court appointed N. L. Allen as foreman of the Grand Jury.

Simon Branstetter was excused from further service as a Grand Juror on 7 Oct 1858.

Grand Jury Report[262]

The Grand Jury empaneled for the term commencing on the 4th of October, having concluded their duties, beg leave to submit the following report.

They have given their constant attention for the last nine days, to the various duties required at their hands, as follows: They have found eight true bills and have ignored two indictments, and dismissed five complaints.

We have investigated the various county offices, and examined both the workings of the system under which they are operating, and the details of their transactions, as thoroughly as the limited time at our disposal would permit.

With one exception, we have found them admirably conducted, and feel constrained to express our gratification at the integrity, capacity and system, which mark the present administration of public affairs, especially when compared with those which we all remember as characterized by the want of system, lack of accountability, and in too many cases, by downright dishonesty.

We regret to say that the Assessor's Book is very badly made up, being impossible for anyone to make anything out of it — we feel that we cannot censure in too strong terms the want of system in making up his Book, as also his negligence in assessing, being thoroughly convinced, that there is quite an amount of property that has not been assessed.

The affairs of the county in regard to the finance, are in a prosperous condition. From all the information we can obtain from the Books of the Treasurer, compared with the books of the Sheriff, Clerk, Recorder and Auditor, we presume the present collection of taxes will clear up the indebtedness of the county; but in the absence of the Treasurer and Auditor, we are unable, without a more thorough investigation than our limited time will admit, to make a positive report. The amount of each separate fund on hand, we are unable to state, in the absence of the Treasurer.

We find the room occupied by the Recorder and Auditor, lacking in too essential requisites — being neither Burglar nor fire proof. It is difficult to estimate the amount of damage that would

---

[262] "Grand Jury Report," *The Sonoma Democrat* (Santa Rosa, California), 14 October 1858, p. 2, col. 6.

be occasioned in either instance. We trust the importance of the matter will induce the proper authorities to adopt the necessary precautions as soon as they can legally do so.

The Jury have visited the County Jail, and find it neatly kept by the present efficient keeper, but deem it insecure, and trust the proper authorities will give it their attention. We found five prisoners confined for various offences. They are provided with good and wholesome food, but are nearly destitute of bedding.

We feel that we cannot close without censuring in strong terms, the negligence of officiating magistrates throughout the county, in making out commitments, for not taking the recognizance of witnesses, holding them to appear before the Grand Jury. This negligence has cost the county hundreds of dollars at the present session of the court.

The roof of the Court House is in a defective condition. We recommend that a new one be put on before the rainy season comes on.

N. L. Allen, Foreman.

H. Fitch, Clerk.

People v. Edward McLaughlin
Assault with intent to commit great bodily injury (case file # 56)

The indictment filed on 7 Oct 1858 accused the defendant of assaulting Patrick Fox with a knife on 20 Mar 1858. Patrick Fox, S. W. Brown, and Richard Harris appeared as witnesses before the Grand Jury. The first trial jury could not agree and was discharged on 12 Oct 1858. The second trial jury found the defendant guilty on 7 Jan 1859. The Court ordered the defendant imprisoned in the State Prison for the term of six months on 10 Jan 1859. He was received by San Quentin on 14 Jan 1859 and discharged on 13 Apr 1859 after being pardoned by Governor John B. Weller.[263] The *Sacramento Daily Union* quoted the Governor as saying about McLaughlin's pardon, "The circumstances connected with the case leave an impression on my mind that he was acting in self-defense" and "His previous character was excellent, and he has a family dependent upon him for support."[264] The pardon was granted conditionally, in that, if McLaughlin violated any of the criminal laws of the State he would be remanded back to the State Prison to serve out the remainder of his term.

People v. Griffin P. Sanders (indicted as Griffith P. Sanders)
Assault with intent to commit great bodily harm (case file # 72)

The indictment filed on 8 Oct 1858 accused the defendant of assaulting Edward Fisher with a knife on 7 Oct 1858. Mrs. H. H. Russell, Mrs. Amanda Williams, Miss Josephine Williams, Dr. J. S. Williams, and Dr. C. C. Green appeared as witnesses before the Grand Jury. The trial jury found the defendant guilty of simple assault on 9 Oct 1858. The Court ordered the defendant to pay a fine of $50 or be imprisoned in the County Jail of Sonoma County until the fine was paid at the rate of $2 per day on 12 Oct 1858.

---

[263] California, State Prison Register (1851–1867), Executive Department, entry no. 1550, Ed. McLaughlin, p. 117, received 14 January 1859; California State Archives, Sacramento.

[264] "News of the Morning," *Sacramento (California) Daily Union*, 14 Apr 1859, p. 2, col. 1.

People v. George W. McFarland
Passing counterfeit gold coin (case file # 74)

The indictment filed on 8 Oct 1858 accused the defendant of passing one piece of false and counterfeit gold coin to Mary Ann Adams with the intention of defrauding her on 6 Jul 1858. Frank Adams, Mary Ann Adams, Samuel Finley, George Tilton, and L. D. Cockrill appeared as witnesses before the Grand Jury. The trial jury found the defendant not guilty on 11 Oct 1858.

People v. William Harris
Grand larceny (no. 1) (case file # 90A)

The indictment filed on 8 Oct 1858 accused the defendant of stealing James Vaughn's roan mare (value $50) on 12 Aug 1858. J. J. Lane, Samuel Thomas, M. B. Cummings, James Vaughn, Daniel Vaughn, Valentine B. Cook, and Valentine M. Cook appeared as witnesses before the Grand Jury. The *Sonoma Democrat* reported the crime as:

> A man by the name of Wm. Harris was brought before Justice Pyatt on a warrant issued by Justice Reddell of Solano Co., upon a charge of Grand Larceny. The testimony upon examination, warranted the Justice in sending the case to the Court of Sessions. Harris was committed in default of bail fixed at $1,000. It appears that on or about the 1st of August a horse was stolen from the premises of D. V. Vaughn residing a few miles from this place. Suspicion fell upon Harris, who was pursued to Benecia, where he sold the animal stolen, giving a bill of sale for the same. J. J. Lane was appointed special Constable who apprehended the prisoner, and brought him to Santa Rosa. Harris confessed stealing the horse in question, and another from the same neighborhood, which he sold in Sacramento City.[265]

The defendant pleaded guilty on 11 Oct 1858. The Court ordered the defendant imprisoned in the State Prison for the term of three years on 14 Oct 1858.

People v. William Harris
Grand larceny (no. 2) (case file # 90A)

The indictment filed on 8 Oct 1858 accused the defendant of stealing Samuel Thomas's grey horse (value $50) on 12 Aug 1858. J. J. Lane, Samuel Thomas, M. B. Cummings, James Vaughn, Daniel Vaughn, Valentine B. Cook, and Valentine M. Cook appeared as witnesses before the Grand Jury. The defendant pleaded guilty on 11 Oct 1858. The Court ordered the defendant imprisoned in the State Prison for the term of five years to commence at the expiration of the first three years he was sentenced to in the first grand larceny case on 14 Oct 1858. San Quentin received the defendant on 15 Oct 1858.[266] He was discharged on 10 May 1866.

---

[265] "Horse Thief Caught," *The Sonoma Democrat* (Santa Rosa, California), 16 September 1858, p. 2, col. 4.
[266] California, State Prison Register (1851–1867), Executive Department, entry no. 1469, William Harris, p. 106, received 15 October 1858; California State Archives, Sacramento.

People v. William (var. Bill) Rains
Assault with intent to kill (case file # 81A)

In a criminal complaint dated 19 Aug 1858 Frank W. Shattuck accused the defendant of stabbing Gallant Rains with a knife or some other deadly instrument in Petaluma Township on 18 Aug 1858. The Grand Jury found no bill and presented the discharge of the defendant on 9 Oct 1858. On 20 Aug 1858 the *Sonoma County Journal* reported the affair as:

> Last Wednesday evening [18 Aug 1858], about 10 o'clock, as Mr. Gallant Rains, and his son William Rains, who live some three miles from town, were on their way home from this city [Petaluma], they got into an altercation, when the old man pronounced the son a thief. Thereupon the young man "pitched in," knocked the old man down, and drawing a pocket knife inflicted two severe cuts in the left side. Young Rains fled back to town, where he was arrested. We are told both father and son were intoxicated at the time of the affray. The wounds, it is feared, will prove fatal.[267]

A week later the same newspaper reported that the defendant had failed to post a bond and had been committed to the county jail, while his father, Gallant Rains, "upon whose person his son William performed a very bad surgical operation," was "very much better" and would "recover from his injuries to the satisfaction of his two wives and numerous progeny."[268]

People v. Louis Piña
Gaming (case file # 90G)

The indictment filed on 9 Oct 1858 accused the defendant of permitting a banking game called monte to be conducted for money at the defendant's house in Mendocino County on 22 Sep 1858. John B. Regan and Henry Fitch appeared as witnesses before the Grand Jury.

People v. Phillips Williams
Gaming (case file # 90I)

The indictment filed on 9 Oct 1858 accused the defendant of conducting a banking game called monte for money in a house owned by Louis Piña on 23 Sep 1858. John B. Regan (var. Reagan) appeared as a witness before the Grand Jury.

People v. Cardelia and Laventina (Indians)
No charges stated

The Grand Jury presented their discharge of the defendants on 9 Oct 1858.

People v. Lewis W. Freeman
Grand larceny (case file # 66)

The indictment filed on 13 Oct 1858 accused the defendant of stealing Timothy McGuire's horse (value $50) on 30 May 1858. John Ellis, Jefferson Thompson, Willis Zane, W. H. Wilson, W. M. Shomake, and W. M. Clay appeared as witnesses before the Grand Jury. The defendant

---

[267] "Cutting Affair," *The Sonoma County Journal* (Petaluma, California), 20 August 1858, p. 2, col. 1.
[268] "Committed," *The Sonoma County Journal* (Petaluma, California), 27 August 1858, p. 2, col. 1. "Better," *The Sonoma County Journal* (Petaluma, California), 27 August 1858, p. 2, col. 1.

pleaded guilty on 13 Oct 1858. The Court ordered the defendant imprisoned in the State Prison for the term of four years on 14 Oct 1858. He was received by San Quentin on 15 Oct 1858, but taken to the Stockton State Hospital insane asylum on 16 Jul 1859.[269] The hospital's commitment register noted that Freeman, a 40-year-old, married, American with no property, was committed by Governor John B. Weller and that he had been insane for six months.[270] He was returned to prison by order of Governor John G. Downey less than a year later on 4 Jun 1860. He escaped from San Quentin on 5 Sep 1860, returned again on 23 Jun 1862, and was finally discharged on 15 Oct 1862.

January term 1859

The Court of Sessions met for eleven days this term, 3–8, 10–13, and 17 Jan 1859.[271]

Hon. William Churchman, County Judge
Hon. L. D. Cockrill, Associate Justice
Hon. Thomas H. Pyatt, Associate Justice
William Ross, District Attorney
Otho Hinton, Special District Attorney
William H. Crowell, Clerk
W. H. Bond, Deputy Clerk
E. L. Green, Sheriff
William Farmer, Grand Jury foreman

Persons called as Grand Jurors but not empaneled: William Conley (excused), James Clark (excused), F. H. Coe (excused), G. A. Cook (excused), James Clyman (excused for being too old for service), Thomas Carson (failed to answer call), and H. J. Clayton (failed to answer call, later excused).

Grand Jurors sworn and empaneled on 3 Jan 1859: John Cavenaugh (var. Cavanagh), James E. Crane, William Farmer, Lancaster Clyman, James G. Cook, John B. Cook, C. W. Brown, S. H. Carriger, George Hawkins, J. W. Calhoun, J. G. Chatham, J. B. Fretwell, J. A. Campbell, Joshua Chadborn, C. Coston, George Davis, E. J. Carson, Winfield Wright, Oliver Craig, and B. Hoen. The Court appointed William Farmer as foreman of the Grand Jury.

---

[269] California, State Prison Register (1851–1867), Executive Department, entry no. 1468, Lewis W. Freeman, pp. 105, 154, and 198, received 15 October 1858; California State Archives, Sacramento.
[270] California, Stockton State Hospital, Commitment Register 1: 445, entry no. 668, Lewis W. Freeman, imaged in "California, State Hospital Records, 1856–1923," database with images, *Ancestry* (http://www.ancestry.com : accessed 5 December 2018), path: Stockton State Hospital > Commitment Registers, vol. 01–02, 1852–1862 > image 233 of 401; California State Archives, Sacramento.
[271] Sonoma County, California, Court of Sessions, Minute Book D: 134–161, January term 1859 proceedings; Sonoma County Archives, Santa Rosa.

Winfield Wright was excused from further service as a Grand Juror on 5 Jan 1859. J. A. Campbell was excused from further service as a Grand Juror on account of sickness in his family on 10 Jan 1859.

Report of the Grand Jury[272]

To the Hon. the Court of Sessions of Sonoma County,

We, the Grand Jury for the January term of the Court, 1859, beg leave to report that they have inquired into and duly considered all business that have come to our notice, and have found the following indictments, to wit, one for manslaughter, one for perjury, two for misdemeanor.

We have also examined the books and papers of the several county offices and also the condition of the Court House and Jail.

We find the books of the County Clerk kept in a neat and businesslike manner and also the books of the Recorder's office.

We are happy to say that the iron shutters on the above offices lately put on adds greatly to the security of the public records, and we would also recommend that the Board of Supervisors order iron doors on those two offices.

We also find that the County Treasurer's office is not kept in the County buildings and that the Board of Supervisors pay rent for the above offices. We therefore recommend that some suitable office be appropriated in the County buildings for the said office. We find from the report of the Treasurer that the finances of the County are in a better condition than we had reason to expect. Deducting the amount now called in for redemption will only leave a balance against the County of six thousand and five hundred or seven thousand dollars on the first of January 1859 which will be more reduced by the collection of taxes yet due to the County.

We find that some revenue due the County accruing from the probate business has not been paid into the Treasury as promptly as could be desired and call the attention of the officer whose duty it is to collect the same to the law governing this source of revenue. We find from the report of the Sheriff that the total amount of taxes for the last year charged to the Sheriff is $87,557. [The] amount collected and paid over to the Treasurer is $67,867. [The] amount yet in the Sheriff's hand is $2,500, leaving a balance not collected of $17,190.

We find the interior arrangement of the Court House not suited nor answering the purpose intended. All the different rooms excepting the Court room we find to[o] small and inconvenient. The Court room we believe to be to[o] large and ill-constructed. We believe the House amply large and substantial to admit of room and convenience and also a successful remodeling of the interior arrangement. We therefore recommend to the consideration of the Board of Supervisors a continuation of the floor above the Clerk's and Recorder's office through the whole building and by that means create a second story which would give ample room for the different offices at the same time improving the Court room.

The Jail we find in a secure and clean condition.

---

[272] Sonoma County, California, Court of Sessions, Report of the Grand Jury January Term 1859, filed 12 January 1859; County Records, Sonoma County, Court Records, Miscellaneous Unprocessed Records, folder "County Records – Sonoma County – Court of Sessions – Reports of the Grand Jury"; California State Archives, Sacramento. "Grand Jury Report," *The Sonoma Democrat* (Santa Rosa, California), 20 January 1859, p. 3, col. 2.

We recommend for the better protection of certain records of brands and marks of stock which are now in a dilapidated condition in the Recorder's office. We recommend an appropriation for the binding or transcribing of them.

All of which is respectfully submitted. We, the Grand Jury, now ask to be discharged.

William Farmer, Foreman

People v. Louis Piña
Gaming (case file # 90G)

The indictment filed on 4 Jan 1859 accused the defendant of permitting Phil Williams to conduct a game played for money called monte in his house on 23 Sep 1858. John B. Reagan appeared as a witness before the Grand Jury. The Court ordered a *nolle prosequi* entered on 4 Jan 1859.

People v. Phil Williams
Gaming (case file # 90I)

The indictment filed on 4 Jan 1859 accused the defendant of conducting a banking game played with cards called monte for money on 23 Sep 1858. John B. Reagan (var. Regan) appeared as a witness before the Grand Jury.

People v. Nathaniel Brown (a colored man)
No charges stated

The Grand Jury dismissed the charge on 7 Jan 1859.

People v. John J. Domes
Manslaughter

The indictment filed on 10 Jan 1859 accused the defendant of assaulting James Hollis with a knife giving him eight mortal wounds which killed him immediately on 25 Dec 1857.[273] W. H. Levally (var. Levalley), M. Fogerty (var. Foggerty), D. M. Smith, J. W. Hartman, William S. Thurogood (var. Thurgood), J. G. Heald, R. Harrison, W. C. Andrews, James Neal, Thomas Broomfield (var. Brumfield), Bird Broomfield (var. Brumfield), and H. S. Engle appeared as witnesses before the Grand Jury. On 31 Dec 1857, the *Sonoma Democrat* reported the fatal assault as:

> We learn that on the evening of the 25th of December, an affray took place in the ball-room at Healdsburg, between James Hollis and J. J. Domes in which the former was almost instantly killed by the latter. Hollis received eight stabs in quick succession in the region of the heart and lived but a few moments. The weapon was a large knife. Hon. Richard Harrison and Gen. Wm. Hartman in attempting to quell the fight, we are sorry to learn, were severely cut, each having received an ugly wound on the left wrist. Domes immediately escaped and has not yet been arrested.

---

[273] Sonoma County, California, District Court, case # 926 (OS), The People v. John Domes, indictment, filed 10 January 1859; County Records, Sonoma County, Court Records, District Court case files; California State Archives, Sacramento.

The circumstances leading to the above encounter were as near as we can learn as follows: Sometime over a year ago, Hollis married a Mrs. Claytor, who, after living with him two or three month[s], left him, since which time she has been living in the family of a respectable citizen of the county, where she got acquainted with Domes, who persisted in marked attentions to her. She went with Domes to the ball on the night of the affray, Hollis being there also. Hollis, it seems, was very much annoyed by Domes' attention to his wife, and some say, forbade her dancing with him, to which however she paid but little attention; and when requested by her husband to dance, she positively refused. On being thus abruptly rejected, he caught hold of her arm, when Domes interfered, which led to a fight, the consequence of which is seen above.

Immediately, on the occurrence of the difficulty, Dr. Bamford of Healdsburg was called in, who rendered every possible assistance. Dr. Bamford added much to the esteem with which he has heretofore been regarded by the promptness and skill with which he ministered to the wants of the wounded. Dr. Boyce of Santa Rosa, also being sent for, arrived at the scene of suffering in time to render valuable assistances, an express having ridden from Healdsburg, and the Doctor returned to that place in three hours from the time of the difficulty.[274]

Domes went to Alameda County after the Grand Jury ignored the bill against him the first time they examined this case on 9 Jan 1858.[275] He was arrested there by Sheriff Green by 4 Feb 1859 and brought back to Sonoma County to be tried. Emily Hollis, the widow of the man Domes had killed, followed him to Alameda County. They were married in the neighboring county of Contra Costa.[276] The case was transmitted to the Sonoma County District Court on 10 Jan 1859. See Sonoma County District Court case # 926 (OS). The District Court trial jury found the defendant guilty on 23 Feb 1859.[277] The District Court sentenced him to six years' imprisonment in the State Prison on 28 Feb 1859.[278] San Quentin received him on 1 Mar 1859.[279] Governor John B. Weller pardoned Domes on 7 Jan 1860 after receiving letters in support of Domes's pardon application from Elam Brown, a neighbor of Domes, William Ross, one of Domes's defense attorneys, and E. L. Green, the former Sheriff of Sonoma County. The Governor noted on the back of Brown's letter:

This man was convicted of manslaughter. His character had always been that of a peaceable and orderly citizen. The circumstances connected with the homicide satisfy me

[274] "Fatal Affray in Healdsburg – One Man Killed and Two Others Wounded," *The Sonoma Democrat* (Santa Rosa, California), 31 December 1857, p. 2, col. 6.

[275] "Again Under Arrest," *The Sonoma County Journal* (Petaluma, California), 4 Feb 1859, p. 2, col. 1.

[276] Contra Costa County, California, Index to Marriage Certificates – Men (May 1851–July 1928, surnames A–M), p. 69, J. J. Domes to Emily L. Hollis, filed 28 April 1858; image, *FamilySearch* (http://www.familysearch.org : accessed 22 December 2018); DGS 7729974, image 579 of 763; FHL microfilm # 1,294,354, item 6.

[277] "District Court," *Sonoma County Democrat* (Santa Rosa, California), 24 February 1859, p. 3, col. 1. Sonoma County, California, District Court, Minute Book B: 182, People v. John Domes, trial jury verdict, 23 February 1859; Sonoma County Archives, Santa Rosa.

[278] "Sentenced," *The Sonoma County Journal* (Petaluma, California), 4 March 1859, p. 2, col. 1. Sonoma County, California, District Court, Minute Book B: 205, People v. John Domes, sentence, 28 February 1859; Sonoma County Archives, Santa Rosa.

[279] California, State Prison Register (1851–1867), Executive Department, entry no. 1582, Jno. Domes, p. 123, received 1 March 1859; California State Archives, Sacramento.

that if all the evidence had been before the jury he would have been acquitted. Let him be pardoned.[280]

People v. James Arlington Delahanty (alias James Arlington)
Perjury (case file # 81B)

The indictment filed on 12 Jan 1859 accused the defendant of giving false testimony concerning the sale of a black cow in the case of James Weir v. Delahanty and Smith in Justice Lewis C. Reyburn's Court in Petaluma Township on 22 Oct 1858. L. C. Reyburn, Edward Latapie, George W. M. Cowles, James Weir, Thomas W. Flavell, and R. K. Smith appeared as witnesses before the Grand Jury. The trial jury found the defendant guilty and recommended him to the mercy of the Court on 5 Apr 1859. The Court ordered the defendant imprisoned in the State Prison for the term of seven years on 9 Apr 1859. The *Sonoma County Democrat* said of the conviction on 14 Apr 1859, "It is so remarkable a circumstance for a man to be convicted of perjury, and punished for it, that we are almost half inclined to believe there is some mistake about it, in some way. But nevertheless, it seems to be true."[281] Delahanty was received by San Quentin on 11 Apr 1859 and died while in prison on 21 Jan 1860.[282] His death and burial at San Quentin were described in a letter dated 23 Jan 1860 that Peter Campbell, a former Justice of the Peace of Sonoma County who had been appointed the head of the medical department of San Quentin, sent to the *Sonoma County Journal*.

> I regret to have to announce to you the demise of your old neighbor Delahanty, the butcher who was buried yesterday [22 Jan 1860]. Since his despair of obtaining a pardon, he sunk gradually, still refusing to enter the Hospital, but enfeebled from acute rheumatism and disease of the viscera, he sunk gradually, until Saturday evening [21 Jan 1860] he died of spasms of the abdomen. If he has any property in Petaluma I should be happy to learn.[283]

April term 1859

The Court of Sessions met for 22 days this term, 4–9, 11–12, and 25–30 April 1859 and 2–7 and 9–10 May 1859.[284]

Hon. William Churchman, County Judge
Hon. Thomas H. Pyatt, Associate Justice
Hon. L. D. Cockrill, Associate Justice

---

[280] California, Pardon Applications, pardon application file # 1355, John J. Domes, Elam Brown to Governor Weller, letter in support of John Domes's pardon application, 6 December 1859; Governor's Office records, Applications for Pardon, Historical Case Files (1850–ca. 1935); California State Archives, Sacramento.

[281] "Sentenced," *Sonoma County Democrat* (Santa Rosa, California), 14 April 1859, p. 2, col. 1.

[282] California, State Prison Register (1851–1867), Executive Department, entry no. 1615, James Arlington Delahanty, p. 127, received 11 April 1859; California State Archives, Sacramento.

[283] Peter Campbell, "Letter from Prison," *The Sonoma County Journal* (Petaluma, California), 27 January 1860, p. 2, col. 4.

[284] Sonoma County, California, Court of Sessions, Minute Book D: 163–189 and 191–225, April term 1859 proceedings; Sonoma County Archives, Santa Rosa.

William Ross, District Attorney
R. C. Flournoy, District Attorney Assistant (appointed by the Court 5 Apr 1859)
William H. Crowell, Clerk
Edward L. Green, Sheriff
R. E. Smith, Grand Jury foreman

Persons called as Grand Jurors but not empaneled: Edward Purdy (not a resident of Sonoma County) and Joseph McMinn (over the age of 60 years).

Grand Jurors sworn and empaneled on 4 Apr 1859: Thomas W. Ingram, M. B. Cummins, Thomas. M. Jones, James Hearn, Caleb Brooks, Joel Crane, A. S. Johnson, Holman Talbot (var. Talbott), Joseph Hastings, William Manion, M. Hayes, J. A. Bradshaw, C. W. Mathews (var. Matthews), J. E. Davidson, George Greegg (var. Gregg), Robert E. Smith, Richard Mayes, Richard Fulkerson, Elijah Dooley, John Powell, J. M. Patrick, and C. C. Money. The Court appointed Robert E. Smith as foreman of the Grand Jury.

Report of the Grand Jury[285]

To the Hon. Court of Sessions of the County of Sonoma, State of California,
The Grand Jury beg leave to make the following report: After a session of eight days, we have inquired into all offences brought to our knowledge, and report eight true bills of indictment. We further report that we have examined into the condition of the County Jail, and find it well kept, but very insecure, and requiring to be constantly guarded. We have examined into the condition of the County Treasury, as far as our time would permit, and find the county money on hand, exclusive of school fund, to be $2,812.36. Outstanding warrants, $7,309.65, to which may be added warrants in the hands of the Auditor not issued amounting to about $700, making the county debt $8,000.
We would call the attention of the Board of Supervisors to the small and crowded condition of the County Offices, and recommend that the Court House be so altered and repaired as to meet the wants of the public.
We recommend to the Board of Supervisors that they put the entire labor at their command upon the public roads in the county, before the next rainy season.
We believe that the practice of horse-racing as at present practiced in this State, tends far more to demoralize and degrade the race of man, than it does to improve the breed of horses, believing that a healthy state of morals is far more needed, and of infinitely more value than any quality or condition of horseflesh.
R. E. Smith, Foreman.

---

[285] "Court of Sessions – April Term, 1859," *The Sonoma County Journal* (Petaluma, California), 15 April 1859, p. 2, col. 5.

People v. Antonio Valasques (var. Valasquez, Velasquez)
Petit larceny (case file # 90)

The indictment filed on 6 Apr 1859 accused the defendant of stealing J. J. Johnson's horse (value $35) on 18 Mar 1859. William Fitch, J. J. Johnson, David Morton, Robert Morton, and Jose Mendoza appeared as witnesses before the Grand Jury. The defendant pleaded guilty on 7 Apr 1859. The Court ordered the defendant imprisoned in the County Jail of Sonoma County for the term of five months on 9 Apr 1859.

People v. John W. Ball, George H. Morrison (alias Tim Ryan), Frank Ward, and William S. Brown (colored)
Grand larceny (case file #s 85 and 90D)

The indictment filed on 7 Apr 1859 accused the defendants of stealing $3,000 of Berthold Hoen's goods and chattels on 7 Nov 1858. Berthold Hoen, Rachel Valley, Louis Mahoney, John Derrick, James C. Russell, William R. Smith, and [James L.] Broadus appeared as witnesses before the Grand Jury. The *Sonoma County Democrat* gave an account of the crime on 11 Nov 1858.

> On Sunday evening last [7 Nov 1858], our community was thrown into quite an excitement, owing to a most daring and extensive robbery, that took place about 8 o'clock in the evening. It seems that one day last week, our fellow townsman, Berthold Hoen, received some $3,500 in cash, in payment for some county script, which was placed in a wallet and deposited in a place of safe keeping. County warrants amounting to $1,500, and promissory notes amounting to $4,000, were deposited in a bureau – in all, amounting to about $9,000.
>
> On Sunday evening, a number of persons spent the evening with Mr. Hoen, who is an accomplished musician, and entertained his visitors with his music. About eight o'clock the company dispersed, and Mr. H. along with the crowd, walked down to Main street. But he had scarcely been absent from the house five minutes, when it was entered by two men, both masked. One of them, with a long knife drawn, approached Mrs. R. Vally, the landlady, and threatened her with instant death, if she made any resistance or alarm. Whilst he kept guard over her, the other villain, who, it seems, knew where to find the money, secured the wallet containing the amount specified above ($100 of which belonged to Mrs. Vally) and the papers. They then left the house, and the lady gave the alarm.[286]

The defendants demanded separate trials on 9 Apr 1859. The trial jury found the defendant John W. Ball guilty on 28 Apr 1859, and the Court ordered the defendant imprisoned in the State Prison for the term of ten years on 3 May 1859. He was received by San Quentin on 5 May 1859, but released back into the custody of the Sheriff of Sonoma County on 15 Oct 1859 after appealing to the California Supreme Court, which, during its October term 1859, reversed the judgment and remanded the cause back to the Court of Sessions for further proceedings on the grounds that the indictment's description of the property stolen ("three thousand dollars, lawful

---

[286] "Two Thousand Dollars Reward!," *Sonoma County Democrat* (Santa Rosa, California), 11 November 1858, p. 2, col. 1.

money of the United States") was not sufficient.[287] The Court of Sessions sustained the defendant's demurrer, set the indictment aside, and ordered the defendant to be discharged on 12 Nov 1859.

The trial jury found the defendant George H. Morrison (alias Tim Ryan) guilty on 30 Apr 1859, and the Court ordered the defendant imprisoned in the State Prison for the term of ten years on 4 May 1859. The *Sonoma County Democrat* gave a lengthy account of his trial in its 12 May 1859 edition.[288] He was received by San Quentin on 5 May 1859, but taken out by an order of the County Judge of Sonoma County on 8 Feb 1860 and never returned.[289] On 18 Jan 1860, the California Supreme Court reversed the judgment of the lower court and remanded the cause back to the Court of Sessions, deciding that the indictment had been "fatally defective within the principle of the People vs. Ball, decided at the last term."[290] Morrison petitioned Judge Churchman for a writ of habeas corpus on 6 Feb 1860 on the grounds that his recent appeal to the California Supreme Court had been successful and he was being illegally held at San Quentin. Judge Churchman ordered the writ to issue on 7 Feb 1860.[291] When Morrison appeared before the Court of Sessions on 9 Feb 1860 the indictment was dismissed, and he was discharged.

The trial jury found the defendant Frank Ward guilty on 5 May 1859, and the Court ordered the defendant imprisoned in the State Prison for the term of ten years on 7 May 1859. He was received at San Quentin on 11 May 1859.[292] Governor John G. Downey pardoned Ward on 11 Jul 1861, citing the facts that Ward had been convicted with John W. Ball and others mainly upon the evidence of Lewis Mahoney, "a pardoned State Prison convict, who has subsequently denied the truth of the evidence given by him" and that Ball's test case to the California Supreme resulted in Ball's discharge.[293]

The trial jury found the defendant William S. Brown guilty on 3 May 1859, and the Court ordered the defendant imprisoned in the State Prison for the term of ten years on 6 May 1859.

---

[287] For the San Quentin dates, California, State Prison Register (1851–1867), Executive Department, entry no. 1636, John W. Ball, p. 129, received 5 May 1859; California State Archives, Sacramento. For the California Supreme Court case and decision, California, Supreme Court, case file # 2489 (WPA # 7353), The People v. John W. Ball, October term 1859; California State Archives, Sacramento. John B. Harmon, reporter, *Reports of Cases Determined in the Supreme Court of the State of California*, vol. 14, 2nd edition (San Francisco: Bancroft-Whitney Company, 1887), 113–114, *The People* v. *Ball* (1859).

[288] "Trial of Morrison, alias Ryan," *Sonoma County Democrat* (Santa Rosa, California), 12 May 1859, p. 1, cols. 5–6 and p. 2, cols. 1–4.

[289] California, State Prison Register (1851–1867), Executive Department, entry no. 1637, Geo. H. Morrison, p. 129, received 5 May 1859; California State Archives, Sacramento.

[290] "Supreme Court Decisions, January Term, 1860," *Sacramento (California) Daily Union*, 20 January 1860, p. 4, col. 2. California, Supreme Court, Minute Book E: 103, People v. Morrison, decision, 18 January 1860; California State Archives, Sacramento.

[291] L. D. Latimer on behalf of George H. Morrison (alias Tim Ryan) to the Hon. William Churchman, County Judge of Sonoma County, petition for writ of habeas corpus, 6 February 1860; County Records, Sonoma County, Court Records, Miscellaneous Unprocessed Records, folder "Miscellaneous to be interfiled – District (1)"; California State Archives, Sacramento.

[292] California, State Prison Register (1851–1867), Executive Department, entry no. 1640, Frank Ward, p. 130, received 11 May 1859; California State Archives, Sacramento.

[293] *The Journal of the Assembly, Thirteenth Session*, 62. Ward's pardon is enumerated in the list of pardons contained in the appendix to the Governor's annual message to the Senate and Assembly dated 8 January 1862.

He was received at San Quentin on 11 May 1859.[294] Governor John G. Downey pardoned Brown on 11 Jul 1861, citing the facts that Brown had been convicted with John W. Ball and others mainly upon the evidence of Lewis Mahoney, "a pardoned State Prison convict, who has subsequently denied the truth of the evidence given by him" and that Ball's test case to the California Supreme resulted in Ball's discharge.[295]

People v. John W. Ball, George H. Morrison (alias Tim Ryan), Frank Ward, and William S. Brown (colored)
Burglary (case file #s 85 and 90D)
The indictment filed on 7 Apr 1859 accused the defendants of breaking and entering the dwelling house of Rachel Valley with the intent of stealing Berthold Hoen's goods and chattels (value $5,000) on 7 Nov 1858. The defendants demanded separate trials on 9 Apr 1859. The defendant John W. Ball's cause was transmitted to the Court of Sessions of Napa County for trial on 8 Nov 1859. The Court ordered the indictment against the defendant George H. Morrison (alias Tim Ryan) dismissed on 9 Feb 1860 because the principal witness, Louis Mahoney, had been rendered incompetent to testify by reason of a felony conviction. Mahoney had been convicted of grand larceny in the Court of Sessions of San Francisco County for stealing a horse and sentenced to four years' imprisonment in the State Prison on 4 Feb 1860.[296]

People v. James S. Oldham (indicted as Sim Oldham)
Murder in the 2nd degree
The indictment filed on 8 Apr 1859 accused the defendant of murdering Thomas Banning by shooting him in the left breast with a pistol killing him instantly on 18 Jan 1859.[297] M. J. Buck [James M. Buck], Milton Brown, Joseph McCracken, J. H. Wassam (var. Wassum), J. M. Dodge, Jesse Talbott, R. Vanderford, and William Patterson appeared as witnesses before the Grand Jury. The *Sonoma County Journal* described the shooting in its 21 Jan 1859 edition as:

> Last Saturday evening [15 Jan 1859], between 6 and 7 o'clock, at the Petaluma Race Course, in Vallejo township, an altercation occurred between Sim Oldham and Tom Bannan, which resulted in the death of the latter.
>
> It appears that while the parties, with several friends, were taking a drink, Bannan took exception to some remark made by Oldham, and commenced throwing glasses. Oldham immediately retreated from the house, accompanied by a friend, while Mr. Brown and others prevented Bannan from following him. Friends here interfered, and as they supposed, settled the difficulty, Bannan in the meantime having left the house, as was supposed, for home. Oldham and friends then returned to the house to take another drink, during which Bannan reentered, stepped up to the bar, and asked in an insulting

---

[294] California, State Prison Register (1851–1867), Executive Department, entry no. 1639, Wm. S. Brown, p. 130, received 11 May 1859; California State Archives, Sacramento.

[295] *The Journal of the Assembly, Thirteenth Session*, 63. Brown's pardon is enumerated in the list of pardons contained in the appendix to the Governor's annual message to the Senate and Assembly dated 8 January 1862.

[296] "Court of Sessions," *Daily Alta California* (San Francisco, California), 5 February 1860, p. 1, col. 8.

[297] Sonoma County, California, District Court, case # 540 (OS), The People of the State of California v. Sim Oldham, indictment, filed 8 April 1859; County Records, Sonoma County, Court Records, District Court case files; California State Archives, Sacramento.

tone, why they were drinking without him? Oldham again stepped toward the door, urged on by a friend, and as he was stepping from the threshold asked, "Tom Bannan, what did you mean by throwing those glasses at me?" To which Bannan replied with a curse, "I meant it," or to that effect. Oldham who was at this time clasped around the waist by a friend, and being hurried into the open air, remarked, "Tom Bannan, you are a damned thief, and I can prove it!" Upon which Bannan sprung toward him, at the same time drawing a knife, furnished him after the first dispute by one Sidney Rathburn. Oldham's right arm being free, he immediately drew his pistol and fired over the shoulder of the man who held him. The shot proved fatal, the ball passing through Bannan's heart. At the time of receiving the wound, Bannan was so near the opposite party, that, dropping the knife, he caught hold of them, and simply remarking "don't let him do it," sank to the earth and instantly expired. To Bannan's entreaty, "don't let him do it," Oldham replied, "Well, don't let him shoot me, then," from which (it being after sundown) it is presumed Oldham supposed him to have been armed with a pistol.

Oldham came to town and gave himself up to Deputy Marshal Latapie. The examination took place on Tuesday and Wednesday [18 and 19 Jan 1859], before Justice Reyburn, and resulted in Oldham's discharge.

The prosecution was conducted by District Attorney Ross, assisted by F. W. Shattuck, Esq.; and the defense by J. B. Southard, Esq.

Deceased, who was a man of family, having a wife and four children residing near the Half Way House, on the Santa Rosa road, was but recently from Oregon, where he and Oldham had long resided, claiming to be warm friends, which facts make the recent transaction the more surprising and mysterious.[298]

The case was transmitted to the Sonoma County District Court for trial on 8 Apr 1859. See Sonoma County District Court case # 540 (OS). After a trial heard before the Hon. J. H. McCune, the judge of the 6th District Court, at the request of the Hon. Elisha W. McKinstry, the trial jury found the defendant not guilty on 22 Jun 1859.[299]

People v. Daniel Brown
Mayhem
The Grand Jury dismissed the charge on 8 Apr 1859.

People v. John W. Ball, George H. Morrison (alias Tim Ryan), Frank Ward, and William S. Brown (colored)
Robbery (case file #s 85 and 90D)
The Court ordered the indictment against the defendants George H. Morrison (alias Tim Ryan) and John W. Ball dismissed on 9 Feb 1860 because the principal witness, Louis Mahoney, had been rendered incompetent to testify by reason of a felony conviction. Mahoney had been convicted of grand larceny in the Court of Sessions of San Francisco County for stealing a horse and sentenced to four years' imprisonment in the State Prison on 4 Feb 1860.[300]

---

[298] "Homicide," *The Sonoma County Journal* (Petaluma, California), 21 January 1859, p. 2, col. 2.
[299] Sonoma County, California, District Court, Minute Book B: 251, The People of the State of California v. James S. Oldham, jury verdict, 22 June 1859; Sonoma County Archives, Santa Rosa.
[300] "Court of Sessions," *Daily Alta California* (San Francisco, California), 5 February 1860, p. 1, col. 8.

People v. Frank Ward
Grand larceny (no. 2) (case file # 90J)

The indictment filed on 9 Apr 1859 accused the defendant of stealing Dudley D. Myers's dark bay horse (value $100) on 18 Sep 1858. Louis Mahoney and Dudley D. Myers appeared as witnesses before the Grand Jury.

People v. James McGowan (alias James Connelly) and Joseph H. Ball
Grand larceny (case file # 87)

The indictment filed on 11 Apr 1859 accused the defendants of stealing $700 of Anthony G. Oakes's gold coins on 9 Jun 1858. Anthony G. Oakes, William Ellis, Louis Mahoney, Ive D. Long, and [William F.] Franklin appeared as witnesses before the Grand Jury. The first trial jury of the defendant Joseph H. Ball could not agree on a verdict on 6 May 1859. A second trial jury found him not guilty on 9 May 1859. The Court discharged the defendant James McGowan (alias James Connelly) after it was proven in Court that, although bearing the same name, he was not the man charged in the indictment.[301]

People v. James Watson
Assault with a deadly weapon with intent to commit bodily injury (case file # 90H)

The indictment filed on 12 Apr 1859 accused the defendant of assaulting James Crittenden with a Bowie knife on 1 Sep 1858. James Crittenden, Jackson Welch, and Lafayette Lansdon appeared as witnesses before the Grand Jury. The trial jury found the defendant not guilty on 8 Nov 1859.

August term 1859

The Court of Sessions met for eight days this term, 1–6 and 8–9 August 1859.[302]

Hon. William Churchman, County Judge
Hon. L. D. Cockrill, Associate Justice
Hon. Thomas H. Pyatt, Associate Justice
William Ross, District Attorney
William H. Crowell, Clerk
E. L. Green, Sheriff
William Farmer, Grand Jury foreman

Persons called as Grand Jurors but not empaneled: F. H. Farley (excused), George McFadden (excused), S. C. Fowler (excused), Ransom Powell (excused), E. A. Rexford (excused), James Fulton (did not answer call), W. W. Ferguson (did not answer call), William Ellis (did not answer call), and J. V. Caldwell (did not answer call).

---

[301] "Court of Sessions," *The Sonoma Democrat* (Santa Rosa, California), 12 May 1859, p. 2, col. 5.
[302] Sonoma County, California, Court of Sessions, Minute Book D: 226–242, August term 1859 proceedings; Sonoma County Archives, Santa Rosa.

Grand Jurors duly sworn and empaneled on 1 Aug 1859: Joseph Ganson, D. P. Fouts, O. F. Ellsworth, J. Holt Fine, Nathan Fike, William F. Franklin, S. C. Hendy, W. A. Eliason, Colman Talbot, John Underhill, William Farmer, I. A. Bradshaw, M. Tarwater, C. C. Money, B. B. Monday, and William E. Cocke.[303] The Court appointed William Farmer as Grand Jury foreman.

Grand Jury Report[304]

Santa Rosa, Aug. 6th, 1859.
To the Hon. the Court of Sessions:
We, the Grand Jury of the County of Sonoma, for the August term of the Court of Sessions, would respectfully submit the following Report:
We have found true bills of indictment for the following crimes, viz.: one for assault and battery, two for grand larceny, and one for assault with intent to kill.
We have examined the County Jail. There are five persons confined in it; one for grand larceny, two for petty larceny, and one held by the requisition of the Court as a witness, subject to bail.
We have examined the books and records of the county, and would recommend that hereafter, there should be a more strict monthly and quarterly settlement between the Auditor's, Sheriff's, and Treasurer's departments.
We have examined the Public Buildings, and are convinced of the necessity of enlarging the Court House, and the erection of a building for the County Jail, which work is now being done.
All of which is respectfully submitted.
No business appearing before us, we respectfully ask to be discharged.
Wm. Farmer, Foreman.

People v. William Harris
Grand larceny (case file # 90A)
The indictment filed on 2 Aug 1859 accused the defendant of stealing James D. Thompson's pinto sorrel mare branded "T. B." on its right hip (value $75) on 3 Jul 1859. James D. Thompson, James Black, and [John M.] Lightner appeared as witnesses before the Grand Jury. The *Sonoma County Journal* reported his arrest on 29 Jul 1859 as:

> A boy of about sixteen years of age, and giving his name as William Harris, was arrested in this city [Petaluma] last Tuesday evening [26 Jul 1859], on the charge of horse stealing. He had but just arrived from Black's ranch, Marin county, near which place he had been arrested by the citizens for horse stealing, robbing of houses, &c., and been sentenced, *a la* Judge Lynch, to a severe whipping; after the inflicting of which the executioners had furnished him with the necessary means, and received an assurance that he would leave this section of the State. From him, among other property, two horses were taken, owners for which have since been found in this vicinity, one belonging to Mr. J. D. Thompson of this city. The prisoner, in consequence of the absence of important

---

[303] S. C. Hendy was empaneled as a Grand Juror, but C. H. Hendy was called. Perhaps this was a clerk's error.
[304] "Grand Jury Report," *Sonoma County Democrat* (Santa Rosa, California), 1 September 1859, p. 3, col. 2.

evidence, had not had an examination on Thursday morning. He says he has been residing in the vicinity of Tomales for the past three or four years.[305]

The trial jury found the defendant guilty of petit larceny and recommended him to the mercy of the Court on 5 Aug 1859. The Court ordered the defendant imprisoned in the County Jail of Sonoma County for the term of sixty days on 9 Aug 1859.

People v. Louis Duthel (indicted as Louis Duchel)
Assault with intent to commit murder (case file # 90E)
The indictment filed on 2 Aug 1859 accused the defendant of shooting Martin Lynch in the left breast with a pistol with the intent to murder him and giving him six severe and dangerous wounds on 2 Jul 1859. John Kenny and James McHenry appeared as witnesses before the Grand Jury. The events of shooting were reported in the *Sonoma County Journal* on 8 Jul 1859 as:

> An affray occurred in this city [Petaluma], at an Italian drinking saloon, near the east end of the Bridge, last Saturday [2 Jul 1859] evening, during which an Irishman named Martin Lynch was seriously, and quite probably, fatally shot, by a Frenchman named Louis Duthel. Like the majority of events of this sort, the difficulty originated in a game of cards, but in which game, however, Duthel had no part. At the commencement of the hostilities, in which Lynch and the barkeeper were the principal actors, Duthel was at work in a lot adjoining the saloon. Hearing a noise, he rushed into the saloon where he found Lynch in the act of severely handling and abusing the barkeeper, who by the way is a friend and countryman of his. The sight appears to have been too much for his French to bear. Rushing into a back room, he seized a common horse-pistol, charged with buck shot, and returning, presented it, and fired upon Lynch as he was in the act of retreating. Six of the charge took effect upon the person of Lynch, entering the left breast, just above the heart, producing a frightful if not a fatal wound. Four of the shot have been extracted, but the other two appear beyond the reach of surgical skill.
>
> Duthel, who was immediately arrested, was brought before Justice Abell, on the 5th inst. [5 Jul 1859], for an examination, the result of which was his commitment to the county jail in failure to procure bail in the sum of $10,000.[306]

The trial jury found the defendant guilty and recommended him to the mercy of the Court on 5 Aug 1859. The Court ordered the defendant imprisoned in the State Prison for the term of two years on 9 Aug 1859. San Quentin received the prisoner on 10 Aug 1859, and he was discharged on 10 Aug 1861 after serving his full sentence.[307]

---

[305] "A Young Horse Thief," *The Sonoma County Journal* (Petaluma, California), 29 July 1859, p. 2, col. 1.
[306] "Shooting Affray," *The Sonoma County Journal* (Petaluma, California), 8 July 1859, p. 2, col. 1.
[307] California, State Prison Register (1851–1867), Executive Department, entry no. 1677, Louis Duthel, p. 134, received 10 August 1859; California State Archives, Sacramento.

People v. John Smith and John N. Steele (var. Steel)
Grand larceny

The *Sonoma County Journal* of 5 Aug 1859 gave the details of Smith and Steele's alleged crime as:

> John N. Steel, a recent graduate from the State Penitentiary, was brought before Justice Reyburn, of this city [Petaluma], by Deputy Sheriff Ellis, last Monday [1 Aug 1859], charged with stealing eighty dollars from E. McLaughlin, of San Antonio Creek; on which charge he was committed to the county jail in fault of $1,000 bail. One of the Smith family, boasting of the uncommon Christian name of John, but a true Digger, was also committed as an accomplice of Steel in the theft.[308]

John N. Steel had been convicted of grand larceny in Shasta County and sent to the State Prison for the term of two years.[309] San Quentin received him for this crime on 10 Jan 1855, and he was discharged on 27 Dec 1856. The Grand Jury dismissed the new charge on 2 Aug 1859.

People v. Fenwick Fisher
Assault and battery (case file # 82)

The indictment filed on 3 Aug 1859 accused the defendant of assaulting James Quinn with a club on 2 Aug 1859. James G. Maxwell, Charles Ames, and James Quinn appeared as witnesses before the Grand Jury. The trial jury found the defendant not guilty on 6 Aug 1859.

People v. William J. Morris
Grand larceny (case file # 88)

The indictment filed on 4 Aug 1859 accused the defendant of stealing George H. Hackett's dark bay horse (value $75) on 11 Jul 1859. George H. Hackett and O. L. Crandall appeared as witnesses before the Grand Jury. Morris had been arrested in San Francisco, "charged with committing several petty thefts at Ukiah city, Mendocino county," examined by Justice Reyburn on the charge of grand larceny, and committed to the Santa Rosa jail.[310] Among the charges against him was "one of having obtained a horse, saddle and bridle at a stable in this city [Petaluma], for the avowed purpose of going to Buckley's Ranch, Marin county, instead of which he proceeded to Ukiah, where he disposed of the horse and bridle."

The trial jury could not agree on a verdict on 8 Aug 1859. The Court ordered the action dismissed because of the insufficiency of the evidence on 9 Aug 1859.

At a convention of Justices of the Peace duly elected and qualified in and for the County of Sonoma held at Santa Rosa on 3 Oct 1859, William Ellis, Esq., of Sonoma Township and William H. Toombs, Esq., of Mendocino Township were elected as Associate Justices of the Court of Sessions for the ensuing year.

---

[308] "Again a Candidate," *The Sonoma County Journal* (Petaluma, California), 5 August 1859, p. 2, col. 1.
[309] California, State Prison Register (1851–1867), Executive Department, entry no. 529, John N. Steel, p. 36, received 10 January 1855; California State Archives, Sacramento.
[310] "Wm. J. Morris," *The Sonoma County Journal* (Petaluma, California), 5 August 1859, p. 2, col. 1.

November term 1859

The Court of Sessions met for six days this term, 7–12 November 1859.[311]

Hon. William Churchman, County Judge
Hon. William Ellis, Associate Justice
Hon. William H. Toombs, Associate Justice
R. C. Flournoy, District Attorney
Frank W. Shattuck, Clerk
William H. Crowell, Deputy Clerk
John J. Ellis, Sheriff
Daniel Rice, Deputy Sheriff
William Farmer, Grand Jury foreman

Persons called as Grand Jurors but not empaneled: Mathew Hetherington (not a United States citizen), Benjamin Hughes (not a United States citizen), William Howard (not a United States citizen), C. W. Ham (failed to appear and the Court fined him $25 with a respite to the next term), Alexander Dunbar (presented "a good and satisfactory excuse under oath" for not serving as a Grand Juror, and the Court discharged him from further service).

Grand Jurors sworn and empaneled on 7 Nov 1859: William Farmer, William Hollis, Mathew Hayes, P. G. Hubbard, John McReynolds, David Hopper, Thomas Johnson, W. A. Hutchinson, Mathew Warmer, James Hosmer, William E. Cocke, L. C. Holloway, Moses Cushenbury, J. C. Hoge, Jeremiah Root, and Ransom Powell. The Court appointed William Farmer as Grand Jury foreman.

Report of the Grand Jury[312]

Our body after a session of five days have ended their task. We find no prisoners in the jail. The jail and court-house being under repair, we deem it inexpedient to report upon their condition.

We have had eight cases presented as public offenses to our body, three of which we find "a true bill." The balance we have dismissed for want of insufficient and unprocurable testimony.

We have heard of no misconduct in office of public officers, and believed it unnecessary to make an examination at this session.

We have acted upon all public offenses triable in this county, which have been presented to our body, and having no more business before us, we beg to be discharged.

William Farmer, Foreman.

---

[311] Sonoma County, California, Court of Sessions, Minute Book E: 4–20, November term 1859 proceedings; Sonoma County Archives, Santa Rosa.

[312] Sonoma County, California, Court of Sessions, Report of the Grand Jury, filed 11 November 1859; County Records, Sonoma County, Court Records, Miscellaneous Unprocessed Records, folder "Grand Jury Reports, 1852–1875"; California State Archives, Sacramento. Sonoma County, California, Court of Sessions, Minute Book E: 18, Report of the Grand Jury, November term 1859, 11 November 1859; Sonoma County Archives, Santa Rosa.

People v. Nathaniel Brown
Assault with intent to inflict bodily injury

No case file for this case has been found at the State Archives. The Grand Jury presented the indictment in Court on 8 Nov 1859. The *Sonoma County Journal* reported on 11 Nov 1859 that the defendant Brown had been sent up from Petaluma for attempting "to split the head of [an] East Indian named Billy."[313] The *Sonoma County Journal* described the assault on 30 Sep 1859 as:

> An East Indiaman, known as Billy, was attacked last Wednesday evening [28 Sep 1859], by a negro named Brown, and quite severely cut on the head. The wound, which was made with an ax, is about three inches in length. Brown was drunk at the time, and is said to have made the attack without provocation.[314]

The trial jury found the defendant guilty on 8 Nov 1859, and the Court ordered the defendant imprisoned in the State Prison for the term of sixty days on 12 Nov 1859. He was received at San Quentin on 14 Nov 1859 and discharged on 13 Jan 1860 after serving his full sentence.[315]

People v. Finis Ewing
Assault with a deadly weapon with intent to inflict bodily injury (case file # 84)

The indictment filed on 9 Nov 1859 accused the defendant of assaulting Milligan Ikenburry (var. Ikenberry) with a knife on 30 Aug 1859. Abram Fine, Dr. P. P. Piper, W. T. Scott, G. W. Grannis (var. Granniss), J. Baker, Thomas Emmerson, and Young Ormsby appeared as witnesses before the Grand Jury. The trial jury found the defendant not guilty on 11 Nov 1859.

People v. R. B. Markle
Assault with an intent to kill (case file # 89)

The defendant was arrested on 11 Aug 1859 for assaulting J. G. Doane of Cloverdale on the evening of 10 Aug 1859. The *Sonoma County Journal* described the assault in its 12 Aug 1859 edition as:

> Marshal Cross of this city [Petaluma], yesterday morning [11 Aug 1859] arrested R. B. Markle, of Cloverdale, on charge of assaulting one J. G. Doane, of the same place, with intent to kill. The assault was made at the residence of Mr. Doane on Wednesday evening [10 Aug 1859] between 8 and 9 o'clock. It would appear, from the statements made to us, that Markle has of late been paying frequent visits to the residence of Mr. D., very much to the annoyance of Mrs. Doane; and that on one of those visits he took away a locket containing the likenesses of Mr. and Mrs. D. On Wednesday evening Markle again called, when Mrs. D. demanded the return of the locket. Mr. D. being present, some words followed, shortly after which M. left the room, before doing which he took from his pocket a percussion cap. This excited Mr. D.'s suspicion, and he also stepped into the open air, when he saw Mr. Markle approaching him with a pistol in one hand and a bowie knife in the other. As he approached Markle fired upon D., but without effect. Doane then

---

[313] "Convicted," *The Sonoma County Journal* (Petaluma, California), 11 November 1859, p. 2, col. 1.

[314] "Cut," *The Sonoma County Journal* (Petaluma, California), 30 September 1859, p. 2, col. 2.

[315] California, State Prison Register (1851–1867), Executive Department, entry no. 1731, Nathaniel Brown, p. 139, received 14 November 1859; California State Archives, Sacramento.

seized a hay rake and belabored his enemy about the head, but failing to cripple him he turned and fled, M. following for a few steps and then retreating to his horse, which stood nearby, mounted and fled, coming directly to this city. Doane in his retreat, fled into the house, and getting his rifle, returned and fired upon M., but without effect. At the time of our paper being put to press Markle had not been examined, consequently we cannot state the result. The foregoing statement, however, is a brief history of the affair as furnished us by the gentleman who followed Mr. M. to this city and caused his arrest.[316]

The *Daily Alta California* reported that Markle had fired a pistol at Doane "and afterwards drove Doane off, then chased his wife [Mercy S. Doane] with a knife, cut his horse's halter and went to Healdsburg, where he took a buggy and driver for Petaluma, when he was arrested, ironed, and taken off the steamer."[317] Markle was examined on 12 Aug 1859 by Justice O'Dell of Washington Township, "who held him for trial in the sum of $2,500. The bail was promptly given, and the prisoner discharged from custody."[318] The Grand Jury dismissed the charge on 10 Nov 1859 and recommended the case to the next Grand Jury. The Grand Jury dismissed the charge again on 9 Feb 1860.

People v. Gilbert Gillett
Assault with a deadly weapon with intent to commit murder (case file # 83)
The indictment filed on 11 Nov 1859 accused the defendant of shooting a man named Robinson (var. Robison) with a pistol wounding him in the head with the intent of murdering him on 1 Nov 1859. G. W. Shoemaker, William Wilson, P. N. Woodworth, Charles Briat, James Buck, and Charles Briard appeared as witnesses before the Grand Jury. An article in the 4 Nov 1859 edition of the *Sonoma County Journal* described the events of the shooting as:

> During a drunken fit, last Tuesday [1 Nov 1859], a fellow named Gilbert Gillett fired four pistol shots at a man named Robbinson, and a Miss Woodworth. The shooting occurred at the Stony Point House. It would appear that Mr. Robbinson, who is a married man and an old friend of the Woodworth family, had that evening arrived from Fraser River. At the hotel he met Miss W. and by invitation started with her for her father's house. Before their leaving the house, Gillett expressed a desire to accompany Miss W., which was promptly declined. So soon as Robbinson and the lady started to leave the house, Gillett stepped to the door, drew a revolver and commenced shooting, firing four shots. The last took effect in the head of Mr. R. The wound fortunately, is but slight. The event occurred after dark. Such, briefly, are the facts as stated to us. Gillett was arrested and taken before Justice Miller, of Sebastopol, on the following day. The examination resulted in his discharge.[319]

---

[316] "Attempt to Kill," *The Sonoma County Journal* (Petaluma, California), 12 August 1859, p. 2, col. 2.
[317] "Sonoma County," *Daily Alta California* (San Francisco, California), 12 August 1859, p. 1, col. 4.
[318] "Held for Trial," *The Sonoma County Journal* (Petaluma, California), 19 August 1859, p. 2, col. 1.
[319] "Shooting," *The Sonoma County Journal* (Petaluma, California), 4 November 1859, p. 2, col. 1.

February term 1860

The Court of Sessions met for fourteen days this term, 6–11 and 13–18 February 1860 and 5–6 March 1860.[320]

Hon. William Churchman, County Judge
Hon. William Ellis, Associate Justice
Hon. William H. Toombs, Associate Justice
R. C. Flournoy, District Attorney
Frank W. Shattuck, Clerk
William H. Crowell, Deputy Clerk
John J. Ellis, Sheriff
E. Latapie, Deputy Sheriff
William Farmer, Grand Jury foreman

Persons called as Grand Jurors but not empaneled: Edward Hilliker (not a United States citizen), George Harrington (a member of the military), Samuel H. Hill, P. B. Hewlett, Henry Beaver, William E. Cocke, and Z. Gossage.

Grand Jurors sworn and empaneled on 6 Feb 1860: Joseph H. Griggs, John Ingram, Zadoc Jackson, John Barry, I. A. Bradshaw, Henry Emerson, C. C. Money, C. G. Dorris, David Grove, John Hughes, William Ayres, Robert Irwin, G. A. Hart, George Hamilton, William M. Jones, and William Farmer. The Court appointed William Farmer as Grand Jury foreman.

Grand Jury Report[321]

To the Honorable Court of Sessions of Sonoma County,

The Grand Jury of Sonoma County, having been in session eight days, and having had under consideration such matters as in their judgment pertained to the peace and prosperity of the County, beg leave to submit the following report:

We have found indictments against eleven persons, for offenses against the law: one for murder; one for assault with [a] deadly weapon with intent to commit murder; one for grand larceny; one for assault with intent to commit bodily injury; two for burglary; one for assault and battery; one for rape; one for petit larceny; and one for passing counterfeit money. Charges were sent up to us against three persons, who, after canvassing the evidence, were discharged.

We would also respectfully report, that we have had under consideration the financial condition of the County, having in view the recent heavy expenses to which she has necessarily incurred, and find that the County debt, against the general and special funds of the County, will amount, at the end of the present term of the Board of Supervisors, to about $53,800.

---

[320] Sonoma County, California, Court of Sessions, Minute Book E: 24–80, February term 1860 proceedings; Sonoma County Archives, Santa Rosa.

[321] "To the Honorable Court of Sessions of Sonoma County," *Sonoma County Democrat* (Santa Rosa, California), 16 February 1860, p. 2, col. 3. Sonoma County, California, Court of Sessions, Minute Book E: 62, Report of the Grand Jury February term 1860, 14 February 1860; Sonoma County Archives, Santa Rosa.

Under these circumstances, and in view of the movement which has recently been made, having for its object the funding of the County debt, we feel it to be our duty to recommend the passage of a judicious law by the State Legislature now in session, for that purpose.

We would also suggest, that information has indirectly reached us, that many persons in the County are carrying on those branches of business which require licenses, without having obtained such licenses, and would recommend the attention of the District Attorney to such cases.

We would further state, that we have examined the several County Offices, and Public Buildings.

The County Jail and Hospital are kept in a clean and neat manner, and from the appearance of the prisoners, they are well cared for. The plan of the County Jail we regard as a good one, but the work badly executed, the walls having been put up with sand instead of lime mortar. Any man, in our judgment, could get out of the cells in fifteen minutes with a jack-knife. In consequence of this insufficient manner of workmanship, the jail is insufficient to retain prisoners without loading them down with irons. We would recommend that the present cells be removed, and that others be built of cut stone, fastened in a way that will keep prisoners safe.

We have also examined the Court House, and find it in good condition, and believe it to be suitable for the purposes for which it was intended.

The Treasurer's Office is well-adapted to its purposes – the safe in good condition and secure, and the vault sufficient for the safe-keeping of the County moneys. The Treasurer's books are kept in a neat and business-like manner.

We find the Clerk's Office well-adapted to its purpose, and well-arranged, but in need of some more furniture, such as pigeon-hole work, in order that documents which are now necessarily bunched up together, may be properly classified and arranged. The Clerk's books are all in good condition, and speak well for the business capacity of that officer.

We also have the satisfaction to give a favorable report of the condition of the Recorder's and Auditor's Office, in both departments of which we find the books kept in a neat, business-like and intelligible manner. We find several of the old books of Record, however, in a dilapidated condition, and would recommend that the same be transcribed. Some additional furniture seems to be necessary for the better preservation of the books, records, &c., and the papers on file in this office.

The Sheriff's Office, the Jury Rooms, the Court Room, County Judge's Office, &c., are all regarded in good condition, and sufficient for the purposes they are intended to serve.

Having completed our labors to the best of our ability, we therefore respectfully ask to be discharged.

Wm. Farmer, Foreman.

People v. Richard Wood
Murder
The indictment filed on 6 Feb 1860 accused the defendant of assaulting Hugh Wiley with a knife giving him two mortal wounds on his left side between his hip and shoulder on 16 Dec 1859. Alexander Wiley, Spenser Currell, Nicholas Mulroy, Charles Galloway, Hugh McArthur, and James H. Curtiss appeared as witnesses before the Grand Jury. On 23 Dec 1859, the *Sonoma County Journal* reported the events of the murder as:

A difficulty occurred at Irish Hill, Bodega, last Friday [16 Dec 1859], between Hugh Wiley and Dick Woods, which resulted in the death of the former. He was stabbed in four different places in the left breast, and survived but a few hours. Woods was taken before Justice Springer, and committed to await his trial.[322]

The case was transmitted to the Sonoma County District Court on 9 Feb 1860. See Sonoma County District Court case # 825 (OS). The District Court trial jury found the defendant guilty of 2nd degree murder on 24 Feb 1860.[323] The Court sentenced him to 15 years' imprisonment in the State Prison on 27 Feb 1860.[324] The *Sonoma County Democrat* devoted almost the entire front page of its 1 Mar 1860 edition to coverage of the trial.[325] San Quentin received Wood on 29 Feb 1860, but he escaped along with numerous other inmates on 22 Jul 1862.[326]

People v. Thomas Haley
Murder
The *Sonoma County Journal* reported on 25 Nov 1859 that James Neary, a native of Ireland, had been found "lying in a pile of wood on the east side of the creek, near the Occidental Mills, with a wound in the left breast."[327] A several-day Coroner's inquest determined that he had come "to his death by a cut from a large knife," but found no "positive proof as to who committed the deed." Neary had been last seen in the company of Thomas Haley about 2 o'clock on the morning of 20 Nov 1859. Haley was arrested for the murder of James Neary on 28 Nov 1859 and committed to prison in Santa Rosa.[328] The Grand Jury dismissed the charge on 7 Feb 1860.

People v. Henry Austin
Assault with a deadly weapon with intent to inflict bodily injury (case file # 86)
The indictment filed on 8 Feb 1860 accused the defendant of assaulting Joseph R. Walker with a knife on 5 Dec 1859. Joseph R. Walker and Irwin R. Morris appeared as witnesses before the Grand Jury. The first trial jury could not agree on a verdict on 11 Feb 1860. The second trial jury found the defendant guilty of a simple assault on 16 Feb 1860. The Court ordered the defendant to pay a fine of $200 and be imprisoned in the County Jail of Sonoma County until the fine was paid at the rate of $2 per day on 18 Feb 1860. The *Sonoma County Democrat* reported on 3 May 1860 that Harvy [sic] Austin was a prisoner in the County Jail serving out his sentence.[329]

---

[322] "Homicide at Bodega," *The Sonoma County Journal* (Petaluma, California), 23 December 1859, p. 2, col. 1.

[323] Sonoma County, California, District Court, Minute Book B: 369, The People of the State of California v. Richard Wood, trial jury verdict, 24 February 1860; Sonoma County Archives, Santa Rosa.

[324] Sonoma County, California, District Court, Minute Book B: 376, The People of the State of California v. Richard Wood, judgment, 24 February 1860; Sonoma County Archives, Santa Rosa.

[325] "Trial of Richard Woods for the Murder of Hugh Wiley!," *Sonoma County Democrat* (Santa Rosa, California), 1 March 1860, p. 1, cols. 2-6.

[326] California, State Prison Register (1851–1867), Executive Department, entry no. 1825, Richard Wood, p. 147, received 29 February 1860; California State Archives, Sacramento.

[327] "A Mysterious Murder," *The Sonoma County Journal* (Petaluma, California), 25 November 1859, p. 2, col. 1.

[328] "The Murder Case," *The Sonoma County Journal* (Petaluma, California), 2 December 1859, p. 2, col. 1.

[329] "The Courts," *Sonoma County Democrat* (Santa Rosa, California), 3 May 1860, p. 2, col. 3.

People v. Juan Seron (indicted as John Serena)
Grand larceny (case file # 105)

The indictment filed on 8 Feb 1860 accused the defendant of stealing one gray horse (value $125) and one roan mare (value $60), property of Adria Godoy, on 26 Oct 1859. Adria Godoy, William Robertson, John B. Owens, L. C. Reyburn, and Jose Maria Peres appeared as witnesses before the Grand Jury. The *Sonoma County Democrat* of 15 Dec 1859 described his arrest on 10 Dec 1859 as:

> John Larema [*sic*], a Mexican, was brought to Santa Rosa by Constable Kavinaugh of Petaluma, on Saturday last [10 Dec 1859], and delivered to Sheriff Ellis, being charged with stealing a horse down on the Laguna. He had been pursued and overtaken in Ukiah valley. On seeing he was about to be overtaken, he undertook to escape by flight, but was brought to by pistol shots, one of which took effect in his leg, another in his arm, and a third in the fleshy part of the breast. He was tried before Justice Rayburn, committed and sent up for trial before the Court of Sessions. For the want of a County [Jail] he and other criminals have been sent for safe-keeping to Napa.[330]

The trial jury found Seron guilty as charged on 10 Feb 1860. The Court ordered the defendant to be imprisoned in the State Prison for the term of four years on 17 Feb 1860. San Quentin received Seron on 22 Feb 1860, and he was discharged on 18 Feb 1864 after serving his full sentence.[331]

People v. James O'Sullivan
Assault with intent to commit murder (case file # 107G)

An indictment was originally filed on 8 Feb 1860, and the case came to trial on 13 Feb 1860. The indictment was resubmitted to the Grand Jury, however, because the manner of the assault was not stated in the indictment. The second indictment filed on 14 Feb 1860 accused the defendant of assaulting James Boylan by shooting at him with a loaded pistol with the intent to murder him on 27 Jan 1860. John K. Brown and James Boylan appeared as witnesses before the Grand Jury. The *Sonoma County Journal* described the shooting in its 3 Feb 1860 edition and added a tongue in cheek comment.

> On Thursday night, 26th ult. [26 Jan 1860], James O'Sullivan sought the couch of James —, a workman in his employ, and fired upon him, wounding the sleeping man in the right arm. Jealousy is said to be the cause. Recorder Abell held O'Sullivan to answer to a charge of murderous assault, and in default of bail, he had to go to jail. He couldn't trust the fellow about his house when he was there himself — phanzy his pheelinks [fancy his feelings] now that he is sixteen miles away, and the object of his suspicions convalescent in his house.[332]

---

[330] "Larceny," *Sonoma County Democrat* (Santa Rosa, California), 15 December 1859, p. 2, col. 1.
[331] California, State Prison Register (1851–1867), Executive Department, entry no. 1820, Juan Seran, p. 146, received 22 February 1860; California State Archives, Sacramento.
[332] "Shooting," *The Sonoma County Journal* (Petaluma, California), 3 February 1860, p. 2, col. 1.

Two different trial juries could not agree on verdicts on 18 Feb 1860 and 6 Mar 1860. The Court dismissed the action because the evidence was insufficient to convict the defendant on 7 May 1860.

People v. Franklin W. Green
Assault with a deadly weapon with intent to commit bodily injury (case file # 98)

The indictment filed on 9 Feb 1860 accused the defendant of assaulting James B. McCallen with an axe on 27 Jan 1860. George W. McAllen (var. McCallen), James B. McAllen (var. McCallen), George Burge, and William Hill appeared as witnesses before the Grand Jury. The trial jury found the defendant not guilty on 15 Feb 1860.

People v. Robert Fawcett and William Harris
Burglary (case file # 100)

The indictment filed on 9 Feb 1860 accused the defendants of burglarizing the store house of Benjamin Goldfish and Henry Wise on 8 Dec 1859. No original indictment has been found at the California State Archives. On 15 Dec 1859, the *Sonoma County Democrat* reported the burglary as:

> Lewis [*sic*] Harris, a boy of about 17 years, and who has recently served an apprenticeship of 60 days in our County Jail, and Bob Faucett, an Irishman, well-known as crazy Bob, were arrested on Thursday morning last [8 Dec 1859], charged with burglariously entering the store of Wise and Goldfish. They had bored a hole through the door, in reach of the lock, and by reaching through turned the key. They then entered, ransacked the store, opened the drawer and helped themselves to the loose change left there overnight. They found the key of the safe, and from all appearance had made considerable effort to unlock it, but failed. The change in the drawer, one pair of shoes, and about a half-gallon of whiskey, is all they took away. The strangest part of this story is, that Mr. Wise was sleeping in the store, but did not hear them.[333]

The defendants demanded separate trials on 9 Feb 1860. The trial jury found the defendant Robert Fawcett not guilty on 11 Feb 1860 after William Harris refused to testify against him. The Court ordered the case against William Harris be dismissed and resubmitted to the Grand Jury on 13 Feb 1860.

People v. Bill (var. William) Williams (a colored man)
Rape (case file #s 90C and 107L)

The indictment filed on 10 Feb 1860 accused the defendant of ravishing and carnally knowing Elisabeth E. Ross, the seven-year-old daughter of Mary E. Ross, on 10 Dec 1859. Dr. J. L. Bond, Mary E. Ross, and Elizabeth E. Ross appeared as witnesses before the Grand Jury. Williams, a native of Bombay, was examined by Justice Hayden of Petaluma on 13 Dec 1859 and delivered

---

[333] "Burglary," *Sonoma County Democrat* (Santa Rosa, California), 15 December 1859, p. 2, col. 1. See case file # 90A for the cause of William Harris's 60-day stay in the County Jail.

to the Sheriff for safe-keeping.[334] On 6 Feb 1860, it was reported that the defendant had escaped from custody by breaking jail while confined in the County Jail of Napa County.

People v. James M. Stevens (indicted as James Stephens)
Assault and battery (case file # 92)

The indictment filed on 10 Feb 1860 accused the defendant of beating, wounding, and ill-treating John E. Rose on 8 Dec 1859. James Stevens, John E. Rose, Uriah Miller, Zeddock Jackson, and Peter Stewart (var. Steward) appeared as witnesses before the Grand Jury. The trial jury found the defendant guilty as charged and recommended him to the mercy of the Court on 14 Feb 1860. The Court ordered the defendant to pay a fine of $200 and be imprisoned in the County Jail of Sonoma County until the fine was paid at the rate of $2 per day on 17 Feb 1860.

People v. William P. Barnes
Assault with intent to commit murder (case file # 96)

On 27 Jan 1860 or early 28 Jan 1860 the defendant got into a quarrel with Daniel Brown at the Magnolia Saloon in Petaluma and "stabbed the latter in the back, causing a severe, but it is thought, not a dangerous wound."[335] The defendant was examined by Recorder Abell and held under a $2,000 bond. The Grand Jury dismissed the charge on 10 Feb 1860.

People v. Uriah Miller
Assault with intent to commit murder

The defendant along with James Stephens was sent up from Analy Township by Justice [Joseph M.] Miller on 9 Dec 1859, "charged with an assault with a deadly weapon with intent to commit murder upon John Rose."[336] The Grand Jury dismissed the charge on 10 Feb 1860. See also case file # 92.

People v. Hiram Hill
Petit larceny (case file # 102)

The indictment filed on 11 Feb 1860 accused the defendant of stealing Curtis C. Edmisson's silver watch (value $25) on 30 Aug 1859. Curtis C. Edmisson (var. Edmonson) appeared as a witness before the Grand Jury. The trial jury found the defendant guilty as charged on 13 Feb 1860. The Court ordered the defendant to pay a fine of $150 and be imprisoned in the County Jail of Sonoma County until the fine was paid at the rate of $2 per day on 17 Feb 1860.

People v. Ramon Arenas
Counterfeiting/passing counterfeit money (case file # 107D)

The indictment filed on 13 Feb 1860 accused the defendant of having in his possession certain false, forged, and counterfeit gold coins with the intention of passing them as true and genuine and thereby defrauding James Slavian on 24 Dec 1859. Stephen Odell appeared as a witness

---

[334] "Crimes," *Sonoma County Democrat* (Santa Rosa, California), 15 December 1859, p. 2, col. 1.
[335] "Stabbing," *Sonoma County Democrat* (Santa Rosa, California), 2 February 1860, p. 3, col. 1. "Serious Fracas," *The Sonoma County Journal* (Petaluma, California), 3 February 1860, p. 2, col. 1.
[336] "Deadly Assault," *Sonoma County Democrat* (Santa Rosa, California), 15 December 1859, p. 2. col. 1.

before the Grand Jury. The *Sonoma County Journal* on 30 Dec 1859 reported the defendant's arrest and described the counterfeit coins in detail.

> Officer Odell last Sunday morning [25 Dec 1859] arrested a Mexican, who gave his name as Ramon, for passing counterfeit gold coin in this city [Petaluma] on the previous day and evening. Upon his person about $20 of this coin was found. How much he had succeeded in passing is unknown – but $25 has as yet come to light. It consists of fives and tens. The former bears date of 1849, and the latter 1850, and purports to be of San Francisco coinage, having the initial letter S. Both denominations are evidently from the same hands and are, without an exception, the poorest attempts at a counterfeit that we have ever seen. They are very roughly milled, of a light brassy complexion, and not quite half the weight of the genuine coin. In addition to the bogus gold coin, several counterfeit American halves were also passed on the same day, and most probably by Ramon. The halves are in no wise likely to deceive, being but a weak imitation of the genuine. Ramon is now in custody, awaiting his examination. He is a newcomer in these parts, and says he is from Bolinas, Napa county, to which point he has sent for witnesses, declaring his ability to prove when, how, and in what manner, the coin came into his possession.[337]

The defendant failed to appear in Court when his case was called on 7 May 1860, and the Court ordered a bench warrant to issue for his arrest.

People v. William Harris
Burglary (case file # 100)
The indictment filed on 14 Feb 1860 accused the defendant of burglarizing the store house of Benjamin Goldfish and Henry Wise on 8 Dec 1859. Dr. John Hendley, John O'Malley, Henry Wise, Benjamin Goldfish, John Hanaha, and Robert Fawcett appeared as witnesses before the Grand Jury. The trial jury found the defendant guilty on 16 Feb 1860. The Court ordered the defendant imprisoned in the State Prison for the term of four years on 18 Feb 1860. San Quentin received the prisoner on 22 Feb 1860.[338] He escaped on 22 Jul 1862, but was recaptured the same day. He was discharged on 18 Feb 1864 after serving his full sentence.

May term 1860

The Court of Sessions met for eleven days this term, 7–12 and 14–17 May 1860.[339]

Hon. William Churchman, County Judge
Hon. William Ellis, Associate Justice
Hon. William H. Toombs, Associate Justice
R. C. Flournoy, District Attorney
Frank W. Shattuck, Clerk

---

[337] "Counterfeit Coin," *The Sonoma County Journal* (Petaluma, California), 30 December 1859, p. 2, col. 1.
[338] California, State Prison Register (1851–1867), Executive Department, entry no. 1819, William Harris, p. 146, received 22 February 1860; California State Archives, Sacramento.
[339] Sonoma County, California, Court of Sessions, Minute Book E: 82–116, May term 1860 proceedings; Sonoma County Archives, Santa Rosa.

William H. Crowell, Deputy Clerk
John J. Ellis, Sheriff
Edward L. Green, Grand Jury foreman

Persons called as Grand Jurors but not empaneled: Charles Merritt (failed to answer call), J. B. Lewis (excused), H. L. Lovell (excused), and Charles Mock (excused).

Grand Jurors duly sworn, examined, and passed upon by the Court on 7 May 1860: Albert Lyon, Charles McHarvey, Hugh Stockdale, H. F. Lambert, Emanuel Light, J. B. Caldwell, Joel Merchant, S. B. Lusk, J. G. Walker, Horace Lamb, I. N. McGuire, E. L. Green, R. H. Lewis, William Ayres, William E. Cocke, and Berthold Hoen. The Court appointed Edward L. Green as Grand Jury foreman.

Grand Jury Report[340]

To the Honorable Court of Sessions of Sonoma County,
The Grand Jury of Sonoma County has been in session five days and had under consideration such matters as in their judgment pertain to the peace and prosperity of the county, beg leave to submit the following report.

We have found eight indictments against persons for offences against the law — one for murder; two for assault with a deadly weapon, with intent to commit murder; one for assault with a deadly weapon, to do bodily injury; two for grand larceny; one for burglary; one for gaming; and one case brought before us, and dismissed, for want of evidence.

We also report, that we have made an examination of the financial condition of the county, and find from the Treasurer's report the whole indebtedness of the county up to the first of May, to be $50,268.93. We also examined the jail, and find the prisoners well-provided for, clean, and comfortable — except for the insecurity of the cells, which compels the jailor to confine them in chains, which, in our judgment, is cruel and wrong, and should be immediately remedied. We conferred with the Board of Supervisors, and hope they will soon devise some plan and make secure the prison, without compelling the jailor to resort to cruel means for their security.

The county hospital, we find kept neat, and one patient in it who is well-provided for. We have also examined the court house, and find it in good condition. The Clerk's office is also in excellent condition — very neat and clean. The books and schedules are very neatly written and well-arranged, and speaks well for the business capacity of that office. We have also the satisfaction to give a favorable report of the Recorder's and Auditor's office. In both departments we find the books kept clean and neat, in business-like manner — plain and intelligible. Some additional furniture appears necessary in that office, such as [a] table and pigeonholes for the better security of his books and papers. We also have the satisfaction to give a favorable report of the Treasurer, whose report and settlement will be published in the next publication of the Board of Supervisors. In examination of the Sheriff's office, we find a full and entire settlement

---

[340] Sonoma County, California, Court of Sessions, Grand Jury Report May term 1860, 11 May 1860; County Records, Sonoma County, Court Records, Miscellaneous Unprocessed Records, folder "County Records – Sonoma County – Court of Sessions – Reports of the Grand Jury"; California State Archives, Sacramento. Sonoma County, California, Court of Sessions, Minute Book E: 101–102, Report of the Grand Jury, 11 May 1860; Sonoma County Archives, Santa Rosa.

with the Auditor for all moneys he is charged with up to the first of March, which, in our judgment, speaks well for that office.

All of which is respectfully submit[ted] and [we] ask to be discharged.

This May the 11th, 1860

E. L. Green, Foreman

People v. George Tomblins (var. Tomlins, indicted as George Tomblin)
Assault with intent to commit murder (case file # 106)

The indictment filed on 8 May 1860 accused the defendant of assaulting Josiah W. Carter with a loaded pistol on 19 Apr 1860. Josiah W. Carter, James T. Crane, and Mary Hardin appeared as witnesses before the Grand Jury. The trial jury found the defendant guilty of an assault with intent to inflict bodily injury on 16 May 1860. The Court ordered the defendant imprisoned in the State Prison for the term of two months on 17 May 1860. Tomblins was received by San Quentin on 18 May 1860 and discharged on 18 Jul 1860 after serving his full sentence.[341]

People v. Joseph Thompson
Burglary (case file # 107O)

The indictment filed on 9 May 1860 accused the defendant of burglarizing the store house of Frederick Duhring and Frederick Leiding on 3 Mar 1860. John A. Rudesill, Frederick Leiding, James Brackett, Frederick Duhring, John Hoffman (var. Huffman), Clovis S. Sayles, and Charles W. Carpenter appeared as witnesses before the Grand Jury. The *Sonoma County Journal* provided the details of Thompson's arrest on 9 Mar 1860.

> Constable Brackett, of Vallejo township, by virtue of a warrant issued by Justice Campbell of Sonoma, and addressed to Justice Payran, arrested a man named Thompson, at Rudesill's landing last Monday morning [5 Mar 1860]. The crime charged was petit larceny, committed at the store of Duhring and Co., of Sonoma City, on the Saturday night previous [3 Mar 1860]. In Thompson's possession was found a quantity of money and goods, amounting to about $[illegible]. The prisoner and goods were taken to Sonoma, where they were duly identified, and after an examination, the prisoner was committed to the county jail.[342]

The trial jury found the defendant guilty on 10 May 1860. The Court ordered the defendant imprisoned in the State Prison for the term of 4 years on 14 May 1860. San Quentin received Thompson on 18 May 1860.[343] He escaped in a prison break on 22 Jul 1862, but was recaptured the same day. He was discharged on 29 Apr 1864.

---

[341] California, State Prison Register (1851–1867), Executive Department, entry no. 1882, Geo. Tomblins, p. 152, received 18 May 1860; California State Archives, Sacramento.

[342] "Burglary," *The Sonoma County Journal* (Petaluma, California), 9 March 1860, p. 2, col. 1.

[343] California, State Prison Register (1851–1867), Executive Department, entry no. 1883, Joseph Thompson, p. 152, received 18 May 1860; California State Archives, Sacramento.

People v. Joseph Thompson

Grand larceny (case file # 1070)

The indictment filed on 9 May 1860 accused the defendant of stealing four pairs of boots (value $14), six pairs of pants (value $8), one coat (value $5), four silk rashes (value $10), twelve silk handkerchiefs (value $8), silk veils (value $3.75), and six pairs of buckskin gloves (value $6), property of Frederick Duhring and Frederick Leiding, on 3 Mar 1860. John A. Rudesill, Frederick Leiding, James Brackett, Frederick Duhring, John Hoffman (var. Huffman), Clovis S. Sayles, and Charles W. Carpenter appeared as witnesses before the Grand Jury. The Court dismissed the action on 15 May 1860 because the defendant had already been convicted of burglary and sentenced to four years' imprisonment in the State Prison.

People v. Amariah Kibbee

Murder

The indictment filed on 9 May 1860 accused the defendant of assaulting Oliver H. Godfrey by shooting him with a gun in the left side of the breast giving him a mortal wound of which he died on 11 Apr 1860.[344] William H. Sansburry (var. Sansbury), William H. Levalley, James M. Eubanks (var. Ewbanks), William Pixley, James R. Mowbray, John P. Buck, Elisha H. Eubanks (var. Ewbanks), James Seright appeared as witnesses before the Grand Jury. The *Sonoma County Journal* of 20 Apr 1860 described the homicide as:

> On Wednesday of last week [11 Apr 1860], as we learn from the Healdsburg *Review*, a difficulty occurred between a Mr. Kibbe, who lives at Sanborn's, on Russian River, and a Mr. Godfrey, who resides near Cloverdale. The dispute was in regard to a land claim, when, in the course of it, Kibbe shot Godfrey with a rifle, killing him instantly, the ball passing through the heart. Much excitement, as a consequence, prevailed in that neighborhood. Kibbe immediately surrendered himself to Sheriff Ellis, who happened to be at Cloverdale at the time, and was taken a prisoner to Santa Rosa. A Cloverdale correspondent of the *Alta*, says: "O. H. Godfrey and A. Kibbe were disputing for the possession of a mountain claim lying about three miles east of this place, and on the eastern slope of the ridge dividing Sulphur Creek from Russian River. Yesterday morning Godfrey proceeded to the ground with a friend or two, and found Kibbe and friends already there as a team. Words passed; Godfrey criticizing, in a jocular way, the fence Kibbe had been making by felling trees; Kibbe retorted, and the witnesses are divided as to whether threats passed between them or not. Godfrey, who was some sixteen paces from Kibbe, drew his revolver, keeping it in his hand, but not raising it higher than his waist. Kibbe called to a friend for his rifle, which was a few yards distant, Godfrey retaining his position and keeping his eye on Kibbe. The rifle was handed him, and Kibbe, bringing it to his shoulder, took deliberate aim and fired; Godfrey fell instantly, without moving a muscle, the ball passing through his heart, and lodging next to the skin below the right shoulder."

---

[344] Sonoma County, California, District Court, case file # 952 (OS), The People of the State of California v. Amariah Kibbee, indictment, filed 9 May 1860; County Records, Sonoma County, Court Records, District Court case files; California State Archives, Sacramento.

In addition to this tragedy, we have to record the accidental death of Mr. Lewis J. Hilt, who was drowned in attempting to ford the river on horseback, while conducting Mr. Godfrey's corpse across the river. Mr. Hilt was a native of Pennsylvania, aged 35 years.[345]

The case was transmitted to the Sonoma County District Court on 9 May 1860. See Sonoma County District Court case # 952 (OS). The District Court trial jury found the defendant guilty of murder in the 2nd degree on 26 Jun 1860.[346] The Court sentenced him to thirty years' imprisonment in the State Prison on 29 Jun 1860.[347] San Quentin received Kibbee on 2 Jul 1860.[348] He was pardoned by Governor Frederick F. Low on 4 Mar 1867 and discharged on 6 Mar 1867 after serving less than seven years of his term.[349] The Governor, on examining the trial evidence, was convinced "that the verdict and sentence of Kibby were an outrage upon justice, [and] that Kibby's crime was not greater than manslaughter, with mitigating circumstances, or, possibly, justifiable homicide."

People v. Joseph Madrad
Assault with intent to kill
    The Grand Jury dismissed the charge on 9 May 1860 in the absence of any evidence.

People v. John Morris
Assault with intent to commit murder (case file # 95)
    The indictment filed on 11 May 1860 accused the defendant of shooting at Asa Ross twice with a double-barreled shotgun on 20 Apr 1860. Asa Ross, John P. Smith, Frederick Rohrer, Alexander W. Sweeney, and Daniel Rice appeared as witnesses before the Grand Jury. The trial jury could not agree on a verdict on 9 Aug 1860, and the Court ordered the action be dismissed as regards to the felony as the proof was insufficient to find the defendant guilty. The defendant pleaded guilty to a simple assault on 9 Aug 1860. The Court ordered the defendant to pay a fine of $400 and be imprisoned in the County Jail of Sonoma County until the fine was paid at the rate of $2 per day on 11 Aug 1860.

---

[345] "Homicide at Cloverdale and Accident," *The Sonoma County Journal* (Petaluma, California), 20 April 1860, p. 2, col. 2.

[346] Sonoma County, California, District Court, Minute Book B: 419, The People of the State of California v. Amariah Kibbee, trial jury verdict, 26 June 1860; Sonoma County Archives, Santa Rosa.

[347] Sonoma County, California, District Court, Minute Book B: 439, The People of the State of California v. Amariah Kibbee, judgment, 29 June 1860; Sonoma County Archives, Santa Rosa.

[348] California, State Prison Register (1851–1867), Executive Department, entry no. 1912, Amariah Kibbee, p. 155, received 2 July 1860; California State Archives, Sacramento.

[349] *The Journal of the Assembly During the Seventeenth Session of the Legislature of the State of California, 1867-8. Began on Monday [2 December 1867], and Ended on Monday [30 March 1868]* (Sacramento: D. W. Gelwicks, State Printer, 1868), 67 (hereafter cited as *The Journal of the Assembly, Seventeenth Session*). Kibbee's pardon and the Governor's decision are contained in a list of pardons from the State Prison granted by Governor Low from 1 November 1865 to 1 December 1867 appended to his second biennial message to the California Senate and Assembly dated 2 December 1867.

People v. Thomas J. Blackwell

Assault with a deadly weapon with intent to inflict bodily injury (case file # 99)

The indictment filed on 11 May 1860 accused the defendant of assaulting Mrs. Catherine Hoffman Unger (var. Ungar) with a piece of wood about 6 feet long, 2 inches thick, and 4 inches broad on 20 Feb 1860. Mrs. Catherine Hoffman Unger (var. Ungar), Charles F. Zimmerman, Justis Rhul, John Gallagher, and Albert H. Unger (var. Ungar) appeared as witnesses before the Grand Jury. The assault was reported in the 17 Feb 1860 edition of the *Sonoma County Journal* as:

> A difficulty occurred in the San Antonio neighborhood, and about four miles from this city [Petaluma], last Wednesday [15 Feb 1860] forenoon, resulting in the serious injury of a Mrs. Ungar, wife of A. Hoffman Ungar. As an examination has not taken place, at the time of going to press, we can only give a statement from rumor. It appears that a dispute in reference to the rights of property in a certain piece of land has for some time existed between Mr. Ungar and a neighbor named Thos. Blackwell, and that the case is yet in litigation. Last Wednesday, Blackwell, aided by several men, and while Ungar was in town, proceeded to fence the disputed land in, whereupon Mrs. Ungar, said to have been armed with a scythe & c., proceeded to warn Blackwell and party off. Hard words passed pro and con, when the woman proceeded to the work of demolishing the fence, upon which Blackwell seized a picket and commenced an assault, inflicting an ugly gash upon the head and breaking one arm. Mrs. U. is quite seriously, but not fatally injured. Blackwell has been arrested, and was to be examined yesterday (Thursday) afternoon.[350]

On 16 Feb 1860 Blackwell was brought before Justice Reyburn on the charge of assault and battery and was fined $100.[351] In the Court of Sessions the defendant pleaded that he had already been convicted of the offence charged in the indictment in the court of L. C. Reyburn, a Justice of the Peace for the Township of Petaluma, on 17 Feb 1860 and further pleaded that he was not guilty on 16 May 1860. The Court continued the case until the first day of the next term of Court. On 6 Aug 1860, the defendant failed to appear when his case was called in the Court of Sessions, and the Court ordered a bench warrant issued for his arrest.

People v. George O. Perkins

Gaming (case file # 107H)

The indictment filed on 11 May 1860 accused the defendant of dealing, playing, opening, and carrying on a game called monte, played with cards and for money, with James S. Oldham and other persons whose names were unknown to the Grand Jury for $20 on 7 Mar 1860. Stephen Odell, George W. Mathews, and James L. Pickett appeared as witnesses before the Grand Jury. The Court sustained the defendant's demurrer to the first indictment of 9 May 1860, and the case was resubmitted to the Grand Jury on 10 May 1860. The defendant was tried twice (11 May 1860 and 16 May 1860), and both times the trial jury could not agree on a verdict. The Court ordered the case continued to the next term of the Court and discharged the defendant on his own recognizance on 16 May 1860. The defendant failed to appear when his case was called on 6 Aug 1860, and the Court ordered a bench warrant issued for his arrest.

---

[350] "Affray at San Antonio," *The Sonoma County Journal* (Petaluma, California), 17 February 1860, p. 2, col. 1.

[351] "Fined," *The Sonoma County Journal* (Petaluma, California), 24 February 1860, p. 2, col. 5.

People v. Charles Tabor (var. Taber)
Grand larceny (case file # 107P)

The indictment filed on 11 May 1860 accused the defendant of stealing one bay horse (value $200), property of James Clyman, on 1 Jan 1860. Lancaster Clyman, Henry Yeagley, and Johnston Ireland appeared as witnesses before the Grand Jury. When his case was called in Court on 11 May 1860, the defendant, who was at large on bail, and his three sureties, failed to appear, and the Court ordered the defendant's recognizance forfeited and a bench warrant to issue for his arrest. Tabor (var. Taber) apparently had not been apprehended by 6 Aug 1860 when his case was again called in Court and he again failed to appear. The Court ordered an alias bench warrant to issue for his arrest.

August term 1860

The Court of Sessions met for six days this term, 6–11 August 1860.[352]

Hon. William Churchman, County Judge
Hon. William Ellis, Associate Justice
Hon. William H. Toombs, Associate Justice
R. C. Flournoy, District Attorney
Frank W. Shattuck, Clerk
William H. Crowell, Deputy Clerk
John J. Ellis, Sheriff
William Farmer, Grand Jury foreman

Persons called as Grand Jurors but not empaneled: George W. Oman (failed to answer call and the Court fined him $10), John O'Hara (alien), G. T. Pauli (alien), and Jacob Philips (alien).

Grand Jurors duly sworn, examined, and passed upon by the Court on 6 Aug 1860: William Farmer, S. T. Power, E. S. Pepper, J. W. Porter, Isaac Baker, William Ayres, J. D. Patton, Henry Beaver, John McReynolds, Charles Offutt, James P. Clark, Joseph Garston, Freeman Parker, Joshua Snow, William Huntley, and S. G. McCullough. The Court appointed William Farmer as Grand Jury foreman.

Grand Jury Report[353]

To the Honorable, the Court of Sessions,
The Grand Jury in and for said County, after a session of (4) four days, would beg to submit the following report: We have found (5) five indictments, (2) two for grand larceny, (2) two for

---

[352] Sonoma County, California, Court of Sessions, Minute Book E: 117-135, August term 1860 proceedings; Sonoma County Archives, Santa Rosa.
[353] Sonoma County, California, Court of Sessions, Grand Jury report for August term 1860, filed 9 August 1860; County Records, Sonoma County, Court Records, Miscellaneous Unprocessed Records, folder "County Records – Sonoma County – Court of Sessions – Reports of the Grand Jury "; California State Archives, Sacramento. "Report of the Grand Jury," *Sonoma County Democrat* (Santa Rosa, California), 16 August 1860, p. 1, col. 5.

assault and battery, and (1) one for vending liquors without a license. Five (5) causes [were] brought before us and dismissed for want of evidence.

We have inquired into the "condition and management of the public prison" with which we are entirely satisfied, but would recommend different and more secure locks and fastenings to the doors thereof. We find one inmate confined for petty larceny, two persons heretofore confined therein on a charge of grand larceny having escaped.

The County Hospital is neat and clean with one inmate whose condition is comfortable as possible.

The public offices, to wit, County Clerk, Sheriff, Recorder, and Treasurer, have all been visited with satisfaction, and with the exception of the Treasurer's books, we find all kept in a neat and creditable manner. With the office of the Treasurer we take pleasure in stating that we find no fault, except in the slovenly manner in which he keeps his books. In the office of County Clerk we think the book containing the official bonds would be improved in convenience by an index.

We find great negligence on the part of our officers whose duty it is to enforce the license laws as well as those whose business requires the taking out of licenses, and would recommend to the next Grand Jury to show no lenity to such persons whatever as the County is by such neglect defrauded annually out of a large amount of revenue.

We would call the attention of the proper officers to the terrible nuisance back of the Court House (the public water closet) and recommend its abatement at once. If it cannot be kept in better condition we recommend its entire removal.

All of which we respectfully submit and ask to be discharged.

Santa Rosa, August 9th, 1860

William Farmer, foreman

People v. John Hunter

Grand larceny (case file # 103)

The indictment filed on 7 Aug 1860 accused the defendant of stealing Spencer C. Way's gold watch with a double case (value $80) on 1 Feb 1860. George W. Mauk and Spencer C. Way appeared as witnesses before the Grand Jury. The defendant escaped from jail while waiting for action by the Grand Jury "by picking the lock on the door leading into the prison yard" on 13 Jul 1860.[354]

People v. James Kelso

Assault and battery (case file # 137)

The indictment filed on 7 Aug 1860 accused the defendant of assaulting Francis B. Green with force and arms on 22 May 1860. Francis B. Green, David Wharff, John Davis, Isaac Underwood, and Zedock Jackson appeared as witnesses before the Grand Jury. F. B. Green petitioned the Court to stay all proceedings in this cause because he had received satisfaction for the injury he had suffered by the acts charged, and the Court stayed all proceedings and discharged the defendant on 9 Aug 1860.

---

[354] "Escaped from Prison," *Sonoma County Democrat* (Santa Rosa, California), 19 July 1860, p. 2, col. 1.

People v. Perez Douglass
Assault with deadly weapon with intent to inflict a bodily injury (case file # 107B)

In a complaint dated and filed on 6 Jul 1860 William E. Weeks accused the defendant of assaulting him with a broad axe on 6 Jul 1860. The Grand Jury dismissed the complaint on 8 Aug 1860.

People v. Andrew J. Markwell
Vending by retail spiritous, malt, and vinous liquors without a license (case file # 94)

The indictment filed on 9 Aug 1860 accused the defendant of vending by retail spiritous, malt, and vinous liquors without a license on 12 May 1860. J. McReynolds, L. C. Cannon, and J. B. Southard appeared as witnesses before the Grand Jury. The defendant pleaded guilty on 5 Nov 1860. The Court ordered the defendant to pay a fine of $30 and stand committed until the fine was paid on 10 Nov 1860.

People v. James W. Porter
Assault and battery (case file # 107I)

The indictment filed on 9 Aug 1860 accused the defendant of assaulting Alden B. Nutting by beating, wounding, and ill-treating him on 28 May 1860. R. C. Flournoy, Alden B. Nutting, Elijah K. Jenner, Charles Hopkins, Lafayette Bond, and Solon P. Derby appeared as witnesses before the Grand Jury. The trial jury found the defendant not guilty on 8 Nov 1860.

People v. Joseph Wood
Grand larceny (case file # 107J)

The indictment filed on 9 Aug 1860 accused the defendant of stealing one dark bay horse, a stallion (value $100), property of William B. White, on 10 Jun 1860. A. A. Dunham, A. Ducker, W. B. White, and A. Leonard Boggs appeared as witnesses before the Grand Jury. When the case was called in Court on 9 Aug 1860 the defendant and his two sureties, Augustus Howell and Gottfried Wohlert, failed to appear, and the Court ordered the defendant's recognizance forfeited.

November term 1860

The Court of Sessions met for eleven days this term, 5, 7–10, and 12–17 November 1860.[355]

Hon. William Churchman, County Judge
Hon. William Ellis, Associate Justice
Hon. William H. Toombs, Associate Justice
R. C. Flournoy, District Attorney
A. Thomas, Acting District Attorney
Frank W. Shattuck, Clerk
William H. Crowell, Deputy Clerk
John J. Ellis, Sheriff

---

[355] Sonoma County, California, Court of Sessions, Minute Book E: 137–166, November term 1860 proceedings; Sonoma County Archives, Santa Rosa.

Robert E. Smith, Grand Jury foreman

Persons called as Grand Jurors but not empaneled: William S. Thurgood (rendered a sufficient excuse), S. D. Towne (rendered a sufficient excuse), J. M. Thornburg (rendered a sufficient excuse), Warren S. Thomas (rendered a sufficient excuse), J. W. Temple (failed to answer call), and William Thompson (failed to answer call).

Grand Jurors duly sworn and empaneled on 5 Nov 1860: Robert E. Smith, A. W. Russell, James McReynolds, T. O. Thompson, William E. Cocke, James McHenry, J. H. Truett, S. G. McCullough, Lancaster Clyman, John D. Thompson, Thomas B. Hood, M. Gillian, A. Tracey, J. G. Cook, Berthold Hoen, and Cornelius C. Money. The Court appointed Robert E. Smith foreman of the Grand Jury.

Lancaster Clyman was discharged from further attendance as a Grand Juror on 12 Nov 1860 "in consequence of [a] sudden and dangerous sickness of a member of his family." Elijah Dooley was examined and sworn to complete the Grand Jury on 12 Nov 1860.

Report of the Grand Jury[356]

To the Honorable, the Court of Sessions,

The Grand Jury submit the following report: That during a laborious session of nine days, they have enquired into all offences brought to their knowledge and have found thirteen indictments. Assault with intent to commit murder, three; grand larceny, two; assault with intent to commit rape, two; altering marks and brands, one; selling liquor within one mile of a campground, one; arson, one; for gambling and keeping a gambling house, three; and one presentment.

They report further that they have examined the County Hospital and find it well-kept, clean and the patients satisfied with the care and attention they receive.

The Jail is also in a neat and healthy condition, but some of the locks used in the Jail are insufficient, and the Grand Jury recommend that some more secure method of fastening the outside doors be adopted. They further report that they have been unable for want of time to make any enquiry into the condition of any of the County Offices.

Robert E. Smith, Foreman.

People v. E. B. Thompson
Forgery (case file # 107Q)

Stephen Smith filed a complaint dated 8 Oct 1860 in Justice William Haydon's Court in Petaluma Township accusing E. B. Thompson of falsely making, forging, and counterfeiting a promissory note for $1,200 by Stephen Smith payable to E. B. Thompson dated 7 Sep 1860. The examination of the defendant and several witnesses by Justice Haydon on 13 Oct 1860 was reported on by the *Sonoma County Journal* in a lengthy two-column article on 19 Oct 1860.[357]

---

[356] "Report of the Grand Jury," *The Sonoma County Democrat* (Santa Rosa, California), 22 November 1860, p. 3, col. 1. Sonoma County, California, Court of Sessions, Minute Book E: 162, Report of the Grand Jury, 14 November 1860; Sonoma County Archives, Santa Rosa.
[357] "Arrest for Forgery," *The Sonoma County Journal* (Petaluma, California), 19 October 1860, p. 2, cols. 3–4.

Stephen Smith testified "that he had never made a note for $1,200 in his life, in favor of [the defendant] Thompson or anybody else." E. B. Thompson, the defendant, claimed he saw Stephen Smith sign the note himself and offered a convoluted explanation of the affair involving a mortgage he, Thompson, held on C. I. Robinson and wife's homestead. The defendant "was held for trial, and bail fixed at $1,500, which was obtained without the least difficulty." The Grand Jury dismissed the case on 7 Nov 1860.

People v. John Linus
Assault with intent to commit murder (case file # 107C)
The indictment filed on 8 Nov 1860 accused the defendant of assaulting Charles Jefferson by shooting at him with a pistol on 10 Sep 1860. Charles Jefferson, Elisabeth Jefferson, and Charles Offutt appeared as witnesses before the Grand Jury. On 13 Sep 1860, the *Sonoma County Democrat* reported the shooting as:

> On Monday last [10 Sep 1860], Mr. John Linus and a Mr. Jefferson, got into a quarrel, near Petaluma, concerning the ownership of some land, in the midst of which Mr. Linus shot Jefferson with a pistol, the ball entering his back and passing out near the hip, inflicting a severe flesh wound. We learn that Mr. Linus had been frequently threatened with injury by Jefferson and his wife, and was compelled to use the weapon in self-defense. Our informant said that the impression prevailed at the scene of the affair, that the act was justifiable. At last advices Mr. Linus had not been arrested.[358]

The next day, on 14 Sep 1860, the *Sonoma County Journal* gave a few more details of the affair and a different cause.

> Dr. J. L. Bond, of this city [Petaluma], was called on Wednesday evening last [12 Sep 1860], to attend to Mr. Charles Jefferson, whose residence is about three miles out of town, on the Santa Rosa road, and who had been shot by Mr. John Linus. An examination of the case, showed that the ball had entered Jefferson just above the left hip, and lodged on the right side, just grazing the spine in its course. The ball was extracted, and the patient is doing well. A writ was issued for the arrest of Linus, but had not been served in consequence of his keeping himself secreted. The shooting is understood to have grown out of a difficulty in relation to some wood.[359]

The trial jury found the defendant not guilty on 14 Nov 1860.

People v. Charles O'Neal
Grand larceny (case file # 107F)
The indictment filed on 8 Nov 1860 accused the defendant of stealing three quilts (total value $50), two white blankets (total value $5), and one pair of pants (value $5), property of William C.

---

[358] "Shooting Affray Near Petaluma," *Sonoma County Democrat* (Santa Rosa, California), 13 September 1860, p. 2, col. 2.
[359] "Shooting Difficulty," *The Sonoma County Journal* (Petaluma, California), 14 September 1860, p. 2, col. 1.

Ragle, on 5 Oct 1860. William C. Ragle and George Ragle appeared as witnesses before the Grand Jury.

People v. James Schivo
Assault with intent to commit murder (case file # 93)

The indictment filed 9 Nov 1860 accused the defendant of shooting at Joseph Schiapacasse with a shot gun with the intent to murder him on 26 Oct 1860. Joseph Schiapacasse, Antonio Schiapacasse, Jose Marie Peres, William Smith, and John A. Young (as interpreter for Antonio Schiapacasse) appeared as witnesses before the Grand Jury. On 2 Nov 1860, the *Sonoma County Journal* described the events of the shooting as:

> A shooting affray occurred at the Italian Garden, near Rudesill's Landing, last Friday morning [26 Oct 1860], between James Schio [Schivo] and Joseph Schiapicasse [Schiapacasse] (brothers-in-law) in relation to the building of a wharf at that point. Schiapicasse, it appears, made the first demonstration by the drawing of his pistol, whereupon, Schio, who had a shot gun in his hand, presented it and fired. From fifty to seventy-five shot took effect in the neck, face and eyes of Joe, inflicting an ugly wound. The left eye is totally ruined, and the right badly injured. Both parties were promptly arrested. Schio had an examination before Justice Reyburn, on Friday, and was held for trial in the sum of $500. Schiapicasse, as soon as able to appear, will be arraigned under a charge of drawing deadly weapons.[360]

The trial jury found the defendant guilty of committing an assault with a deadly weapon, to wit, a double-barreled shotgun, with the intent to inflict bodily injury on 13 Nov 1860. The Court ordered the defendant to pay a fine of $400 and in the case of non-payment of the fine to be imprisoned in the County Jail of Sonoma County for the term of 200 days until the fine was satisfied on 17 Nov 1860. The *Sonoma County Democrat* reported on 22 Nov 1860 that "the fine was promptly paid, and the prisoner released."[361]

People v. Frederick G. Blume
Assault with intent to commit murder (case file # 117)

The indictment filed on 9 Nov 1860 accused the defendant of assaulting Robert Dobson by shooting him with a pistol with the intent to murder him on 1 Nov 1860. John A. Young, David McAfee, Elijah McAfee, James L. Merrill, and Irving R. Morris appeared as witnesses before the Grand Jury. The *Sonoma County Democrat* reported the shooting and its cause on 8 Nov 1860 as:

> We are informed by a gentleman from Sebastopol that a shooting affray occurred in Analy Township last Monday [5 Nov 1860], in which, F. G. Bloome shot R. Dobson. It seems that Bloome has had good cause to suspect Mrs. Bloome of infidelity and of being *too* intimate with Dobson; and on last Monday found them together and fired upon Dobson; the ball taking effect in Dobson's back and passed through the left lung. He then attempted to shoot his wife, but some person struck his arm, and the ball passed over

---

[360] "Shooting," *The Sonoma County Journal* (Petaluma, California), 2 November 1860, p. 2, col. 1.
[361] "Sentenced," *The Sonoma County Democrat* (Santa Rosa, California), 22 November 1860, p. 3, col. 2.

them. Dobson's wound is supposed to be mortal. Bloome then went before a magistrate and gave himself up. We have not heard the result of the examination.[362]

The trial jury found the defendant not guilty on 13 Feb 1861.

People v. Spencer P. Emerson
Assault with intent to commit rape (case file # 107A)
The indictment filed on 10 Nov 1860 accused the defendant of assaulting Mary E. Thurston by attempting to pull and jerk her down from her horse by violently thrusting his hand under her clothes and trying to ravish and carnally know her on 29 Jan 1860. Mary E. Thurston, Lurissa Thurston, and William McReynolds appeared as witnesses before the Grand jury. The trial jury found the defendant not guilty on 9 Aug 1861.

People v. Charles Jefferson
Altering marks and brands (case file # 119)
The indictment filed on 10 Nov 1860 accused the defendant of marking, altering, and defacing the mark of one of P. K. Rackliff's hogs on 10 Oct 1860. P. K. Rackliff and Charles Merrit appeared as witnesses before the Grand Jury. The first trial jury found the defendant guilty and recommended him to the mercy of the Court on 5 Feb 1861. The Court granted the defendant a new trial on 8 Feb 1861. The second trial jury could not agree on a verdict on 6 Mar 1861. The third trial jury found Jefferson not guilty on 9 Mar 1861, and he was discharged from custody.

People v. Richard (var. R. D.) Wilson
Grand larceny
The presentment was filed on 10 Nov 1860, and the Court ordered a bench warrant issued for the defendant returnable before the Hon. L. C. Reyburn, a Justice of the Peace of Petaluma Township, on 17 Nov 1860. The bench warrant was issued on 19 Nov 1860. It was returned and filed on 8 Dec 1860. The defendant was required to give a bond in the sum of $500 to answer to the Court and was committed to the custody of the Sheriff until the bond was given.

People v. George W. Hagenmeyer
Assault with intent to commit a rape (case file # 104)
The indictment filed on 14 Nov 1860 accused the defendant of assaulting Ida Ludolph by trying to ravish and carnally know her on 10 Jul 1860. Henry Ludolph, Mary Ludolph, and Dr. C. C. Green appeared as witnesses before the Grand Jury.

People v. Hiram White
Grand larceny (case file # 107N)
The indictment filed on 14 Nov 1860 accused the defendant of stealing one bay mare (value $65) and one saddle (value $15), property of Obediah Rippetoe, on 7 Aug 1860. Nathaniel W. Bostwick and S. G. McCollough appeared as witnesses before the Grand Jury. White was arrested

---

[362] "Shooting," *The Sonoma County Democrat* (Santa Rosa, California), 8 November 1860, p. 2, col. 1. The date of the shooting as reported in newspapers of the time vary.

by the Mendocino County Sheriff and taken to Healdsburg for examination. He escaped his confinement in the brick cellar of Hooper's Block there sometime before the morning of 3 Sep 1860.[363] He apparently was recaptured and placed in the County Jail from which he escaped again on 24 Oct 1860. The *Sonoma County Democrat* gave the details of the escape on 25 Oct 1860 and added a note to the Board of Supervisors.

> Hiram White, committed by Justice Ireland, of Mendocino Township, to await trial on charge of grand larceny, in stealing horses, made his escape from the County Jail last night [24 Oct 1860], by picking the lock on the door leading to the prison yard. Sheriff Ellis has offered a reward [$25] for his arrest, and a full description of his person will be found in our advertising columns. We are informed that this is the third time the lock on the yard door has been picked; and we hope the Supervisors will make the necessary appropriation to enable the Sheriff to repair the locks.[364]

The $25 Sheriff's reward notice for the arrest of White described him as: "He has light hair, blue eyes, is of spare build, about 5 feet 8 inches high, and was dressed in light woolen pants, check shirt, and black hat. He had a pale sallow look, and is about 25 years old."[365] The Grand Jury dismissed the case on 14 Nov 1860.

People v. Thomas Finchley
Selling liquor within one mile of a camp meeting (case file # 113)

The indictment filed on 14 Nov 1860 accused the defendant of erecting and keeping a tent, booth, stall, and contrivance for the purpose of selling and otherwise disposing of spiritous and fermented liquors (whiskey and brandy) within one mile of a camp meeting for religious worship during the time of the holding of the meeting on 30 Sep 1860. Thomas Crowley, William Barnes, James Seawell (var. Sewell), William Parker, and V. J. Ballou appeared as witnesses before the Grand Jury. The defendant pleaded guilty on 5 Feb 1861. The Court ordered the defendant to pay a fine of $50 and in the case of non-payment of the fine to be imprisoned in the County Jail of Sonoma County for the term of 25 days until the fine was satisfied on 8 Feb 1861.

People v. John Morand
Gaming house (case file # 97)

The indictment filed on 15 Nov 1860 accused the defendant of knowingly permitting the games of faro, monte, roulette, lansquenet, rouge et noir, and ronds to be played, conducted, and dealt in a house rented by the defendant on 10 Oct 1860. James W. Turney, William M. Howard, P. F. Decker, B. Hoen, S. G. McCullough, and Henry Beaver appeared as witnesses before the Grand Jury. For related cases, see case file #s 101 and 137C.

---

[363] "Escaped," *The Sonoma County Journal* (Petaluma, California), 7 September 1860, p. 2, col. 3.
[364] "Escape from Prison," *The Sonoma County Democrat* (Santa Rosa, California), 25 October 1860, p. 2, col. 5.
[365] "$25 reward," *The Sonoma County Democrat* (Santa Rosa, California), 25 October 1860, p. 2, col. 6.

People v. Milton Hall
Gaming (case file # 101)

The indictment filed on 15 Nov 1860 accused the defendant of playing, opening, carrying on, and conducting as owner and employee a game called rondo played with balls and other devices for money on 10 Oct 1860. James W. Turney, W. N. Howard, P. F. Decker, B. Hoen, and S. G. McCullough appeared as witnesses before the Grand Jury. For related cases, see case file #s 97 and 137C.

People v. Fenwick Fisher
Gaming (case file # 137C)

The indictment filed on 15 Nov 1860 accused the defendant of knowingly permitting the games of faro, monte, roulette, lansquenet, rouge et noir, and rondo, games played with cards, dice, and other devices for money, checks, credit, and other representatives of value, to be played, conducted, and dealt in a house rented by him on 10 Oct 1860. James W. Turney, Henry Beaver, William N. Howard, P. F. Decker, B. Hoen, and S. G. McCollough (var. McCullough) appeared as witnesses before the Grand Jury. The trial jury could not agree on a verdict on 13 Aug 1861. The Court dismissed the indictment for want of sufficient testimony on 12 Nov 1861. For related cases, see case file #s 97 and 101.

People v. George Edgar
Arson

The indictment filed on 15 Nov 1860 accused the defendant of setting fire to and burning down the barn of Rufus King on the night of 17 Sep 1860.[366] Rufus King, William Faught, Medora Travor, and William Patterson appeared as witnesses before the Grand Jury. The *Sonoma County Journal* reported on 21 Sep 1860 that George Edgar had been arrested and charged with setting fire to and burning down the barn of R. H. King containing hay, grain, farming tools, and over 100 hens on the morning of 18 Sep 1860.[367] Edgar was examined by Justice Hayden and released on bail of $600. The case was transferred to the Sonoma County District Court on 15 Nov 1860. The District Court sustained the defendant's demurrer on 19 Feb 1861 and ordered that the case be submitted to the next Grand Jury.[368]

On 3 Dec 1860, the Hon. L. C. Reyburn and the Hon. William Ellis were elected as Associate Justices of the Court of Sessions at a convention of the Justices of the Peace of Sonoma County.

---

[366] Sonoma County, California, County Court, case file # 32 (OS), People v. George Edgar, indictment, 15 November 1860; California State Archives, Sacramento. The District Court case file for this suit has been erroneously filed with the County Court case files although there were no County Court proceedings.
[367] "Fire," *The Sonoma County Journal* (Petaluma, California), 21 September 1860, p. 2, col. 1.
[368] Sonoma County, California, District Court, Minute Book B: 511 and 525, People v. George Edgar, case proceedings, 1861; Sonoma County Archives, Santa Rosa.

February term 1861

The Court of Sessions met for twenty-two days this term, 4–9, 11–16, and 18 February 1861, 4–9 and 18–19 March 1861, and 1 April 1861.[369]

Hon. William Churchman, County Judge
Hon. William Ellis, Associate Justice
Hon. L. C. Reyburn, Associate Justice
Hon. D. D. Myers, Acting Associate Justice
Hon. Joel Miller, Acting Associate Justice
R. C. Flournoy, District Attorney
William H. Jones, Acting District Attorney
Frank W. Shattuck, Clerk
William H. Crowell, Deputy Clerk
John J. Ellis, Sheriff
E. Latapie, Deputy Sheriff
William L. Anderson, Grand Jury foreman

Persons called as Grand Jurors but not empaneled: Hugh Brun (failed to answer call), A. W. Acker (failed to answer call), and Henry Babcock (failed to answer call).

Grand Jurors duly sworn and empaneled on 4 Feb 1861: William L. Anderson, William Ayers, Jr., William T. Allen, I. A. Bradshaw, Robert Aiken, Norman Fay, Edward Barry, A. W. Russell, S. J. Agnew, J. B. Cook, J. N. Barry, Z. Jackson, John A. Abbay, William M. Roberts, David Ayers, and J. B. Fretwell. The Court appointed William L. Anderson as Grand Jury foreman.

The Court excused J. N. Barry from further attendance as a Grand Juror on 9 Feb 1861 after "showing to the Court under oath good and sufficient cause why he should be so excused." James P. Clark was sworn as Barry's replacement as a Grand Juror on 9 Feb 1861.

Report of the Grand Jury[370]

To the Honorable Court of Sessions of Sonoma County,

The Grand Jury of Sonoma County, during a session of nine days, beg leave to report as follows: After having examined all matters presented to us, we have found seventeen indictments, viz.: For murder, three; for grand larceny, two; for assault with intent to commit great bodily injury, one; for misdemeanor, eleven; and have ignored one charge.

We have examined the offices of the county, and find them well-kept. The offices of Recorder, Auditor and Clerk, are kept in a manner alike creditable to the respective officers and the county.

---

[369] Sonoma County, California, Court of Sessions, Minute Book E: 169–232 and 234, February term 1861 proceedings; Sonoma County Archives, Santa Rosa.

[370] Sonoma County, California, Court of Sessions, Minute Book E: 194, Report of the Grand Jury, 13 February 1861; Sonoma County Archives, Santa Rosa. "Report of the Grand Jury," *The Sonoma County Democrat* (Santa Rosa, California), 14 February 1861, p. 2, col. 4.

The books, maps, papers, &c., are clean and properly arranged—the writing well executed. The Treasurer's and Sheriff's offices are also properly kept; the books are kept in a good and business-like manner.

The present indebtedness of the county, in bonds issued, is $54,900; in county scrip, not redeemed by the bonds, a small amount—it is not known the exact amount. At this time there are in all the funds on hand $33,241.96. The amount of county bonds redeemed since the funding act took effect, is $4,500. Thus showing that the actual indebtedness of the county is about one-half what it was last May.

The Hospital we find neat, as kept by the contractor. At this time there are three persons in the hospital, under the charge of the County Physician. We find that the County Physician is conducting the arduous duties of his office with honor to himself and credit to the county. The jail, like the hospital, is properly kept, and prisoners well cared for. There are at this time confined in the jail seven prisoners. The jail is very insecure; the cells are frequently dug out of by the prisoners.

We would recommend [to] the Supervisors to furnish for the Court House the necessary number of chairs; also, drugget for the bar floor. We also call immediate attention to the roofs of the Court House and Jail, which are in a very bad condition; the jail yard is a public nuisance in its present condition, as it is not high enough to prevent the escape of prisoners—hence it is used as a common reservoir. It appears that the Court House is occasionally used for religious and other purposes; we would therefore recommend [to the] Supervisors to instruct parties thus using the room, to adopt some means for the better preservation of the furniture and cleaning the room.

W. L. Anderson, Foreman of the Grand Jury.

People v. John Doe
Charge unstated (case file # 116A)
The Grand Jury dismissed the case February term 1861.

People v. William H. Meiering
Assault with a deadly weapon with intent to inflict bodily injury (case file # 108)
The indictment filed 7 Feb 1861 accused the defendant of assaulting William B. Pearson by shooting him with a gun on 2 Jan 1861. William B. Pearson and Henry Campbell appeared as witnesses before the Grand Jury. The first trial jury could not agree on a verdict on 5 Mar 1861. The second trial jury found the defendant not guilty on 8 Mar 1861.

People v. James R. Graham
Receiving stolen property knowing it to be stolen (case file # 110)
The indictment filed on 7 Feb 1861 accused the defendant of receiving stolen property knowing it to be stolen (480 pieces of gold commonly known as slugs, each of the value of $50, for a total value of $24,000), the property of Granville P. Swift, on 20 Jul 1860. G. P. Swift, Robert Ayers, Stephen Odell, W. R. Cluness, Smith D. Towne, J. Q. Shirley, James S. Hutchinson, Henry S. Babcock, James Leary, Mrs. Margaret O'Sullivan, James O'Sullivan, and William H. Jones appeared as witnesses before the Grand Jury. The Court ordered the action transferred to the Court of Sessions of Napa County on 5 Mar 1861. Graham was apparently convicted in that Court of

receiving stolen goods and sentenced to five years' imprisonment in the State Prison.[371] San Quentin received him on 19 Sep 1861. After petitioning the California Supreme Court for a writ of habeas corpus, he was discharged three and a half years later on 6 Mar 1865 by an order of that Court "on account of informalities in the commitment and other kindred reasons."[372] For related cases, see also case file #s 111 and 112.

People v. John Sweeny (alias Long John) and James R. Graham
Grand larceny (case file # 112)

The indictment filed on 7 Feb 1861 accused the defendants of stealing 480 flat pieces of gold of the octagon form commonly known as and called slugs, each of the value of $50 (total value $24,000), the property of Granville P. Swift, on 20 Jul 1860. G. P. Swift, George S. Tate, Charles Patten, F. S. Jones, Robert Ayers, Stephen Odell, J. C. Gardener, W. R. Cluness, Charles Arthur, John Tate, O. M. LeFever, Smith D. Towne, J. Q. Shirley, James S. Hutchinson, Henry S. Babcock, Mrs. Ann Graham, James Leary, Margaret O'Sullivan, James O'Sullivan, James R. Graham, and William H. Jones appeared as witnesses before the Grand Jury. The Court granted the defendants separate trials on 8 Feb 1861. A *nolle prosequi* was entered for the defendant James R. Graham, and the indictment was dismissed for the purpose of obtaining his testimony against his co-defendant John Sweeny on 15 Feb 1861. The *Sonoma County Democrat* devoted two and a half columns reporting John Sweeny's trial on 21 Feb 1861, stating that the evidence was "so voluminous that we can only present abstracts of the main points of testimony in the case."[373] The trial jury found the defendant John Sweeny guilty on 16 Feb 1861. The Court ordered him imprisoned in the State Prison for the term of eleven years on 18 Feb 1861. San Quentin received Sweeny on 22 Feb 1861, and he was discharged on 22 May 1870.[374] For related cases, see also case file #s 110 and 111.

People v. William Manion
Assault with intent to inflict bodily injury

The Grand Jury dismissed the charge on 7 Feb 1861.

People v. Thomas Stewart, James Stewart, and Samuel Stewart
Murder

The indictment filed on 9 Feb 1861 accused the defendant Thomas Stewart of assaulting Lina Davenport Helm (var. Helms) by shooting him in the right side of the breast with a gun giving him

---

[371] California, State Prison Register (1851–1867), Executive Department, entry no. 2240, James R. Graham, p. 184, received 19 September 1861; California State Archives, Sacramento.

[372] "Discharged," *Sacramento (California) Daily Union*, 7 March 1865, p. 3, col. 1. California, Supreme Court, Minute Book 1: 360, application of James R. Graham for discharge, court order discharging the prisoner, 6 March 1865; California State Archives, Sacramento.

[373] "Granville P. Swift vs. John Sweeny," *The Sonoma County Democrat* (Santa Rosa, California), 21 February 1861, p. 2, cols. 2-4.

[374] California, State Prison Register (1851–1867), Executive Department, entry no. 2106, John Sweeny, p. 173, received 22 February 1861; California State Archives, Sacramento.

a mortal wound of which he died on 24 Nov 1860.[375] The indictment also accused the defendants James Stewart and Samuel Stewart of abetting and assisting Thomas Stewart in the murder of Lina Davenport Helm on 24 Nov 1860. The indictment further accused the defendant Thomas Stewart of murdering Lina Davenport Helm on 24 Nov 1860 in the manner stated previously and further accused the defendants James Stewart and Samuel Stewart of inciting, advising, and encouraging Thomas Stewart to murder Lina Davenport Helm on 23 Nov 1860. H. T. Helm, George Currier (var. Currin, Curran), Ira Mapes, Enos Parks, James Mulatt, Christopher Stingle, and E. Webber appeared as witnesses before the Grand Jury. The *Sonoma County Democrat* described the shooting in its 29 Nov 1860 edition as:

> On Saturday morning last, 24th inst. [24 Nov 1860], while Mr. L. D. Helms, of Salt Point Township, was setting in front of his house, in company with two persons, he was suddenly shot dead, by some unknown person. As yet, it is impossible to get the exact particulars of this horrible affair. Report was made to Sheriff Ellis, and he has dispatched officers to the neighborhood who will use every means to ferret out the murder and bring to justice the cold-blooded fiend who has deliberately taken the life of Mr. Helms. Mr. Geo. Currin, one of the party who was with Mr. Helms when he was shot, informed us that the weapon used was a rifle, and that he saw the smoke rise from the bushes immediately after the unfortunate man fell, about fifty yards from the house. The ball struck the right arm, above the elbow, and lodged in the breast. Mr. Helms exclaimed, "I am shot," and fell dead. The murdered man has no family, but a brother residing in the Salt Point Township. An inquest will be held upon the body. We will probably be able to give a fuller report of the lamentable affair in our next issue.[376]

Two weeks later on 13 Dec 1860, the *Sonoma County Democrat* reported at length on Justice Myers' examination of witnesses in the case.[377] He "held James Stewart and Samuel Stewart to answer before the Court of Sessions, and fixed their bonds at $1,000." Thomas Stewart had initially been arrested by Deputy Sheriff Daniel Rice in Point Arenas, but escaped from custody on the trip down to Santa Rosa.[378]

The case was transferred to the Sonoma County District Court on 9 Feb 1861. See Sonoma County District Court case #s 237 (OS) and 1050 (OS). The District Court granted the defendants James Stewart and Samuel Stewart separate trials on 19 Feb 1861.[379] The District Court granted the defendants a change of venue for trial and ordered the cases transferred to the District Court

---

[375] Sonoma County, California, District Court, case # 237 (OS), The People of the State of California v. Thomas Stewart et al., certified copy of the indictment, 15 March 1861; County Records, Sonoma County, Court Records, District Court case files; California State Archives, Sacramento.

[376] "Brutally Assassinated," *The Sonoma County Democrat* (Santa Rosa, California), 29 November 1860, p. 2, col. 2.

[377] "The People versus Stewart et al.," *The Sonoma County Democrat* (Santa Rosa, California), 13 December 1860, p. 2, cols. 2–3.

[378] "Arrests in the Helm Case," *The Sonoma County Democrat* (Santa Rosa, California), 6 December 1860, p. 2, col. 2.

[379] Sonoma County, California, District Court, Minute Book B: 525, The People of the State of California v. Samuel and James Stewart, court order for separate trials, 19 February 1861; Sonoma County Archives, Santa Rosa.

of Napa County on 22 Feb 1861.[380] These two Stewart brothers were apparently acquitted of the charges in this Court.[381]

The third Stewart brother, Thomas, was rearrested four years later on 19 Dec 1864 at the home of his father near Vallejo in Solano County.[382] He was brought "before a Justice of the Peace at Vallejo and admitted to bail in the sum of $5,000." After posting the necessary bond, he was released from custody and went to Mendocino County to work on a farm, "where he was arrested again, on the ground that being charged with a capital offence, he could not legally be admitted to bail."[383] In the Sonoma County District Court, the Hon. E. D. Sawyer, judge of the 4th Judicial District Court, presiding, the trial jury found him guilty of murder in the 2nd degree on 23 Jun 1865.[384] The District Court sentenced Stewart to life imprisonment in the State Prison on 29 Jun 1865.[385] San Quentin received Stewart on 1 Jul 1865, but he was discharged by an order of the Court on 15 Oct 1865 after he appealed to the California Supreme Court.[386] This Court reversed the District Court's judgment and granted Stewart a new trial because the District Court "erred in excluding the testimony offered by the defendant for the purpose of proving his character for peace and quiet to be good."[387] Because the judge of the Sonoma County District Court, the Hon. J. B. Southard, had been consulted in the cause prior to his election as the District Court judge, the Sonoma County District Court transferred the case to the Contra Costa County District Court on 19 Oct 1865.[388] An article in the *Daily Evening Bulletin* of 23 Apr 1866 summarized Stewart's Contra Costa County District Court case proceedings and trial jury verdict as:

> The trial of Thomas J. Stewart for the murder of Davenport Helms in Sonoma County in 1860 has occupied the attention of the Fifteenth District Court for Contra Costa county, sitting at Martinez, Judge Dwinelle presiding, during nearly all of last week, and

[380] Sonoma County, California, District Court, Minute Book B: 549, The People of the State of California v. James Stewart and The People of the State of California v. Samuel Stewart, court order for a change of venue for trial, 22 February 1861; Sonoma County Archives, Santa Rosa.

[381] "Charged with Murder," *Daily Evening Bulletin* (San Francisco, California), 15 February 1865, p. 3, col. 2.

[382] "Re-Arrested – Out on Bail," *The Sonoma County Democrat* (Santa Rosa, California), 24 December 1864, p. 2, col. 1.

[383] "To Be Tried For Murder," *Daily Alta California* (San Francisco, California), 15 February 1865, p. 1, col. 1.

[384] "District Court – June Term 1865," *The Sonoma County Democrat* (Santa Rosa, California), 24 June 1865, p. 2, col. 3. Sonoma County, California, District Court, Minute Book C: 402, The People of the State of California v. Thomas Stewart, trial jury verdict, 23 June 1865; Sonoma County Archives, Santa Rosa.

[385] "Sentence of the Court in the Murder Cases," *The Sonoma County Democrat* (Santa Rosa, California), 1 July 1865, p. 3, col. 2. Sonoma County, California, District Court, Minute Book C: 420, The People of the State of California v. Thomas Stewart, judgment, 29 June 1865; Sonoma County Archives, Santa Rosa.

[386] California, State Prison Register (1851–1867), Executive Department, entry no. 3050, Thomas Stewart, p. 255, received 1 July 1865; California State Archives, Sacramento.

[387] Charles A. Tuttle, reporter, *Reports of Cases Determined in the Supreme Court of the State of California*, vol. 28 (Sacramento: O. M. Clayes & Co., 1866), 395–396, *The People* v. *Thomas J. Stewart* (1865). This case was argued before the California Supreme Court during the Court's July term 1865 on 15 August 1865. See, California, Supreme Court, Minute Book 1: 545, People vs. Stewart, proceedings of the case, 15 August 1865; California State Archives, Sacramento.

[388] "District Court," *The Sonoma County Democrat* (Santa Rosa, California), 21 October 1865, p. 3, col. 2. Sonoma County, California, District Court, Minute Book C: 448–449, The People of the State of California v. Thomas J. Stewart, court order transferring case to the Contra Costa District Court in the 15th Judicial District, 19 October 1865; Sonoma County Archives, Santa Rosa.

terminated late on Saturday afternoon [21 Apr 1866] in a verdict of not guilty. There had been some squatter feuds between the families in that neighborhood, and Helms was shot early in the morning while sitting on a log of wood in front of his door by some person concealed in the brush some yards distant. Suspicion fastened upon Stewart, at that time only 19 years of age, on account of a fight he had previously had with Helms, in which the latter appeared to have got the worst of it; and on account of threats by Helms that he would shoot Stewart on sight, having come to Stewart's knowledge. Helms appeared to have been regarded as a desperate, dangerous sort of man; and there was some evidence (although it was strongly controverted) to the effect that Stewart had declared after the shooting that he had killed Helms. Aside from this disputed evidence, the testimony was purely circumstantial; and Stewart was able to show that both previous to and subsequent to the killing he had borne an excellent character. He had been once tried on the same indictment in Sonoma county, and convicted of murder in the second degree, but a new trial was granted by the Supreme Court, upon which state of facts Judge Dwinelle decided that the jury could not find a verdict of murder in the first degree.[389]

After a long discussion about whether Stewart's Point, the place of the murder, was under the jurisdiction of Sonoma County at the time of the murder or not, the article concluded, "The verdict of not guilty, returned by the jury after an absence of only 20 minutes, was received by an irrepressible outburst of applause in the crowded courtroom—several ladies present showering bouquets of flowers upon the prisoner and his counsel."

People v. James R. Graham
Vending liquor without a license (case file # 110)
The indictment filed on 13 Feb 1861 accused the defendant of vending by retail spiritous, malt, and vinous liquors in quantities less than a quart without a license on 8 Jan 1861. Stephen Odell and John Henley appeared as witnesses before the Grand Jury. For related cases, see also case file #s 111 and 112.

People v. Patrick Sweeny and Jeremiah Sweeny (indicted as John Sweeny)
Vending by retail spiritous, malt, and vinous liquors in quantities less than a quart without a license (case file # 111)[390]
The indictment filed on 13 Feb 1861 accused the defendants of vending by retail spiritous, malt, and vinous liquors in quantities less than a quart without a license on 5 Feb 1860. James O'Sullivan, James M. Gray, and John Henley appeared as witnesses before the Grand Jury. A *nolle prosequi* as to Jeremiah Sweeny was entered, and Patrick Sweeny pleaded guilty on 16 Feb 1861. The Court ordered Patrick Sweeny to pay a fine of $76 and in the case of the non-payment of the fine to be imprisoned in the County Jail of Sonoma County for the term of 38 days until the fine was satisfied on 18 Feb 1861. For related cases, see also case file #s 110 and 112.

---

[389] "Murder Trial at Martinez – A Novel Question of Law," *Daily Evening Bulletin* (San Francisco, California), 23 April 1866, p. 5, col. 5.
[390] Most of the documents in case file # 111 actually pertain to case file # 112, People v. John Sweeny and James R. Graham.

People v. Andrew J. Markwell
Vending spiritous liquors without license (case file # 115)

The indictment filed on 13 Feb 1861 accused the defendant of vending by retail spiritous, malt, and vinous liquors in quantities less than a quart without a license on 5 Feb 1861. James P. Clark, Isaac Baker, and John A. Abby appeared as witnesses before the Grand Jury. The trial jury found the defendant guilty on 7 Mar 1861. The Court ordered the defendant to pay a fine of $150 and in the case of non-payment to be imprisoned in the County Jail of Sonoma County until the fine was satisfied at the rate of $2 per day on 8 Mar 1861. A. J. Markwell was the proprietor of the Stony Point House according to newspaper advertisements of the day.[391]

People v. James Culligan (indicted as James Calligan)
Vending spiritous liquors without a license (case file # 124)

The indictment filed on 13 Feb 1861 accused the defendant of vending by retail spiritous, malt, and vinous liquors in quantities less than a quart without a license on 10 Jan 1861. James O'Sullivan, Jacob C. Peavey, J. J. Pennypacker, and John Henley appeared as witnesses before the Grand Jury. The defendant pleaded guilty on 4 Mar 1861. The Court ordered the defendant to pay a fine of $70 and in the case of non-payment to be imprisoned in the County Jail of Sonoma County until the fine was satisfied at the rate of $2 per day on 5 Mar 1861.

People v. William C. Jordan
Vending spiritous liquors by retail without a license (case file # 126)

The indictment filed on 13 Feb 1861 accused the defendant of vending by retail spiritous, malt, and vinous liquors in quantities less than a quart without a license on 25 Jan 1861. Stephen Odell, J. J. Pennypacker, and John Henley appeared as witnesses before the Grand Jury. The defendant pleaded guilty on 16 Feb 1861. The defendant withdrew his guilty plea and pleaded not guilty on 18 Feb 1861. After two jury trials on 7 Mar 1861 and 9 May 1861 in which the trial juries could not agree on a verdict, a *nolle prosequi* was entered, and the defendant was discharged on 10 May 1861.

People v. William R. Dodge (indicted as Henry Dodge)
Vending spiritous liquor without a license (case file # 128)

The indictment filed on 13 Feb 1861 accused the defendant of vending by retail spiritous, malt, and vinous liquors in quantities less than a quart without a license on 24 Feb 1861. Michael Barnes and John Hendley appeared as witnesses before the Grand Jury. The defendant pleaded guilty on 16 Feb 1861. Because the offense was committed subsequent to the filing of the indictment the Court ordered an arrest of judgment, and the defendant was discharged on 18 Feb 1861.

---

[391] For example, see "Stony Point House," *The Sonoma County Journal* (Petaluma, California), 8 February 1861, p. 4, col. 7.

People v. Jesse Blanchard
Selling spiritous, malt and vinous liquors by retail without a license (case file # 135)

The indictment filed on 13 Feb 1861 accused the defendant of vending by retail spiritous, malt, and vinous liquors in quantities less than a quart without a license on 10 Jan 1861. Enos Park (var. Parks) and John Hendley appeared as witnesses before the Grand Jury. Because the principal prosecuting witness Enos Parks had died and a conviction could not be had the Court dismissed the indictment on 5 Aug 1861.[392]

People v. Samuel Eberhart (var. Eberheardt) and Peter Gleason
Vending spiritous liquors without a license (case file # 136)

The indictment filed on 13 Feb 1861 accused the defendant of vending by retail spiritous, malt, and vinous liquors in quantities less than a quart without a license on 3 Feb 1861. S. J. Agnew, William Ellis, James P. Clark, and John Henley appeared as witnesses before the Grand Jury. A *nolle prosequi* was entered, and the Court dismissed the indictment due to the insufficiency of the evidence on 15 Feb 1861.

People v. Francis Post (indicted as Frank Post)
Vending spiritous liquors by retail without a license (case file # 137D)

The indictment filed on 13 Feb 1861 accused the defendant of vending spiritous, malt, and vinous liquors by retail in quantities less than a quart without a license on 20 Jan 1861. Stephen Odell, J. J. Pennypacker, and John Henley appeared as witnesses before the Grand Jury. The trial jury found the defendant not guilty on 7 Mar 1861.

People v. William J. Reynolds
Vending spiritous liquors by retail without a license (case file # 137E)

The indictment filed on 13 Feb 1861 accused the defendant of vending spiritous, malt, and vinous liquors by retail in quantities less than a quart without a license on 10 Jan 1861. S. J. Agnew, William Ellis, and John Hendley appeared as witnesses before the Grand Jury. The trial jury found the defendant guilty on 6 Mar 1861. The Court ordered the defendant to pay a fine of $120 and in the case of non-payment to be imprisoned in the County Jail of Sonoma County until the fine was paid at the rate of $2 per day on 7 Mar 1861.

People v. John Wilson
Vending spiritous liquors without a license (case file # 137H)

The indictment filed on 13 Feb 1861 accused the defendant of vending spiritous, malt, and vinous liquors by retail in quantities less than a quart without a license on 13 Jan 1861. S. J. Agnew, William Ellis, and John Henley appeared as witnesses before the Grand Jury. The trial jury found the defendant not guilty on 6 Mar 1861.

---

[392] Enos Parks may have been the E. Parks who died on 15 Mar 1861 after being stabbed by an unknown party while playing cards at Timber Cove on 9 Mar 1861. See, "Murder at Timber Cove," *The Sonoma County Democrat* (Santa Rosa, California), 21 March 1861, p. 2, col. 3.

People v. James Holivan
Vending liquors without a license

The Court ordered the defendant to be discharged from custody as he was not the party described in the indictment on 16 Feb 1861.

People v. Ira Berry
Grand larceny

The Grand Jury could not take any action on this case because of the lack of material witnesses, and the Court ordered the case resubmitted to the next Grand Jury on 18 Feb 1861. The *Sonoma County Journal* of 1 Feb 1861, quoting an article from the *Petaluma Argus,* described Berry's arrest as:

> Wm. H. Ray and J. P. Smith arrested a man by the name of Ira Berry, in Mendocino county, and brought him to town [Santa Rosa] on last Saturday [26 Jan 1861]. He is charged with stealing two valuable mares from Henderson Willson, a respectable farmer living near that place. But one of the mares was recovered, at the time, though hopes are entertained of finding the other one. Since then a man named [George] Vanderpool has been arrested, charged with being concerned in the same theft, and has been lodged in the jail.[393]

Berry did not remain in jail long. His escape on 20 Mar 1861 was reported in the *Petaluma Argus* on 26 Mar 1861 as:

> Ira Berry, who was confined in jail on the charge of stealing two mares from Mr. Wilson, near Santa Rosa, in December last, made his escape on last Wednesday [20 Mar 1861] between two and three o'clock from the county jail at Santa Rosa, in broad daylight. He cut the staple, through which the padlock was passed, by means of some instrument furnished him for that purpose. He was not confined in the cells, except at night, and could easily have received assistance from the outside. This is not the first instance of the kind; three or four others have "done like-wise" during the past year.[394]

---

[393] "From Santa Rosa," *The Sonoma County Journal* (Santa Rosa, California), 1 February 1861, p. 2, col. 3. George Vanderpool was arrested on Sansberry's Ranch on the charge of stealing two of Mr. Wilson's mares near Santa Rosa and was confined in the Sonoma County Jail by 31 Jan 1861. See, "Another One of Them," *The Sonoma County Democrat* (Santa Rosa, California), 31 January 1861, p. 2, col. 1. "County Jail," *The Sonoma County Democrat* (Santa Rosa, California), 31 January 1861, p. 2, col. 2.
[394] "Escaped," *The Petaluma (California) Argus*, 26 March 1861, p. 2, col. 1.

May term 1861

The Court of Sessions met for eight days this term, 6–11 and 13–14 May 1861.[395]

Hon. William Churchman, County judge
Hon. William Ellis, Associate Justice
Hon. L. C. Reyburn, Associate Justice
Hon. Joel Miller, Acting Associate Justice
R. C. Flournoy, District Attorney
Frank W. Shattuck, Clerk
William H. Crowell, Deputy Clerk
John J. Ellis, Sheriff
Zadok Jackson, Grand Jury foreman

Persons called as Grand Jurors but not empaneled: H. F. Bates (failed to appear and answer when called and later rendered a good and sufficient excuse for not serving), H. F. Brockman (rendered a good and sufficient excuse for not serving), James Billett (rendered a good and sufficient excuse for not serving), Edward Barnes (rendered a good and sufficient excuse for not serving), Edward Conley (rendered a good and sufficient excuse for not serving), and Berthold Hoen (rendered a good and sufficient excuse for not serving).

Grand Jurors duly sworn and empaneled on 6 May 1861: Zadock Jackson, J. E. Davidson, A. M. Brown, H. Valentine, William Brians, William Roberts, J. D. Binns, C. C. Money, John C. Bedwell, M. Blodgett, J. J. Lane, James B. Fretwell, Julio Carrillo, James E. Crane, Joseph Wright, and O. B. Mathews. The Court appointed Zadock Jackson as Grand Jury foreman.

Report of the Grand Jury[396]

State of California, County of Sonoma, May Term A. D. 1861
To the Hon. Court of Sessions of said County,
We, the Grand Jury, would respectfully submit to this Hon. Court the following report:
We have found ten indictments, six of which were for felony and four for misdemeanor.
We have examined and Jail and Hospital and find them in proper order with the exception of the roof of the Jail and its back door to which we would respectfully call [to] the attention of the Board of Supervisors.
We have examined the offices of the Clerk and Sheriff and find that these officers have faithfully discharged their duties in all respects as far as we can judge.

---

[395] Sonoma County, California, Court of Sessions, Minute Book E: 235–257, May term 1861 proceedings; Sonoma County Archives, Santa Rosa.
[396] Sonoma County, California, Court of Sessions, Report of the Grand Jury, May term 1861, filed 10 May 1861; County Records, Sonoma County, Court Records, Miscellaneous Unprocessed Records, folder "County Records – Sonoma County – Court of Sessions – Reports of the Grand Jury"; California State Archives, Sacramento. Sonoma County, California, Court of Sessions, Minute Book E: 249, Report of the Grand Jury, 10 May 1861; Sonoma County Archives, Santa Rosa.

The office of the Recorder is well kept as well as his books, everything is cleanly and business-like.

The office of the Treasurer is alike kept in good condition, and we feel satisfied that business in that department is met with uniform promptness.

After a session of five days, we, the Grand Jury, wish to submit the foregoing report and ask the Hon. Court to be discharged.

Zadock Jackson, Foreman of the Grand Jury.

People v. Herbert Mitchell
Attempting to aid and assist a prisoner to escape (case file # 109)

The indictment filed on 7 May 1861 accused the defendant of aiding and assisting Ira Berry, a prisoner in the County Jail of Sonoma County, to make his escape from jail by taking a note from Berry to John W. Ball requesting Ball to furnish Berry with a file, a saw, some wax, and other things on 6 Feb 1861.[397] J. W. Ball appeared as a witness before the Grand Jury. The trial jury found the defendant guilty on 13 May 1861. The Court ordered the defendant to pay a fine of $300 and in the case of non-payment to be imprisoned in the County Jail of Sonoma County until the fine was paid at the rate of $2 per day on 14 May 1861. After sentencing, the defendant was taken to Marin County to serve as a witness in the case of the People v. [George] Vanderpool. Since Mitchell had not paid his fine, he was returned to Sonoma County to serve out his time.[398]

People v. John Hargrave
Grand larceny (case file # 130)

The indictment filed on 7 May 1861 accused the defendant of stealing one sorrel mare (value $100), the property of Robert Clark, on 22 Mar 1861. Robert Clark, David Odell, and Samuel Hadlock appeared as witnesses before the Grand Jury. The trial jury found the defendant not guilty on 10 Aug 1861.

People v. Ira Berry
Grand larceny

The indictment filed on 8 May 1861 accused the defendant of stealing one sorrel mare (value $250) and one gray mare (value $300), property of Henderson Wilson, on 13 Dec 1860. William H. Ray and Herbert Mitchell appeared as witnesses before the Grand Jury. Since the defendant was still at large after escaping from the County Jail on 20 Mar 1861 the Court issued a bench warrant for his arrest on 21 May 1861. In the beginning of October 1861, Berry was "nabbed" in San Francisco, "where he had just arrived 'from the plains' with horses for sale."[399] On the evening of 14 Oct 1861, he once again escaped from the Sonoma County Jail "as the Under Sheriff, who acts as jailer, was entering the jail with food for the prisoners, Berry rushed past him and fled to the hills."[400] The Sonoma County Sheriff, J. M. Bowles, offered a $50 reward for Berry's

---

[397] In the note included as evidence in the case file the prisoner Berry actually asks Mitchell for "a fine little saw to cut iron and a small piece of shoemaker's wax" wrapped in a piece of newspaper.

[398] "Convicted," *The Sonoma County Democrat* (Santa Rosa, California), 16 May 1861, p. 2, col. 4.

[399] "Nabbed," *The Sonoma County Democrat* (Santa Rosa, California), 3 October 1861, p. 2, col. 5.

[400] "Broke Jail," *The Sonoma County Democrat* (Santa Rosa, California), 17 October 1861, p. 3, col. 1.

"arrest and delivery in Santa Rosa."[401] Berry was described in the reward notice "as a man of medium height, genteel in appearance, dark hair and whiskers, had on a dark coat and pants, calico shirt, and shoes, and black slouch hat." He was arrested by Ike Smith and W. H. Ray, but broke jail again along with Thomas Stennet on the evening of 27 May 1864 by removing his "shackles and the iron bars from the window by means of a saw made of a butcher's knife."[402] He was captured again less than a month later in Carson City.[403] Berry was convicted of grand larceny in the County Court of Sonoma County on 7 Jul 1864. See County Court case # 10 (OS). The Court ordered the defendant imprisoned in the State Prison for the term of six years on 9 Jul 1864. He was received by San Quentin on 11 Jul 1864, pardoned by Governor Frederick F. Low, and discharged on 29 Oct 1867.[404] In granting Berry's pardon, Governor Low cited "a statement made by the [County Court] Judge showing that the offense was not clearly proven, that the Judge had determined to impose a sentence of two or three years at most, that he was induced by [the] prisoner's counsel to make the sentence six years instead of two or three because it was thought [that the] prisoner would be more likely to obtain a pardon with a longer sentence, and because he has already suffered a longer imprisonment than was intended."[405]

People v. Henry Thornley
Assault with a deadly weapon with intent to commit murder (case file # 114)
The indictment filed on 8 May 1861 accused the defendant of assaulting Charles Brannon (var. Brennan) with a knife with the intent to murder him on 6 May 1861. William D. Gray and William L. Wilson appeared as witnesses before the Grand Jury. The altercation was described in the *Sonoma County Democrat* on 9 May 1861 as:

> During the municipal election at Sonoma, on Monday [6 May 1861], a difficulty arose between Henry Thornly and Charles Brennan, which occasioned a recourse to knives. Thornly received a stab in the right breast, and Brennan received a cut that severed a vein connected with the brachial artery of his left arm. They will probably survive their wounds.[406]

The trial jury found the defendant guilty on 13 Aug 1861, and the Court granted the defendant a new trial on 17 Aug 1861. The case was continued to the next term for trial on 11 Nov 1861, but there are no further proceedings of the case in the Court minutes. For a related case, see case file # 140.

---

[401] "$50.00 Reward!," *The Sonoma County Democrat* (Santa Rosa, California), 31 October 1861, p. 4, col. 3.
[402] For arrest, "In Town," *The Sonoma County Democrat* (Santa Rosa, California), 7 May 1864, p. 3, col. 2. For escape, "Give the Alarm!," *The Sonoma County Democrat* (Santa Rosa, California), 28 May 1864, p. 3, col. 2.
[403] Untitled, *Marysville (California) Daily Appeal*, 19 June 1864, p. 2, col. 1.
[404] California, State Prison Register (1851–1867), Executive Department, entry no. 2771, Ira Berry, p. 230, received 11 July 1864; California State Archives, Sacramento.
[405] "Pardoned by the Governor," *Sacramento (California) Daily Union*, 9 November 1867, p. 2, col. 1.
[406] "Stabbing Affray," *The Sonoma County Democrat* (Santa Rosa, California), 9 May 1861, p. 2, col. 4.

People v. Edmond T. Pepper
Murder

The indictment filed on 8 May 1861 accused the defendant of murdering Wladislaw Zboinski by stabbing him with a knife on his left side between his hip and shoulder giving him one mortal wound on 22 Mar 1861. Martha A. Zboinski, Judson A. Gaston, Overton B. Mathews, John M. Symonds, Joseph Browning, and Tandy Browning appeared as witnesses before the Grand Jury. On 6 Apr 1861, *The Marin County Journal*, quoting *The Sonoma County Journal* of 29 Mar 1861, reported the affray as:

> About half past six o'clock last Friday evening [22 Mar 1861], a difficulty occurred one mile from town, between W. Zboinski and Edwin and George Pepper, aged respectively 17 and 14 years, sons of E. S. Pepper, and which resulted in the death of Mr. Z.
>
> It would appear from the evidence adduced on examination, that an ill feeling had for some time existed between the family of Mr. Pepper and Mr. Zboinski, growing mainly out of the construction of a line fence; the breaking into Mr. P.'s enclosure of Z.'s cows; that on the day of the stabbing, Zboinski had discovered his cow in Pepper's field and had just driven her out, when the Pepper boys came up and commenced calling him hard names. This exasperated Zboinski, and he threatened chastisement, at the same time stepping upon the fence between himself and the boys with the evident intention of making good his threat. No sooner was he upon the fence than the eldest of the boys, Edwin, drew from his pocket a stone, which he hurled at Z. striking his hat. As Z. approached, young Pepper drew a second stone from his pocket and threw it, hitting Z. in the eye and blinding him, when he turned to run. At this stage of affairs his assailant rushed upon him and with a bowie-knife, inflicted a fatal wound in the back, near the left side. The wounded man survived his injury some eight hours. He was a native of Poland, and aged about thirty-three years.
>
> His remains were followed to the grave, on Sunday [24 Mar 1861], by a large number of our citizens.
>
> On Monday [25 Mar 1861], Edwin and his brother were arraigned before Justice Reyburn for examination. District Attorney Flournoy appearing in behalf of the state, and Geo. Pearce, Esq., for the prisoners. The result of the examination was the discharge of George and the holding for trial of Edwin, who was accordingly conveyed to Santa Rosa on Tuesday [26 Mar 1861] and committed to prison.[407]

The case was transferred to the Sonoma County District Court on 8 May 1861. The District Court trial jury, after deliberating for three hours, found the defendant not guilty on 25 Jun 1861.[408] *The Sonoma County Democrat* published almost three full columns of testimony from the trial on 4 Jul 1861.[409] See Sonoma County District Court case # 1102 (OS).

---

[407] "Sad and Fatal Affray," *The Marin County Journal* (San Rafael, California), 6 Apr 1861, p. 2, col. 3.
[408] "Acquitted," *The Sonoma County Democrat* (Santa Rosa, California), 27 June 1861, p. 2, col. 1.
[409] "Evidence in the Trial of Edward T. Pepper, Charged with the Murder of Wladislaw Zboiniski," *The Sonoma County Democrat* (Santa Rosa, California), 4 Jul 1861, p. 2, cols. 2–4.

People v. George Edgar

Arson

The indictment filed on 9 May 1861 accused the defendant of burning down a barn, a stock of wheat (value $100), and a stock of oats (value $100), all property of Ann C. King, on the night of 17 Sep 1860.[410] Rufus H. King, Ann C. King, William Faught, and James Forte appeared as witnesses before the Grand Jury. The case was transferred to the Sonoma County District Court on 10 May 1861, and the District Court trial jury found the defendant not guilty on 21 Jun 1861.[411]

People v. James D. Barnes

Assault with a deadly weapon with intent to commit murder (case file # 120)

The indictment filed on 10 May 1861 accused the defendant of assaulting James Hendry by drawing, pointing, and leveling a loaded gun at him with the intent of murdering him on 8 May 1861. James Hendry and Samuel J. Finley appeared as witnesses before the Grand Jury.

People v. Darias Clark

Selling spiritous, malt, and vinous liquors without a license (case file # 121)

The indictment filed on 10 May 1861 accused the defendant of vending by retail spiritous, malt, and vinous liquors in quantities less than a quart without a license on 6 May 1861. Joseph D. Binns, Sebastian R. Dickey, and Timothy Buel appeared as witnesses before the Grand Jury.

People v. B. F. Tilton

Selling spiritous liquors without a license (case file # 137A)

The indictment filed on 10 May 1861 accused the defendant of vending spiritous, malt, and vinous liquors by retail in quantities less than a quart without a license on 8 May 1861. William Brians appeared as a witness before the Grand Jury. The defendant entered a plea of guilty on 5 Aug 1861. The Court ordered the defendant to pay a fine of $55 and in the case of non-payment to be imprisoned in the County Jail of Sonoma County until the fine was paid at the rate of $2 per day on 9 Aug 1861. Tilton paid the $55 fine and was discharged on 9 Aug 1861.

People v. Almer Clark (indicted as Adam Clark)

Selling spiritous liquors without a license (case file # 138)

The indictment filed on 10 May 1861 accused the defendant of vending spiritous, malt, and vinous liquors by retail in quantities less than a quart without a license on 7 May 1861. Joseph D. Binns appeared as a witness before the Grand Jury. The defendant entered a plea of guilty on 5 Aug 1861. The Court ordered the defendant to pay a fine of $35 and in the case of non-payment to be imprisoned in the County Jail of Sonoma County until the fine was paid at the rate of $2 per day on 9 Aug 1861. Clark paid the $35 fine and was discharged on 9 Aug 1861.

---

[410] Sonoma County, California, County Court, case file # 32 (OS), People v. George Edgar, indictment, 9 May 1861; California State Archives, Sacramento. The District Court case file for this suit has been erroneously filed with the County Court case files although there were no County Court proceedings.

[411] Sonoma County, California, District Court, Minute Book B: 537, 563, 578, 592–593, and 596, People v. George Edgar, case proceedings, 1861; Sonoma County Archives, Santa Rosa.

August term 1861

The Court of Sessions met for eleven days this term, 5–10, 12–15, and 17 August 1861.[412]

Hon. William Churchman, County Judge
Hon. L. C. Reyburn, Associate Justice
Hon. William Ellis, Associate Justice
William F. Smith, District Attorney (appointed by the Court 5 Aug 1861)
Frank W. Shattuck, Clerk
William H. Crowell, Deputy Clerk
John J. Ellis, Sheriff
M. Barnes, Under Sheriff
E. Latapie, Deputy Sheriff
S. T. Coulter, Grand Jury foreman

Persons called as Grand Jurors but not empaneled: George Campbell (excused), James Blyth (did not possess the necessary qualifications), B. L. Cook (did not possess the necessary qualifications), Joseph Carpenter (did not possess the necessary qualifications), and S. D. Pomeroy (rendered a good and sufficient excuse).

Grand Jurors sworn on 5 Aug 1861: S. T. Coulter, J. J. Badger, C. Carlton, W. E. Cocke, Samuel Duncan, T. B. Hood, L. Cox, B. M. Fetter, A. S. Cartwright, D. B. Shaw, Samuel Colbroth, C. C. Money, T. B. Clark, G. W. Arnold, J. M. Carter, and W. P. Barnes. The Court appointed S. T. Coulter as Grand Jury foreman.

Report of the Grand Jury[413]

To the Hon. Court of Sessions, Sonoma County, State of California, at the August term eighteen hundred and sixty-one, we respectfully submit our report.

During our session we have found the following bills of indictment: murder, one; grand larceny, two; assault with deadly weapon, two; assault and battery, one; mayhem, one; bigamy, four.

We have examined the Hospital and Jail. In the Hospital we found three patients all improving under the care of the officers. The rooms we found in good condition. In the Jail we found four criminals, all of whom speak well of the attention of the officers. The Privy we find broken, which needs immediate repairs, for the comfort and health of the inmates. Otherwise we commend the officers for the good condition of the building.

---

[412] Sonoma County, California, Court of Sessions, Minute Book E: 259–290, August term 1861 proceedings; Sonoma County Archives, Santa Rosa.

[413] Sonoma County, California, Court of Sessions, Report of the Grand Jury, August term 1861, filed 10 August 1861; County Records, Sonoma County, Court Records, Miscellaneous Unprocessed Records, folder "County Records – Sonoma County – Court of Sessions – Reports of the Grand Jury"; California State Archives, Sacramento. Sonoma County, California, Court of Sessions, Minute Book E: 277, Report of the Grand Jury, August term 1861, 10 August 1861; Sonoma County Archives, Santa Rosa.

A committee have examined the offices of the Court House and report them in good condition.

Complaints have come before us in regard to gates across public highways in different parts of the county. We would respectfully call the attention of the different Road Masters to such nuisances.

For the able advice and prompt attention of the Hon. W. F. Smith, our District Attorney, we feel indebted to return our unanimous thanks. The sheriff and his deputies have given us their closest attention for which we return our thanks. Returning our thanks for the attention of your Hon. and the Court, we most respectfully submit our report.

S. T. Coulter, Foreman

People v. Edward S. Emerson
Assault and battery (case file # 152B)

The indictment filed on 6 Aug 1861 accused the defendant of assaulting James M. Hannah with force and arms by beating, wounding, and ill-treating him on 2 Jul 1861. James M. Hannah appeared as a witness before the Grand Jury. In his complaint dated 2 Jul 1861 taken, subscribed, and sworn before Justice Marvin Buckland, a Justice of the Peace for Russian River Township, James M. Hannah accused Emerson of violently assaulting him with an axe on 2 Jul 1862 at the Kentuck ranch in Annally Township. The defendant pleaded guilty on 9 Aug 1861. The Court ordered the defendant to pay a fine of $25 and in the case of non-payment to be imprisoned in the County Jail of Sonoma County until the fine was satisfied at the rate of $2 per day on 12 Aug 1861. Emerson paid the $25 fine on 12 Aug 1861, and the Court discharged him from custody and all further restraint. For a related case, see case file # 129.

People v. James B. Boggs
Murder

The indictment filed on 7 Aug 1861 accused the defendant of stabbing Hugh McLaughlin with a knife on the left side of his body immediately below the left nipple and between the fourth and sixth ribs giving him a mortal wound of which he died on 6 Jul 1861. The *Sonoma County Democrat* of 11 Jul 1861 gave an account of the fatal affray:

> Hugh McLaughlin, keeper of a livery stable at Healdsburg, was fatally stabbed on Saturday last [6 Jul 1861] in a rencontre with James B. Boggs. Several versions of the affair have appeared in print, none of which is correct. One of the parties at least had been drinking to excess, as persons who saw him a short time previous to the lamentable affair, remarked, such was the effect of the liquor he had drank upon him, that he "seemed to be merry," but both were undoubtedly under its influence. The parties met in front of Foss's livery stable at about 6:30 in the afternoon, when Boggs remarked, upon seeing a horse that was being groomed before the door, that the animal was "not of much account." McLaughlin rejoined in effect, "Of course not, it came from Pike. Nothing from there is of any account." Boggs made the pleasant retort, "O, yes. I came from Pike, and you know that I'm a good fellow." To which McLaughlin replied calling him a liar. What followed will be found in the testimony of the witnesses for the prosecution at the examination, which took place before Justice Ireland on the 9th, the substance of which we subjoin:

Mr. Hinkle [sic], sworn—Testified that the parties were talking in his stable. McLaughlin gave Boggs the lie and knocked the latter down and struck him several times while down. McL. was taken off, but soon knocked him down again. McL. afterward left the stable and went into a saloon. He was followed soon after by Boggs, who was urged by Mr. Hudson. The parties came together at the saloon door, where somebody said Boggs had a knife. McL. backed into the saloon, Mr. Hudson urging Boggs up to him. The combatants struck at one another at about the same time. Boggs staggered back about three steps, McL. following him up and both striking again, when McL. fell against Boggs. Someone took McL. away. Boggs left and I saw no more. Saw blood come from his wound, and saw the knife, which was a common pocket knife. Heard Boggs use no threatening language.

The testimony of Messrs. Voorhies, Collins, Cunningham, Ley, Foss, and Lancaster, so far as they were eyewitnesses of the affair, was substantially the same. F. S. Poor testified that he heard [the] deceased say to Boggs, "Mr. Boggs, go away from me. I am good enough for you at any time or anyplace." Mr. Bloom testified in accordance with the foregoing.

Boggs was held to answer before the Court of Sessions on [a] charge of manslaughter, bail being fixed at $10,000. We may add that Mr. Boggs gave himself up promptly to the authorities after the affair.[414]

James Albertson, James H. Hickle, T. Z. Cunningham, H. D. Ley, Garrett Voorhies, D. Bloom, Edmund Collins, Dr. B. B. Bonham, William S. Grey, Dr. S. S. Todd, Henry Sargent, O. C. Ormsby, John W. Howe, and P. G. Hubbard appeared as witnesses before the Grand Jury. The case was transferred to the Sonoma County District Court on 7 Aug 1861. See Sonoma County District Court case # 1176 (OS). The first District Court trial jury found the defendant guilty of manslaughter on 26 Oct 1861. The District Court granted the defendant a new trial on 29 Oct 1861 "on the ground of some informality on the part of the Court in submitting the case to the jury."[415] The second District Court trial jury also found the defendant guilty of manslaughter on 20 Feb 1862. The District Court ordered the defendant imprisoned in the State Prison for the term of four years and six months. The case was appealed to the California Supreme Court which affirmed the judgment of the lower court on 16 Jun 1862.[416] See California Supreme Court case # 3520 (WPA # 9458). The defendant was received at San Quentin State Prison on 10 Mar 1862.[417] Governor Leland Stanford pardoned Boggs on 14 Aug 1863, citing letters he had received attesting to Boggs's good character and good behavior while in prison.[418]

---

[414] "Fatal Affray at Healdsburg," *The Sonoma County Democrat* (Santa Rosa, California), 11 July 1861, p. 2, col. 4.

[415] "Criminal Trial," *The Sonoma County Journal* (Petaluma, California), 1 November 1861, p. 2, col. 1.

[416] "Supreme Court," *Sacramento (California) Daily Union*, 17 June 1862, p. 3, col. 1.

[417] California, State Prison Register (1851–1867), Executive Department, entry no. 2327, James B. Boggs, p. 193, received 10 March 1862; California State Archives, Sacramento.

[418] *The Journal of the Assembly, During the Fifteenth Session of the legislature of the State of California, 1863-4, Began on Monday, [7 December 1863], and Ended on Monday, [4 April 1864]* (Sacramento: O. M. Clayes, State Printer, 1864), 77. Boggs's pardon is enumerated in the list of pardons granted by Governor Stanford during the year 1863 contained in the appendix to the Governor's second annual message to the California Senate and Assembly dated 9 December 1863.

People v. F. W. Hudson
Murder

The Grand Jury dismissed the charge on 8 Aug 1861. This case is related to the case of the People v. James B. Boggs above. See Sonoma County District Court case # 1176 (OS).

People v. Isaac Talbot (indicted as Isaac Tolbert)
Mayhem (case file # 137B)

The indictment filed on 8 Aug 1861 accused the defendant of assaulting John Patton (var. Patten) by biting off the lower part of his left ear disfiguring him on 15 Jun 1861.[419] John Patton, John Cantrell, E. V. Cofer, Charles Morgan, and M. V. Hickson appeared as witnesses before the Grand Jury. The Court sustained the defendant's demurrer and discharged the defendant on 12 Aug 1861.

People v. James M. Hannah
Assault with a deadly weapon with intent to inflict bodily injury (case file # 129)

The indictment filed on 9 Aug 1861 accused the defendant of assaulting Edward S. Emerson with a knife on 2 Jul 1861. Edward S. Emerson appeared as a witness before the Grand Jury. The trial jury found the defendant not guilty on 9 Nov 1861. For a related case, see case file # 152B.

People v. David Wharf and Francis Green (indicted as William Green)
Grand larceny (case file # 137G)

The indictment filed on 9 Aug 1861 accused the defendants of stealing three of Thomas S. Paige's merino lambs (value $100) on 6 Mar 1861. Daniel McLeod, Adam Ross, and Alexander Lockwood appeared as witnesses before the Grand Jury. The Court granted the defendants separate trials on 4 Nov 1861. The trial jury found the defendant David Wharf not guilty on 11 Nov 1861. The Court dismissed the indictment against the defendant Francis Green due to the insufficiency of the evidence, and a *nolle prosequi* was entered on 12 Nov 1861.

People v. Charles Brennan (var. Brannan)
Assault with a deadly weapon with intent to inflict a bodily injury (case file # 140)

The indictment filed on 9 Aug 1861 accused the defendant of assaulting Henry Thornley with a knife attempting to cut and stab him on 6 May 1861. John Prater, Henry Thornley, David Rupe, William M. Wood, B. A. Snoddy, William Foster, and William P. Campbell appeared as witnesses before the Grand Jury. The altercation was described in the *Sonoma County Democrat* on 9 May 1861 as:

> During the municipal election at Sonoma, on Monday [6 May 1861], a difficulty arose between Henry Thornly and Charles Brennan, which occasioned a recourse to knives. Thornly received a stab in the right breast, and Brennan received a cut that severed a vein connected with the brachial artery of his left arm. They will probably survive their wounds.[420]

---

[419] In his complaint filed with the Hon. L. D. Cockrill, a Justice of the Peace for Analy Township, on 3 Jun 1861, John Patten states that the assault took place on 1 Jun 1861 at his premises in Bloomfield.

[420] "Stabbing Affray," *The Sonoma County Democrat* (Santa Rosa, California), 9 May 1861, p. 2, col. 4.

The trial jury found the defendant not guilty on 6 Feb 1862. For a related case, see also case file # 114.

People v. Nancy A. Culbertson (formerly Nancy A. Moore and Nancy A. Bray)
Bigamy (case file # 118)

The indictment filed on 10 Aug 1861 accused the defendant of feloniously and unlawfully marrying William F. Culbertson in Sonoma County on 20 Oct 1859, her former husband, Fulmer Moore, then still being alive. S. Payran, B. B. Bonham, H. Bray, Sr., and S. T. Coulter appeared as witnesses before the Grand Jury. The Court sustained the defendant's demurrer and dismissed the indictment on 4 Nov 1861. For a related case, see also case file # 125 below.

People v. William F. Culbertson
Bigamy (case file # 125)

The indictment filed on 10 Aug 1861 accused the defendant of feloniously and unlawfully marrying Nancy A. Moore, wife of Fulmer Moore, in Sonoma County on 20 Oct 1859, her former husband still being alive. S. Payran, B. B. Bonham, H. Bray, Sr., and S. T. Coulter appeared as witnesses before the Grand Jury. The Court sustained the defendant's demurrer and dismissed the indictment on 4 Nov 1861. For a related case, see also case file # 118 above.

People v. Mary Frances Hopper (formerly Mary Frances Johnson and Mary Frances Groves)
Bigamy (case file # 123)

The indictment filed on 10 Aug 1861 accused the defendant of marrying John B. Hopper in Sonoma County on 13 May 1861, her former husband, Allison Johnson, then still being alive. Thomas H. Pyatt, Ira Johnson, David Groves, and Robert Dickinson appeared as witnesses before the Grand Jury. A bench warrant was issued for the defendant's arrest on 14 Aug 1861. For a related case, see also case file # 131 below.

People v. John B. Hopper
Bigamy (case file # 131)

The indictment filed on 10 Aug 1861 accused the defendant of unlawfully and feloniously marrying Mary Frances Johnson, the true and lawful wife of Allison Johnson, he being alive, in Sonoma County on 13 May 1861. Thomas H. Pyatt, Ira Johnson, David Groves, and Robert Dickinson appeared as witnesses before the Grand Jury. A bench warrant was issued for the defendant's arrest on 14 Aug 1861. For a related case, see also case file # 123 above.

The Hon. Stephen Payran and the Hon. William Ellis were elected as Associate Justices of the Court of Sessions at a convention of the Justices of the Peace of Sonoma County on 7 Oct 1861.

November term 1861

The Court of Sessions met for ten days this term, 4-9 and 11-14 Nov 1861.[421]

Hon. William Churchman, County Judge
Hon. William Ellis, Associate Justice
Hon. Stephen Payran, Associate Justice
William Henry Jones, District Attorney
Joseph A. Woodson, Acting District Attorney
William L. Anderson, Clerk
William H. Crowell, Deputy Clerk
J. M. Bowles, Sheriff
D. Campbell, Under Sheriff
Zadock Jackson, Grand Jury foreman

Persons called as Grand Jurors but not empaneled: Abijah Evans (failed to appear and answer when called), George Eldridge (failed to appear and answer when called), M. R. Evans (failed to appear and answer when called), William F. Franklin (rendered a good and sufficient excuse), L. G. Ellsworth (rendered a good and sufficient excuse), Thomas Edwards (rendered a good and sufficient excuse), William J. Ellis (not a citizen of the United States), R. E. Smith (rendered a good and sufficient excuse), and G. T. Espy.

Grand Jurors sworn on 4 Nov 1861: George H. Eadis, J. F. Kessing, J. G. Edwards, J. H. Holman, David Espy, G. W. Arnold, William Foster, William R. Smith, E. Elliott, J. Leslie, Zadock Jackson, E. C. Bray, W. M. Roberts, William E. Cowper, J. B. Cook, and James Fretwell.

Report of [the] Grand Jury[422]

To the Hon. Court of Sessions, Sonoma County, State of California, at November Term A. D. eighteen hundred sixty-one, we respectfully submit the following report:

During our session of six days we have found the following indictments, for misdemeanor eleven (11).

We have examined the Hospital and Jail and all the different County offices. The Hospital and Jail are in excellent order, but for the greater comfort of the prisoners we recommend that a stove be furnished the Jail.

The Treasurer's, Clerk's, and Recorder's offices we find well-arranged and great credit is deserved for the neat manner in which the books are kept. We recommend the records in the County Surveyor's office which were injured by a fire that occurred in said office be transcribed and the damage sustained by the room repaired.

---

[421] Sonoma County, California, Court of Sessions, Minute Book E: 292–320, November term 1861 proceedings; Sonoma County Archives, Santa Rosa.
[422] Sonoma County, California, Court of Sessions, Minute Book E: 305, Report of [the] Grand Jury, November term 1861, 9 November 1861; Sonoma County Archives, Santa Rosa.

We recommend that the Sheriff's office be supplied with such furniture as may be necessary for the better preservation of books and papers. We also recommend that the License book be kept in alphabetical order or in some convenient manner so that [the] names of those paying licenses may be found without trouble.

For the advice and prompt attention of the District Attorney we return our thanks. We are also indebted for the promptness and attention of the Sheriff and his deputies. Returning our thanks for the attention of [your] Honor and the Court we respectfully submit our report and ask to be discharged.

Zadock Jackson, Foreman.

People v. Paul Heisel
Selling certain goods, wares, and merchandise by retail without a license (case file # 122)

The indictment filed on 6 Nov 1861 accused the defendant of vending by retail goods, wares, and merchandise (boots and shoes in single pairs) without a license on 28 May 1861. Henry Wise, Andrew Ester, and William M. Roberts appeared as witnesses before the Grand Jury. The trial jury found the defendant not guilty on 11 Nov 1861.

People v. Jacob B. Palmer
Keeping, renting, and letting horses and carriages and saddle horses, etc. for hire without a license/violation of section 79 of the Revenue Act of 1861 (case file # 80)[423]

The indictment filed on 7 Nov 1861 accused the defendant of keeping, renting, and letting out for hire horses and carriages without a license on 4 Nov 1861. Jacob Peavy and John Van Doren appeared as witnesses before the Grand Jury. The defendant pleaded guilty on 11 Nov 1861. The Court ordered the defendant to pay a fine of $50 and in the case of non-payment to be imprisoned in the County Jail of Sonoma County until the fine was paid at the rate of $2 per day on 14 Nov 1861. Palmer paid the $50 fine and was discharged on 14 Nov 1861.

People v. Jerry Linehan
Keeping, renting, and letting horses and carriages and saddle horses for hire without a license/violation of section 79 of the Revenue Act of 1861 (case file # 127)

The indictment filed on 7 Nov 1861 accused the defendant of keeping, renting, and letting for hire horses and carriages (saddles horses, single horses and buggies, and carriages with 2 horses) without a license on 6 Nov 1861. William Ellis and William Fleming appeared as witnesses before the Grand Jury. The defendant pleaded guilty on 11 Nov 1861. The Court ordered the defendant to pay a fine of $50 and in the case of non-payment of the fine to be imprisoned in the County Jail of Sonoma County until the fine was paid at the rate of $2 per day on 14 Nov 1861. Linehan paid the $50 fine and was discharged on 14 Nov 1861.

---

[423] The Revenue Act of 1861, approved 17 May 1861, in its section 79, required persons who sold or vended "any goods, wares, or merchandise, wine, or distilled liquors, drugs, or medicines, jewelry, or wares of precious metals" and persons who kept "horses, or carriages, for rent, or hire, except mules, horses, or animals, used in [the] transportation of goods" to obtain licenses from the Tax Collector of the county in which the business was conducted. See, *The Statutes of California, Twelfth Session*, pp. 419–457, Chap. CCCCI, "An Act to provide Revenue for the support of the Government of this State," specifically pp. 444–445, section 79.

People v. Manville Doyle
Keeping, renting, and letting horses and carriages and saddle horses for hire without a license/violation of section 79 of the Revenue Act of 1861 (case file # 132)

The indictment filed on 7 Nov 1861 accused the defendant of keeping and letting for hire horses and carriages (saddle horses, single horses and buggies, and carriages with 2 horses) without a license on 1 Aug 1861. Jacob Peavy appeared as a witness before the Grand Jury. The defendant pleaded guilty on 11 Nov 1861. The Court ordered the defendant to pay a fine of $46 and in the case of non-payment to be imprisoned in the County Jail of Sonoma County until the fine was paid at the rate of $2 per day on 14 Nov 1861. Doyle paid the $46 fine and was discharged on 14 Nov 1861.

People v. J. B. Hinkle
Renting and letting horses and carriages and saddle horses without a license (case file # 133)

The indictment filed on 7 Nov 1861 accused the defendant of keeping, renting, and letting for hire horses and carriages (single buggies and horses, 2 horses and carriages, and saddle horses) at a stable known as "Rough and Ready" without a license on 1 Apr 1861. John F. Kessing and William L. Van Doren appeared as witnesses before the Grand Jury. The defendant pleaded guilty on 7 Nov 1861. The Court ordered the defendant to pay a fine of $50 and stand committed until the fine was paid on 11 Nov 1861.

People v. Parker E. Weeks (indicted as P. Weeks)
Keeping, renting, and letting for hire horses and carriages and saddle horses, etc. without a license/violation of section 79 of the Revenue Act of 1861 (case file # 137F)

The indictment filed on 7 Nov 1861 accused the defendant of keeping, renting, and letting for hire horses and carriages (saddle horses, single horses and buggies, and carriages with two horses) without a license on 4 Nov 1861. John Van Doren and Jacob Peavy appeared as witnesses before the Grand Jury. The defendant pleaded guilty on 11 Nov 1861. The Court ordered the defendant to pay a fine of $50 and in the case of non-payment to be imprisoned in the County Jail of Sonoma County until the fine was paid at the rate of $2 per day on 14 Nov 1861. Weeks paid the $50 fine and was discharged on 14 Nov 1861.

People v. J. W. Henderson
Violation of section 79 of the Revenue Act of 1861 (case file # 147)

The indictment filed 7 Nov 1861 accused the defendant of keeping, renting, and letting for hire horses and carriages (saddle horses, single horses and buggies, and carriages with two horses) without a license on 1 Aug 1861. William Drew and Daniel Sink appeared as witnesses before the Grand Jury. The defendant pleaded guilty on 5 Feb 1862. The Court ordered the defendant to pay a fine of $50 and in the case of non-payment to be imprisoned in the County Jail of Sonoma County until the fine was paid at the rate of $2 per day on 8 Feb 1862.

People v. B. F. Bonnell (var. Bonnel)
Violation of section 79 of the Revenue Act of 1861 (case file # 139)

The indictment filed on 8 Nov 1861 accused the defendant of dealing in and vending goods, wares, and merchandise (stoves, stove furniture, lead pipe, tin ware, cutlery, and carpenter's hardware) without a license in a fixed place of business (west side of Main Street in Healdsburg) on 1 Sep 1861. Bennett Ellis and J. B. Roney appeared as witnesses before the Grand Jury. The defendant pleaded guilty on 4 Feb 1862. The Court ordered the defendant to pay a fine of $50 and in the case of non-payment to be imprisoned in the County Jail of Sonoma County until the fine was paid at the rate of $2 per day on 8 Feb 1862. Bonnell paid the $50 fine and was discharged on 8 Feb 1862.

People v. William M. Main
Vending certain goods, wares, and merchandise without a license (case file # 116)
    The indictment filed on 8 Nov 1861 accused the defendant of dealing in and vending goods, wares, and merchandise (harnesses, bridles, whips, and saddler's hardware) without a license on the south side of Washington Street in Petaluma on 4 Nov 1861. Jacob Peavey and John S. Van Doran appeared as witnesses before the Grand Jury. The trial jury found the defendant not guilty on 12 Nov 1861.

People v. William Allen, John McCombs, R. Combs, Walter Currier, Ed H. Grover, William Rodgers, and John Grennan
Resisting, opposing, and obstructing a duly authorized Deputy Sheriff in the execution of his duty (case file #s 134 and 152I)
    The indictment filed on 9 Nov 1861 accused the defendants of obstructing, resisting, and opposing with force and arms W. P. Mahoney, a duly authorized Deputy Sheriff of Sonoma County, while he was serving a writ of execution issued in the case Alfred Borel v. Phillip Kalkman and Cesar C. Schnepel by the 12th Judicial District Court in and for the City and County of San Francisco against the property of Phillip Kalkman and Cesar C. Schnepel, by placing their bodies between the Deputy Sheriff and the property he demanded on 21 Oct 1861. Jake Peavey, J. M. Bowles, and John Ingram appeared as witnesses before the Grand Jury. A bench warrant dated 19 Dec 1861 was issued for all the defendants mentioned in the indictment, but the Sonoma County Sheriff returned with only William Rodgers, not finding any of the others, on 10 Feb 1862. The Court dismissed the action on 8 May 1862 because the evidence was not sufficient to warrant a verdict against the defendant.

People v. William Allen, John McCombs, R. Combs, Walter Currier, Ed H. Grover, William Rodgers, and John Grennan
Unlawfully assembling to do an unlawful act and not dispersing on being commanded to do so by a duly authorized Deputy Sheriff (case file #s 134 and 152I)
    The indictment filed on 9 Nov 1861 accused the defendants of wrongfully and unlawfully assembling for the purpose of committing an unlawful act (resisting and obstructing W. P. Mahoney, a duly authorized Deputy Sheriff of Sonoma County, while he was serving a writ of execution issued in the case Alfred Borel v. Phillip Kalkman and Cesar C. Schnepel by the 12th Judicial District Court in and for the City and County of San Francisco against the property of Phillip Kalkman and Cesar C. Schnepel) and refusing to disperse on 21 Oct 1861. Jake Peavey, J. M. Bowles, and John Ingram appeared as witnesses before the Grand Jury. A bench warrant dated 19 Dec 1861 was issued for all the defendants mentioned in the indictment, but the Sonoma

County Sheriff returned with only William Rodgers, not finding any of the others, on 10 Feb 1862. The trial jury found the defendant William Rodgers not guilty on 7 May 1862.

People v. Henry Yeagley
Keeping horses and carriages not used in the transportation of goods for rent and hire without a license (case file # 1371)

The indictment filed on 9 Nov 1861 accused the defendant of keeping horses and carriages not used in the transportation of goods for rent and hire at a fixed place of business in Sebastopol without a license on 1 Oct 1861. P. N. Emerson and Smith F. Hood appeared as witnesses before the Grand Jury. The Court dismissed the indictment on 12 Nov 1861 due to the insufficiency of the evidence and the fact that the defendant did indeed have a license at the time the indictment was found.

February term 1862

The Court of Sessions met for eight days this term, 3–8 and 10–11 February 1862.[424]

Hon. William Churchman, County Judge
Hon. William Ellis, Associate Justice
Hon. Stephen Payran, Associate Justice
Hon. Z. Middleton, Acting Associate Justice
William Henry Jones, District Attorney
J. A. Woodson, Acting District Attorney
William L. Anderson, Clerk
William H. Crowell, Deputy Clerk
J. M. Bowles, Sheriff
O. T. Baldwin, Under Sheriff
E. Latapie, Deputy Sheriff
Sterling T. Coulter, Grand Jury foreman

Persons called as Grand Jurors but not empaneled: Edward Fitzgerald (rendered a good and sufficient excuse).

Grand Jurors sworn on 3 Feb 1862: Edward Gillian, Hiram T. Fairbanks, Joseph Fitch, Patrick Fox, T. J. Gould, Joseph Badger, A. Farris, C. B. Cook, Willis Faught, R. E. Smith, Thomas A. Fields, James E. Crane, Peter Engle, Sterling T. Coulter, S. P. Emerson, and O. Rippetoe. The Court appointed Sterling T. Coulter as Grand Jury foreman.

---

[424] Sonoma County, California, Court of Sessions, Minute Book E: 322–342, February term 1862 proceedings; Sonoma County Archives, Santa Rosa.

To the Honorable the Court of Sessions of Sonoma County, February Term A. D. 1862,

The Grand Jury would respectfully report that they have examined the various County offices and the Hospital and Jail. We find them all kept in good order.

For the better security of the public records we recommend that an iron door be placed at the entrance of the Recorder's Office from the hall.

We find also that the public buildings have been greatly damaged by the wet weather in consequence of the insufficiency of the roofing, and the Jail uncomfortable for want of glass windows inside the grating.

We recommend to the Board of Supervisors that the County buildings be roofed with some better material than that now in use, as we are advised by competent judges, that a reliable roof cannot be made of such material as that now in use.

The Grand Jury recommend to the Legislature that the laws for the observance of the Sabbath be so amended as to operate equally on all classes of the community or altogether abolished.

Having found two bills of indictment and disposed of all the business before the Grand Jury we respectfully ask to be discharged.

S. T. Coulter, Foreman.

People v. John McCune (indicted as Jack Murray)
Assault with a deadly weapon with intent to inflict bodily injury (case file # 152E)

The indictment filed on 6 Feb 1862 accused the defendant of assaulting John Dowd with a knife cutting and stabbing him with the intent to inflict a bodily injury on 7 Dec 1861. John Dowd, James Slaven, and D. F. Strother appeared as witnesses before the Grand Jury. On 13 Dec 1861, the *Sonoma County Journal* reported the affray, giving Dowd's name as Dow.

> John Dow and Jack Murray were sparring in Slaven's saloon, in this city [Petaluma], last Saturday night [7 Dec 1861], when Murray discovering his antagonist to be a little too hard for him, drew his knife and commenced using it in no agreeable manner to Dow. Before they were separated, three frightful wounds were inflicted upon the latter—two between the shoulders and one on the breast. They are all flesh wounds, however, and consequently not dangerous. Murray was examined before Justice Reyburn, on Monday morning [9 Dec 1861], and was required to give bond in the sum of $500, for his appearance at the next Court of Sessions, but failing to do it, was sent up the flume—no, up to Santa Rosa, where the jail has gone his security for his appearance at Court.[426]

---

[425] Sonoma County, California, Court of Sessions, Report of the Grand Jury, February term 1862, filed 7 February 1862; County Records, Sonoma County, Court Records, Miscellaneous Unprocessed Records, folder "County Records – Sonoma County – Court of Sessions – Reports of the Grand Jury"; California State Archives, Sacramento. Sonoma County, California, Court of Sessions, Minute Book E: 334, Report of the Grand Jury, February term 1862, 7 February 1862; Sonoma County Archives, Santa Rosa.
[426] "Cutting Affray," *The Sonoma County Journal* (Petaluma, California), 13 December 1861, p. 2, col. 2.

The trial jury found the defendant guilty of a simple assault on 10 Feb 1862. The Court ordered the defendant imprisoned in the County Jail of Sonoma County for the term of three months on 11 Feb 1862.

People v. H. H. Cooper
Vending and selling by retail spiritous, malt, vinous, and distilled liquors without a license (case file # 151)

The indictment filed on 7 Feb 1862 accused the defendant of vending and selling spiritous, malt, vinous, and distilled liquors by retail in quantities less than a quart at the Petaluma House without a license on 4 Jul 1861. O. T. Baldwin and D. F. Strother appeared as witnesses before the Grand Jury. The defendant pleaded guilty on 7 May 1862. The Court ordered the defendant to pay a fine of $35 and in the case of non-payment to be imprisoned in the County Jail of Sonoma County until the fine was paid at the rate of $2 per day on 10 May 1862.

May term 1862

The Court of Sessions met for six days this term, 5–10 May 1862.[427]

Hon. William Churchman, County Judge
Hon. Stephen Payran, Associate Justice
Hon. William Ellis, Associate Justice
Hon. Z. Middleton, Acting Associate Justice
William Wilks, District Attorney
William L. Anderson, Clerk
William H. Crowell, Deputy Clerk
J. M. Bowles, Sheriff
M. Barnes, Grand Jury foreman

Persons called as Grand Jurors but not empaneled: Thomas Gifford (rendered a good and sufficient excuse).

Grand Jurors sworn and empaneled on 5 May 1862: M. Barnes, Holman Talbot, J. H. Fowler, Edwin Peterson, David Hall, William M. Roberts, Robert Gorrell, Henry Gibbs, Thomas C. Gray, J. H. Raney, Martin Gaston, J. Whaley, John Haig, E. H. Gates, Robert Ferguson, and Julio Carrillo. The Court appointed M. Barnes as Grand Jury foreman.

---

[427] Sonoma County, California, Court of Sessions, Minute Book E: 344–362, May term 1862 proceedings; Sonoma County Archives, Santa Rosa.

Report of the Grand Jury[428]

To the Hon. Court of Sessions of Sonoma County,

We, the Grand Jury empaneled at the May Term of said Court, beg leave to submit the following report. We have found three true bills during our session, all of which have been for felonies. We have examined into the several offices in the county, and the books kept by each officer, and find that they are kept in a neat and correct manner. We have also examined into the condition of the Court House, and find that the roof of the same is leaky and should be immediately repaired; and unless the same is done, we are of the opinion that the Court House will suffer material injury therefrom. We call the especial attention of the Board of Supervisors to the condition of the same, and that particular care be taken to have the same effectually repaired, conceiving it to be useless to expend money for simply patching as heretofore.

We have examined into the condition of the revenue of the county license, and recommend that the District Attorney and Tax Collector of the county proceed to collect the license under the Revenue Act of 1861, before the Justices of the Peace, they having concurrent jurisdiction with this body, and deeming that course less expensive both to the county and the delinquents.

We also find that the Hospital is kept in a clean, neat and satisfactory manner; but the roof of the building is in a miserable condition, leaking almost like a sieve, and unless the same is substantially repaired the building will be rendered useless. The Jail is also kept in a clean, neat and safe manner, and the prisoners are well cared for.

We also took an account of the money in the Treasurer's office, and found the same to correspond with his accounts.

Having completed the business before us, we respectfully ask to be discharged.

M. Barnes, Foreman of the Grand Jury.

People v. N. R. Ellis
Grand larceny (case file # 152C)

The indictment filed on 6 May 1862 accused the defendant of stealing one bay horse (value $75), property of Isaac Smith, on 15 Apr 1862. Isaac Smith, D. Jones, and John Griffin appeared as witnesses before the Grand Jury. On 24 Apr 1862, the *Sonoma County Democrat* reported the theft and Smith's arrest as:

> N. R. Ellis was lodged in the jail at Santa Rosa on Monday last [21 Apr 1862] by Sheriff Bowles, on the charge of stealing a horse from Mr. Thomas Smith, on Mark West Creek. Ellis was first arrested at Sebastopol, by Deputy Sheriff Harrington, on Saturday, and placed in charge of a guard to await an examination before Justice Morris, of Analy Township, on Monday, that Justice having issued the warrant for his arrest. On Saturday the prisoner made his escape from the guard who had him in charge. On Monday he was again arrested – this time by Mr. Lewis Lucas, who had seen a description of him at the Sheriff's office. He was arrested on the road leading from Santa Rosa to Sonoma, and delivered over to the Sheriff, who placed him in the "lock-up," as stated above.

---

[428] Sonoma County, California, Court of Sessions, Minute Book: E: 356, Report of the Grand Jury, May term 1862, 8 May 1862; Sonoma County Archives, Santa Rosa. "Grand Jury Report," *The Sonoma County Democrat* (Santa Rosa, California), 15 May 1862, p. 2, col. 6.

Since the above was written, Ellis has had an examination before Justice Middleton, which resulted in his being held to answer to the charge of horse stealing before the Court of Sessions. Bail fixed at $1,500, which he has not yet given.[429]

The defendant pleaded guilty on 7 May 1862. The Court ordered the defendant imprisoned in the State Prison for the term of nine years on 10 May 1862. San Quentin received Ellis on 13 May 1862.[430] After receiving a petition signed by numerous Sonoma County officials, Governor Frederick F. Low pardoned Ellis on 30 Nov 1867, noting in his decision that Ellis had "already suffered over five years' imprisonment, a punishment which seems ample for the offence."[431] The Governor's pardon was granted on the condition that Ellis depart from California before 15 Dec 1867, "never to return."

People v. Henry P. Ferguson (indicted as H. P. Fergurson)
Assault with a deadly weapon with intent to inflict a bodily injury (case file # 152D)
The indictment filed on 7 May 1862 accused the defendant of assaulting William Adams with a knife and another deadly weapon unknown to the Grand Jury with the intent to inflict a bodily injury on 1 Mar 1862. James Doyle, Dr. William Burnett, Fernando Upham, Thomas Stephens, William L. Lummers, and William Potter appeared as witnesses before the Grand Jury. The *Sonoma County Democrat* reported the details of the stabbing and its cause on 6 Mar 1862 as:

> Harry Ferguson stabbed Wm. Adams at Petaluma, eleven times, with a small penknife, on Friday night last [28 Feb 1862]. The difficulty that caused the stabbing, as we are informed, originated as follows: Ferguson is a barber, and a short time since Adams went to his shop and got shaved on credit, telling Ferguson that he would pay him as soon as he got the money. On Friday night, Ferguson went into the Exchange Saloon at Petaluma, where Adams was playing cards. On seeing Ferguson enter the room, Adams turned to him and gave him twenty-five cents, remarking that he owed him for shaving. Ferguson became offended at the remark, and commenced an assault upon Adams, with the result stated. The wounds are considered dangerous. Ferguson was arrested and admitted to bail in the sum of $300.[432]

The trial jury found the defendant not guilty on 10 May 1862.

People v. William Hendrickson
Assault with a deadly weapon with intent to inflict bodily injury (case file # 150)
The indictment filed on 8 May 1862 accused the defendant of assaulting Joseph Hooser by shooting at him with a pistol with the intent of inflicting bodily injury on 5 Apr 1862. J. M. Peterson, John Young, Evan S. Stockwell, J. J. Piper, E. H. Smith, John W. Clack, H. M. Wilson,

---

[429] "Arrested for Horse Stealing," *The Sonoma County Democrat* (Santa Rosa, California), 24 April 1862, p. 2, col. 2.

[430] California, State Prison Register (1851–1867), Executive Department, entry no. 2365, N. R. Ellis, p. 196, received 13 May 1862; California State Archives, Sacramento.

[431] *The Journal of the Assembly, Seventeenth Session*, 78. Ellis's pardon and the Governor's decision are contained in a list of pardons from the State Prison granted by Governor Low from 1 November 1865 to 1 December 1867 appended to his second biennial message to the California Senate and Assembly dated 2 December 1867.

[432] "Cutting Affray," *The Sonoma County Democrat* (Santa Rosa, California), 6 March 1862, p. 3, col. 3.

William Fitch, J. R. Rany, P. N. Hogan, F. G. Poor, W. S. Thurgood, and Charles Michell appeared as witnesses before the Grand Jury. The encounter, which resulted in the death of Hooser, alias "Big Joe," was reported in the *Sonoma County Democrat* of 10 Apr 1862 as:

> On last Saturday evening [5 Apr 1862], Joseph Hooser, alias "Big Joe," was killed at Healdsburg by Officer [Henry] Sargent, a constable of Mendocino township. The particulars of the tragedy are, as near as we can ascertain from reliable sources, as follows: Hogan and Hendricks, keepers of a restaurant at Healdsburg, placed a bill for board against Hooser in the hands of Sargent for collection. The officer attached a mule belonging to Hooser, when the latter went to see Hendricks concerning the matter. As he approached, Hendricks, supposing he was about to make a personal attack, fired upon him with a revolver. Hooser returned the fire, and from six to ten shots were then exchanged between them, when, Hendricks's ammunition becoming exhausted, he retreated, followed by Hooser, who continued to fire upon his antagonist, one ball taking effect in his left arm. Just then Sargent arrived, and in attempting to arrest Hooser, who resisted with a knife, shot him through the heart, instantly killing him.[433]

August term 1862

The Court of Sessions met for fifteen days this term, 4–9, 11–14, and 18–22 August 1862.[434]

Hon. William Churchman, County Judge
Hon. William Ellis, Associate Justice
Hon. Stephen Payran, Associate Justice
William Wilks, District Attorney
William L. Anderson, Clerk
William H. Crowell, Deputy Clerk
J. M. Bowles, Sheriff
E. Latapie, Deputy Sheriff
Z. Middleton, Grand Jury foreman

Persons called as Grand Jurors but not empaneled: W. Fowler (failed to appear and answer), J. G. Heald (presented a good and sufficient excuse), George H. Jacobs (presented a good and sufficient excuse), William Gleason (presented a good and sufficient excuse), Richard Grey (presented a good and sufficient excuse), and A. W. Gates (presented a good and sufficient excuse).

Grand Jurors sworn, examined, and empaneled on 4 Aug 1862: Patrick Hayne, William B. Cockrill, B. Hall, Richard Fulkerson, Calvin M. Garrison, Z. Middleton, David Grove, John Farmer, Adam Fickas, Holman Talbot, David Green, G. M. Sacry, W. J. Hardin, Thomas L. Gault, Hamilton Gaston, and Robert Ferguson.

---

[433] "Man Killed by an Officer," *The Sonoma County Democrat* (Santa Rosa, California), 10 April 1862, p. 2, col. 2.
[434] Sonoma County, California, Court of Sessions, Minute Book E: 364–389, August term 1862 proceedings; Sonoma County Archives, Santa Rosa.

On 8 August 1862, the Court discharged Patrick Hayne as a Grand Juror as he was intoxicated and unable to transact the business of the Grand Jury. The Court examined Francis B. Green, found him duly qualified, and duly swore him as a Grand Juror in replacement of Patrick Hayne on 8 Aug 1862.

Report of the Grand Jury[435]

To the Honorable Court of Sessions, Sonoma County, California, August term 1862,
We respectfully submit the following report.
During our session of six days we have found indictments as follows:
For an assault with an attempt to commit rape, one
For an assault with a deadly weapon with intent to do bodily injury, one
For an assault and battery, one
For petit larceny, one
For resisting a public officer in the discharge of his duties in executing an order of [the] Court, (thirty-two persons), 32
For refusing to disperse when commanded to do so by the Sheriff (thirty-two persons), 32
We have also examined the Court House, Jail and Hospital and find the Jail and Hospital in good order.
The books of the County Officers [are] all in good order and kept in a manner calculated to reflect credit upon our County Officers.
We would respectfully call the attention of our Board of Supervisors to the dilapidated condition of the roofs of our Court House, Hospital and Jail. We think the time has come when patch work is insufficient to protect our public buildings from the peltings of the winter storms, especially our Jail and Hospital and their unfortunate inmates.
All of which is respectfully submitted.
August 9th, 1862
Z. Middleton, foreman Grand Jury

People v. D. M. Graham
Assault with intent to commit rape
The indictment filed on 5 Aug 1862 accused the defendant of assaulting Nevada Ann Hickle, a six-year-old girl, with the intent to commit rape on 30 Jun 1862. J. H. Hickle, Elizabeth Jane Hickle, and Dr. J. J. Piper appeared as witnesses before the Grand Jury. On 10 Jul 1862, the *Sonoma County Democrat*, quoting the *Healdsburg Review*, reported Graham's arrest as:

D. M. Graham, for several years a schoolmaster at this place [Healdsburg], and a supposed exemplary member of the church, was arrested on Wednesday [9 Jul 1862] on a charge of attempt to commit rape upon the person of a girl six years of age, the daughter of Mr. J. H. Hickle. The examination of the case took place before Justice [Thomas]

---

[435] Sonoma County, California, Court of Sessions, Grand Jury Report, August term 1862, 9 August 1862; County Records, Sonoma County, Court Records, Miscellaneous Unprocessed Records, folder "Reports – Grand Jury"; California State Archives, Sacramento. Sonoma County, California, Court of Sessions, Minute Book E: 374–375, Report of the Grand Jury, 9 August 1862; Sonoma County Archives, Santa Rosa.

Spencer, which resulted in the accused being committed to jail in default of $1,000 bonds. This affair, of course, created great surprise for the moment, and gave occasion for the usual amount of gossip. The schoolmaster has not proved himself a very moral man nor a pattern of a good Christian, for, as he himself says, "the d–l got in him." Convicted or acquitted, the scandal itself will drive him from this community.[436]

The first trial jury could not agree on a verdict on 14 Aug 1862. The second trial jury found the defendant guilty on 20 Aug 1862, and the Court ordered the defendant imprisoned in the State Prison for the term of 12 years on 22 Aug 1862. San Quentin received Graham on 25 Aug 1862.[437] He was discharged on 24 Apr 1863 by an order of the California Supreme Court after appealing his case to that Court, which had reversed the lower Court's decision and remanded the case back to Sonoma County for a new trial on 17 Mar 1863.[438] On 5 Sep 1863, the *Sonoma County Democrat* reported Graham's escape from the County Jail as:

> D. M. Graham who was returned to this county some time ago from the State Prison to undergo a second trial for a rape upon a child at Healdsburg, and whose case had been continued to [the] next term of [the] Court of Sessions, escaped from the county jail on Wednesday night or Thursday morning [2 or 3 Sep 1863], the doors to the jail were found locked as usual, and the prisoner gone. As to how he escaped is a mystery. The prison keys were found in the morning just where they had been left the night previous. The officers in charge of the prison entertain the opinion that the doors were opened by means of false keys.[439]

On 7 Nov 1863, the *Sonoma County Democrat* reported that Graham had been seen by John Prewitt on 1 Nov 1863 "in the mountains adjacent to Windsor."[440] He was arrested "while engaged in partaking of supper" on 11 Nov 1863 by Constable John H. Farmer, Ransom Powell, and several others near the place he had been seen.[441] The case was retried in the Sonoma County District Court, and the District Court trial jury found the defendant not guilty on 18 Feb 1864.[442] See Sonoma County District Court case # 285 (NS) and California Supreme Court case # 3737 (WPA # 7396).

---

[436] "The Graham Rape Case," *The Sonoma County Democrat* (Santa Rosa, California), 10 July 1862, p. 2, col. 2.

[437] California, State Prison Register (1851–1867), Executive Department, entry no. 2422, D. M. Graham, p. 200, received 25 August 1862; California State Archives, Sacramento.

[438] Curtis J. Hillyer, reporter, *Reports of Cases Determined in the Supreme Court of the State of California*, vol. 21, 2nd edition (San Francisco: Bancroft-Whitney Company, 1887), 266–273, *People v. Graham* (1862). California, Supreme Court, Minute Book F: 577, People v. Graham, judgment, 17 March 1863; California State Archives, Sacramento.

[439] "Another Prisoner Gone," *The Sonoma County Democrat* (Santa Rosa, California), 5 September 1863, p. 2, col. 1.

[440] "D. M. Graham Still in the County," *The Sonoma County Democrat* (Santa Rosa, California), 7 November 1863, p. 2, col. 1.

[441] "Arrest of Graham," *The Sonoma County Democrat* (Santa Rosa, California), 14 November 1863, p. 2, col. 1.

[442] Sonoma County, California, District Court, Minute Book C: 265, The People of the State of California v. D. M. Graham, trial jury verdict, 18 February 1864; Sonoma County Archives, Santa Rosa.

People v. A. Myers
Assault with intent to kill
The *Sonoma County Democrat* reported the assault in its 15 May 1862 edition as:

> At Bodega Corners, in this county, on Thursday last [8 May 1862], a dispute arose between A. Myers and S. J. Findley, which led to a fight between the parties, resulting in the stabbing of the latter with a pocket knife, Findley having eleven stabs, one of which penetrated the cavity of the chest. The dispute commenced about a bet that had been made between the parties on the election last fall. After the difficulty Myers was arrested by constable Ellison, and upon examination before Justice Sherman was held to bail in the sum of one thousand dollars, and having failed to give the required bonds, was on Wednesday last [14 May 1862] brought to Santa Rosa, by constable Ellison, and turned over to the Sheriff.
>
> Our informant states the people were very much exasperated during the examination, and while Myers was in the hands of the constable. Threats of lynching were freely made, and it was with great difficulty the officers succeeded in keeping the peace.[443]

The Grand Jury dismissed the charge on 5 Aug 1862. See also case file # 144.

People v. Alexander Skaggs, A. M. Green, I. N. Stapp, Elisha Givens, S. B. Martin, Warham Easley, James S. Buchanan, James Miller, Robert Neeley, Gip Young, C. C. Clark, George Lawrence, Daniel Prouse (var. Prowse), Sylvester Prouse (var. Prowse), John Hatfield, Peter T. Archambeau, [?] Phipps, William T. Garrison, Thomas Prince, K. Maxwell, Jesse Houghton (var. Hooton), George Clark, Isaac Miller, William Freshour, C. C. Freshour, B. W. Scott, Walker Wilson, Franklin Burk, Joseph Baugh, William Walters, Josiah McKinley, and Marion Anderson
Resisting an officer (case file # 141)
The indictment filed on 9 Aug 1862 accused the defendants of obstructing, resisting, and opposing J. M. Bowles, Sheriff of Sonoma County, while he attempted to serve a writ of execution issued by the 7th District Court dated 11 Jun 1862 against Cornelius Bice, Robert Neely, and James Miller on 15 Jul 1862. J. M. Bowles, N. Fike, William McP. Hill, E. Latapie, P. N. Emerson, H. M. Wilson, E. T. Espy, Alexander Wilson, John Prewitt, J. J. May, B. F. Tucker, B. W. Scott, George J. Greenwood, William Scott, Joseph Binns, Martin Bunch, Anderson Delzell, and G. W. Arnold appeared as witnesses before the Grand Jury. The Court sustained the defendants' demurrer and ordered the case be resubmitted to the Grand Jury on 5 Nov 1862. See also case file # 158.

---

[443] "Cutting Affray at Bodega," *The Sonoma County Democrat* (Santa Rosa, California), 15 May 1862, p. 2, col. 2.

People v. Alexander Skaggs, A. M. Green, I. N. Stapp, Elisha Givens, S. B. Martin, Warham Easley, James S. Buchanan, James Miller, Robert Neeley, Gip Young, C. C. Clark, George Lawrence, Daniel Prouse (var. Prowse), Sylvester Prouse (var. Prowse), John Hatfield, Peter T. Archambeau, [?] Phipps, William T. Garrison, Thomas Prince, K. Maxwell, Jesse Houghton (var. Hooton), George Clark, Isaac Miller, William Freshour, C. C. Freshour, B. W. Scott, Walker Wilson, Franklin Burk, Joseph Baugh, William Walters, Josiah McKinley, and Marion Anderson
Unlawful assembly (case file # 141)

The indictment filed on 9 Aug 1862 accused the defendants of unlawfully assembling for the purpose of obstructing, resisting, and opposing J. M. Bowles, Sheriff of Sonoma County, while he attempted to serve a writ of execution issued by the 7th District Court dated 11 Jun 1862 against Cornelius Bice, Robert Neely, and James Miller on 15 Jul 1862. The Court sustained the defendants' demurrer and ordered the case be resubmitted to the Grand Jury on 5 Nov 1862. See also case file # 158.

People v. John S. Taylor
Assault with a deadly weapon with intent to commit a bodily injury (case file # 142)

The indictment filed on 9 Aug 1862 accused the defendant of assaulting Rufus Temple with a pistol by shooting him with the intent of inflicting a bodily injury on 1 Aug 1862. Rufus Temple, John McArthur, and H. H. Lewis appeared as witnesses before the Grand Jury. The trial jury found the defendant not guilty on 5 Feb 1863.

People v. Samuel J. Finley
Assault and battery (case file # 144)

The indictment filed on 9 Aug 1862 accused the defendant of assaulting Alexander Myers with force and arms by unlawfully beating, wounding, and ill-treating him on 10 May 1862. Alexander Myers, John Waters, Alfred Law, and E. T. Thurston appeared as witnesses before the Grand Jury. The trial jury found the defendant not guilty on 5 Nov 1862.

People v. George Pitts
Petit larceny (case file # 152H)

The indictment filed on 9 Aug 1862 accused the defendant of stealing one horse colt (value $45), property of Ambrose Dellenger, on 25 Nov 1861.[444] Ambrose Dellenger, Mike Barnes, and George McCain appeared as witnesses before the Grand Jury. The indictment was set aside and resubmitted to the November term 1862 Grand Jury on 3 Nov 1862. The Grand Jury failed to find a bill against the defendant on 10 Nov 1862.

The Hon. Thomas Spencer and the Hon. Josiah Chandler were elected as Associate Justices of the Court of Sessions at a convention of the Justices of the Peace of Sonoma County on 6 Oct 1862.

---

[444] The indictment actually states the theft took place on 25 November 1862, but this is clearly a clerical error.

November term 1862

The Court of Sessions met for thirteen days this term, 3–8, 10–11, 13–14, and 18–20 November 1862. A special term of the Court of Sessions was convened for two days on 27–28 January 1863 "for the purpose of proceeding with the criminal trials which had grown out of the Healdsburg squatter troubles."[445]

Hon. William Churchman, County Judge
Hon. Josiah Chandler, Associate Justice
Hon. Thomas Spencer, Associate Justice
William Wilks, District Attorney
William L. Anderson, Clerk
William H. Crowell, Deputy Clerk
John N. Bailhache, Deputy Clerk
J. M. Bowles, Sheriff
O. T. Baldwin, Under Sheriff
P. N. Emerson, Deputy Sheriff
E. Latapie, Deputy Sheriff
J. D. Binns, Deputy Sheriff
L. C. Lewis, Coroner
Charles Patton, Grand Jury foreman

Persons called as Grand Jurors but not empaneled: James A. Kleiser (failed to appear and answer when called), Andrew Johnson (not a citizen of the United States), William Johnson (rendered a good and sufficient excuse), J. Jordan (rendered a good and sufficient excuse), Jonathan Jones (rendered a good and sufficient excuse), and C. H. Ivans (var. Ivins) (rendered a good and sufficient excuse).

Grand Jurors sworn, examined , and empaneled on 3 Nov 1862: William Jellings, Allison Johnson, J. Illingworth, James Ingles, Robert Irwin, William Jameson, Lorenzo Jackson, Charles Patton, Joseph Badger, I. A. Bradshaw, D. P. V. Ogan, John W. Jones, B. Forsythe, T. W. Ingram, James Fretwell, and John Leslie. The Court appointed Charles Patton as foreman of the Grand Jury.

---

[445] Sonoma County, California, Court of Sessions, Minute Book E: 393–430 and 432–437, November term 1862 and special term 1863 proceedings; Sonoma County Archives, Santa Rosa. "Special Term of the Court of Sessions," *The Sonoma County Democrat* (Santa Rosa, California), 17 January 1863, p. 2, col. 1.

Report of the Grand Jury[446]

To the Hon. Court of Sessions of Sonoma County,

The Grand Jury have been in session from Monday 3ᵈ instant [3 Nov 1862] till the present time [8 Nov 1862]. A number of cases have come up before us which have been dismissed, as the evidence did not warrant (in the opinion of the necessary number) indictments being found. In connection with these cases, we will only refer particularly to the charge of rape against one Wm. Taylor. In this case, we are happy to say, that no evidence came before us to induce us to believe that any such offence had been committed at all.

We have found seven true bills. One for assault and battery. One assault with a deadly weapon. One assault with intent to commit murder. One for exhibiting a deadly weapon. One against twenty-two persons for resisting the Sheriff in the discharge of his duty, an indictment for the same offence having been set aside by the Court of Sessions for the present term. One for doing business without license, and one for assault with intent to do bodily injury.

Our attention has been called to a County road in Santa Rosa which is stopped up – in connection with this matter we refer the Overseers to the statutes of 1855 where it will be seen to be the duty of Overseers of road districts to prosecute in such cases before Justices of the Peace. We will here remark, that we sincerely hope that in these times when sectional and political feeling seem to create a constant danger of collision among our fellow citizens, that every man among us, having the good of our common country at heart, will use his utmost influence in inducing everyone to yield that deference, and ready obedience, to the laws, which are so essential, to prevent the scenes of discord, strife, and civil war, among us, which, in the Atlantic States are endangering the very existence and structure of our Government.

We have examined the Jail building both as a Hospital and a Jail, to both of which uses it is applied. We found the hospital very clean and comfortable, with but one patient, and he is convalescent. We also examined the Jail and found it in good order as to comfort of the prisoners, who may be there from time to time, but think it needs some improvements to make it secure. The windows on the west side are perfectly easy of access from the outside, so that liquor or other small articles can be passed to prisoners on the inside, who are usually allowed the liberty of the passages in the day time.

We think it would be well to erect a strong fence, extending along the west side of the Jail lot, about ten feet west of the Jail, and about ten feet high, and joining the Jail at the ends, of 2 inch fir. This would prevent intercourse through these windows between prisoners and persons on the outside in the day time when prisoners have the liberty of the passage in which the windows are.

We also think it necessary to cover the inside of the outside walls of the Jail with two thicknesses of two inch fir – the second thickness nailed to the first with 5 inch spikes about one inch apart. The spikes would make it almost impossible to cut through the plank, and would also prevent its liability to take fire, and we think would make the jail much more secure than at

---

[446] Sonoma County, California, Court of Sessions, Report of the Grand Jury, November term 1862, 8 November 1862; County Records, Sonoma County, Court Records, Miscellaneous Unprocessed Records, folder "Reports – Grand Jury"; California State Archives, Sacramento. Sonoma County, California, Court of Sessions, Minute Book E: 406–408, Report of the Grand Jury, 8 November 1862; Sonoma County Archives, Santa Rosa.

present. We think it would be well to plate two of the cells with boiler Iron so as to make a secure place in which to confine the most desperate class of offenders. We think the fencing and wooden lining of the walls referred to could be done within three hundred and fifty dollars cash. We cannot say what it would cost to plate the cells with Iron. We are glad to be able to say, that at present our Jail is empty.

We have called the attention of the County Attorney to the names of persons who are said to be doing business without license. We have also examined the Offices of the County Clerk, Recorder, and Treasurer, as well as that of the Sheriff, and find everything appears to be in good order and the books properly kept. We have concluded the business before us and respectfully ask to be discharged.

Santa Rosa, Nov. 8th, 1862

Charles Patton, foreman of the Grand Jury

People v. John Kelly

Grand larceny

On 28 Aug 1862 the *Sonoma County Democrat* reported Kelly's arrest as:

> John Kelly was brought to town [Santa Rosa] last Thursday [21 Aug 1862] and lodged in the County Jail by officer [William N.] Ferrell of Petaluma, on [a] charge of grand larceny—stealing a gold watch. He was examined before Justice [Josiah] Chandler and held to answer before the Court of Sessions. Bail placed at $500.[447]

The Grand Jury ignored the case on 4 Nov 1862. The day before, on 3 Nov 1862, the Sheriff reported to the Court that the defendant had escaped by breaking jail along with John Wood on 14 Sep 1862. See also case file # 152G.

People v. William Taylor

Rape (case file # 143)

In a complaint dated 17 Oct 1862, District Attorney William Wilks accused the defendant of having carnal knowledge of Nancy Churchill, a child under the age of 10 years old, on 10 Oct 1862. The *Petaluma Argus* of 22 Oct 1862 reported William Taylor's arrest as:

> At one of the hell-holes in East Petaluma, a most heart-sickening object was discovered on Friday last [17 Oct 1862]. A little girl eight years old was found—nearer dead than alive—with a loathsome disease. Drs. Carpenter and Martin made an examination and ascertained that an attempt had been made to ravish the child. The statement of the mother, Mrs. Churchill, led to the suspicion of one Wm. Taylor, who was immediately arrested by constable Cavanagh and taken before Justice Chandler, who held the prisoner to bail in the sum of $1000—in default of which he was lodged in the County jail to await the action of the Grand Jury.[448]

---

[447] "Grand Larceny," *The Sonoma County Democrat* (Santa Rosa, California), 28 August 1862, p. 2, col. 4.

[448] "Revolting," *The Petaluma (California) Argus*, 22 October 1862, p. 2, col. 2.

The Hon. Josiah Chandler, a Justice of the Peace of Petaluma Township, after hearing testimony from John C. Sherman, Mrs. A. Churchill, Joseph Miller, E. J. Martin, and W. W. Carpenter, held the defendant over to answer to the charge on 18 Oct 1862. The Grand Jury dismissed the charge for lack of evidence on 5 Nov 1862.

People v. Catherine Waters
Perjury

The *Sonoma County Journal* reported on 22 Aug 1862 that Mrs. Catherine Waters of Petaluma, "upon the complaint of Mr. C. A. Hough," had "been bound over in the sum of $1,000 to appear before the next Grand Jury and answer to the charge of perjury."[449] The Grand Jury dismissed the charge on 5 Nov 1862.

People v. Arnold Stump and Lewis W. Stump
Illegal voting

On 12 Sep 1862, the *Sonoma County Journal* reported that the two Stump brothers had "been arrested and bound over in the sum of $800, charged with double voting at the late election, first at the Freestone Hotel precinct, and lastly at Bodega Corners."[450] The Grand Jury could not agree on this case on 6 Nov 1862.

People v. Alexander Skaggs, I. N. Stapp, George Lawrence, Sylvester Prouse, and James Miller
Destroying the County Jail locks, hasps, bolts, and fastenings to cells (case file # 141)

On 25 Oct 1862, the District Attorney William Wilks, swore out a complaint before Justice of the Peace Z. Middleton accusing the defendants of willfully and intentionally breaking down and destroying the locks, hasps, bolts, and fastenings to cells and places of confinement in the County Jail on 25 Oct 1862. After an examination of the witnesses, Justice Middleton held the defendants over to answer to the charges on 27 Oct 1862. The Grand Jury dismissed the case on 6 Nov 1862.

People v. John Wood
Assault with a deadly weapon with intent to inflict a bodily injury (case file # 152G)

The indictment filed on 6 Nov 1862 accused the defendant of assaulting John B. Ford at Tibbett's Saloon in Sebastopol with a Bowie knife giving him one severe wound in the left breast near the shoulder on 9 Sep 1862. Mathew Heatherington (var. Matthew Hetherington), Thomas W. Clark, James Ingles, and J. B. Ford appeared as witnesses before the Grand Jury. On 3 Nov 1862 the Sheriff reported to the Court that the defendant had escaped on 14 Sep 1862 by breaking jail along with John Kelly. On 18 Sep 1862, the *Sonoma County Democrat* described the escape as:

> John Kelley and John Wood, confined in our county prison to await the action of the grand jury – the first upon [a] charge of grand larceny, and the latter for an assault with a deadly weapon upon one Ford – made their escape from jail on Sunday night [14 Sep 1862]. The feat was accomplished by taking the brick from a particular wall dividing the

---

[449] "Perjury," *The Sonoma County Journal* (Petaluma, California), 22 August 1862, p. 2, col. 1.
[450] "Illegal Voting," *The Sonoma County Journal* (Petaluma, California), 12 September 1862, p. 2, col. 1.

prison from an ante-room, and then removing the bolt from an outside door. The wall through which the hole was made, large enough to admit of the passage of the prisoners, is about five inches in thickness and is constructed entirely of brick and mortar, and since an examination of the place, we are only surprised that such an escape has not been effected by others who have been confined in the prison. Steps should be taken by the Supervisors to make the jail more secure. As it now is, the only guarantee against outbreak will be the ball and chain, or handcuffs, either of which would be brutal, except in extreme cases. No reward has been offered for the apprehension of the escaped prisoners, as yet. Much astonishment has been expressed that Sheriff Bowles has made no effort to apprehend them.[451]

People v. John Scanlon
Drawing and exhibiting a gun in an angry and threatening manner (case file # 152J)

The indictment filed on 6 Nov 1862 accused the defendant of drawing and exhibiting a gun in the presence of Charles Roberts, Armsted Goatley, and Kate Unger in a rude, angry, and threatening manner, not in necessary self-defense, on 21 Oct 1862. Charles Roberts, Armsted Goatley, and Kate Unger appeared as witnesses before the Grand Jury. The trial jury found the defendant guilty on 10 Nov 1862. The Court ordered the defendant to be imprisoned in the County Jail of Sonoma County for the term of six months and pay the costs of the prosecution on 11 Nov 1862. The Governor of California, Leland Stanford, pardoned the defendant on 18 Nov 1862. Stanford noted on his pardon that "a large number of respectable citizens of Sonoma County, including an Associate Justice of the Court of Sessions [Josiah Chandler]" had represented to him that Scanlon was "a temperate, peaceable, and industrious citizen without property" who supported well "a large family, who are entirely dependent upon him" and "that the weapon exhibited by Scanlon was empty and was drawn without any intention on his part of committing a crime."[452]

People v. James R. Glasscock
Assault with intent to commit murder (case file # 153)

The indictment filed on 6 Nov 1862 accused the defendant of assaulting Sylvester McClintock with a knife giving him two dangerous wounds with the intent of killing him on 17 Sep 1862. James Ramey, Sylvester McClintock, John Gall, Thomas B. Jones, and E. Ray appeared as witnesses before the Grand Jury. On 19 Sep 1862, the *Sonoma County Journal* reported the assault as:

> A stabbing affray occurred in Cloverdale on Wednesday night [17 Sep 1862], in which Sylvester McClentick [*sic*] was stabbed twice by one Glascock. One wound was over the hip and the other on the left side of the neck. They will probably prove fatal. Glascock was taken under arrest. The difficulty originated in a dispute about stock.[453]

The trial jury found the defendant not guilty on 5 Feb 1863.

---

[451] "Broke Jail," *The Sonoma County Democrat* (Santa Rosa, California), 18 September 1862, p. 2, col. 2.
[452] Governor Stanford's pardon of John Scanlon is included in Scanlon's case file.
[453] "Stabbing Affray," *The Sonoma County Journal* (Petaluma, California), 19 September 1862, p. 2, col. 1.

People v. John Adrain
Assault and battery (case file # 142A)

The indictment filed on 8 Nov 1862 accused the defendant of assaulting William Flemming by beating, wounding, and ill-treating him on 3 Nov 1862. William Flemming appeared as a witness before the Grand Jury.

People v. Lancaster Clyman
Keeping stallions to be used for propagation for hire and profit without a license/violation of the Revenue Act (case file # 145)

The indictment filed on 8 Nov 1862 accused the defendant of keeping and permitting two stallions to be used for the purposes of propagation for hire and profit without a license on 1 Jun 1862. Frank Halley and Felix Stout appeared as witnesses before the Grand Jury. The defendant pleaded guilty on 2 Feb 1863. After being shown that the defendant had taken out the necessary license and paid all the costs of the prosecution, the Court ordered the defendant to pay a fine of 6 cents on 5 Feb 1863.

People v. Budd Gann
Assault with a deadly weapon with intent to inflict bodily injury (case file # 148)

The indictment filed on 8 Nov 1862 accused the defendant of assaulting Charles Spurgen (var. Spurgeon) with a sheath knife giving him a severe wound upon the left breast on 1 Nov 1862. F. Halley and Felix Stout appeared as witnesses before the Grand Jury. The *Sonoma County Democrat* reported the stabbing in its 6 Nov 1862 edition as:

> Saturday evening [1 Nov 1862] C. A. Spurgeon of Cloverdale was severely stabbed by J. N. Gann. We are informed the difficulty grew out of a dispute about dancing. The parties had been good friends previous to the dispute, and the weapon used was a pocket knife.[454]

The Justice's Court documents in the case file give the defendant's name as Isaac W. Gann.

People v. Warham Easley, Sylvester Prouse (var. Prowse), I. N. Stapp, James Miller, George Young (indicted as Gip Young), Isaac Miller, Joseph Baugh, B. W. Scott, Elisha Givens, A. M. Green, [?] Phipps, S. B. Martin, Joseph Derrick, Walker Wilson, William Freshour, George Lawrence, William Garrison, Peter T. Archambeau, Alexander Skaggs, John Hatfield, Franklin Burk, and C. C. Freshour
Unlawful assembly (case file # 158)

The indictment filed on 8 Nov 1862 accused the defendants of wrongfully and unlawfully assembling for the purpose of obstructing, resisting, and opposing Joseph M. Bowles, Sheriff of Sonoma County, while he attempted to serve a writ of execution against Cornelius Bice, Robert Neeley, and James Miller on 15 Jul 1862. Joseph Binns, Joseph M. Bowles, William Scott, and L. D. Latimer appeared as witnesses before the Grand Jury. The trial jury found thirteen of the defendants (Alexander Skaggs, Peter T. Archambeau, S. B. Martin, Joseph Baugh, Warham Easley, William Garrison, Elisha Givens, B. W. Scott, John Hatfield, James Miller, I. N. Stapp, Sylvester

---

[454] "Stabbing Affray," *The Sonoma County Democrat* (Santa Rosa, California), 6 November 1862, p. 2, col. 1.

Prouse, and George Lawrence) not guilty on 28 Jan 1863. The Court dismissed the charge against defendants A. M. Green, Isaac Miller and George Young (indicted as Gip Young) on 6 Feb 1863. See also case file # 141.

People v. Warham Easley, Sylvester Prouse (var. Prowse), I. N. Stapp, James Miller, George Young (indicted as Gip Young), Isaac Miller, Joseph Baugh, B. W. Scott, Elisha Givens, A. M. Green, [?] Phipps, S. B. Martin, Joseph Derrick, Walker Wilson, William Freshour, George Lawrence, William Garrison, Peter T. Archambeau, Alexander Skaggs, John Hatfield, Franklin Burk, and C. C. Freshour Resisting an officer in the discharge of his duty (case file # 158)

The indictment filed on 8 Nov 1862 accused the defendants of obstructing, resisting, and opposing Joseph M. Bowles, Sheriff of Sonoma County, while he attempted to serve a writ of execution against Cornelius Bice, Robert Neeley, and James Miller on 15 Jul 1862. Joseph Binns, Joseph M. Bowles, William Scott, and L. D. Latimer appeared as witnesses before the Grand Jury. The trial jury found thirteen of the defendants (Alexander Skaggs, Peter T. Archambeau, S. B. Martin, Joseph Baugh, Warham Easley, William Garrison, Elisha Givens, B. W. Scott, John Hatfield, James Miller, I. N. Stapp, Sylvester Prouse, and George Lawrence) not guilty on 20 Nov 1862. The Court dismissed the charge against defendants A. M. Green, Isaac Miller and George Young (indicted as Gip Young) on 6 Feb 1863. See also case file # 141.

February term 1863

The Court of Sessions met for six days this term, 2–7 February 1863.[455]

Hon. William Churchman, County Judge
Hon. Josiah Chandler, Associate Justice
Hon. Thomas L. Spencer, Associate Justice
William Wilks, District Attorney
William H. Crowell, Deputy Clerk
O. T. Baldwin, Under Sheriff
E. Latapie, Deputy Sheriff
Adam Shane, Grand Jury foreman

Persons called as Grand Jurors but not empaneled: John Long (under twenty-one years of age) and Charles Kennedy (rendered a good and sufficient excuse).

Grand Jurors sworn, examined, and empaneled on 2 Feb 1863: George C. Jewett, A. H. Kirkpatrick, J. E. Lamb, E. Katlin, R. Keyes, Isaac Long, Tilford Lindsley, August Kohle, O. Rippetoe, William Roberts, Adam Shane, N. R. Davidson, J. G. Cook, H. Wise, Joel Miller, and W. B. Cockrill. The Court appointed Adam Shane as Grand Jury foreman.

---

[455]Sonoma County, California, Court of Sessions, Minute Book E: 438–459, February term 1863 proceedings; Sonoma County Archives, Santa Rosa.

To the Honorable Court of Sessions,

The Grand Jury in and for Sonoma County after a session of six days would beg to submit the following report. We have found three indictments, and one presentment, also four dismissals.

We have enquired into the management of the Public Prison and find no occupants at present. We find the rooms to be in an uncleanly and neglected condition and not altogether calculated to insure the safety or comfort of prisoners.

The Hospital we find to be occupied by four patients. They appear to be as comfortably situated as could be expected. The roof of the building is undergoing repairs at present, which we consider necessary, and when completed will, we believe, render the same in a good condition.

The Public Offices, to wit, County Clerk, Sheriff, Recorder, and Treasurer, have all been visited with satisfaction, and [we] take pleasure in reporting the books [are] kept in a neat and business-like manner.

On examination of the license Book, we find some delinquents and would call special attention to the same by the proper Officers whose duty it is to attend thereto.

We also find on examination of the Court House some necessary repairs required, especially plastering, and would recommend to the Board of Supervisors their immediate attention to the same.

All of which is respectfully submitted, and [we] ask to be discharged.

February 7th, 1863

Adam Shane, Foreman, Grand Jury.

People v. Hiram N. Green (indicted as H. N. Green)
Assault with a deadly weapon with intent to commit murder (case file # 149)

The indictment filed on 3 Feb 1863 accused the defendant of assaulting J. M. Hooper by shooting him with a pistol with the intent of killing him on 11 Dec 1862. J. M. Hooper, Jacob Mitty, and H. W. Isbel appeared as witnesses before the Grand Jury. The affray was described in the *Sonoma County Democrat* in its 20 Dec 1862 edition as:

> We are indebted to a friend for the following particulars of a shooting affray which occurred recently in the upper end of this county: On Wednesday, 10th inst. [10 Dec 1862], when C. C. Green [sic], of Mendocino, was passing the ranch of Murdoch Hooper, who resides on the road leading from Geyserville to Cloverdale, he was observed by Hooper, who had some grudge against him, and followed a mile or so upon the road, when an altercation took place between the parties, in which Colt's five shooters were freely used, and resulted in both being severely, though not dangerously, wounded. Hooper was shot in the leg and Green in the shoulder. After having exhausted the loads in his pistol, Hooper

---

[456] Sonoma County, California, Court of Sessions, Grand Jury report, February term 1863, 7 February 1863; County Records, Sonoma County, Miscellaneous Unprocessed Court Records, folder "County Records – Sonoma County – Court of Sessions – Reports of the Grand Jury "; California State Archives, Sacramento. Sonoma County, California, Court of Sessions, Minute Book E: 457–458, Grand Jury report, 7 February 1863; Sonoma County Archives, Santa Rosa.

drew a large Bowie knife, with which he inflicted a severe cut upon Green's arm. Notwithstanding his wounds, our informant says Green held on to his pistol, and finally Hooper believing that Green had reserved one charge, was made by Green to acknowledge himself in error, etc. After the fight Green proceeded to Dry Creek, where his wounds received the attention of Dr. Martin, of Healdsburg, and on Wednesday he was arrested by the Constable of Mendocino Township, and taken before Justice Spencer of Healdsburg upon a warrant gotten out by Hooper. It is said the difficulty originated from jealousy. Of course there was a woman concerned in the affair.[457]

The trial jury found the defendant not guilty on 7 Feb 1863. See also case file # 158B below.

People v. J. M. Hooper
Assault with intent to commit murder (case file # 158B)
In a complaint filed in the Justice's Court of the Hon. Thomas Spencer, a Justice of the Peace of Mendocino Township, dated 14 Jan 1863, H. N. Green accused J. M. Hooper of assaulting him on the high road between the towns of Geyserville and Cloverdale with a pistol by shooting him in the right shoulder giving him a severe and dangerous wound with the intent of killing him and assaulting him with a knife giving him a severe and dangerous wound on the right arm with the intent of killing him on 11 Dec 1862. The Grand Jury dismissed the charge on 3 Feb 1863. See also case file # 149 above.

People v. Jacob Weingartner
Assault with a deadly weapon with intent to inflict a bodily injury
On 27 Dec 1862, the Sonoma County Democrat reported the assault of Thomas Donnelly by Jacob Weingartner as:

> Thos. Donnelly, a painter in the employ of Jas. McCoy, and Jake Wiengartner [sic], a man who does odd jobs about town, engaged in a broil last Friday evening [26 Dec 1862], which ended in the former being severely stabbed by the latter. The following are the particulars of the affair as near as we can learn them. The parties were friends, and on Friday afternoon visited a wine cellar together, where they indulged freely in the pure juice of the grape. Donnelly, not being provided with funds at the time, requested his companion to "foot the bill," and promised to refund his share on the day following. This proposition was accepted, and they left for home. On the road to town they had some dispute about a duck which Wiengartner was carrying, the latter charging Donnelly with having cut the string with which his game was tied. In town they separated, and Donnelly went immediately home, to the residence of Mr. McCoy. Shortly after he had been indoors Wiengartner came to the house and demanded the money which he had paid out for him. Donnelly replied that he did not have it. Some words then ensued between the principals, and Mr. McCoy observing that they were both in liquor came between them as moderator, and quieted the dispute by promising Wiengartner that he would see him paid in the morning, not however before having received a slight cut upon the hand in an attempt to wrench a knife from the hand of the latter. Mr. McCoy then accompanied Wiengartner down town, who promised to go home provided McCoy would take a drink

[457] "Shooting Affray," The Sonoma County Democrat (Santa Rosa, California), 20 December 1862, p. 2, col. 1.

with him. They went in a saloon and got a drink, and Mr. McCoy returned home, but it seems Wiengartner did not. About 7 o'clock in the evening he and Donnelly again met, this time in Reichardt and Harrison's restaurant, and Donnelly tendered Wiengartner the money he had borrowed and demanded a bit, which was coming to him in change. As to what followed the demand there seems to be a diversity of opinion, some who witnessed the difficulty say that Donnelly was very abusive to Wiengartner and struck him several blows with his fist. Donnelly says himself that Wiengartner commenced the assault upon him. Be this as it may, the proprietor of the house separated them and compelled them to go into the street. Getting outside, Donnelly says he started up town, and as he stepped from the sidewalk he stumbled, and while in a falling attitude he was stabbed by Wiengartner. Three blows appear to have been struck with a knife, there being one cut upon the head and two a little below the right shoulder blade. The most severe wound is on the back and is about four inches in length and one and a half in depth. The case is now in course of examination before Justice Middleton, having been postponed from time to time, on account of Donnelly's being unable to attend. He will probably be about in a few days.[458]

The Grand Jury dismissed the case on 3 Feb 1863.

People v. M. Nathanson
Grand larceny
    The Grand Jury dismissed the case on 5 Feb 1863.

People v. John Mann
Grand larceny
    The Grand Jury dismissed the case on 6 Feb 1863.

People v. A. M. Green, Isaac Miller, and George Young (indicted as Gip Young)
Resisting an officer while in the discharge of his duty (case file # 158)
    The Court dismissed the charge on 6 Feb 1863.

People v. A. M. Green, Isaac Miller, and George Young (indicted as Gip Young)
Unlawful assemblage (case file # 158)
    The Court dismissed the charge on 6 Feb 1863.

People v. Oliver Williams
Assault with intent to commit murder (case file # 158E)
    The indictment filed on 7 Feb 1863 accused the defendant of assaulting "Dutch Joe," whose true name was unknown to the Grand Jury, by shooting at him with a pistol with the intent to murder him on 30 Jan 1863. James B. White appeared as a witness before the Grand Jury.

---

[458] "Stabbing Affray," *The Sonoma County Democrat* (Santa Rosa, California), 27 December 1862, p. 2, col. 1.

People v. Alexander Lockwood
Perjury

The indictment filed on 7 Feb 1863 accused the defendant of giving false testimony in the case of F. B. Green v. Alexander Lockwood before the Hon. J. Snow, a Justice of the Peace for Vallejo Township, concerning the borrowing of a gun on 27 Dec 1862. David Warfe, L. F. Collins, F. B. Green, T. Lavin, and R. Mock appeared as witnesses before the Grand Jury. While awaiting trial the defendant escaped from the County Jail on 27 Feb 1863 by removing a brick in the wall of the jail, making a hole large enough to crawl through. The *Sonoma County Democrat* noted that this was the identical manner of escape used by the prisoner John Wood just months earlier (see case file # 152G).[459] Nine and a half years later Lockwood was arrested in San Bernardino County, and the case was finally tried in the County Court of Sonoma County.[460] See County Court case # 611 (NS) for the indictment and other papers.[461] The County Court trial jury found the defendant guilty and recommended him to the clemency of the Court on account of his age on 12 Oct 1872. The County Court ordered the defendant imprisoned in the State Prison for the term of four years on 17 Oct 1872. The defendant was received at San Quentin State Prison on 18 Oct 1872 and discharged on 11 Mar 1876.[462]

People v. Robert G. Meeks, Adam A. Bushnell, John B. Stamps, Winslow H. Bowen, and Benjamin Williams
Malicious mischief (case file # 153)

The presentment filed on 7 Feb 1863 accused the defendants of taking two nuts off of a buggy belonging to James Williamson and Co., taking the nuts off a wagon belonging to M. Gillam and throwing them away, and cutting the tails off of five horses and one mule, two of the horses the property of James Williamson and Co., on 25 Dec 1862. William Nelson, Lemuel Chenowoth (var. Chenoweth), James Griggson, Otis Allen, Lancaster Kleiman (var. Clyman), and M. Gillam appeared as witnesses before the Grand jury.

May term 1863

The Court of Sessions met for eight days this term, 4–9 and 26–27 May 1863.[463]

Hon. William Churchman, County Judge
Hon. Josiah Chandler, Associate Justice
Hon. Thomas Spencer, Associate Justice
Hon. Z. Middleton, Acting Associate Justice (26–27 May 1863 in place of Hon. Thomas Spencer)
William Wilks, District Attorney

---

[459] "Another Prisoner Gone," *The Sonoma County Democrat* (Santa Rosa, California), 7 March 1863, p. 2, col. 1.

[460] "Local Waifs," *The Sonoma Democrat* (Santa Rosa, California), 5 October 1872, p. 5, col. 1.

[461] Sonoma County, California, County Court, Minute Book F: 187, 188–189, 191, 193, 204–205, and 220–221, People v. Alexander Lockwood, case proceedings, 1872; Sonoma County Archives, Santa Rosa.

[462] California, State Prison Register (1867–1875), Executive Department, entry no. 5403, Alex. Lockwood, p. 169, received 18 October 1872; California State Archives, Sacramento.

[463] Sonoma County, California, Court of Sessions, Minute Book E: 462–477, May term 1863 proceedings; Sonoma County Archives, Santa Rosa.

J. M. Bowles, Sheriff
O. T. Baldwin, Under Sheriff
J. D. Binns, Deputy Sheriff
E. Latapie, Deputy Sheriff
William L. Anderson, Clerk
John N. Bailhache, Deputy Clerk
William H. Crowell, Deputy Clerk
S. T. Coulter, Grand Jury foreman

Persons called as Grand Jurors but not empaneled: William Lowry (failed to appear and answer to his name when called), Jasper Linville (offered a good excuse), John Lee (offered a good excuse), and William McDonald (offered a good excuse).

Grand Jurors sworn, examined, and empaneled on 4 May 1863: William Keys, James Lavin, R. T. Mitchell, Charles Lampkin, John Morris, R. M. Morris, Milas Laton, John Hendley, H. Jackson, S. T. Coulter, A. B. Glover, John Limbaugh, William Smith, H. Hall, J. C. Hoag, and Z. Middleton. The Court appointed S. T. Coulter as Grand Jury foreman.

Report of the Grand Jury[464]

To the Hon. Court of Sessions of Sonoma County,

The Grand Jury would respectfully submit to the Court the following report.

We have inquired into all Public Offenses committed in the County of which we could procure the evidence.

We have found six Indictments. We have examined the Public Offices, Court House and Jail. We find the Recorder's, Treasurer's, Sheriff's and Clerk's Offices well-kept and in good order and the Grand Jury takes this method to return their thanks to the Public Officers for the courtesy received from them during our labors and especially to the Deputy Sheriffs who have been in attendance on the Grand Jury.

We have examined the Jail, and feel called upon to remind our Board of Supervisors of its unsafe condition and recommend to adopt such measures as shall render it more secure.

We have examined the Hospital and find [it] in sad need of repairs.

We are of [the] opinion that some improvement might be made in the management of the Hospital, by which it would present a more neat and cleanly appearance.

The following resolution was adopted by the Grand Jury.

Resolved, that the Grand Jury, having the subject of the Act of the Legislature in reference to a County map before them, after due deliberation would recommend to our Board of Supervisors

---

[464] Sonoma County, California, Court of Sessions, Grand Jury report for May term 1863, 8 May 1863; County Records, Sonoma County, Court Records, Miscellaneous Unprocessed Records, folder "County Records – Sonoma County – Court of Sessions – Reports of the Grand Jury "; California State Archives, Sacramento. Sonoma County, California, Court of Sessions, Minute Book E: 469–470, Grand Jury report, 8 May 1863; Sonoma County Archives, Santa Rosa.

to make no contract under said Act, considering as we do, that the action of the Legislature was hasty, and <u>did</u> <u>not</u> express the will of the County.[465]

We also consider that no County map could be made at this time that would be of much value to the County, for the reason, that our County is young and growing in population, and the lands are not yet subdivided as they are bound to be.

Having completed our labors we ask to be discharged.

Santa Rosa, May 8th, 1863

S. T. Coulter, Foreman.

People v. Brede Brady
Grand larceny (case file # 158A)

The indictment filed on 5 May 1863 accused the defendant of stealing a horse (value $75), property of Calvin H. Holmes and Henderson P. Holmes, on 1 Mar 1863. F. G. Poor, H. P. Holmes, S. R. Emerson, and James Kruse appeared as witnesses before the Grand Jury. The trial jury found the defendant guilty on 26 May 1863. The Court ordered the defendant imprisoned in the State Prison for the term of 3 years on 27 May 1863. San Quentin received Brady on 29 May 1863, and he was discharged per Act on 14 Jan 1866.[466]

People v. Neville Lewis and Oliver H. Lewis
Grand larceny

The indictment filed on 6 May 1863 accused the defendants of stealing 50 head of cattle (value $2,000), property of Winfield S. M. Wright, on 3 Apr 1863.[467] Joseph Wright, James B. Fretwell, Ludolph Wittenberg, Wesley Monroe, W. S. M. Wright, and E. Latapie appeared as witnesses before the Grand Jury. The theft of the cattle and the defendants' arrest were described in the *Sonoma County Democrat* on 25 Apr 1863 as:

> Levi [*sic*] and Oliver Lewis, cousins, aged respectfully about 19 and 24 years, arrived in town Thursday [21 Apr 1863], in charge of Sheriff Latapie. They are charged with stealing 100 head of cattle, most of them belonging to Winfield Wright, of this township. The cattle were taken from Mr. Wright's ranch, near the mouth of [the] Russian River, three weeks ago, and were traced into Contra Costa county, where most of them were found in the possession of these young men, they having disposed of a few head on the route. When arrested they were about completing an arrangement with San Francisco butchers for the remaining cattle. They traveled most of the distance at night, and the

---

[465] The Act of the Legislature to which the Grand Jury is referring was approved by the California Legislature on 28 March 1863 and was to take effect immediately. Section 1 of this Act states, "The Board of Supervisors of the County of Sonoma are hereby authorized and empowered, and it is hereby made their duty, to contract with A. B. Bowers for the completion and publication of his map of said county, and to pay for the same the sum of five thousand dollars, on or before the delivery to them of twenty copies of the aforesaid map." See, *The Statutes of California, Fourteenth Session*, p. 130, Chap. CXIV, "An Act to authorize the Board of Supervisors of Sonoma County to appropriate money for a Map."

[466] California, State Prison Register (1851–1867), Executive Department, entry no. 2556, Brede Brady, p. 210, received 29 May 1863; California State Archives, Sacramento.

[467] Sonoma County, California, County Court, case file # 63 (OS), The People of the State of California v. Oliver Lewis, indictment of N. and Oliver Lewis, 6 May 1863; California State Archives, Sacramento.

second day herded the stock within five miles of Mr. Wright's residence, near Sebastopol. For boldness and daring this theft is unparalleled in the history of the State. One of the parties [Oliver Lewis] is a son and the other, we are informed, a nephew of L. C. Lewis, County Coroner. The prisoners state that they bought the cattle from a man named Welch, at Sonoma bridge. An examination took place before Justice Middleton at 2 o'clock yesterday [24 Apr 1863], and resulted in the accused being held to await the action of the Grand Jury. Bail placed at $1,000 each.[468]

Both defendants escaped from the County Jail on the night of 7 Jun 1863 "by digging through three different walls of the prison" and leaving "a letter addressed to the public."[469] Oliver Lewis, the author of the letter, claimed that he was innocent of the charge and had escaped in order to find the witnesses to prove this.[470] He vowed to "most assuredly return" if successful and stand his trial. Instead, the Lewis boys apparently continued their thieving ways. They were arrested and placed in jail again by 5 Mar 1864 for stealing cattle in Colusa County and were also charged with horse stealing in Oregon.[471] Neville Lewis managed to escape from the Colusa County jail on the afternoon of 3 Apr 1864.[472] Oliver Lewis's demurrer to the indictment was sustained by the Colusa County Court.[473] He was discharged from the Colusa County jail, but immediately arrested by a Sonoma County Deputy Sheriff on 22 Apr 1864 and brought back to Sonoma County to stand trial.

As the Court of Sessions had been abolished while the defendants were at large, the case was transferred to the County Court. See County Court case # 63 (OS). The County Court ordered the defendants to be tried separately on 9 May 1864. The County Court trial jury found the defendant Oliver H. Lewis guilty on 10 May 1864, and the County Court ordered him imprisoned in the State Prison for the term of three years on 14 May 1864.[474] San Quentin received Lewis on 16 May 1864.[475] He was discharged on 11 Dec 1866 before serving out his full term and after being pardoned by Governor Frederick F. Low by virtue of an Act of the Legislature.[476]

---

[468] "Stealing on a Large Scale," *The Sonoma County Democrat* (Santa Rosa, California), 25 April 1863, p. 2, col. 1.

[469] "Escaped," *The Sonoma County Democrat* (Santa Rosa, California), 13 June 1863, p. 2, col. 2.

[470] "Letter from an Escaped Prisoner," *The Sonoma County Democrat* (Santa Rosa, California), 20 June 1863, p. 2, col. 4.

[471] "Cattle Thieves," *The Weekly Colusa (California) Sun*, 5 March 1864, p. 2, col. 3.

[472] "Escaped," *The Weekly Colusa (California) Sun*, 9 April 1864, p. 3, col. 1.

[473] "Proceedings of the County Court," *The Weekly Colusa (California) Sun*, 23 April 1864, p. 3, col. 1.

[474] For the trial jury verdict, Sonoma County, California, County Court, Minute Book D: 254, The People of the State of California v. Oliver Lewis, trial jury verdict, 10 May 1864; Sonoma County Archives, Santa Rosa. For the judgment, Sonoma County, California, County Court, Minute Book D: 263, The People of the State of California v. Oliver Lewis, judgment, 14 May 1864; Sonoma County Archives, Santa Rosa.

[475] California, State Prison Register (1851–1867), Executive Department, entry no. 2742, Oliver Lewis, p. 227, received 16 May 1864; California State Archives, Sacramento.

[476] "Pardoned by Act of the Legislature," *Sacramento (California) Daily Union*, 1 January 1867, p. 8, cols. 2–3. The Act, approved 4 April 1864, authorized the Governor to deduct five days from prisoners' terms for each month of good behavior and steady labor and grant pardons for the remainder of the prisoners' terms. See, *The Statutes of California, Fifteenth Session*, pp. 356–357, Chap. CCCXXIV, "An Act to confer further powers upon the Governor of this State in relation to the Pardon of Criminals."

People v. Henry Hegeler
Trespassing (case file # 156)

The indictment filed on 8 May 1863 accused the defendant of trespassing on the land of George Henckell and cutting down and taking away a tree, underwood, and timber on 10 Feb 1863. George Henckell, John Vanderliet, and Milas Laton appeared as witnesses before the Grand Jury. The case was transferred to the County Court.[477] After a County Court trial jury could not agree upon a verdict and the District Attorney, William Wilks, moved to dismiss the case, the County Court dismissed the indictment on 8 Jan 1864.

People v. William Eller
Murder (case file # 153)

The indictment filed on 8 May 1863 accused the defendant of shooting Jesus Piña in the head with a pistol giving him a mortal wound 6 inches in depth and one-half inch in width and killing him instantly on 7 Mar 1863. William E. Richards, Tennessee Bishop, Louis Piña, Francisco Piña, Lester Feliz, and Henry Lavally appeared as witnesses before the Grand Jury. Giving the name of the murderer as Ben Allard, the *Sonoma County Journal* reported the affray on 13 Mar 1863 as:

> On Saturday last [7 Mar 1863] a Californian named Jesus Piña, was shot and instantly killed at Dry Creek, near Healdsburg, by a man named Ben Allard, of Geyserville. The shooting, we are told, occurred at a horse race, and came of Piña's interfering to prevent a fight between Allard and another person; whereupon A. drew a pistol and shot Piña through the head, killing him instantly. Immediately after the shooting Allard fled, and up to last accounts had not been taken.[478]

A day later on 14 Mar 1863, the *Sonoma County Democrat* added a few more details, naming the murderer as William Eller and giving the date of the affair as 9 Mar 1863.

> Jesus Penia was murdered by Wm. Eller, in the upper part of this county, Monday, last [9 Mar 1863]. An eye-witness states that Eller and a Spaniard were in a quarrel about a horse race; that someone had struck the Spaniard on the head with a tumbler, when Penia interfered to settle the difficulty, and someone sung out to Eller to shoot him, whereupon he drew his revolver and fired, the ball entering Penia's head, who died in a few minutes. The murderer then jumped upon a horse and made good his escape. No arrests have yet been made.[479]

The case was transferred to the Sonoma County District Court for trial on 8 May 1863, however, no mention of the case can be found in the Sonoma County District Court minute books nor the local newspapers of the time.

---

[477] Sonoma County, California, County Court, Minute Book D: 161, 166, 168, and 170, People v. Henry Hegeler, case proceedings, 1864; Sonoma County Archives, Santa Rosa.

[478] "Man Shot at Healdsburg," *The Sonoma County Journal* (Petaluma, California), 13 March 1863, p. 2, col. 1.

[479] "A Cold Blooded Murder," *The Sonoma County Democrat* (Santa Rosa, California), 14 March 1863, p. 2, col. 1.

People v. [unnamed]
Murder

The case was transferred to the Sonoma County District Court for trial on 8 May 1863. No mention of the case can be found in the Sonoma County District Court minute books nor the local newspapers of the time.

People v. Mathew Dillon
Grand larceny (case file # 154)

In a complaint filed in the Justice's Court of the Hon. T. W. Phinney, a Justice of the Peace of Salt Point Township, dated 3 Apr 1863, William Rogers accused Mathew Dillon of stealing a gray horse (value $75) left in his charge by William Wright on 2 Apr 1863. The Grand Jury dismissed the charge May term 1863.

August term 1863

The Court of Sessions met for four days this term, 3–4 and 10–11 Aug 1863.[480]

Hon. William Churchman, County Judge
Hon. Josiah Chandler, Associate Justice
Hon. Thomas Spencer, Associate Justice
William Wilks, District Attorney
O. T. Baldwin, Under Sheriff
E. Latapie, Deputy Sheriff
John N. Bailhache, Deputy Clerk
A. C. Bledsoe, Grand Jury foreman

Persons called as Grand Jurors but not empaneled: John Churchman, B. M. Fetter, R. A. Harvey, J. W. Calhoun, Wesley Mock, William Beckman, M. Hinman, Hamilton Gaston, T. W. Close, T. A. Cravins, S. Correll, A. W. Barnes, G. L. Crane, N. Carriger, and W. J. Annis.

Grand Jurors sworn and empaneled on 10 Aug 1863: H. Meacham, J. J. Van Allen, H. H. Attwater (var. Atwater), A. W. Riley, Willis Goodman, D. P. Cook, Josiah Brown, A. C. Bledsoe, M. J. Davock, J. W. Carter, P. B. McGuire, J. W. Dittimore, William Cofer, Samuel Potter, and J. A. Hardin. The Court appointed A. C. Bledsoe as Grand Jury foreman.

---

[480] Sonoma County, California, Court of Sessions, Minute Book E: 478–484, August term 1863 proceedings; Sonoma County Archives, Santa Rosa.

Report of [the] Grand Jury[481]

To the Honorable Court of Sessions of Sonoma County,

We the Grand Jury for the August Term have transacted the following business. Two cases were presented for our action, one for grand larceny, and one for highway robbery, both of which cases were ignored. In regard to the Sheriff's, Recorder's, Treasurer's, and Clerk's offices, we found the books clean and everything appertaining thereto in order.

In respect to the Jail, we find the cells dirty and the Jail in a miserable condition and insufficient as a prison. On the condition of the Hospital, we simply and earnestly state it is a nuisance.

We do find on overlooking the Sheriff's book that quite a number of persons in the county are delinquent, so far as procuring their licenses, and that we call the attention of the District Attorney to the fact, and take action in the matter. We extend our thanks to the District Attorney for his kind attentions during our term. Nothing more appearing before us, we beg of the honorable Court to be discharged.

A. C. Bledsoe, Foreman.

People v. John Brotts
Grand larceny
The Grand Jury dismissed the case on 10 Aug 1863.

People v. William Clark
Highway robbery
The Grand Jury dismissed the charge on 11 Aug 1863.

November term 1863

The Court of Sessions met for eight days this term, 2–7 and 9–10 Nov 1863.[482]

Hon. William Churchman, County Judge
Hon. Josiah Chandler, Associate Justice
Hon. Thomas Spencer, Associate Justice
William Wilks, District Attorney
M. Johnson, Deputy Clerk
E. Latapie, Deputy Sheriff
George W. Frick, Grand Jury foreman

---

[481] Sonoma County, California, Court of Sessions, Grand Jury report for August term 1863, filed 14 August 1863; County Records, Sonoma County, Miscellaneous Unprocessed Court Records, folder "County Records – Sonoma County – Court of Sessions – Reports of the Grand Jury "; California State Archives, Sacramento. Sonoma County, California, Court of Sessions, Minute Book E: 483, Grand Jury report, 11 August 1863; Sonoma County Archives, Santa Rosa.

[482] Sonoma County, California, Court of Sessions, Minute Book E: 486–501, November term 1863 proceedings; Sonoma County Archives, Santa Rosa.

Persons called as Grand Jurors but not empaneled: John Churchman (incompetent on account of defective hearing), J. B. Hinkle (a mail carrier), L. Carter (his business would be materially injured if he were to serve), John Kron (written excuse mislaid by the Court), Robert Giles (could not be found in the county), Thomas Brookshire, W. E. Flanery, William B. Atterbury, John Fulkerson, John Folks, Edward Cummins, James E. Crane, Henry Gibbs, Jack Gordon, and J. W. Calhoun.

Grand Jurors sworn and empaneled on 2 Nov 1863: Jonathan R. Ellis, James Lyon, J. B. Cook, J. G. Edwards, C. Clark, Henry Dudley, Freeman Parker, George W. Frick, S. R. Emerson, A. B. Nally, J. E. Fowler, H. B. Hasbrouck, J. G. Cook, M. Hinman, and S. F. Cowen. The Court appointed George W. Frick as Grand Jury foreman.

Grand Jury Report[483]

To the Honorable Court of Sessions of Sonoma County,

We the Grand Jury for the November Term have transacted the following business. Two causes of Grand Larceny were presented, one of which was sustained, the other discharged. One cause of murder was considered and discharged. One cause of assault with a deadly weapon with intent to kill, discharged. One cause of carrying concealed weapons, charge sustained and a true bill found; and one bill found for misdemeanor.

In respect to the Jail we find the same adequate and safe but would report that the plan of ventilation or bar windows offer no sufficient obstruction to the passing of instruments to the prisoners, even when in their cells. We, therefore, recommend metallic blinds on the inside, or some plan that will preclude no passing of tools or implements into the jail.

We further report that we found a disgraceful nuisance, used as a privy, in the back part of the jail, which should have immediate attention; also, the flue of the stove needs immediate attention without which the building is liable to take fire. We also represent that from the best information we can obtain, the keys of the jail have been kept in a very reprehensible manner, having been left in the hands of others than the hands of the officer entitled to them; in fact in the keeping of irresponsible persons. We would further recommend that a jailor be appointed, whose duty it shall be to reside at the jail and to take charge of the keys and other paraphernalia thereunto belonging, and not resign them to *anyone*, unless by proper authority. The Hospital we represent as being in good condition, we would, however, suggest that closet should have more attention.

In regard to the Sheriff's, Recorder's, Clerk's, Treasurer's and Supervisor's offices, we find everything in proper condition.

We would also recommend that parties doing business without license should be proceeded against immediately.

There not appearing any more business before us, we would ask to be discharged, returning our thanks to the various county officers for their assistance in our investigations.

Geo. W. Frick, Foreman.

Santa Rosa, Nov. 7, 1863.

---

[483] "Grand Jury Report," *The Sonoma County Democrat* (Santa Rosa, California), 14 November 1863, p. 2, col. 4.

People v. J. William Fossett
Grand larceny
    The Grand Jury found no bill and dismissed the case on 3 Nov 1863.

People v. Harrison Meacham
Murder
    On 23 Oct 1863, the *Sonoma County Journal* reported that Harrison Meacham had shot and killed Albert C. Vanwyck on 16 Oct 1863 with a double-barreled shot gun.

> Our citizens were startled last Friday morning [16 Oct 1863] by the report that Harrison Meacham, of Two Rock Valley, a man extensively and favorably known in this community, had shot and instantly killed Albert C. Vanwyck. A few minutes later Mr. Meacham arrived in town and delivered himself into the hands of the civil authorities. The circumstances attending this sad affair, so far as we can learn them, were as follows: Vanwyck and a partner named David Bicknell were occupying and working a piece of land—under a lease to Bicknell—belonging to Meacham; that Bicknell, without consulting with Vanwyck, sold to Meacham a lot of grain, some forty sacks, which Vanwyck claimed to have himself sold to another party, and on better terms. On the morning of the shooting—according to the statement of Lewis, a man in Meacham's employ, and who witnessed the affair—at an early hour Meacham and Lewis proceeded to the field in which the grain was stacked, and loading it upon their wagon, drove into the street in front of Vanwyck's house. Seeing no signs of Vanwyck, Meacham proceeded to the house and calling to Vanwyck, said, "I have got that grain." Vanwyck, who had not yet arisen, immediately made his appearance (undressed) at the door, and catching up a double-barreled shot gun that stood near, declared the grain should come off the wagon, else he or Meacham should die. As Vanwyck stepped from the door, Meacham seized the gun from his hands and commenced retreating, backward, towards and through the gate, Vanwyck following him up. As Vanwyck approached the gate and attempted to pass out, Meacham fired, having first warned Vanwyck that he would pass it at his peril. Both barrels of the gun were evidently discharged at [the] deceased, but at what precise point of the proceedings is at this time a matter of conjecture.[484]

    The article continued with the findings of the Coroner's Jury and mentioned that Vanwyck was a native of Fishkill, New York, aged about forty years old. His remains were taken to San Francisco where he had a brother living and interred in Lone Mountain cemetery. The Grand Jury dismissed the charge on 4 November 1863. The *Petaluma Argus* of 11 Nov 1863 reported that "[t]he Jurymen were unanimously of the opinion that it was a perfect case of self-defense."[485]

People v. J. W. Barton (indicted as J. W. Barker)
Grand larceny (case file # 155)
    The indictment filed on 5 Nov 1863 accused the defendant of stealing five double eagle gold coins (value $100), one eagle gold coin (value $10), and two half eagle gold coins (value $ 10), the personal goods and property of B. F. Tilton, on 6 Oct 1863. B. F. Tilton, F. G. Blume, and W.

---

[484] "Fatal Affray," *The Sonoma County Journal* (Petaluma, California), 23 October 1863, p. 2, col. 2.
[485] "Grand Jury," *The Petaluma (California) Argus*, 11 November 1863, p. 2, col. 1.

D. Burhaus appeared as witnesses before the Grand Jury. The case was transferred to the County Court.[486] The County Court trial jury found the defendant not guilty on 5 Jan 1864.

People v. Frederick T. Hedges
Carrying a concealed weapon (case file # 157)

The indictment filed on 5 Nov 1863 accused the defendant of carrying a concealed pistol on 18 Aug 1863. Adam McConnell, P. E. Weeks, Mason Southard, Patrick Flynn, and Dr. W. R. Wells appeared as witnesses before the Grand Jury. The defendant pleaded guilty on 6 Nov 1863. The Court ordered the defendant to pay a fine of $76 and be imprisoned in the County Jail of Sonoma County until the fine was paid at the rate of $2 per day on 10 Nov 1863.

People v. Eucebio Alvarado and John Vanderlieth
Illegal voting (case file # 159)

The indictment filed on 7 Nov 1863 accused the defendants of fraudulently voting at the Freestone Precinct in Bodega Township on 21 Oct 1863. Charles Kennedy, James Hendry, George Henckel, and F. G. Blume appeared as witnesses before the Grand Jury. The case was transferred to the County Court.[487] The County Court trial jury found the defendant John Vanderlieth not guilty on 7 Jan 1864.

People v. Frederick T. Hedges
Assault with a deadly weapon with intent to commit murder (case file # 157)

In a complaint filed in the Justice's Court of Petaluma Township dated 19 Aug 1863, Adam McConnell accused the defendant of shooting him in the chest and abdomen with a pistol with the intent of killing him on 18 Aug 1863. The *Petaluma Argus* reported the shooting on 19 Aug 1863 as:

> About 8 o'clock yesterday evening [18 Aug 1863] an unfortunate difficulty occurred, near Weeks' Livery Stable, on Washington street, which resulted in a man named Adam McConnell being shot by Fred. Hedges, a lad about 16 years of age. At the time of our going to press last night, it was not known whether McConnell's wound would prove fatal or not. The ball, a pistol shot, took effect near the lower rib, on the right side and coursed downward. Hedges was arrested.[488]

The Court dismissed the charge on 10 Nov 1863.

---

[486] Sonoma County, California, County Court, Minute Book D: 158, 159, and 161, People v. J. W. Barton, case proceedings, 1864; Sonoma County Archives, Santa Rosa.

[487] Sonoma County, California, County Court, Minute Book D: 152, 160, and 163–164, People v. John Vanderlieth, case proceedings, 1864; Sonoma County Archives, Santa Rosa.

[488] "Shooting Affray," *The Petaluma (California) Argus*, 19 August 1863, p. 2, col. 3.

Name Index

A

Abbay
   J., 74
   John A., 139
Abbey
   J. A., 97
   John, 97
Abby
   John A., 145
Abell, 113, 121, 123
Acker
   A. W., 139
Adams
   F., 97
   Frank, 99
   Jesse, 97
   John, 97
   Joshua, Jr., 63
   Joshua, Sr., 63
   Mary Ann, 99
   William, 166
Adler
   Lewis, 4, 40, 97
Adrain
   John, 21, 177
Agnew
   S. J., 139, 146
Aiken
   Robert, 139
Albany
   John, 6
Alberdine
   Frederick, 97
Albertson
   James, 155
Alejandro, 5, 53, 58
Alexander, 58
Alford
   G. S., 97
Allard
   Ben, 186
   William, 97
Allen
   John, 5
   M. T., 97
   N. L., 96, 97, 98
   Otis, 182
   S., 97
   S. N., 97
   William, 18, 161
   William T., 139
Allman
   John, 16
Alvarado
   Eucebio, 24, 191

Ames
   Charles, 114
   Moses, 97
Anderson
   Harriet, 43, 44, 47
   Marion, 20, 170, 171
   Robert, 34, 37
   W. L., 97, 140
   William L., 139, 158, 162, 164,
      167, 172, 183
Andres
   John, 39
Andrews
   J., 74
   John, 41
   T. E. L., 50
   W. C., 103
Annis
   W. J., 187
Anser
   E. W., 97
Antonio
   Jose, 6, 56, 58
Archambeau
   Peter T., 20, 23, 24, 170, 171,
      177, 178
Arenas
   Ramon, 15, 123, 124
Arlington
   James, 11, 105
Arnold
   G. W., 153, 158, 170
   Joseph, 9
Arr
   William, 6
Arthur
   Andrew, 26, 85
   C., 74
   Charles, 141
   Charles R., 6
Asbury
   Coleman, 39
Asher
   James, 97
Atterberry
   William B., 97
Atterbury
   William B., 189
Attwater
   H. H., 187
Atwater
   H. H., 187
Austin
   Harvy, 120
   Henry, 13, 120
Ayers
   David, 139

   Robert, 140, 141
   William, Jr., 139
Ayres
   William, 118, 125, 130

B

Babb
   John, 6
Babcock
   Henry, 139
   Henry S., 140, 141
Backman
   George, 81
Badger, 11, 89
   J. J., 153
   Joseph, 162, 172
Bailhache
   John, 97
   John N., 172, 183, 187
Baker
   Isaac, 130, 145
   J., 116
Baldwin
   O. T., 24, 162, 164, 172, 178,
      183, 187
Ball
   J. D., 71
   J. W., 149
   John W., 11, 12, 13, 107, 108,
      109, 110, 149
   Joseph H., 13, 111
Ballou
   V. J., 137
Bamford, 104
Bannan
   Tom, 109, 110
Banning
   Thomas, 109
Barker
   J. W., 23, 190
Barnard
   Lafayatt, 5
Barner
   Lafayatt, 5
Barnes, 65, 71
   A. W., 187
   Baronet, 71
   C. H., 74
   Edward, 148
   James D., 18, 152
   M., 9, 16, 153, 164, 165
   Michael, 145
   Mike, 17, 171
   Reason, 71
   Rergan, 71, 72
   W. P., 153

William, 137
William P., 14, 123
Barnett
William B., 76
Barns
Baronet, 8, 64, 65, 70
Baronett, 70, 72
Reason, 8, 64, 65, 70, 72
Barratt
Basil, 4, 50
Barry
Edward, 139
J. N., 139
John, 90, 118
Bartlett
C. H., 3, 38
Bartlette, 6
Barton
J. W., 23, 190, 191
Bassett
H., 74
Bates
H. F., 148
Baugh
Joseph, 20, 23, 24, 170, 171, 177, 178
Bayer
A. J., 61
Baylis
Thomas, 4, 40
Baylis and Flogdell, 4
Baylor, 70, 71
George W., 7, 25, 70, 72
Bean
Peter, 50
Beans, 44
Beasley
Edward, 37
J., 5
Jesse, 43
Beasly
Woodson, 62
Beason
Henry, 54
Beaver
H., 74
Henry, 118, 130, 137, 138
Beck
Robert, 51, 58
Beckman
William, 187
Beckwith
S., 6
Bedwell
John C., 148
Beeler
William, 45

Beldon
J. W., 7
Bell, 19
G. R., 74
Benitz
William, 15
Benjamin
Fordyce J., 9
Bennett
J. N., 90
James N., 89, 91
Nathaniel, 80
Bennt
J. M., 35
Beronda
Juan, 4, 45
Berry
B. B., 77
Ira, 25, 147, 149, 150
James, 93
Bice
C., 74
Cornelius, 170, 171, 177, 178
Bicknell
David, 190
Bidwell
William, 74
Big Joe, 167
Bigelow
George W., 26, 81
Bigler
John, xxx, xxxi, 58
Bihler
William, 4, 45, 51
Biles
Barbara, 51
Bill
Sherman, 83
Billett
James, 57, 148
Bills
Sherman, 83, 97
Billy, 116
Binns
J. D., 22, 148, 172, 183
Joseph, 22, 170, 177, 178
Joseph D., 152
Bird
G. W., 97
Bishop
T. C., 85, 87, 92
Tennessee, 186
Blachen, 4, 41, 45
Adolph, 3, 40
Blachen and Ducollet, 4
Blachier, 3, 38
Black, 112
James, 112

Blackwell
T., 74
Thomas, 129
Thomas J., 14, 129
Blakely
J. C., 51
Blakesly
J. C., 35
Blanchard
Jesse, 18, 146
Blashen
Adolph, 3, 40
Bledsoe
A. C., 61, 66, 72, 75, 79, 187, 188
Blodgett
M., 148
Bloom, 155
D., 155
Bloome
F. G., 135
Blume
F. G., 45, 47, 49, 190, 191
Frederick G., 17, 135
Blyth
James, 153
Boak
Samuel A., Capt., 50
Boake
S. H., 49
Bodger
Edmond, 45
Edward, 37, 46, 47, 53
Boggs
A. L., 17, 88
A. Leonard, 132
J. B., 5, 40, 51
James, 43
James B., x, 11, 26, 55, 92, 154, 155, 156
John M., 37
L., 17
L. W., 31, 33
Leonard, 94
Theodore, 37
W. M., 39
William M., 41
WIlliam M., 35
Bolier, 5
Bolieu
Oliver, 8, 68
Bolio
Oliver, 3, 35, 38
Bond
J. L., Dr., 122, 134
Lafayette, 132
W. H., 93, 96, 101
William, 51
William F., 50

198

Coleman
    M., 35
    O. H. P., 25, 64, 65, 70, 71, 72
Collins, 155
    Edmund, 155
    L. F., 182
Combs
    R., 18, 161
Comstock
    Walter, 4, 48, 49
    William G., 4, 48
Concklin
    W. R., 47, 48
Coneghan
    Condy, 8, 78
Conklin
    William H., 3, 4, 43, 44, 45, 47
Conley
    Edward, 148
    William, 101
Connelly
    James, 13, 111
Conrad
    Bruno, 50
Conuto, 77
Cook
    B. L., 153
    C. B., 162
    D. P., 187
    G. A., 101
    H. F., 6
    J. B., 139, 158, 189
    J. G., 83, 133, 178, 189
    James G., 101
    James N., 3, 37
    John B., 101
    Valentine B., 99
    Valentine M., 99
Cooke
    Franklin, 46
    Israel, 55
    Martin E., xxx, xxxi, 44
Coolbroth
    S. W., 6
Cooper
    H. H., 21, 164
    James, 68, 69
Correll
    S., 187
Coston
    C., 101
Coulter, 71
    J. C., 73
    S. J., 73
    S. T., 83, 84, 153, 154, 157, 163,
        183, 184
    Sterling T., 73, 162
Counts, 72

Cousens
    Davenport, 8, 76
Cousins, 4, 46
    Davenport, 8, 76
Cowan
    Samuel F., 53
Cowen
    S. F., 189
Cowles
    George W. M., 10, 85, 105
Cowper
    William E., 158
Cox
    A. J., xii, 17
    L., 153
Craig
    Oliver, 101
Crandall
    O. L., 114
Crane
    G. L., 187
    James E., 72, 75, 97, 101, 148,
        162, 189
    James T., 126
    Joel, 106
Cravins
    T. A., 187
Crazy Bob, 122
Crenshaw
    James, 37
Crist
    William, 67
Crittenden
    James, 111
Crofts
    James, 88
Cross, 116
Crowell
    W. H., 73
    William H., 78, 79, 83, 89, 93,
        96, 101, 106, 111, 115, 118,
        125, 130, 132, 139, 148, 153,
        158, 162, 164, 167, 172, 178,
        183
Crowley
    Thomas, 137
Culbertson
    Nancy A., 17, 157
    William F., 18, 157
Culligan
    James, 18, 145
Cummings
    M. B., 99
    M. M., 5, 55
Cummins
    Edward, 189
    M. B., 106
    Madison B., 73

Cummons
    Matthew, 83
Cunningham, 155
    Robert, 74
    T. Z., 155
Curran
    George, 142
Currell
    Spenser, 119
Currier
    George, 142
    Walter, 18, 161
Currin
    George, 142
Curtis
    Tyler, 52
Curtiss
    James H., 119
Cushenbury
    Moses, 115

D

Dampier
    William, 6
Danforth
    William, 57
Dashields
    T. W., 14
Davenport
    Alfred, 6, 61
Davidson
    Daniel, 45
    Daniel D., 50
    J. E., 106, 148
    N. R., 178
    Smith, 80
Davis, 52
    George, 94, 101
    J., 87
    J. W., 37
    James, 10, 85
    John, 131
Davock
    M. J., 187
Dayton
    John, 9, 95
Deavenport
    Alfred, 6, 61
Decker
    P. F., 137, 138
Delahanty
    James Arlington, 11, 105
    John, 9
Delahenty
    John, 9, 11
Dellebach
    Anton, 81

148, 153, 157, 158, 159, 162,
164, 167, 171
William J., 158
Ellison, 170
Ellsworth
L. G., 158
O. F., 112
Elson
William, 57
Ely
Elisha, 5, 55
Emerson
Edward S., 22, 154, 156
Henry, 63, 118
King, 7, 62
P. N., 162, 170, 172
S. P., 162
S. R., 184, 189
Spencer P., 15, 19, 136
Emmerson
Thomas, 116
Engle
H. S., 103
Peter, 162
Esparsa
Francisco, 6, 59
Espy
David, 158
E. T., 170
G. T., 158
Ester
Andrew, 159
Estis, 65, 71
Jackson, 8, 64, 65, 70
Eubanks
E. H., 17, 79
Elisha H., 127
James M., 127
Evans
Abijah, 158
M. R., 158
Ewbanks
E. H., 67
Elish H., 127
James M., 127
Ewing
Finis, 11, 116
W. P., 44, 47

F

Failis
Lorenzo, 8, 81
Fair
J. G., 6
Fairbanks
Hiram T., 162

Fallen
Luke, 24
Farley
F. H., 111
Farmer
E. T., 22
John, 97, 167
John H., 169
William, 101, 103, 111, 112, 115,
118, 119, 130, 131
Farrar
George B., 3, 35, 37
Farris
A., 162
Faucett
Bob, 122
Faught
William, 6, 138, 152
Willis, 162
Fawcett
Robert, 14, 122, 124
Fay
Norman, 139
Feliz
Lester, 186
Fergurson
H. P., 22, 166
Ferguson
Harry, 166
Henry P., 22, 166
Josiah, 35
Robert, 164, 167
W. W., 111
Ferrell
William N., 174
Fetter
B. M., 153, 187
Fickas
Adam, 167
Field
J. S., 50, 62, 73, 88
Fields
Thomas A., 162
Fife
Andrew, 62
Fike
N., 170
Nathan, 112
Finchley
Thomas, 17, 137
Findley
S. J., 170
Fine
Abram, 116
J. Holt, 112
Finley
Joseph, 7, 66
L. G., 39

S. J., 40
Samuel, 7, 8, 63, 99
Samuel J., 21, 152, 171
William, 7, 66
Fisher
Edward, 98
F., 74, 77
Fenwick, 11, 19, 20, 25, 94, 114,
138
Fitch, 53
F., 83
Frederick, 46, 48, 49
Guillermo, 37
H., 98
Henry, 46, 49, 97, 100
Joseph, 67, 162
Josepha C., 46
William, 67, 107, 167
Fitzgerald
Edward, 162
Flanery
W. E., 189
Flavell
Thomas W., 105
Fleming
William, 159
Flemming
William, 177
Fletcher
Charles, 96
Flogdell, 4, 40
Flood
John, 60
Flournoy, 151
R. C., 17, 106, 115, 118, 124,
130, 132, 139, 148
Flying Duchman, 6
Flynn
Patrick, 191
Fogerty
M., 103
Foggerty
M., 103
Folks
John, 189
Ford
J. B., 175
John B., 175
Forrester
A. J., 8, 78
Jack, 8, 78
Forrister
A. J., 8
Jack, 8, 78
Forsee
Peter A., 8
Forsythe
B., 172

Forte
James, 152
Fortis
Nicholas, 26, 82
Foss, 154, 155
Fossett
J. William, 190
J. WIlliam, 27
Foster
R. D., 47
William, 156, 158
Fouts
D. P., 112
Fowler
Henry, 9
J. E., 189
J. H., 164
John S., 15
Richard, 4, 40
Robert, 7, 8, 9, 52, 67
S. C., 111
S. L., 74
Stephen L., 73, 74
W., 167
Fox
Frank, 95
Patrick, 95, 98, 162
Franklin
William F., 111, 112, 158
Fraseir
William, 4, 48
Frazer
William, 4, 48
Freeland
A. C., 8, 76
William, 8, 76
Freeman
L. W., xi
Lewis, 95
Lewis W., 10, 100, 101
Freshour
C. C., 20, 23, 24, 170, 171, 177,
178
William, 20, 23, 24, 170, 171,
177, 178
Fretwell
J. B., 97, 101, 139
James, 158, 172
James B., 148, 184
Frick
George W., 188, 189
Frost
Elisha, 6
Thomas, 6
Fulkerson
John, 189
Richard, 72, 106, 167

Fulton
James, 111
Funk
George, 60

G

Gaines
W. C., 67
William C., 67
Galager
J., 68
Gall
John, 176
Gallagher
Jacob, 68
Jacob M., 79
John, 129
Galland
Dr., 6
Galloway
Charles, 119
Galusha
Norman, 3, 44
Gann
Budd, 21, 177
Isaac W., 177
J. N., 177
Ganson
Joseph, 112
Gardener
J. C., 141
Gardner
John, 88
Garlich
James, 71
Garrison
Calvin M., 167
William, 23, 24, 177, 178
William T., 20, 170, 171
Garson
William, 17
Garston
Joseph, 130
Gaskill
Silas E., 95
Gaston
Hamilton, 167, 187
Judson A., 151
Martin, 164
Gates
A. W., 167
E. H., 164
Gault
Thomas L., 167
George
J. D., 37

Gibbs
Henry, 164, 189
Gifford
Thomas, 164
Gile
Daniel, 34
Giles
Robert, 189
Gillam
M., 182
Gillespie
Eugene F., 15
Gillett
Gilbert, 11, 117
Gillian
Edward, 162
M., 133
Gilliland
J. M., 37
Gillis
William, 13
Gird
Henry S., 10, 95
Givens
Elisha, 20, 23, 24, 170, 171, 177,
178
Glascock, 176
Glasscock
James R., 23, 176
Gleason
Peter, 19, 146
William, 167
Gllen
Ed, 35
Glover
A. B., 183
Goatley
Armsted, 176
Godfrey
O. H., 127
Oliver H., 127, 128
Godoy
Adria, 121
Godwin, 4, 45
A. C., 38
Goldfish
Benjamin, 122, 124
Goldsmidt
Meier, 9
Goldsmith
M., 9
Meier, 9
Goodman
W. C., 39
William, 40
Willis, 50, 51, 187
Gordon
Jack, 189

204

Hopkins
  Charles, 94, 132
  Robert, 31, 36
Hopper
  David, 115
  John, 80
  John B., 18, 157
  Mary Frances, 18, 157
Horrell
  Johnson, 9
Hosmer
  James, 115
Hotel
  David, 80
Houck
  John, 17
Hough
  C. A., 175
Houghton
  Jesse, 20, 170, 171
Houx
  John, 17
Howard
  Frank, 96
  W. N., 138
  William, 47, 49, 115
  William M., 137
  William N., 138
Howe
  John W., 155
Howell
  Augustus, 132
Hubbard, 41
  P. G., 115, 155
Hubble
  O., 80
Hudson, 155
  F. W., 26, 156
  Thomas, 83
  William, 37
Hudspeth
  C. M., 49
  Charles, 31
  Charles M., 7, 41, 57, 59
Huff
  John, 90
Huffman
  J. A., 95
  John, 80, 81, 84, 126, 127
Hughes
  Benjamin, 115
  John, 118
Hunt
  Charles, 94
Hunter, 5, 57
  John, 15, 131
Huntley
  William, 130

Hurd, 36
Hutchinson
  James S., 140, 141
  W. A., 115
Hutton
  Arnold, 37
Hylton, 68, 75
  Thomas A., 66

I

Ikenberry
  Milligan, 116
Ikenburry
  Milligan, 116
Illingworth
  J., 172
Ingles
  James, 172, 175
Ingram, 70, 71
  A. B., 7, 25, 64, 65, 72, 80
  Amos B., 7, 25, 70, 72
  John, 24, 25, 118, 161
  T. W., 172
  Thomas W., 106
Ireland, 137
  Johnston, 130
Irwin
  C., 5
  Robert, 118, 172
  W. C., 57
Isbel
  H. W., 179
Ivans
  C. H., 172
Ivins
  C. H., 172

J

Jackson
  C. R., 33
  H., 183
  James, 4, 47, 49
  Jesse, 14, 86
  John, 4, 47
  Lorenzo, 172
  William, 49
  Z., 139
  Zadoc, 118
  Zadock, 148, 149, 158, 159
  Zadok, 6, 148
  Zeddock, 123
  Zedock, 131
Jacobs
  George H., 167
Jameson
  James W., 37

William, 172
Jarbo
  W. S., 79
  Walter S., 79
Jarboe
  W. S., 79, 96
  Walter S., 10, 85
Jefferson, 134, 136
  Charles, 6, 17, 58, 59, 134, 136
  Charles, wife of, 6
  Elisabeth, 134
Jellings
  William, 172
Jenkins
  J. H., 50
Jenner
  Elijah K., 132
Jewett
  George C., 178
Johns
  H. L., 39, 40
Johnson
  A. S., 106
  Allison, 157, 172
  Andrew, 172
  C. A., 89
  Fred, 11, 87
  G. A., 88
  George, 8, 80
  George A., 8, 80, 88
  Ira, 157
  J. J., 107
  J. N., 61
  J. Neely, 62
  M., 188
  Mary Frances, 18, 157
  Thomas, 115
  William, 95, 172
Johnston
  John, 13
Jones
  D., 165
  F. S., 141
  John W., 172
  Jonathan, 172
  Thomas B., 176
  Thomas M., 106
  William H., 139, 140, 141
  William Henry, 158, 162
  William M., 118
Jordan
  J., 172
  William C., 18, 145
Jordon
  Michael, 5

K

Kalkman
    John, 83
    Phillip, 161
Kamp
    H. L., 37, 39
Katlin
    E., 178
Kavinaugh, 121
Kay
    Elisha, 17
Kearney, 37
Kelley
    John, 175
Kellogg
    G. P., 83
Kelly
    John, 26, 174, 175
Kelsey
    Samuel, 55
Kelso
    James, 19, 131
Kendall
    J., 88
    John, 88
    John W., 8
Kendig
    M. H. N., 9
Kennedy
    Charles, 178, 191
    James, 83
Kenny
    John, 113
Kent, 48
    W. D., 37, 66, 83, 84
    Walter D., 66
Kern
    Samuel, 10, 88
Kessing
    J. F., 158
    John F., 160
Keyes
    R., 178
Keys
    William, 183
Kibbe
    A., 127
    Amariah, 78, 127
Kibbee
    Amariah, 25, 127, 128
Kibby. *See* Kibbee
King, 10, 86
    Ann C., 152
    E. L. N., 69
    R. H., 16, 138
    Rufus, 138
    Rufus H., 152

    William O., xxx
Kirkpatrick
    A. H., 178
Kleiman
    Lancaster, 182
Kleiser
    J. A., 17
    James A., 172
Kline
    George, 83
Knowles
    James, x, 10, 88
Kohle
    August, 178
Kron
    John, 189
Kruse
    James, 184

L

Lamar
    J. B., 71
Lamb
    Horace, 125
    J. E., 178
    John, 76
    Joshua, 76
    Thomas J., 23
Lambert
    Charles L., 9, 67
    H. D., 19
    H. F., 125
    S. D., 19
    Vincent, 9, 74, 75
Lamkin, 64
Lampier, 6
Lampkin, 64
    Charles, 183
Lampkins
    James, 64, 65
Lancaster, 155
Lane
    J. J., 99, 148
Lansdon
    Lafayette, 111
Larrabee
    H. P., 80
Larry
    William, 9, 76
Latapie, 110, 184
    E., 16, 19, 118, 139, 153, 162,
        167, 170, 172, 178, 183, 184,
        187, 188
    Edward, 105
Latimer
    L. D., 22, 108, 177, 178

Laton
    Milas, 183, 186
Laurence
    Henry H., 9
Lavally
    Henry, 186
Laventina, 26, 100
Lavin
    James, 183
    T., 182
Law
    Alfred, 171
Lawrence
    George, 20, 23, 24, 170, 171,
        175, 177, 178
Laymance
    J. C., 83
Leary
    Jack, 4, 51
    James, 140, 141
    John, 4, 51
    William, 9, 76
Leavenworth
    T. M., 5, 10, 25, 55, 88, 89, 93
    William, 5, 55
Lebret
    Joseph, 35
LeBrett
    Joseph, 5
Lee, 43
    John, 183
LeFever
    O. M., 141
Legendre
    Lewis, 5, 35
    Louis, 36
Leiding
    Frederick, 126, 127
Lennox
    Robert, 69
Leonak
    Robert, 6
Leprince
    Joseph, 3, 38
Leslie
    J., 158
    John, 172
Levalley
    W. H., 79, 103
    William H., 127
Levally
    W. H., 103
Lewis, 190
    H. H., 83, 171
    Hiram, 83
    J. B., 125
    Joshua, 7, 69
    L. C., 6, 21, 172, 185

M. G., 43, 46
Neville, 26, 184, 185
Oliver, 184, 185
Oliver H., 26, 184, 185
R. H., 125
Ley, 155
H. D., 155
Lidstrom
H. L., 3, 38
Light
Emanuel, 125
Lightner
John M., 112
Lille, 45
Lillie, 4
Limbaugh
John, 183
Lindsley
Tilford, 178
Linehan
Jerry, 18, 159
Linn
J., 94
Linus
John, 15, 134
Linville
Jasper, 183
Liquore
Sebastiano, 6
Livreau
Joseph, 5
Lockwood
Alexander, 26, 156, 182
Lonel
Samuel D., 35
Long
Isaac, 178
Ive D., 59, 111
John, 178
N. J. T., 92, 93
Nicholas, 41
Nicholas J. T., 3, 44
Nick, 85, 87, 92
Long John, 17, 141
Louis
Caper, 6
Casper, 6
Lovell
H. L., 125
Low
Frederick F., 128, 150, 166, 185
Lowell
S. D., 39, 83
Samuel D., 35
Lowry
William, 183
Loyd
J., 88

Lubeck
Emil, 51
Emuel, 51
Lucas
James, 20
Lewis, 165
Ludolph
Henry, 136
Ida, 136
Mary, 136
Luman
John, 55
Lummers
William L., 166
Lunceford
Reuben, 61
Lusis
Gaspar, 6
Lusk
S. B., 125
Lynch
Martin, 113
Lyon
Albert, 125
James, 189
Lyons
Albert G., 83
Robert B., 83

M

Macpherson
A. W., 96
Charles, 96
Maddox
P., 83
Madison
Daniel, 76
Madrad
Joseph, 26, 128
Mahoney
Lewis, 13, 108, 109
Louis, 107, 109, 110, 111
W. P., 22, 161
Maille
Joseph, 31
Main
William M., 17, 161
Major
John, 49
Malay
Israel M., 8, 81
Manion
William, 26, 106, 141
Woodson, 40
Mann, 33
John, 26, 81, 84, 181

Mapes
Ira, 142
Markle
John, Capt., 17
R. B., 13, 70, 83, 116
Markwell
A. J., 145
Andrew J., 14, 17, 132, 145
Marsh
Edward, 35
Marshal
Richard, 39
Martin, 174, 180
E. J., 175
S. B., 20, 23, 24, 170, 171, 177, 178
S. M., 85
Maso
Antonio, 49
Mason
Cornelius, 6
Mathews
C. W., 106
George W., 129
O. B., 148
Overton B., 151
Matthews
C. W., 106
Mauk
George W., 131
Maupin
Milton, 71
Maxey
P. L., 67
Maxwell
James G., 114
K., 20, 170, 171
May
J. J., 170
S., 86, 87, 89
Mayes
Richard, 106
Mayfield
Frank, 61
McAfee
David, 135
Elijah, 135
McAllen
George W., 122
James B., 122
Robert, 39
McArthur
Hugh, 119
John, 171
McCain
George, 171
McCallen
George W., 122

Stephen, 123, 124, 129, 140,
141, 144, 145, 146
Offutt
Charles, 130, 134
Ogan
D. P. V., 72, 80, 83, 172
Old Dad, 65
Oldham
James S., 25, 109, 110, 129
Sim, 25, 109
Olmstead
A. O., 90
Hanson, 37
Olmsted
L. W., 90
Oman
George W., 130
Ormsby
J. S., 8, 78
O. C., 155
William M., 7, 53
Young, 116
Orr
Samuel, 50, 60, 61
Osborn
Jeptha, 90
Owens
John B., 121
Owins
Charles, 39

P

Paige
Thomas S., 156
Palmer
B., 85, 86, 87, 89
J. M., 94
Jacob B., 11, 89, 159
Pancho, 3, 41
Park
Enos, 146
Parker
F. A., 90
Freeman, 130, 189
William, 137
Parks
E., 146
Enos, 142, 146
Patrick
J. F., 97
J. M., 106
Patten
Charles, 141
John, 156
Joseph, 40, 41
Robert, 7, 61

Patterson
A. S., 90
Archer, 89
William, 109, 138
Patton
Charles, 14, 59, 60, 61, 172, 174
Hugh, 43
J. D., 90, 130
John, 156
Joseph, 39, 41
Robert, 7, 61
T. B., 60, 61
Pauli
G. T., 3, 40, 130
Pauli and Schultz, 3
Payran, 126
S., 157
Stephen, 60, 61, 157, 158, 162,
164, 167
Peabody
E. T., 53
Pearce
B. M., 90
George, 33, 89, 151
Pearson
William B., 140
Peavey
Jacob, 161
Jacob C., 145
Jake, 22, 161
Peavy
Jacob, 159, 160
Peck
John R., 60, 61
Pellicee
Joseph, 46
Pena, 48
Antonio, 48
Peña
Antonio, 5, 46
Penia
Jesus, 186
Pennypacker
J. J., 86, 145, 146
Peobode
E. T., 53
Peoples
A., 60, 61
Pepper
E. S., 130, 151
Edmond T., 25, 151
Edward T., 151
Edwin, 151
George, 151
Peres
Jose Maria, 121
Jose Marie, 135

Perkins
A. T., 90, 93
G. R., 90
George O., 15, 129
Joshua, 8, 68
Peter
Jordan, 60, 61
Petersen
Peter, 81, 84
Peterson
Aug., 60, 61
Edwin, 164
J. M., 166
Peter, 25, 26, 81, 82, 84, 85
Petra
G. W., 90
Philips
Jacob, 130
William, 90
Phinney
T. W., 187
Phipps, 20, 23, 24, 170, 171, 177,
178
Pickett
James L., 129
Pickle
C. J., 73
Pierce, 5, 46
Pierson
David, 88
Piña
Antonio, 5, 46
Francisco, 186
Jesus, 186
Louis, 14, 100, 103, 186
Piper
Dr., 17
J. J., 166
J. J., Dr., 168
P. P., Dr., 116
Pitts
George, 22, 171
Pixley, 17
William, 127
Pomeroy
S. D., 153
Poor
F. G., 167, 184
F. S., 155
Porter
J. W., 130
James W., 16, 132
Post
Francis, 19, 146
Frank, 19, 146
Potter
Samuel, 187
William, 5, 35, 94, 166

Powell
    George, 8, 80
    John, 75, 106
    Milroy, 6, 58, 59
    Ransom, 111, 115, 169
    William, 78
Power
    S. T., 130
Prater
    John, 156
    John B., 68
Prather, 7, 70
    William, 7, 64, 65, 72
Prewett
    James, 77
Prewitt
    James, 43
    John, 169, 170
Price
    J. B., Jr., 79
Prier, 93
Prime
    M. S., 50
Prince
    Thomas, 20, 170, 171
Prouse
    Daniel, 20, 170, 171
    F. M., 76
    Frank M., 76
    Sylvester, 20, 23, 24, 170, 171,
        175, 177, 178
Prowse
    Daniel, 20, 170, 171
    Sylvester, 20, 23, 24, 170, 171,
        177, 178
Pugh
    J. P., 90
Purdy
    Edward, 106
Pyatt, 99
    Thomas, 76
    Thomas H., 3, 37, 41, 47, 54, 72,
        73, 76, 79, 82, 89, 93, 96,
        101, 105, 111, 157

Q

Quesenbery
    M., 60, 61
Quinn
    James, 114

R

Rackliff
    P. K., 136
Ragle
    George, 60, 61, 135

William C., 135
Rains
    Bill, 11, 100
    Gallant, 100
    William, 11, 100
Ramer
    H., 6
Ramey
    James, 176
Ramirez
    Fernando, 78
Ramy
    James, Dr., 17
Randall
    Gibbs, 44
Randolph, 5, 46
    Isaac, 45
    Isaac N., 5, 38, 47
Raney
    J. H., 164
Rany
    J. R., 167
Rauschert
    George, 85, 87, 92
Ray
    E., 176
    John G., 35, 53
    W. H., 150
    William, 53
    William H., 147, 149
Rayburn, 121
Read
    J. F., 60, 61
Reagan
    John B., 100, 103
Reddell, 99
Reed
    E. L., 80
Regan
    John B., 100
Reichardt, 181
Remeris
    Fernando, 8, 77
    Jose, 8, 77
Rexford
    E. A., 111
Reyburn, 110, 114, 129, 151, 163
    L. C., 105, 121, 129, 136, 138,
        139, 148, 153, 171
    Lewis C., 105
Reynolds
    J. A., 37, 51
    James A., 79
    William J., 19, 146
Rhoads
    J. L., 6
Rhul
    Justis, 129

Rice
    Daniel, 20, 89, 92, 93, 115, 128,
        142
Richards
    William E., 186
Richardson
    James, 51
    John H., 10, 88
    W. H., 9
    William H., 9
Rickman
    M., 3, 38
Riley, 17
    A. W., 187
Rippetoe
    O., 162, 178
    Obediah, 136
Roach
    Patrick, 88
Robbinson, 117
Roberts
    Charles, 176
    John M., 6
    W. M., 158
    William, 148, 178
    William M., 139, 159, 164
Robertson
    William, 121
Robinson, 117
    C. I., 10, 16, 60, 61, 88, 134
    Frank, 17
    George, 6
    Henry E., 15
    Robert, 17
    William, 55
Robison, 117
Rodgers
    William, 18, 22, 161, 162
Roe
    Richard, 4, 47
Rogers
    William, 187
Rohrer
    Calvin, 60, 61
    Frederick, 128
Romin
    John, 93
Romine
    John, 93
Roney
    J. B., 161
Root
    Jeremiah, 115
Rose
    John, 123
    John E., 123
Rosell
    Stephen, 93

www.ingramcontent.com/pod-product-compliance
Lightning Source LLC
Chambersburg PA
CBHW082353270326
41935CB00013B/1605